Hindu
Gods and Goddesses
Truth and Myth

Hindu Gods and Goddesses

Truth and Myth

As narrated by Sathya Sai Baba
Compiled by Catherine Kapahi

Kapahi Books
Halifax, Canada

First Edition, 2010

Published by:
Kapahi Books
6194 Inglis St
Halifax, N.S
Canada B3H 1L8

Printed through:
Northern Book Centre
Publishers of Scholarly Reference Books
4221/1, Ansari Road, Daryaganj
New Delhi-110002, India
Phones: 23264519, 23271626, 23280295; Fax : 011-23252651
E-mail: nbcnd@bol.net.in, Website: http://www.northernbook.com

BLESSED BY BABA IN INTERVIEW MARCH 16, 1998.

Dedicated

to

Sri Sathya Sai Baba
the Eternal Witness
the Merciful Guru
and

the Divine Mother and Father of All

Acknowledgements

I wish to express my deep heartfelt gratitude to the Poorna Avatar of this age, Bhagavan Sri Sathya Sai Baba, for making available to the world His Beautiful Words of Love and Wisdom contained in this volume, and for giving me His Blessing to compile them.

I wish to thank the Sri Ramakrishna Math, Mylapore, Chennai, 600-004, India, for granting permission to use excerpts from *Hindu Gods and Goddesses* by Swami Harshananda; and to the Central Chinmaya Trust, Bombay, for permission to quote excerpts from *Symbolism in Hinduism*, compiled by R. S. Nathan.

I wish to thank artist Anirudda Goswami for his beautiful illustrations of the Hindu Gods and Goddesses depicted in this book, as well as the front cover illustration.

I am grateful to Yasa Malaviarachchi for her help to research the appropriate excerpts from Bhagavan Baba's Discourses for this book.

Table of Contents

x

A Word from
the Author

I began this compilation of Sathya Sai Baba's teachings after He gave His Permission and Blessing to do so in April, 1996, in Kodaikanal. On May 27, 1997, in Whitefield, India, He placed His palm atop the draft copy to bless.

On March 17, 1998, in an interview in Whitefield, India, Baba signed the frontispiece photo of Himself, "With Love, Baba". I had handed this book to Baba saying, "It is a compilation of your words on Hindu Gods and Goddesses." Baba replied, "Hindu Gods, Canadian Gods, Christian Gods: all the same. God is one."

Some of the words in the Introductions and Summaries of Chapters 2 to 8 are larger than the words of Sri Sathya Sai Baba in the larger portion of this book. This was done to enable the reader to distinguish more clearly the difference between Sri Sathya Sai Baba's words and those of this compiler.

Introduction

I first conceived of the idea for this book entitled *Hindu Gods and Goddesses: Truth and Myth* around 1992 when I came to know that many Hindus as well as most adherents of other faiths had little idea of the deep inner truth the gods and goddesses of Hinduism represented. I felt a strong desire to make this beautiful universal knowledge available to all peoples of all faiths. To this end I have gathered the words of Bhagavan Sri Sathya Sai Baba, Avatar of this Age, presented in this volume from dozens of volumes of His Divine teachings delivered over the past forty years. The gods and goddesses of Hinduism represent the deepest truth of this universe; they are not separate entities as one may at first glance imagine them to be due to their separate names and forms, but are interconnected aspects of the one Godhead, both transcendent, and intrinsic to all religions. They express and describe the play of the Infinite among the finite objects of the world. They call our attention to the unseen power that supports and moulds the happenings in life. The following are the words of Bhagavan Baba regarding the different names and forms of Godhead:

◊ ◊ ◊ ◊ ◊

You may give God any name or form. The Divine has been given various names. Even the *Rishis* have called God by many names — Shiva, Sankara, Adithya, Sambhava and Bhagavan. These names were given to Him; He did not give Himself any name. All that you see may be called God. Nature is God. Energy is God. Nothing is God. But, it is really not Nothing; it is Everything. In what you call everything, there is nothing. What you call Nothing has Everything. Everything is Nothing and Nothing is Everything. Some say: "There is no God." But everything is in God. The atheist denies the existence of what is. In saying, *"There is no God," "There is"* comes first. This means that he is denying what is. He is blind.[1]

◊ ◊ ◊ ◊ ◊

People dare describe Her or Him (God or Goddesss), as thus and thus; that reveals only their faculty to guess. No description can picture the portrait in full. When direct realisation is won, the tongue is rendered dumb; the portrait is unlimitable. It is beyond the reach of human intelligence or imagination. But, man seeks to picture the vast magnificence within a limited frame and locate it in *Ayodhya* or *Dwaraka* or *Madurai* or Kanyakumari or some such spot, and give it a name and a form, so that he can approach It and adore It. The name and form identify It; they do not limit It. When you dive into the Sea at one place, you are diving into the Full, not a Fraction, for the ocean is the same everywhere. You cannot separate it into sections by drawing lines on it. Plunge anywhere; you are plunging into the self–same Bliss.[2]

◊ ◊ ◊ ◊ ◊

---

[1] *Sai Baba Discourses* (West Indies), Volume I, p. 57.

[2] *Sathya Sai Speaks*, Vol. 7, pp. 160–61.

God is all names and all forms, the integration of all these in harmonious charm! Gods designated in different faiths, adored by different human communities, are all limbs of the One God that really is. Just as the body is the harmonious blending of the senses and the limbs, God is the harmony of all the forms and names that man gives Him![1]

◊ ◊ ◊ ◊ ◊

God is one without a second. You can adore Him according to your fancy and pleasure. He does not change. He is not changed, when the names you adore Him by are changed or the forms you picture Him by, are changed. We have many kinds of sweets — many names and forms. But sugar is the one substance that makes each one sweet. You may prefer one sweet thing more than another; you are welcome to prefer it, but do not condemn or prevent others' preferences.

You may adore Krishna, for that Name and Form gives you the greatest joy, the maximum thrill; but do not find fault with a brother who worships the same God through another Name–Form: Rama, Shiva or Vishnu, or any such other. He has as much right as you, to worship God in the form he likes. The effectiveness lies not in the *mantra* or in the Name and Form it is centred upon. It lies in the heart, in the yearning, in the thirst. God will assume the form and answer to the Name for which you thirst! That is the measure of His Grace.

When the child in the cradle starts weeping and wailing, the mother who is on the terrace of the house will run down the steps to fondle it and feed it She will not stop to discover whether the wail was in the correct key or on the proper note! So also, the Supreme Mother of the Universe will come down from Her Sovereign Throne to fondle, caress and console Her child, provided the yearning comes spontaneously from a full heart, a pure heart. She will not investigate

---

[1] *Sathya Sai Speaks*, Vol. 8, p. 95.

the correctness or otherwise of the pronunciation of the *manthra* or the perfection of the picture formed in the mind of the Divine Ideal yearned for. It is the feeling in the heart that is the crucial test — not the length of time devoted or the amount of money spent.[1]

◊ ◊ ◊ ◊ ◊

Do not proclaim that this Name of God is superior or more efficacious than the other. To assert that Rama is superior or that Shiva is superior, or even that Sai Baba is the *Avatar* that is the fullest of all — all this only reveals that you have not understood what Divinity is. Rama is a Name that combines the *ra* of Narayana and the *ma* of *namashivaya*, the *mantras* of the Vaishnavas and that of the Shaivites. So, Rama means the quality of Shiva or Vishnu. Or, Rama has the *ra* of *Hara* (Shiva) and the *ma* of *Uma* (the *shakti* aspect of Shiva); so, Rama is the name of Shivashakthi! How can faction arise when each name is so resonant with the lesson of the unity of all Names?[2]

◊ ◊ ◊ ◊ ◊

There is nothing so grand and so sublime as the Lord in whom you find refuge. Call on Him by any Name or speak of Him as the Nameless one. It is both *Saakara* and *Nirakara* (with Form and Formless). The ocean takes the form of the vessel which contains a part of it. When that is done, the Formless takes Form; the Absolute is reduced to the Particular. You will find out, however, that all the joy is derived from the Formful aspect of God; the Formless causes no joy or grief; it is beyond all duality.

Jewels give joy, not gold. You can experience the Name, you can imbibe the Form; you can take them to heart and dwell upon them and fill yourself with the joy that they evoke. That is why Jayadheva,

---

[1] *Sathya Sai Speaks*, Vol. 10, pp. 217–18.

[2] *Sathya Sai Speaks*, Vol. 10, p. 18.

Gouranga, Ramakrishna and others wished to remain ants, tasting Sugar rather than becoming Sugar Itself. The Name is like the seed, implanted in your heart; when the shower of His Grace falls upon it, it sprouts into a lovely tree. All trees that sprout from the Names of the Lord are equally lovely and shady. If you have Krishna–*nama*, the vision that you win and the form that you evoke is that of Krishna; if you have Rama–*nama*, it is the Rama–form that sprouts.[1]

◊ ◊ ◊ ◊ ◊

Though God is one, as a result of our love for Him, we establish different kinds of relationship with God. Some may address him as Father, others as Mother, others as Christ, others as Shiva, others as Hari and so on. It is only the difference which is born out of illusion, but there is only one God behind all these relationships.[2]

◊ ◊ ◊ ◊ ◊

Most of the Names of the Divine have but two letters or syllables; the significance of the number two (Rama, Krishna, Hara, Hari, Datta, Shakti, Kali, etc.) is that the first syllable represents *agni* (fire principle), which burns up accumulated demerit or sin, and the second, represents the *Amritha* principle, the Restorative, the Refreshing, the Reformation force. The two processes are necessary; removal of obstructions and construction of the structure.[3]

◊ ◊ ◊ ◊ ◊

---

[1] *Sathya Sai Speaks*, Vol. 1, p. 217.

[2] *Summer Showers in Brindavan* (1972), p. 239.

[3] *Sathya Sai Speaks*, Vol. 9, p. 129.

A second reason that I became very interested in putting together a book about the deep inner meaning of Hindu gods and goddesses was Sathya Sai Baba's great emphasis on devotional singing, that is, the singing of the names and glories of God, as a means to purify the mind and transform and divinize one's entire nature. Through my own experience I saw that if the singer or listener of the *bhajans* (devotional songs) knew the deep inner meaning of the gods and goddesses and their equipments (for example, the *damaru* or drum of Shiva represents *Om*, the primordial sound of energy as creation or universe), the *bhajan* would be a basis for deep contemplation on the Truth of the Universe and one's own Divinity. One would begin to gain the awareness that oneself was Divine and thus realize the goal of human lif Sathya Sai Baba says the following about the need for man to do spiritual practice in order to discover one's own Divinity:

◊ ◊ ◊ ◊ ◊

Man is God, reawakening of man is at hand — reawakening to the knowledge that man himself is God. The human body is not you, it simply houses the Soul, or the spark of Divinity within, for God dwells in the heart of every man and that indwelling spark of the Divine is you — yourself. All else is illusion. Contemplate on that thought and when the Truth unfolds, you will find your true identity; then your whole life pattern will change, and you will see everyone in the same Light.[1]

---

[1] *Sathya Sai Speaks*, Vol. 4, p. 258.

◊ ◊ ◊ ◊ ◊

God is neither distant, nor distinct from you. You are God. You are *Sath–Chit–Ananda* (Being, Awareness and Bliss Absolute). You are *Asthi* (Being), *Bhati* (Awareness), *Priyam* (Bliss). You are All. When do you cognise this Truth? When you shake off the delusions which hide the Truth. If your yearning to experience *Brahmananda*, the *Sath–Chit–Ananda*, is sincere and pure, from this day, keep ever in your memory what I am about to tell you:

(1) "I am God; I am not different from God." Be conscious of this always. Keep it ever in mind. "I am God; I am God. I am not different from God." Be reminding yourself of this. Pray that you may not fail in this *sadana* (spiritual exercise).

(2) "I am the *Akanda Para Brahman* (Indivisible Supreme Absolute)." This is the second Truth to be established in the consciousness by unremitting repetition and prayer.

(3) I am *Sath–Chit–Ananda* ("Being Awareness, Bliss").

(4) "Grief and anxiety can never affect me." Develop this Faith and convince yourselves of this Truth by repeated assurance and prayer.

(5) "I am ever content; fear can never enter me." Feel thus forever. Pray that this conviction grows stronger and stronger. Exhort yourself, "O self! Utter '*Om Tat Sat*,' '*Om Tat Sat*, ('*Om is That Truth*'), the threefold symbol of *Brahman* (Supreme Absolute). As the physical body is maintained healthy and strong by the five *prana* (vital airs), these five prayers will endow you with the "awareness of *Brahman*," which is the same as "the status of *Brahman* Itself."[1]

◊ ◊ ◊ ◊ ◊

The very first lesson I gave when I declared My Identify at Uravakonda was: "*Manasa bhajare Gurucharanam, Dusthara bhava sagara tharanam.*" That is to say, first know that you are in *bhavasagaram*, this

---

[1] *Sathya Sai Speaks*, Vol. 16, pp. 170–71.

cycle of birth and death; then, resolve on *tharanam*, crossing it; then fix on a Guru or the Name and Form of God which appeals to you; lastly, dwell on His Glory, do *bhajan* (devotional singing), but do it with all your mind. He who is deluded by this relative reality is the samsari (worldly person); he who is aware that it is only relatively real is the *sadhaka* (spiritual seeker).[1]

Rama was *Dharma* embodied; Krishna was God sporting a human form, but how does that affect you? Have you felt that you too are kith and kin of Rama and Krishna, that every *manava* (human) can be a Madhava (God), that every *nara* (man) can be a Narayana? Unless you adhere a little to Rama *Dharma*, how can you claim to be a *bhakta* (devotee) of Rama? Unless you evince a little of the *Prema* (Divine Love) that Krishna had how can you pride yourself on being a Krishna–*bhakta* (devotee)? Do not be different from your ideal; approach it as close as you can. You must be as golden as the gold you idealise, though you may be a tiny jewel and He, a vast treasure. The *bhakta* must form himself on the model of Bhagavan; otherwise, he can lay no claim for *swarupa* (sameness of the Form of the Lord).[2]

◊ ◊ ◊ ◊ ◊

The third motivation to prepare this book was to help dispel the ignorant notion held by many throughout the world that Hinduism is a primitive religion comprised of idol worshippers, people who may or may not believe or experience that one Self or God is the basis of this universe. The basis of Hinduism definitely is One omnipresent, omniscient, omnipotent Self has many functions or aspects or incarnations repre-

---

[1] *Sathya Sai Speaks*, Vol. 3, pp. 152–53.

[2] *Sathya Sai Speaks*, Vol. 4, pp. 234–35.

sented as gods and goddesses; the entire creation consists of the multiple forms of the one God. Sathya Sai Baba says the following about the origin, meaning and necessity of "idol" worship or worship of a "form" of God leading to realization of the One formless God:

◊ ◊ ◊ ◊ ◊

The entire phenomenal universe is a manifestation of the atom. The water you drink, the air you breathe, and the sounds you hear are all composed of atoms. The five basic elements (space, air, water, fire, and earth) are all made up of atoms and pervade the universe. The Cosmos is the embodiment of the five elements. For this reason, the ancients regarded the universe as a manifestation of God.

Long before men started exploring the secrets of the atom and discovering the nature of atomic energy, even before scientists began to understand the nature of spirituality, *Bharatiyas* (Indians) worshipped the Earth (*Bhoomi*) as Divine. Because the five elements were present in the Earth, they adored the Earth as Bhoodevi, the Earth Goddess.

Moreover, they worshipped water as *Ganga Devi*, recognising the divine element in water, the Fire God, the Lord of Wind (*Vayudeva*), and *Sabda Brahman*, the Divine as sound. Thus, all the five elements were considered manifestations of the Divine and worshipped as such by the *Bharatiyas*. Outsiders who did not understand the profound significance of the worship of the elements, treated them with levity.

Every atom has a form. There is no object in the universe without a form. The form is an expression of the Divine (*vigraha* or idol). Members of other faiths considered idol worship as irrational. They ridiculed idol worship as a form of superstition, but they made no attempt to explain the worship of the formless.

Every person begins to learn about all objects only in relation to their forms. Most people could not conceive of God as omnipresent, in every object and in every individual. I point my finger at the mike and tell you: "This is a mike." After you have seen the mike you don't need the finger to point it out. I point to a flower and say: "This is a flower." After you have seen the flower, there is no need for the finger to point it. Likewise, idols were used to point out God. Until God–realisation comes, idols are essential. After God–realisation there is no need for idols.

After worshipping an idol and gaining experience of Divinity by such worship, one would be able to describe one's experience of God. Before worshipping God and gaining spiritual experience, how can anyone say anything about the nature of the Divine? Hence, it is necessary to develop faith in idol worship. It should be realised that every object is a manifestation of God. Every atom is Divine.

Some people ask whether it is not foolish to worship an inanimate inconscient figure as God. This question is born of ignorance. Today ninety *crores* (one crore = 10,000,000) of *Bharatiyas* (Indians) hoist the National Flag and revere it. Before the Flag could attain this status, many sacrificed their all for the freedom of the country. Many suffered long terms of imprisonment. They went through all this suffering so that they could have their own flag in a free country. On August 15th or January 26th, in India, the National Flag is hoisted all over the country and revered as the symbol of national freedom. In the same manner people in other countries revere their respective national flags. Moreover, people respect even their party flags.

Is this flag animate? Has it any vitality or power in it? When you enquire like this you discover that it is the faith in the flag that makes it adorable.

Likewise, if the question is asked whether a stone idol that is worshipped has any life or consciousness in it, they will find the answer from the example of the honour done to the national flag. How does a square yard of cotton cloth made into a flag acquire its value? The value is derived from the fact that the flag is a symbol of the victory achieved in the freedom struggle. That victory has no form. The flag demonstrates the achievement of that victory. Without the flag how do you demonstrate the victory in the freedom struggle?

The idols that are worshipped are the answers to those who go about asking, "Where is God?" The truth is, God is present in every atom. Every atom represents the power of the Divine. Every atom deserves to be worshipped. All objects in Creation have to be respected. Men have to cultivate this feeling of reverence for all things.

But, believing that the physical body is permanent and is all in all, men are wasting their lives in the pursuit of the ephemeral and the transient. There can be no action without the body. Without action there can be no fruits. Hence the body is at the base of everything. The body is a form (*"vigraha"*). The mother is a form. The preceptor is a form. All are forms (*"vigrahas"*). The term *vigraha* also means an idol that is an object of worship. But these *"vigrahas"* have a certain value. It is through them that we can realise the Divine. It is impossible to conceive in this world any kind of worship (*aradana*) without a form. Worship of the formless is misconceived. It is these misguided persons who preach against idol worship.

In every religion there is a distinct form for worship. For example: Nature (*Prakriti*). Nature has the power of attraction. It contains all the five elements (earth, air, fire, water, ether). It is from Nature that we get our food. Nature is the source of all minerals. Nature is the sustainer of man in ordinary life. That being the case, what is there wrong in adoring Nature? Should we not be grateful to that which provides so many things for our needs? That gratitude is a form of worship.

Every man is composed of the five elements. Man cannot exist without these elements. Is there no obligation to express one's gratitude to them?

Nature has the power of attraction. This is called magnetism. Nature has immense magnetic power. Every object is affected by this magnetic power. The object also gets magnetised in the process and acquires magnetic power.

Today scientists are trying to understand this power of attraction in Nature. Take, for instance, a temple. Thousands of people go to the temple for worship. The magnetic power in the earth extends to the idol in the sanctum. The thoughts of the worshippers are also attracted by the idol. Thereby the power of attraction in the idol gets intensified. The rituals performed for the idol also enhance its power of attraction. This process can be noticed if a couple of nails are kept near a magnet. After two days it will be found that the nails also have been magnetised. In the same manner when worshippers go to a temple and the power goes forth from thousands of worshippers, the power of attraction in the idol gets immensely intensified. The idol surcharged with this power is able to energise the worshippers.

Thus, in this world there is no object without this power. Atomic energy is present everywhere. It is only when the true character of this atomic power is understood that the power of the Divine can also be understood.

Idol worship should not be regarded as a meaningless exercise. It is a good practice because on the basis of the idol the higher consciousness is attained. In a home, there are pictures of grandparents and great–grandparents. The present generation has not seen them. But they offer garlands to the pictures and revere the ancestors. Is there life in the pictures? Do they exhibit any love? Do the pictures by themselves reveal any relationship? Not at all. But the pictures are revered out of the feeling that they represent one's ancestors. If such a loving feeling did not exist, the pictures will not be kept in the house. Likewise it is the attachment for an object that inspires respect and reverence. This is termed devotion. This devotion should be shown towards all objects because the Divine is in everything, in every atom. It may be difficult to cultivate such devotion. But once its rationale is properly understood, the practice of devotion will become easy.

There have been controversies and doubts about this in the past. For instance, a school of philosophers known as Charvakas used to deride idol worship. But later on, they also recognised its value. They realised that everything in the world has a form, from the atom onwards, and that everything with a form was an idol (*vigraham*) fit for worship. What is the form of water? Here in this tumbler is some water and its form is derived from the tumbler. Likewise air acquires the form of the balloon in which it is confined. Similarly, when the body is filled with Divine energy, the Divine acquires the human form. The all–pervading Divine thus acquires the form in which It manifests Itself. Perform your worship to the Divine with awareness of the truth that the Divine is omnipresent and is therefore in the idol that is worshipped. And then you are bound to have a vision of the Divine.[1]

Worship of a Divine Form is a Necessary Precondition to Awareness of the Formless Divinity

In spiritual matters, it is experience alone that is the deciding factor. Reason is rendered dumb before the testimony of actual experience. All the arguments of logic, all the tricks of dialectics are powerless to nullify the direct effect of that inner evidence. For example, take the question of image worship. Many people laugh at those who practise it and condemn it as superstition. But, those who do worship idols have the faith that the Omnipresent Almighty is present in the symbol before them. For them, it is not a mere external adjunct or apparatus or object. It is a part of the inner mechanism of devotion and faith. Of course, all the "worship" carried out with the idea that the idol is lifeless wood or stone or bronze, is so much waste of time. But, if it is done in the full confidence that the image or idol is alive, saturated with consciousness and power, then image worship can bestow the Realisation of Godhead itself. ... The *sadaka* should see, not the stone which is the material stuff of the idol, but the Power that

---

[1] *Sanathana Sarathi*, March 1995, pp. 57–62.

is inherent in it, that is symbolised by it, the same Power that is inherent in his own heart and that pervades and transcends all creation.[1]

◊ ◊ ◊ ◊ ◊

The saints and sages ... have been teaching the people of East and West manifold ways to lift the veil of ignorance that hides God from Man. One such "means" is the worship of "idols," symbolising God. This method has been grossly misinterpreted by many fanatics with one-track minds. The significance of the idol is simple and can be easily understood. When you desire to drink something, say, milk, you need a cup! The milk then fills the cup and takes the form of the cup. When you have the *Linga* as the idol, you feel it is filled with Divine effulgence, glory and grace. When you worship the Krishna idol, you have a more ornate cup wherein you fill the same Divine essence, so that you may quaff it and slake your thirst.[2]

◊ ◊ ◊ ◊ ◊

Vemana did not visit any temple for years; for years he was laughing at those who considered that the image was a symbol of Divinity. But when his daughter died, he was one day holding her picture in his hand weeping over the loss. Then the idea suddenly struck him that if the picture could cause sorrow in him and bring tears, the image too can evoke joy and bring tears to those who know the beauty and the glory of the Lord. The image was just a reminder of the Presence of the Lord everywhere and in everything.[3]

---

[1] *Sathya Sai Speaks*, Vol. 2, pp. 18–19.

[2] *Sathya Sai Speaks*, Vol. 8, p. 36.

[3] *Sathya Sai Speaks*, Vol. 1, pp. 170–71.

◊ ◊ ◊ ◊ ◊

We in India see God in trees, in plants, in birds and beasts; we worship Him everywhere, in all things. People laugh at you when you worship a picture; and, some weak–minded persons feel ashamed themselves, when they do so. But, we are treating the picture as God, and not treating God as a picture. Worship the stone as God, not treat God as stone![1]

◊ ◊ ◊ ◊ ◊

When you see the idol as God, you transmute the stone out of which it is carved, of which it is composed, out of existence; the stone has been eliminated, when you see only God in the shrine! Purify and cleanse the mind so that wherever you turn, not only in the shrine, not only in the idol, but, in everything, at all times, you will cognise only God; then, the mind becomes your best friend, your most efficient instrument of liberation.[2]

◊ ◊ ◊ ◊ ◊

Again, the worship of idols has to be looked upon as but the worship of the Formless. Water or milk has no form as such; they assume the form of vessel which contains it, is it not? Take milk in a cup or a flask, or a kettle or jug or mug, it assumes those forms. So also the form of Krishna is the form of a vessel in which you fill the formless entity; the form of Rama, Shiva, Linga, Chamundeshwari, Ganesha — all are forms of vessels in which, according to your fancy,

---

[1] *Sathya Sai Speaks*, Vol. 109, p. 4.

[2] *Sathya Sai Speaks*, Vol. 10, p. 63.

you take the Formless, Unpicturable! The *nama* is the nectar, the *nama* is the cup, the idol.[1]

◊ ◊ ◊ ◊ ◊

The seeker elevates the stone image into a replica of God; he does not reduce God into a stone. The idol is just a container, prompter, a base, a reminder, a residence which God is invited to occupy. The Supreme is not squeezed into the small; the small is recognised as symbolic of the Supreme. Through the seen to the unseen, from the drop to the sea, from the patent to the latent — that is how idol–worship helps the aspirant. In fact, no one can conceive of the Almighty without picturing it as Power, Light, Mercy, Wisdom, Energy, Intelligence, Purity. And, these qualities can enter the consciousness only through some concrete experience, as the Sun, the Lotus, the Sky, the Ocean and the Wave, etc. The name is a vocal image, the image is a visual base. The seed contains the tree; the *Linga* contains the manifestable and the manifested Universe, including the Creator whose Will it is.

When the name is pronounced by the tongue, and the image is adored by the mind, these should not degenerate into mechanical routine; the meaning of the Name and the content of the Form must, at the same time, inspire and illumine the consciousness. ... involve yourselves in the attitude of worship deeply and sincerely. That is the way to earn peace and content, for which all human activity ought to be dedicated and directed.[2]

The content of this book is mainly informative, comprised almost exclusively of the words of Sathya Sai

---

[1] *Sathya Sai Speaks*, Vol. 4, p. 243.

[2] *Sathya Sai Speaks*, Vol. 8, p. 37.

Baba. Chapter I entitled "The Goal of Life" consists of a series of excerpts related to the goal of human life, that is, the realization of *Atma* as the only Truth. Without knowledge of this goal, and dedication to it through worship and spiritual practices, human life is predominantly a meaningless waste of a great opportunity given for Self–realisation.

I hoped to convey to the reader the most important underlying theme of all of Sathya Sai Baba's words in this book: that all of the Hindu gods and goddesses are potentialities or capacities within man and aspects of both his Divine and human nature, and as such need only be cultivated and realized. The end of evolution is not humanity, but Divinity. The following words of Sathya Sai Baba express the urgent need for man to seek liberation from ignorance about Reality to realize not only the goal of human life for himself but also as a means to aid the transformation of this earth of hate, delusion, lust (desire), greed and jealousy to a place where Truth, Love, Peace and Righteousness reign.

◊ ◊ ◊ ◊ ◊

Man has, through the ages, sought liberation, struggled for freedom from bondage. But, he has no correct appreciation of what he has to liberate himself from, what the bondage is from which he has to be freed. Many are not even aware that they are imprisoned and are bound. So, they do not even try to free themselves. Is the family, the wife and children, the prison? Are riches, properties and possessions the bonds? Are attractions and aversions the bonds that curb him? No. No one of these binds him. The tightest bond that limits his feelings and deeds is his ignorance of who he really is.

Until one is aware of the *Atma* (Divine Soul), one is certain to be tossed from grief to grief, with intervals of joy. The grief has three sources, and so it has three characteristics: (1) grief caused by the unreality of the apparent, (2) grief caused by want of knowledge or wrong apprehension on account of the limitations of our instruments of perception and inference or on account of the mystery of the Divine phenomenon that subsists in everything, and (3) the grief caused by the death, disintegration or dissolution of things which we held to be real! When one is established in the awareness of the truth of the *jeeva* (the individual being), the *jagat* (cosmos) and God, the Creator, he need have no grief or fear anymore.

Let us consider *jagat* — the visible cosmos around us, which we can cognise. The things we experience in dreams disappear when we wake. The things we see when awake are also short–lived. During sleep, we are not aware of the world at all. Though the body is in the bedroom, we dream, and the dream is direct and dramatic, that we are busy shopping in Mount Road, Madras! So, the waking, dreaming and sleeping stages are all only relatively real, deludingly real. When you come towards the hostel at dusk singing *bhajans*, the boy in the front row shouts in fear, "Snake! Snake!" and fear overtakes all. Fear made them step back. But, was it a snake? A boy looked at it with a lit torch, and found that it is only a rope! Ignorance caused it, knowledge removed it. When the torch lights up the world, it is seen to be really God, Vishnu, the Divine Body, sacred substance, *Sat–Chit–Ananda* (Existence, Awareness, Bliss Absolute). The *Asat* (unreal) is realised as *Sat* (Real).

The process of living is the swinging of a pendulum from smile to tear. Childhood is too tender and innocent; youth is too full of folly and faults; middle age is muddled with problems and possible remedies; old age is spent in regret over past failings and falterings. When can man taste some little sincere joy? Nature is the vesture of God. It images the Supreme. It shines through the machinations of the mind. The inner core of each living thing is God. Joys and sorrows are the result of the mind's involvement in the transient and the trivial. Like the Sun, Divine Grace falls. The Sun is not tarnished by anything harmful which it falls upon. The Self, too, is unaffected by the effects of the mind pursuing the senses wherever they lead it. When one becomes aware that the Self is God, there can be no fear of death haunting him. The building may collapse, but the basis is safe. When does man die? Every moment he dies; every moment he is born. When the next tick does not happen, it is death. When it beats again, one is born anew. Faith is life; absence of faith is death. Only the body dies; the *Atma* (Divine Self) is beyond birth and death. Aware of this, one is soaked in *Ananda* (Divine Bliss).

Give up what has to be cast away, know what has to be attained, then, *Ananda* becomes your unruffled nature. So give up the idea of the world being valid; know the reality of the Self and attain the Source, the *Brahman*. This is the significance of the *Upanishadic* Prayer, which you use every day before the lessons start at the Institute:

Asatho ma sath gamaya (Lead me from the Unreal to the Real)
Thamaso ma Jyothir gamaya (Lead me from darkness to light)
Mruthyor ma amrutham gamaya (Lead me from death to immortality)

This is a prayer asking to be led from the *jagat* (mundane world), which is constantly being built and rebuilt, resolved and dissolved, into the Divine whose Being undergoes no change. The darkness symbolises the ignorance which induces identification with the body–senses–mind–reason complex. The light reveals the Divine core, over which all the rest is superimposed by the fog of faulty vision. Death affects only the body–mind complex. When we are led into the light, we become aware that we are the undying *Atma*, and so we become immortal. Live in God, with God, live on God and for God. Drink God, eat God, see God, reach God. God is the Truth, the substance of the Heart of Man. "I am the occupant of your heart," says Krishna. Every cell in the human body is God, though under a microscope you cannot find Him. You are now recording my speech in the cassette. But can you see my voice or words now on the cassette? No. When you play it back, you can hear the words. So, too, the body is the tape, the voice of God is immanent. Equip it with faith and tune it with Love. Then, you can imbibe My voice and words. A pure heart, a cleansed mind, a God–filled consciousness will help you to listen to the voice of the God within you.[1]

◊ ◊ ◊ ◊ ◊

Life is a market.
In life, giving and taking,
bargaining and speculating,
is a part of the game.
Life has
its ups and downs,
its profits and losses,
its joys and sorrows,
depreciations and appreciations
and balance sheets.
But the giving of *bhakti* (devotion)
exchanging for *mukti* (liberation)
is the most powerful business for all.[2]

◊ ◊ ◊ ◊ ◊

The gods and goddesses described in this book have been the most popularly worshipped by Hindus over millennia. I included Sathya Sai Baba as a Deity in this book because of His great poplarity throughout the world as a living God. He comprises all Deities and is the embodiment of all names and forms.

---

[1] *Sathya Sai Speaks*, Vol. 16, pp. 11–14.

[2] *Sathya Sai Speaks*, Vol. 5, p. 94.

Chapter 1

The Goal of Life

After long searches, here and there,
in temples and in churches,
in earths and in heavens,
at last you come back.
Completing the circle from where you started,
to your own soul, and find that
He, for whom you have been seeking
all over the world,
for whom you have been weeping and praying,
in churches and temples,
on whom you were looking
as the mystery of all mysteries,
shrouded in the clouds,
in the nearest of the near,
is your own self, the reality of your life,
body and soul. [1]

---

[1] *Sathya Sai Speaks*, Vol. 4, p. 192.

Chapter 1

The Goal of Life

Introduction

According to Sai Baba, the goal of human life is spiritual liberation, known by such names as *moksha*, *nirvana*, *mukthi*, etc. Spiritual liberation comprises the ending of the cycle of birth and death based on *karma* and is attained when all desires end. Spiritual liberation happens when one realizes the *Atma*, Spirit, or Self (Consciousness) that permeates everywhere, and knows that one's Self is that one *Atma*. The following words of Sathya Sai Baba describe the process and state of *Atmic* awareness or spiritual liberation, the goal of human life and the importance of striving to attain it.

◊ ◊ ◊ ◊ ◊

1.

The State of Atmic Awareness: How and Why to Attain It

You must have heard of people seeking *moksha* (liberation) and getting *moksha*; many may be under the impression that it is some rare honour that only a few secure or that it is some area like Paradise or a Colony of the Elect or a Height that some heroic souls alone can climb up to. No, *moksha* is something which all must achieve, whether they are heroic or not; even those who deny it have to end by realising it. For, every one is even now seeking it when he seeks joy and peace; and, who does not seek joy and peace? *Moksha* is when you have lasting joy and lasting peace. Tired with temporary joys and transient peace, man will at last endeavour to know the secret of permanent joy and peace, that is to say, *moksha*, liberation from the cycle of birth and death.

If only men knew the path to permanent joy and peace, they will not wander distracted among the bye–lanes of sensual pleasure. Just as the joy felt in dreams disappears when you wake, the joy felt in the waking stage disappears when you wake into the higher awareness, called *Jnana*. So, the *Upanishads* say, "Get up, arise, awake"; time is fleeing fast. Use the moment while it is available, for the best of uses, the awareness of the Divine in all. When you die, you must die not like a tree or a beast or a worm, but like a Man who has realised that he is *Madava* (God). That is the consummation of all the years you spend in the human frame.[1]

◊ ◊ ◊ ◊ ◊

---

[1] *Sathya Sai Speaks*, Vol. 5, p. 82.

Struggle to realise *Atma*
to visualise God;
even failure in this struggle
is nobler
than the success
in other worldly affairs.[1]

◊ ◊ ◊ ◊ ◊

Students and spiritual seekers have to learn these lessons from the farmer. The stage of youth is the season for mental and intellectual culture. These years should be intensively and intelligently cultivated; for, once wasted, they can never be retrieved or regained. One must decide to use them for one's progress, irrespective of difficulties and obstacles. Of course, obstacles have to be overcome. The clamour of the senses has to be silenced; hunger and thirst have to be controlled; the urge to sleep and relax has to be curbed.

The attainment of the goal is the aim. When the valuable years are frittered away in petty pleasure, flimsy gossip, feast and festivity, idleness and sleep, one becomes unfit to receive or retain spiritual knowledge — the vital harvest one has to gain. This is the reason why in past ages, sages left hearth and home and retired into forest hermitages and achieved Divine grace. Without concentrated effort, success can never be attained. Laziness is a demon that possesses man and debilitates him. Its brother's name is conceit. When both of them join to dominate *nara* (man) he is transfigured into a *naraka* (demon). One becomes a demon or God or human; ...

Man acquires during his life three types of visions — The earliest is *A–jnana drishti*, the vision through the eye of ignorance. He is able to visualise only his own body and its needs, his own kith and kin and their fortunes and his own class, caste, community or creed and its value and validity. The second vision sees beyond these considerations

---

[1] *Sathya Sai Speaks*, Vol. 5, p. 102.

and pays attention to character and virtues only. The eye that sees the good in all, irrespective of personal relationship, is the *jnana drishti*, the Eye of Wisdom. The third stage is *vijnana drishti*, the highest Universal Wisdom, the Eye of Divine Love. It sees the entire Cosmos as the Body of the living God. Beyond this stage lies the Stage of Total Mergence.
...

Lamps are many but light is ONE. Every patch of water on earth has the reflection of the sun in it but the original sun is ONE. Just as the one sun is seen in a million pots or lakes, or wells or cisterns, the one *Paramjyothi* (Supreme Divine Light) shines as wisdom in a million hearts, whether noticed or unnoticed. When the water in the pot or other receptacle evaporates, the image too disappears. But the sun is not affected in the least. So, too, the *Atma* appears in the body (the pot) which contains desires (water). When identification with the body is given up and when, in consequence, desires dry up, the image *Atma* merges in the genuine *Atma*. This is the Eternal Consummation.

This is the *sadhana* (spiritual practices) that should be undertaken today. You must learn to understand that the *Atma* in all containers is the reflection of the One Overself or *Paramatma*. But, the tragedy is that the one is misinterpreted as the manifold! The fault lies in the prominence given to the petty desires of the puny self. How can one, attached to the self, turn towards the higher Self? Detachment alone can lead one to the awareness of the immortal Self. That is the price one has to offer to receive the reward. Give up and gain, that is the Divine Law.[1]

◊ ◊ ◊ ◊ ◊

Though it seems to be the centre of all activities and agitations, the *Atma* is unaffected. It is consciousness, pure and unsullied. The body and its accessories and equipment have birth and death, they develop and decline. But the *Atma* is free from change.

---

[1] *Sathya Sai Speaks*, Vol. 15, pp. 149–153.

> The Eternal, with no birth and death,
> No beginning, no middle nor end;
> It does not die, it is not born,
> It can never be destroyed;
> It is the Witness, the Self, the *Atma*.

The man who strives to attain the awareness of this *Atma* has indeed fulfilled the destiny of man. But, out of sheer ignorance, man today has no inclination towards it nor does he proceed in that direction. His march is not steady and straight. Sankaracharya once poured out his heart in prayer, to have three errors pardoned by God. "Lord," he said, "Knowing that You are beyond the intellect and even beyond imagination, I am committing the error of meditating on You. Knowing that You are indescribable by word, I am trying to describe Your glory. Knowing that You are everywhere and I have been preaching so, yet I have come on pilgrimage to Kasi. My action belies my speech." Beware of this great error that is prevalent — saying one thing and endeavouring to achieve the opposite.

Man builds a frail nest on the sands, prompted by the delusion of certainty; a monstrous force upsets his hopes, without mercy. A sudden storm plucks the petals of a blossoming flower and scatters them on the dust beneath. Sunk in ignorance, man does not learn the lessons these disasters convey. He clings pathetically to his desires and designs. So the result he reaps is quite contrary to the plans he framed! He can get the success he planned for, only when his efforts and actions are in consonance with the results he seeks. The supremest result of spiritual effort is "beyond the reach of speech, thought and imagination," as the *Vedas* declare.

The *Vedas* use two words to indicate that goal: *Nithya* and *Swagatha*. *Nithya* means that which undergoes no change, in the past, present and future. *Swagatha* means that which, from one unchanging position, illumines the awareness (*jnana prakash*) for all from everywhere. The One sun, from where it is, spreads His splendour in all directions. The lamp, though on one spot, sheds light on the entire home. The *Atma*, likewise, is only ONE; but it awakens all by the light of wisdom.[1]

◊ ◊ ◊ ◊ ◊

Embodiments of the Universal *Atma*! Man has in him the capacity to grow into a pure Divine personality. But, due to ignorance and waywardness, he has become stunted. He has chained himself to low ideals and so, he has fallen into fear and grief. The *Upanishads* exhort man to awaken and become master of himself. "*Utthishtta, jagrata, prapya varan nibodhatha*" — they warn. Man is overcome by the sleep of ignorance. He has to be aroused and taught by elders who know the precious heritage he is losing. The sleep is caused by the *eeshana* or attachments — to the mate, to the children and to riches. Of course, a person must have enough to lead a simple life. But, wealth accumulated beyond reasonable levels intoxicates the self and breeds evil desires and habits. Wealth has to be held in trust for activities that are beneficial, for promoting righteous living and for fulfilling one's duties to Society.[2]

◊ ◊ ◊ ◊ ◊

Everyone of you has in possession a ticket for liberation from the cycle of birth and death. But, most do not know the train which they have to board; many get down at intermediate stations, imagining them to be the terminus and wander helplessly in the wilderness or are carried away by sights and scenes.[3]

◊ ◊ ◊ ◊ ◊

---

[1] *Sathya Sai Speaks*, Vol. 15, pp. 190–91.

[2] *Sathya Sai Speaks*, Vol. 15, p. 29.

[3] *Sathya Sai Speaks*, Vol. 15, p. 32.

What is realisation? The moment you see your own beauty and are so filled with it that you forget all else, you are free from all bonds. Know that you are all the beauty, all the glory, all the power, all the magnitude of the Universe. This Nature is but an infinitesimal fraction of His Glory; yet, you feel content with the pleasure it gives, the knowledge you gather about it, the wonder it reveals.[1]

◊ ◊ ◊ ◊ ◊

You must tread the spiritual path with an uncontrollable urge to reach the Goal; you must cultivate the yearning for liberation from all this encumbrance.

Remember that you have to dwell in a house built on four stout pillars: *Dharma, artha, kama* and *moksha* (righteousness, wealth, desire and liberation); *Dharma* supporting *artha,* and *moksha* being the only *kama* or desire.

However much you may earn either wealth or strength, unless you tap the springs of *Ananda* (Bliss) you cannot have peace and lasting content.[2]

◊ ◊ ◊ ◊ ◊

Rarely does man realise that he is the crown of creation. Rarely is he aware of his innate glory. If he dwells in the constant consciousness of his uniqueness, his life would be lighter, more beneficial and fully saturated with ecstatic delight. Man, then, will strive unceasingly to reach higher and higher levels of consciousness enveloping both the objective and subjective worlds. He will not allow himself to slide into lower levels of animality, which he is now able to subdue and rule over through the use of his intelligence.

---

[1] *Sathya Sai Speaks*, Vol. 4, p. 238.

[2] *Sathya Sai Speaks*, Vol. 1, p. 219.

Of the traditional 84 *lakhs* (a *lakh* is 100,000) of living species, man is the last and the most significant. He is the only animal that is capable of knowing not only itself but also its Creator and Master, not only its own potentialities but the potence of God. Other living beings strive to preserve and prolong life. Man is prepared in pursuit of an ideal or in answer to a call to sacrifice and surrender life.

Man alone can posit for his consolation a series of past lives and for his guidance a series of future lives. He can peep into the past as well as into the future and profit thereby. He has the power of choice to rise or fall, to become a God or a beast or a demon. he can use his unique intelligence and memory enshrined in language to widen his vision, to adjust his reactions to nature and society and to benefit by the knowledge and experience of others. He can influence society as much as society influences him.

Man is the only animal that can transform his own nature, along lines consciously laid down. A beast continues to be stupid or cruel until death but man can by spiritual effort or godly company deal with himself as a problem and modify his feelings and actions. The dacoit who became Valmeeki and the highway robber Angulimala who became a staunch Buddhist are illustrations of this characteristic of man. By association, through teaching and faith, sinners become saints.

Again, man alone is capable of awakening the serpent–power of the life–energy that lies dormant in him as the *Kundalini Shakti* and elevate it through *chakras* (higher fields of awareness), up to the thousand–spoked wheel on the very crest of the head. This is the *Urdwa Gati* (the Upward Path). This *yoga sadhana* is possible for man, since he has a straight body and can sit with his trunk and head held in a straight vertical line. Quadrupeds and bipeds other than man are severely handicapped. They cannot tap the vital *Kundalini Shakti*.

The Sanskrit word *Manava* for Man means *Ma* (not), *nava* (new). That word intimates that man has had a series of births and deaths and is heavily laden with burdensome heritages of good and bad. He doesn't land on earth for the first time. His task is to discard this burden and become free. For that he must concentrate on another meaning of the word *Manava*, where *Ma* stands for "nescience, delusion and mistaken identity", *na* stands for "without" and *va* stands for "*Varthana*" (Action). Man must act, speak and think without being deluded by the apparent, in preference to the real. Man ignores the *Atma* (Divine Soul), which is the only Reality, and allows himself to be fascinated by *Maya* (illusory energy), which scintillates and deceives.[1]

◊ ◊ ◊ ◊ ◊

Bhagavan has seven chief characteristics: *Aishwarya, Keerthi, Jnana, Vairagya, Srishti, Sthithi* and *Laya* (prosperity, glory, wisdom, non–attachment, creation, preservation and dissolution). Whoever has these seven, you can consider as having Divinity in Him. These seven are the unfailing characteristics of *Avatars*, of the *Mahashakti* (Supreme Power) which persists fully when it has apparently modified itself with *Mayashakti* (deluding power). Wherever these are found, you can identify Godhead.

You are also of the same nature as the *Atma* with *Mahashakti*, but like the Prince who has fallen into a den of robbers and is growing up there, the *Atma* has not recognised its true identity, that is all. Though he does not know, he is nevertheless a Prince, whether he is in the palace or in a forest or in the robber's cave. Very often, the Prince will have got intimations of his real status, a craving for the *Ananda* that was his heritage, a call from his inner consciousness to escape and become himself. That is the hunger of the soul; the thirst for lasting joy. You are like the man who has forgotten his name. The hunger of the mind can be appeased only by the acquisition of *Jnana*.[2]

◊ ◊ ◊ ◊ ◊

---

[1] *Sathya Sai Speaks*, Vol. 16, pp. 84–86.

[2] *Sathya Sai Speaks*, Vol. 1, pp. 200–201.

Winnow the real from the apparent. Look inside the event, for the kernel, the meaning. Dwell ever on your *Atmic* reality; you are pure, you are indestructible; you are unaffected by the ups and downs of life; you are the true, the eternal, the unchanging *Brahman*, the entity which is all this. A mere five–minute inquiry will convince you that you are not the body, or the senses, the mind or the intelligence, the name or the form, but that you are the *Atma* Itself, the same *Atma* that appears as all this variety. Once you get a glimpse of this truth, hold on to it; do not allow it to slip. Make it your permanent possession.[1]

◊ ◊ ◊ ◊ ◊

What is this destination, the goal and the aim of life? The *Bhagavatha* and the *Bhagavad–Geetha* have made this clear. Our destination is the source from which we came. As long as the individual is caught up in the *Prakriti* (phenomenal world), his mind will be unsteady and vacillating. As long as there is life in the body it is *Shivam* (sacred). Once life goes out, it is nothing. The *Vedic* declaration, "*So–ham*" ("He is I") is demonstrated by the inhaling done during breathing. When you exhale and utter "*Aham*," you are giving up the "I." "*So–ham*" proclaims the identity of the individual and the Divine ("I and He"). This identity will not be understood as long as one is caught up in the tentacles of the material world.[2]

◊ ◊ ◊ ◊ ◊

Your reality is the *Atma*, a wave of the *Paramatma* (Supreme Self). The one object of this human existence it to visualise that reality, that *Atma*, that relationship between the wave and the sea. All other activities are trivial; you share them with birds and beasts; but, this is

---

[1] *Sathya Sai Speaks*, Vol. 5, p. 31.

[2] *Sathya Sai Speaks*, Vol. 16, pp. 28–29.

the unique privilege of Man. He has clambered through all the levels of animality, all the steps in the ladder of evolution, in order to inherit this high destiny. If all the years between birth and death are frittered away in seeking food and shelter, comfort and pleasure, as animals do, man is condemning himself to a further life-sentence.[1]

◊ ◊ ◊ ◊ ◊

Kama (desire) is the cause of birth; *Kala* (Time) is the cause of death; Rama (God) is the guardian of life. On account of desire, birth takes place. By, Time, which flows unceasingly on, respecting none, the thread of life is cut. Through the constant chanting of the Name of God, life is made worthwhile. Life is a battle; the battle is fought until victory. The goal of victory is the "Crown" of *Atma*, the "Sovereignty" of the Realm of Liberation. That is attained and won by the process laid down in *Vedanta*.[2]

◊ ◊ ◊ ◊ ◊

Always have the meaning and purpose of life in view. And experience that purpose and that meaning. You are That; that is the truth. You and the Universal are One; you and the Absolute are One; you and the Eternal are One. You are not the Individual, the Particular, the Temporary. Feel this, know this. Act in conformity with this. Some one came to Ramana Maharishi and asked him thus: "Swami! I have been doing intense *dhyana* (meditation) for the last 18 years; but I have failed to realise the Ideal on which my *dhyana* is concentrated. How many more years should I continue thus?" Ramana answered, "It is not a question of a certain number of years. You have to continue *dhyana* until the awareness that you are doing *dhyana*

---

[1] *Sathya Sai Speaks*, Vol. 8, p. 114.

[2] *Sathya Sai Speaks*, Vol. 7, p. 44.

disappears." Forget the ego; let it melt and merge, with all its layers of consciousness.[1]

◊ ◊ ◊ ◊ ◊

Vedanta means the final product of the fund of knowledge — liberation. The final product of milk is ghee — for, when milk is heated, curdled, churned and the resultant butter is clarified, ghee is secured and it cannot be turned into anything else. That is the end–product. *Vedanta* is *Jnana* — the knowledge that reveals, that loosens "the knots of the heart" and the bondage to external objects, that discloses in a flash the Unity that is the Truth of all this multifarious Creation. That alone can give *shanti* and *sukha* (peace and happiness). Man can be happy only in vastness, in overflowing into greater and greater power and magnificence. People run up to Nainital or Kodaikanal or Mussorie during summer, in order to escape the heat of the plains. So, too, people seek vastness, in order to escape the stuffiness of "individualised" life. They want the Eternal, the Absolute; not the temporary and the particular.[2]

◊ ◊ ◊ ◊ ◊

You have come from God; you are a spark of His Glory; you are a wave of that Ocean of Bliss; you will get peace only when you again merge in Him. Like a child who has lost his way, you can have joy only when you rejoin your mother. The ocean drop rose as vapour, joined the congregation called cloud, fell on the earth, flowed along the ravines, and at last reached the ocean. Reach likewise the ocean you have lost. Start on that journey and travel quick and light.[3]

---

[1] *Sathya Sai Speaks*, Vol. 5, p. 22.

[2] *Sathya Sai Speaks*, Vol. 7, p. 172.

[3] *Sathya Sai Speaks*, Vol. 6, p. 154.

◊ ◊ ◊ ◊ ◊

Life is a pilgrimage, where man drags his feet along the rough and thorny road. With the Name of God on his lips, he will have no thirst; with the Form of God in his heart, he will feel no exhaustion. The company of the holy will inspire him to travel in hope and faith. The assurance that God is within call, that He is ever near, will lend strength to his limbs and courage to his eye.

Remember that with every step, you are nearing God; and God, too, takes ten steps towards you when you take one step towards Him. There is no stopping place in this pilgrimage; it is one continuous journey, through day and night; through valley and desert; through tears and smiles; through death and birth, through tomb and womb.

When the road ends, and the Goal is gained, the pilgrim finds that he has travelled only from himself to himself, that the way was long and lonesome, but the God that led him unto it was all the while in him, around him, with him, and beside him! He himself was always Divine. His yearning to merge in God was but the sea calling to the Ocean! Man loves, because He is Love! He craves for melody and harmony, because He is melody and harmony. He seeks Joy, for he is Joy. He thirsts for God, for he is composed of God, and he cannot exist without Him.

...

If you know the road and the goal, then you can discover whether you are progressing or not; otherwise how can you? The goal is to enlarge your vision, your sympathy, your love to the extent that God has spread His Love, His Compassion and His Grace. So, be ever watchful to see that you strive to take in more and more of God into you.[1]

◊ ◊ ◊ ◊ ◊

---

[1] Sathya Sai Speaks, Vol. 8, p. 39.

To be born as a human being is a great piece of luck. For, man alone can attain the status of the Divine, by recognising the reality of his being. No beast or bird can reach that height of realisation. But, it is tragic that instead of valuing the chance and utilising it, man fritters his years here and dies, without seeing the light. He is disgracing himself and denying his destiny. A minute's reflection will reveal how far he is from the goal, the precious stage of Self–realisation. Man is neither a picture, nor a sculpture, which are both lifeless and have no aspiration of their own. He has activity, attainment, a hunger for expansion, for immortality. But, what a pity, he does not dedicate his life to the Divine, he is caught up in the vain pursuit of comfort and cosy living. And to style himself as a son of *Bharat Matha* (Mother India) and yet behave so foolishly is a greater shame. He is simply converting a fine moonlit night into a night of thick blackness.[1]

◊ ◊ ◊ ◊ ◊

The mind can be pulled down by systematic efforts and you can become master of yourself. ... The ladder must be as tall as the height to which you want to climb, is it not? Your spiritual practice to curb the mind must be carried on step by step until *Sakshathkaram* (Realisation) is gained. The rice in the pot must be well boiled and become soft and sweet. Until that happens, the fire must burn. In the vessel of "body," with water, that is to say the "senses," boil the mind and make it soft. The fire is the *sadhana* (spiritual practice). Keep it burning bright; the *jeeva* (individual soul) will at last become *Deva*.[2]

◊ ◊ ◊ ◊ ◊

---

[1] *Sathya Sai Speaks*, Vol. 6, p. 84.

[2] *Sathya Sai Speaks*, Vol. 4, p. 107.

Behind the seen, there is a sublime unseen. The seen and the unseen are two halves of the One, or rather, two phases of the One. From the Full, the full has emerged, leaving the Full ever Full. The Created is as full of the One as the One whose manifestation it is. The Experiencer is as Full as the Experienced. A grain of sand is as full as a star in the sky. The *Paramatma*, who is the One Fullness, has willed mankind which is co-sharer of that Fullness. Man has to fulfil himself, half through the Grace of the effort and half through the Grace of the indwelling Divine. Awareness of this Fullness, escaping from the illusion of incompleteness, is the goal, the destination of human life. When man knows, visualises and experiences the Creator, he becomes as mighty, as majestic and as knowledgeable as the Creator. The ultimate cause cannot be the object of direct vision, nor can it be discovered by logical inference. One has to rely on the Word, the *Sabda*, the *Vedas*, and proceed along the path laid down therein.[1]

◊ ◊ ◊ ◊ ◊

Man has to become Divine, the Divine from which he has come. So, he has to lessen his attachment to the world, not by cutting himself off, but, by being in it as an instrument in His hands; by subduing all tendencies towards egoism that raise their heads in him; by single-minded attention to the dictates of God called *Dharma*. Edison the scientist concentrated so much on the solution of the problems that worried him that he left untouched for days together the food and drink that was pushed in through the doors of his laboratory. You must have the same concentration and *shradda* (faith) while engaged in *sadhana* (spiritual practice).

The best *sadhana* is to discover your *Atmic* reality and to recognise your kinship in the *Atmic* fold with all others. The body has to be kept trim until this is achieved; its purpose too is just this. Keep it light and bright. It is a boat which can take you across the sea of illusion, of false

---

[1] *Sathya Sai Speaks*, Vol. 15, p. 26.

multiplicity. Don't add to its weight by attachment to things and others; then, it is in danger of sinking during the voyage.

Namasmarana (repetition of the name of God) is the most effective *sadhana*. Remember with each name the glory behind the name. Escape from the clutches of anger, jealousy, hatred, malice and greed. Do not seek to discover others' defects; do not gloat over them; when others point out your defects, be thankful; or keep quiet as Buddha did.[1]

◊ ◊ ◊ ◊ ◊

You are the whole, the infinite, the all. You as body, mind and soul are a dream; but what you really are is Existence, Knowledge and Bliss. You are the God of the Universe. You are creating the whole Universe and drawing it in.[2]

◊ ◊ ◊ ◊ ◊

Perfect freedom is not given to any man on earth. Lesser the number of wants, the greater is the freedom. Hence perfect freedom is absolute desirelessness.[3]

◊ ◊ ◊ ◊ ◊

---

[1] *Sathya Sai Speaks*, Vol. 5, p. 256.

[2] *Sathya Sai Speaks*, Vol. 5, p. 154.

[3] *Sathya Sai Speaks*, Vol. 5, p. 200.

2.

The Manifestation of Atma through the Human Form

The following words of Sathya Sai Baba describe the state of one who has attained spiritual liberation and has thus become master of himself:

◊ ◊ ◊ ◊ ◊

God is Truth, Truth is Goodness, Goodness is Beauty. Truth, Goodness, Beauty, Sathyam, Shivam, Sundaram is yourself. Be yourself.[1]

◊ ◊ ◊ ◊ ◊

Man is fundamentally Divine, and so, naturally, the more he manifests the Divine attributes of Love, Justice, Truth and Peace, the more *Ananda* (Bliss) he is able to enjoy and impart. The less he manifests them, the more ashamed he ought to be, that he is living counter to his heritage.

The tree of Life has to be watered at the roots, but now, those who plan to raise the standard of living, water the branches, the leaves and the blossoms. The roots are the virtues; they have to be fostered so that the flowers of actions, words and thoughts may bloom in fragrance and yield the fruit of *seva* (service), full of the sweet juice of *Ananda*. Planning for food, clothing and shelter is only promoting the well–being of the cart; plan also for the horse, the mind of man which has to use the food, the clothing, the shelter and other material

---

[1] Sathya Sai Speaks, Vol. 5, p. 227.

instruments for the high purpose of "escaping from the ego into the universal."[1]

◊ ◊ ◊ ◊ ◊

The traditional number of created beings is 84 *lakhs* (a *lakh* is 100,000), and man is the final item of the evolutionary procession; but, why did the number stop at 84 *lakhs*? It stopped because man is the zenith, the fullness; he is *Madava* in fact, though he has ignored the truth and holds fast to the belief that he is just a man. He is endowed with *manas, buddhi, chitta* and *ahamkara* (mind, intelligence, reasoning faculty and ego), all four, in an integrated personality, whereas the birds and beasts and all other species have mostly *ahamkaram* (ego) alone. The lives of the latter are centred round the *aham* and its desires and demands. But, man has the capacity to follow *Sathya* (Truth), *Dharma* (Righteousness), *Shanti* (Peace) and *Prema* (Divine Love); man alone has it. If he does not evince that capacity and develop it, he is as bad as a *vanara* or a *danava* (ape or ogre). When man was created, there remained nothing higher to create.[2]

◊ ◊ ◊ ◊ ◊

The new year is called Vishwavasu and you must take it as a call to strengthen your *Vishwasa* (Faith); faith in your own *Atma*, your own Divinity, which manifests itself as Love, as desire for immortality, as detachment, as admiration of virtue, the awe and wonder that Nature provokes. But, man is neglecting a grand opportunity, the opportunity of imbibing his own genuine grandeur. He prefers to burn the sandalwood trees for sale as charcoal, for, he does not know the value of the wood. The Divine he takes to be just human; the goal he has set

---

[1] *Sathya Sai Speaks*, Vol. 6, p. 104.

[2] *Sathya Sai Speaks*, Vol. 6, p. 81.

before himself is the winning of *Sukha* (Happiness) and *Shanti* (Peace); that is the proper thing to do, but, he stops after a few steps, mistaking the pseudo for the real, that is the tragedy. He believes that if he gets two full meals a day, a few yards of cloth to wear, and a roof over his head, with a few sundry superfluities, he has reached the goal; but the joy he derives is paltry, mixed with grief, easily turning into pain, harmful to others, full of pride, envy, malice, greed and other harmful ingredients. The body that is sustained on food which will not keep fresh for even a few hours, how can it be fresh for long? That which is made and marred cannot for that very reason be Truth; for, Truth cannot be made and marred. It is, was and will be, without any modification.

What is the immortal part of man? Is it the wealth he has accumulated, the residences he has built, the physique he has developed, the health he has acquired, the family he has reared? No, all that he has done, developed or earned are destroyed; he has to leave them all to the ravages of time. He cannot take with him even a handful of earth, the earth he loved so much. If only the dead could take with them a handful each, earth would have become so scarce that it should have been rationed by now! Discover the immortal "I" and know that it is the spark of God in you; live in the companionship of the vast measureless Supreme and you will be rendered vast and measureless.[1]

◊ ◊ ◊ ◊ ◊

Man did not come here to sleep and eat; he has come to manifest, by disciplined processes, the Divine in him. That is why he is called *vyakthi* (individual), he who makes *vyaktha* (clear) the *shakti* (power) that is in him — the Divine energy that motivates him.

For this purpose he has come endowed with this body and the intelligence needed to control it and divert it to useful channels of

---

[1] *Sathya Sai Speaks*, Vol. 5, pp. 150–51.

activity. You must achieve this by *Dharma–nishtha* and *Karma–nishtha* — steady pursuit of morality and good deeds.[1]

◊ ◊ ◊ ◊ ◊

You must feel that all this is just a passing show, that you are the central figure, the only figure, the entire figure. *Tat Twam Asi:* That thou art. That is this. The external world is fundamentally One, is really *Brahman*, appearing as many. *Twam* is you, yourself. And, what does the experience of all the sages tell him? What is the profound discovery embodied in the wisdom of the *Vedas*? *Tat* is *Twam*, *Twam* is *Tat*; there is no second, there is only One.

If you act or feel or talk contrary to your nature you demean yourself; you deny your reality. The *Brahmatatwam* (Reality of *Brahman*) is *Vimalam*, *Achalam* — Pure, Unshakable; be pure and unshakable. It is *thriguna rahitham*, devoid of the three qualities: dull, active or balanced; it is pure consciousness. You too must not be agitated by the storms of feeling, or the fog of dullness and sloth. Play your role, as a puppet does; the unseen Director unfolds the drama, which He has willed.[2]

◊ ◊ ◊ ◊ ◊

The discovery of Truth — that is the unique mission of Man. Man is a mixture of *Maya* and *Madava*; the *Maya* (illusion) throws a mist which hides the *Madava* (God); but through the action of the healthy impulses inherited from acts performed while in previous bodies or through the cleansing done by austerities in this body or through the Grace of the Lord Himself, *Maya* melts away; for it is just a mist which flees before the sun. Then *Nara* (human) is transformed into *Narayana*

---

[1] *Sathya Sai Speaks*, Vol. 1, p. 165.

[2] *Sathya Sai Speaks*, Vol. 5, p. 168.

(God) and this *Bhuloka* (world) is elevated into a *Prashanti Nilayam* (place of tranquillity).[1]

◊ ◊ ◊ ◊ ◊

3.

Worship, Dedicated Action, Self Inquiry, Meditation and Contemplation Lead to Spiritual Wisdom and Liberation

Even to place one foot forward, man needs an inner urge, a purpose, a prompting. His will is moved by his wish. Therefore, man must endeavour to wish for higher and holier goals. His mind is a bundle of wishes; turned hither and thither by the dictates of each wish, man wastes the time allotted to him and the skills he is endowed with. He enslaves his conscience believing that he is acting right.

But, man has to recognise the preciousness of time. Not even a fraction of a second should be wasted. He must be engaged always in the investigation of his own Truth and his own Duty to himself. Life is dripping away, drop by drop, from the leaking pot! Time hangs over every head like a sharp sword, ready to inflict the mortal slash. But, man pays no attention to this ever–present calamity.

Cynics declare that statements like "Man is the crown of Creation" are only for text–books and platform. But really speaking, human life

---

[1] *Sathya Sai Speaks*, Vol. 2, p. 175.

is holy, sublime, sacred, ever–new, ever–fresh. The *Upanishads* try to arouse and awaken man into the awareness of this Truth for man is slumbering in ignorance, wrapped in his ego and his desires. "Awake and adore the Sun and recognize your Reality in the light of His rays," that is the call reverberating from the *Upanishads*. But, man is deaf to this entreaty.

Three *eshanas* (ardent desires) are holding man back: he is enamoured of wealth, wife and children. These obstruct him at each step and act as handicaps to spiritual advance. Of course, wherewithal is essential for the process of life and labouring for it cannot be avoided. But, beyond a limit riches foul the mind and breed arrogance. They must be used for good purposes, promoting virtue and well–being, fostering *Dharma* (Virtue) and fulfilling one's duties along the Divine path.[1]

◊ ◊ ◊ ◊ ◊

What is the purpose of life? Is it to struggle in the mire or march straight on to the Eternal? You will get millions to tell you what is pleasing to you; but, it is difficult to get one in a million who can tell you what is good for you. What is good for you is akin to Truth; Truth is hard but beneficial. It is unpleasant advice to tell a man to stick to Truth at all costs; but, Truth alone pays dividends that satisfy.

Sit quiet for just a moment and inquire within yourself what is it that stays and what is it that does not. You try to know the news of the world, the changing fortunes of men and movements, in all the countries of the world; but you have no thirst to know about the conditions and conflicts of your own inner world happening against the permanent backdrop of the unchanging *Atma*, which is your innermost core. Know that and everything becomes known; act and no other act is needed; possess that and all things are possessed by you!

---

[1] *Sathya Sai Speaks*, Vol. 15, pp. 33–34.

...

There is a deep urge in man to visualise the One behind the many; scientists seek to find a law that will explain all sources of energy and all forms of matter. You can also know that, which, if known, all else can be known; only, you have to get immersed in the Bliss of *Atma*. In the grindstone the base is steady, unmoving; the upper grinder moves; but both are stones. So too, the *chara* and the *achara* (the fixed and the changing), the base and the superstructure, are all *Brahman*. *Prakriti* (objective world) moves; *Brahman* (Supreme Being) is steady; both are inextricably inter–related, the one with other in *Avinabhava–sambanda* (relationship of interdependent existence).

God should be the bedrock on which you resolve; then, life would be smooth. The physical, the mental, the objective world — these revolve around God, and if that close relationship with God is recognised, they lead you into Light. Like the strokes of the hammer, which lend shape and beauty to gold, *Atma* gets Name and Form through the strokes of multifarious *karma*, from birth to birth. The *Akaram* makes it *Vikaram* (Form makes it deformed). The deformity has to be set right by *Adhyatmic* rigour — spiritual discipline.

No effort is made now for this kind of discipline, no lessons are given in the educational institutions of the country. It is wrong to lay the blame on want of time; time can never obstruct it. You are the obstructor, not time. The monkey that cannot pull out its clenched fist from the narrow neck of the pot lays the blame on the pot or the maker of the pot. But, if only it releases the hold on the peanuts it has grasped in that fist, it can easily take its hand out. The fault lies in itself. So too man's greed is the reason for this want of time. No one thrust the hand into the pot; no one forced the monkey to grab the nuts. It has become the victim of its own rapacity, that is all.[1]

◊ ◊ ◊ ◊ ◊

---
[1] *Sathya Sai Speaks*, Vol. 4, pp. 259–261.

Unaware of your Divine Status, you revel in low company; you toil and sweat as the slave of mean passions which drag you into disgrace. Be the Prince you really are. Be like the lotus, which though born in the slush at the bottom of the lake, by sheer will–power rises above the waters to see the Sun and be inspired by its rays. The lotus discards contact with water, though it is born and bred in that element; so, you too should avoid being attached to the elemental passions, that the elements constituting you urge you into. How long are you to sit content with the minor role of a clown or a clout? Are you not ashamed? Have you no ambition? Why smother your genuine talents under a self–imposed mask? All these are zero roles; take on the role of the hero which is your right, and shine![1]

◊ ◊ ◊ ◊ ◊

You are the Formless (*Nirakaram*) come in the form of Man (*Narakaram*), the Infinite, come in the role of the finite, the Formless Infinite appearing as the formful infinitesimal, the Absolute pretending to be the Relative, the *Atma* behaving as the body, the Metaphysical masquerading as the merely physical. The Universal *Atma* (Self) is the basis of all being. the sky was there before houses were built under it; it penetrated and pervaded them for some time; then, the houses crumbled and became heaps and mounds; but, the sky was not affected at all. So too, the *Atma* pervades the body and subsists even when the body is reduced to dust.

The same inexplicable, invisible, electric current, when it enters a bulb, a fan, a stove, a cooler, or a sprayer, activates each one of them or all of them together. Similarly, *Ishwara sarva bhoothanam*: the Divine Principle activates all beings. That is the inner core, the Divine Spark, more minute than the minutest, more magnificent than the most magnificent. To observe the minute you must use a microscope; to bring the remote nearer your eye, you seek the help of a telescope;

---

[1] *Sathya Sai Speaks*, Vol. 4, p. 47.

these are *yantras* (material instruments). The instruments that help you to visualise the Core that has such strange contradictory attributes are called *mantras* — formulae that save you when you meditate on them They are also called *tantras* (ceremonies and rites) when their practical application has to be emphasized. Faith in the efficacy of these *mantras* and in the utility of the procedure prescribed, as well as in the existence of the Core are all essential for success in the great adventure, just as faith in the efficacy of the *yantra*, in the correctness of the procedure, and in the existence of the material he is seeking to know more about are essential for the scientist.

You must tackle this problem, straight from where it starts. Ignorance can be cured only by knowledge; darkness can be destroyed only by light. No amount of argument or threat or persuasion can compel darkness to move away. A flash, that is enough; it is gone. Prepare for that flash of illumination; the light is there already, in you. But, since it is heavily overladen by repressing factors, it cannot reveal itself. "The liberation from night" which happens when the light is revealed, is called *moksha*. Every one has to achieve it, whether he is striving for it now or not. It is the inevitable end to the struggle, the goal to which all are proceeding.[1]

◊ ◊ ◊ ◊ ◊

Life must have an ideal before it, it must proceed towards a goal; it must be a constant march. Life has as its sole purpose the divinising of man, the transformation of the "man" we profess to be into the God we really are. *Gu* in the word *Guru*, indicates the quality of *gunatheetha*, that is, unaffected by attributes and attitudes, not associated with any one particular characteristic. And *Ru* means *rupa–rahitha*, that is, not limited to any form, pervasive in all forms. In this context, the

---

Universe and all its components are to be looked upon as one's preceptors and lessons learnt from each.[1]

◊ ◊ ◊ ◊ ◊

Just reflect on this for a minute: How did man forget his Divinity? How did he fall into this delusion of littleness? Then you will know that it must be as a result of the mind running after momentary pleasures. What then is the remedy? The answer is just one word — "Worship." Do everything as worship. *Yath bhaavam thath bhavathi* — "You become that which you feel." You can get the feeling for the Divine only if you have a taste of the *Prema* (Divine Love) of the Divine. That is why the *Avatar* has come to give you a taste of that *Prema*, so that the yearning for the Lord will be planted in your heart.

...

By means of the Name, you can keep God ever near you. Prayer and *puja* (worship) follow the recital of the Name, for the Glory and grace of God draw you to adore Him and to rely on Him for all your needs. In the beginning, the Adored and the Adorer are distant and different; but, as the *sadhana* (spiritual practice) becomes more confirmed and consolidated, they commingle and become more and more composite. For, the individual and the Universal are one; the wave in the sea. Merging fulfils. When merged, the ego is dissolved; all symbols and signs of the particular like name, form, caste, colour, creed, nationality, church, sect and the rights and duties consequent thereon will fade.

For such individuals, who have liberated themselves from the narrowness of individuality, the only task is the uplift of humanity, the welfare of the world and the showering of love. Even if they are quiet,

---

[1] *Sathya Sai Speaks*, Vol. 15, p. 83.

the state of Bliss in which they are, will shower Bliss on the world. Love is in all, Love is of all, Love is all.[1]

◊ ◊ ◊ ◊ ◊

Know that which, if known, makes known everything that has to be known. This was the advice given to Uddalaka by his *Guru*, as mentioned in the *Upanishads*. You are the core, the centre of your world. Without you there is no world for you. Unless you know yourself, you cannot know the world which is your creation. Now, you ask every one you meet, "How do you do?" But have you ever asked the question to yourself, "How do I do?" You ask every third person, "Who is he?" But, have you asked the first person, "Who am I" and searched for the answer? That is what the *Vedanta* teaches, that is what these Pandits are eager to tell you.[2]

◊ ◊ ◊ ◊ ◊

All acts must be done as offerings to Him, dedicated to Him, prompted, planned, executed and blessed by Him. The *smarana* (remembrance) of the Name will help this *sadhana*. The Name has to be repeated with the heart yearning for the Named. It should not be like a tape–recorder reeling off the names of a gramophone plate that has stuck, repeating the same note. Know that this life is for realising Him, not for winning petty triumphs. Your ideal, your determination and your activity, all three must be directed to the same consummation, the attainment of Supreme Bliss. The Name will make all activity as welcome as worship; it will add witness to worship itself;

---

[1] *Sathya Sai Speaks*, Vol. 7, p. 240.

[2] Sathya Sai Speaks, Vol. 5, p. 134.

it will concretise the Named. It will confer the Wisdom that reveals the Truth.[1]

◊ ◊ ◊ ◊ ◊

Seeing one's own reality is the opening of the doors of liberation; for this, the mirror of the heart has to be prepared, by coating the back of the heart with *Sathya* (Truth) and *Dharma* (Righteousness). Otherwise, the image will not appear. In every act of yours, if you observe Truth and Justice, then you can see your own reality revealed. You may say that the burden of past acts and their inevitable consequences have to be borne; but, the Grace of the Lord can burn that burden in a flash; the revelation of reality will, in a flash, save you from that burden. If you see yourself in all and all in you, then, you have known the reality, says Krishna in the Geetha. Therefore, you have to develop the same quantity and quality of Love that you have for Me, towards all others. When you are the Universal, where can you say your street is or your house is? You are then no longer an individual; you are the Universal. Get that idea fixed in your mind. The Lord will be easily moved; He is like butter, a little warmth is enough to melt His heart.[2]

◊ ◊ ◊ ◊ ◊

The *Vedas* have three sections: *Karma, upasana* and *jnana. Karma* or activity engaged in with a dedicatory attitude, regardless of the benefit it may result in, builds up purity of mind. *Upasana* or systematic worship of God contemplating on the glory and splendour of His manifold expressions equips you with concentration. These two lead to a clear grasp of the Reality, that is to say, you acquire *jnana* (spiritual wisdom); the veil of delusion drops and glory stands revealed. Now, these three are neglected and even scoffed at.[1]

◊ ◊ ◊ ◊ ◊

The secret is, discover the fountain of joy within; that is a never–failing, ever–full, ever–cool fountain, for it rises from God. What is the body? It is but the *Atma* encased in five sheaths, the *Annamaya* (the one composed of food), the *Pranamaya* (the one composed of vitality), the *Manomaya* (the one composed of mind), the *Vignanamaya* (the one composed of the intellect), and the *Anandamaya* (the one composed of Bliss). By a constant contemplation of these sheaths or *koshas*, the *sadaka* attains discrimination to recede from the outer to the inner and the more real. Thus, step by step, he abandons one *kosha* after another and is able to dissolve away all of them, to achieve the knowledge of his unity with *Brahman*.[2]

◊ ◊ ◊ ◊ ◊

Of the four *yugas*, the present *Kali yuga* is far more congenial than the previous three (*Kritha*, *Thretha* and *Dwapara yugas*) for the acquisition of wisdom and the cultivation of discrimination (*viveka*) for, we now have many simple paths available for liberating ourselves. The scriptures say, "No, no, dear sirs, no age is equal to the *Kali* age! Through just *smarana* and *chinthana*, we can reach the Goal. *Smarana* is the process of keeping the Lord ever in the memory and *chinthana* is the process of thinking of His glory all the time. Many people are scared because they believe that the *Kali yuga* in which we live will witness the ultimate Deluge. Others call it the *Kalaha yuga*, the Age of

---

[1] *Sathya Sai Speaks*, Vol. 5, p. 123.

[2] *Sathya Sai Speaks*, Vol. 5, p. 191.

Conflict, for it is now well-nigh omnipresent. No, no. This age is the Golden Age for the seekers of God, for earning and learning *viveka*.[1]

◊ ◊ ◊ ◊ ◊

Individual effort and Grace, both are essential. *Sankara* says, "*Ishwara anugrahath eva pumsam adwaitha vasana*" — "through the Grace of the Lord alone can man develop a desire for the non-duality of the Universe," for the One without a second. Seeing only the One is *jnana* (spiritual wisdom); and *jnana* alone confers *kaivalyam* (liberation).

Note down all the things for which you have cried so far. You will find that you have craved only for paltry things, for momentary distinctions, for fleeting fame; you should cry only for God, for your own cleansing and consummation. You should weep, wailing for the six cobras that have sheltered themselves in your mind, poisoning it with their venom: Lust, anger, greed, attachment, pride and malice. Quieten them as the snake charmer does with his swaying flute. The music that can tame them is the singing aloud of the Name of God. And when they are too intoxicated to move and harm, catch them by the neck and pull out their fangs as the charmer does. Thereafter, they can be your playthings; you can handle them as you please.[2]

◊ ◊ ◊ ◊ ◊

You have to read the newspaper to know how mad and foolish the world is; how futile is heroism, how momentary the glory; and after perusing it for the information it conveys, you throw it aside; it is now a tasteless waste. So too, live but once; so live that you are born but once. Do not fall in love with the world so much that your false fascination brings you again and again into this delusive amalgam of

---

[1] *Sathya Sai Speaks*, Vol. 15, p. 157.

[2] *Sathya Sai Speaks*, Vol. 8, p. 55.

joy and grief. Unless you stand back a little, away from entanglement with the world, knowing that it is all a play whose director is God, you are in danger of being too closely involved. Use the world as a training ground for sacrifice, service, expansion of the heart, cleansing of the emotions. That is the only value it has.[1]

◊ ◊ ◊ ◊ ◊

4.

Complete Surrender to the Divine is Necessary to Achieve Spiritual Liberation, the Goal of Life

Without surrender, there can be no liberation. So long as you cling to the narrow "I," the four prison walls will close in on you. Cross out the "I" and you are free. How to kill the "I?" Place it at the feet of the Lord and say, "You," not "I" — and you are free of the burden that is crushing you. Associate always with the *Niranjana* — the vast, the unlimited, the Divine; dream and plan to merge with the Absolute; fill your ears with the call from the beyond and the boundless. Transcend the walls, the bars and bolts, the locks and chains. You can do so easily by fixing your mind on your own infinity.[2]

◊ ◊ ◊ ◊ ◊

---

[1] *Sathya Sai Speaks*, Vol. 7, p. 67.

[2] *Sathya Sai Speaks*, Vol. 2, p. 224.

You have been born for one purpose: to die. That is to say, to kill the "I." If *bhrama* (delusion) dies, you become *Brahman* (the Supreme Spirit), or rather, you know that you are *Brahman*. All this literature, all this effort, all this *yajna*, all this teaching is just to hold a mirror before you, so that you may see Yourself.[1]

◊ ◊ ◊ ◊ ◊

Man too has a unique quality which marks him out from others. It is *Thyaga*, the capacity and the willingness to give up, renounce, sacrifice. He is endowed with that quality for a high purpose.

What exactly is that purpose? The *Vedas* declare it in clear terms. "By renunciation alone can immortality be gained." Immortality, not death, is the genuine *Dharma* or nature of the human being. This is the reason why humans are the crown of created beings. But man has lost hold of this precious quality and he lives in bondage to selfishness. When man attaches himself to the ego (*swartha*) he loses access to the higher levels of consciousness (*parartha*). This downfall results in his losing grip of the Reality (*yatharta*). And, when the Reality eludes him, he is confronted by a crowd of contradictory conclusions (*nanartha*). This calamity (*anartha*) in the thought process results in mental confusion (*ashanti*).[2]

◊ ◊ ◊ ◊ ◊

Such statements like surrendering body, mind and heart are only - rhetoric sanctioned by tradition and long usage. The act of surrender is often highlighted as *Atma*–arpana. The expression is even more ridiculous. When you are *Atma* in essence, how can *Atma* (Self) offer Itself to Itself? "The body is a composite of the five elements; it cannot avoid

---

[1] *Sathya Sai Speaks*, Vol. 2, p. 242.

[2] *Sathya Sai Speaks*, Vol. 15, p. 65.

disintegration, but the dweller within the body has no birth or death, no desire or despair, no attachment or bondage. In truth, that dweller is the God of Gods who resides as *Atma* in you." This is what the seers have experienced. So *Atma*–arpana is a meaningless expression. You have nothing in you or belonging to you that you can claim as yours to offer to God.

Then, what does surrender of the self signify or imply? To experience God as Omnipresent, to be aware of nothing other than God — this is true surrender. To see God in everything, everywhere, at all times, is true *Sharanagati*. He gives, He enjoys, He experiences. If you offer, and God accepts, you become superior; how can God be all-powerful? You should not reduce the glory of God through such high–sounding statements.[1]

---

[1] *Sathya Sai Speaks*, Vol. 15, pp. 147–48.

Chapter 2

Ganesha

LORD GANESHA

Chapter 2

Ganesha

Introduction

The following words of Swami Chinmayananda lend meaning to the illustration of Ganesha:

Lord Shiva's first son is described as the Supreme Leader (*Vinayaka*) or as the leader of the *Ganas (Ganapathi)* who attends upon and follows at all times Lord Shiva, or as the Lord of all obstacles (*Vigneswara*). These names clearly show that he is a Master of all circumstances and not even the Divine forces can obstruct His path. Since He is thus the Lord of all obstacles, no Hindu ritual or auspicious act is ever undertaken without invoking Him. With His grace it is believed that no undertaking can fail due to subjective or objective obstacles.

He is considered as having married both Lakshmi and Saraswati, the Goddesses of Wealth and Knowledge, so he is the Master of Knowledge (*Vidya*) and the champion of worldly achievements (*Avidya*).

Sri Ganapathi represents a man of perfect wisdom, and a fully realized *Vedantin* ... To a *Vedantic* student, since his "path of knowledge" is essentially intellectual, he must have a great head to conceive and understand the logic of the *Vedantic* thought, and, in fact, the truth of *Vedanta* can be comprehended only through listening to a teacher and therefore, *sravana* (listening) is the initial stage to be mastered by the new initiate. Therefore, Sri Ganapathi has large ears representing continuous and intelligent listening to the teacher.

After "listening" to the truths of the *Upanishads*, the *Vedantic* student must independently "reflect" (*manana*) upon what he has heard, for which he needs a sensitive intelligence with ample sympathy to discover in himself sufficient accommodation for all living creatures in the universe.

His intellect must have such depth and width in order to embrace in his vision the entire world of plurality. Not only must he in his visualization, embrace the whole cosmos, but he must have the subtle discriminative power (*viveka*) in him to distinguish the changing perishable, matter–vestures from the Eternal, Immutable, All Pervading Consciousness, the Spirit. This discrimination is possible only when the intellect of the student has consciously cultivated this power to a large degree of perfection.

The trunk coming down the forehead of the elephant face, has got a peculiar efficiency and beats all achievements of man and his ingenuity in the mechanical and scientific world. Here is a "tool" which can at once uproot a tree or pick up a pin from the ground .... Like the elephant's trunk, so should be the perfect discriminative faculty of an evolved intellect so that it can use its discrimination fully in the outer world for resolving gross problems, and at the same time, efficiently employ its discrimination in the subtle realms of the inner personality layers.

The discriminative power in use functions only where there are two factors to discriminate between: these two factors represent the tusks of the elephant and the trunk growing down between them. Between good and evil, right and wrong, and the dualities we must discriminate and come to our own judgements and conclusions in life

.... The broken tusk indicates that a real *Vedantin* student is one who has gone beyond the pairs of opposites ....

A man of Perfection must have a big belly to stomach peacefully, as it were, all the experience of life, auspicious and inauspicious ....

In the representation of Sri Vinayaka we always find a mouse .... The mouse is a small animal with tiny teeth and yet, in a barn of grain a solitary mouse can bring disastrous losses by continuously gnawing and nibbling at the grain. Similarly there is a "mouse" within each personality which can eat away even a mountain of merit in us and this mouse is the power of desire. The man of perfection is one who has so perfectly mastered this urge to acquire, possess and enjoy, this self–annihilating power of desire, that it is completely held in obedience to the will of the master. And yet, when the master wants to play his part in blessing the world, he rides upon the mouse — meaning it is a desire to do service to the world that becomes his vehicle to move about and act ....

Ganesha has four arms. In His hands he often has a rope, an axe, rice balls (*modakas*), or a lotus or tusk. With the axe he cuts off the attachments of his devotees to the world of plurality and thus ends all the consequent sorrows, and with the rope pulls them nearer and nearer to the Truth, and ultimately ties them down to the Highest Goal. He holds rice balls (*modakas*) representing the reward of the joys of *sadhana* which He gives his devotees. With another hand He blesses all His devotees and protects them from all obstacles on their spiritual path of seeking the Supreme.[1]

◊ ◊ ◊ ◊ ◊

Further meanings of specific aspects of the form of Ganesha such the tusk, mouse, book and rosary, the

---

[1] *Symbolism in Hinduism*, Swami Chinmayananda, compiled by R. S. Nathan, pp. 171-177.

elephant head, white cloth, ash grey body, gram flour sweets and the large belly are explained in this chapter by Sathya Sai Baba.

The role of spiritual practices (*sadhanas*) as self–effort to remove obstacles to Self–realization as aspects of the Ganesha principle within each human being is presented through excerpts from Sathya Sai Baba's Divine Discourses under the headings; A. the control and purification of the senses, mind and emotions; B. the need for spiritual discipline; C. the need for skill, capacity, will, courage, confidence, perseverance and wisdom; D. the need for self–inquiry; E. the need for good, pure actions.

The role of God's Grace or the Guru's Grace and the *Gayatri Mantra* as aspects of Ganesha to remove obstacles in life and in the pursuit of Self–realization are also presented through excerpts from Sathya Sai Baba's Divine Discourses.

◊ ◊ ◊ ◊ ◊

1.

Vinayaka and Ganapathi: Interchangeable Aspects of Ganesha

Ganesha is the symbol of optimum coordination of mind and intellect; therefore, He is worshipped before all other deities when any work or worship is initiated. This is to indicate that mind and intellect should have all the virtues and qualities of Ganesha and should first be well controlled and well coordinated when one applies oneself to any work or worship.

Ganesha is the Lord of the Intellect. His form itself symbolizes and signifies all the proper activities of the intellect.[1]

◊ ◊ ◊ ◊ ◊

Vinayaka or Ganesha or Ganapathi or Vigneswara — all indicate the elephant–God, who is popular among young and old, and who is worshipped as the very first deity, before regularly beginning any ceremony or *samskar*, any *yaga* or *yajna*, any vow or fast or pilgrimage. He is the Lord of the *Ganas* or Divine Forces, inside and outside the human body; He is the Lord, who masters and overwhelms *vighna* (obstacle), however imminent or eminent. This is the natural effect of the fact that Ganapathi is the God of Intelligence, *Vidya* or *Buddhi* (learning or intellect).

Ganapathi is a God revered in *Tantric* (ritualistic) lore, and also, by various *Vedic mantras*.[2]

◊ ◊ ◊ ◊ ◊

How did Vinayaka acquire *siddhis* (supreme powers)? His parents held a contest for their two sons — Ganesha and Subramanya. They said they will offer their grace in the form of a fruit to whoever came first in circumambulating the universe. The younger son, Subramanya, set out immediately on his peacock to go round the universe. On seeing Subramanya approaching his parents, almost at the end of his trip, Vinayaka, who had been quietly sitting all the while, got up and

---

[1] *The Words of Sathya Sai Baba: Life is a Dream, Realize It*, Joy Thomas, p. 132.

[2] *Sathya Sai Speaks*, Vol. 11, p. 210.

went round the parents and sat down. Parvathi (symbol of Creation) observed that Subramanya, who had taken so much trouble to go round the universe, should be declared the winner. Parameswara (Shiva) asked Vigneswara what was the inner significance of his going round the parents. Ganesha replied: "The entire universe is permeated by both of you. The entire creation is a manifestation of the Shiva–Shakti form. It is an act of delusion to attempt to go round this phenomenal universe. To go round both of you is the true circumambulation of the cosmos." Then Parvathi exclaimed: "Yours is the fruit." Ganesha became the Lord of the Divine hosts (*ganas*). Easwara (Shiva) was so much impressed with the supreme intelligence of Vinayaka that he told him: "All those who wish to worship Me, will offer their worship first to you." Such was the grace showered on Vinayaka. What is the reason? Ganesha's faith in the Lord and His omnipresence. The right path for all people is to develop faith in God and lead godly lives.[1]

◊ ◊ ◊ ◊ ◊

Vinayaka is the Lord of all learning (*vidya*). Does learning mean bookish scholarship? No. Everything pertaining to the cosmos is included in the term learning (*vidya*). Walking, talking, laughing, sitting, eating, strolling, thinking — every kind of activity is related to learning. Vinayaka is the master of every kind of learning. Today learning is identified with acquisition of information. But apart from knowledge of the physical world, we have many other kinds of knowledge relating to chemistry, the fine arts and other skills.

Vinayaka is the master of every kind of knowledge. Learning is related to the intellect (*buddhi*). It is not mere scholarship. Familiarity with books is not knowledge. One's entire life is a continuous process of learning. Any process of enquiry is related to learning. But basically

---

[1] *Sanathana Sarathi*, October 1991, p. 276.

our enquiry should be concerned with finding out what is transient and what is permanent. This is true knowledge.[1]

◊ ◊ ◊ ◊ ◊

Vinayaka is the Lord of life. Men should learn to shed selfishness and cultivate Love of the Supreme Self. This is the inner Truth about Vinayaka. Vinayaka should not be considered as merely an elephant–headed deity riding on a mouse.[2]

◊ ◊ ◊ ◊ ◊

Today were are celebrating *Ganesh Jayanthi*, the birthday of Vighneswara. Who is He? What is His greatness? What has He taught to the world? We celebrate the *Jayanthi* but do not make any effort to understand the *tatwa* or principle behind it. His supreme teaching by His own example is oneness of the Universe. When He was asked to go round the universe to get a prize from his parents, He just circumambulated His parents, Lord Shiva and Parvathi and claimed that He had completed the trip around the universe by going around them, as Lord Shiva and Parvathi represented the Universe.[3]

◊ ◊ ◊ ◊ ◊

... Ganapathi ... means ... the lord of the *ganas* — a class of Divine entities. This term also means that he is the master of the intellect and discriminating power in man. He possesses great intelligence and knowledge. Such knowledge issues from a pure and sacred mind. This knowledge leads to wisdom (*vignana*). Because he is the master of

---

[1] *Sanathana Sarathi*, October 1995, p. 255.

[2] *Sanathana Sarathi*, October 1995, p. 259.

[3] *Sanathana Sarathi*, November 1993, p. 296.

buddhi (intelligence) and *siddhi* (wisdom or realisation), he is described as the Lord of *buddhis* and *siddhi*. *Buddhi* and *siddhi* are referred to as the consorts of Vinayaka.[1]

◊ ◊ ◊ ◊ ◊

Vighneswara is called Ganapathi because he is the Supreme Lord of the *ganas*. The *ganas* are the embodiment of the organs of perception (*jnanendriyas*) and of action (*karmendriyas*). The mind is the master of these ten senses. The presiding deity of the mind is called Indra as he is the Lord of the *Indriyas* (the senses). The master over the mind is the intellect (*buddhi*).

What does the name *Ganapathi* signify? *Ga* means *buddhi* (or intellect), *Na* means *Vijnana* (wisdom). As Vighneswara is the Lord of the Intellect and Wisdom, he is called *Ganapathi*.

It follows from this that what are called *ganas* are parts of the human body. The individual (*vyakti*) is a part of creation (*srishti*). Hence, Divinity, of which the cosmos is a projection, is immanent in the human being. *Vigatho nayaka Vinayaka* ("Vinayaka has no master over him.") This means that Vinayaka is a totally autonomous and independent deity. He has no Lord above him. In the world, any individual or authority has someone superior above him. But Vinayaka has no overlord.

The worship of Vinayaka has been in existence from times immemorial in *Bharat*. The *Rig Veda*, the *Narayanopanishad* and the *Thaithiriya Upanishad* have passages referring to Vinayaka. It is embedded also in the *Gayatri Mantra*.

Tatpurushaya Vidmahe
Vakrathundaya dheemahi
Thanno Danthi Prachodayath

---

[1] *Sanathana Sarathi*, October 1991, p. 275.

This *mantra* indicates that Vinayaka's Divinity is glorified in this *Gayatri Mantra*. Hence Ganapathi signifies an all–pervading Divine potency.

In everyday parlance, Ganapathi is described as the son of Parvati. Parvati represents *Prakriti* (Nature). Man is a child of nature. Hence every human being is a Vinayaka. He is a spark of the Divine Shiva–Sakti, the union of the Lord and Nature. Everything in the world has emanated from nature (*prakriti*). All things are aspects of nature. It is to reveal this sacred truth that holy festivals are observed.[1]

◊ ◊ ◊ ◊ ◊

Whatever you see in the external world is *drisya* (that which is seen). The Sun, Moon, stars, the five elements which are constituents of the universe are all *drisya*. You are seeing your body too as you see other things. So the body is also *drisya*, that which is seen by you. Who is then the seer? The seer is *drashta*. The body is the object and you are the seers. Without a seer there is no question of anything being "seen." Some people talk about *soonya* or emptiness or nothingness. Unless this has been seen, how can they talk about *soonya*? Knowledge of the seer and the seen is the great message of Ganapathi, whose advent we are celebrating today. *Ga* means *buddhi* or intelligence, *na* means *vignana* or wisdom, and *pathi* means master. So, Ganapathi is the master of all knowledge, intelligence and wisdom. There is also another significant meaning for the word, that He is the Leader of all the *ganas* who are celestial beings. He is also called *Vinayaka*, which term means that he is one who has no master above him. He is the Supreme Master. He is beyond the mindless state. One who has stilled the mind cannot have any master.[2]

---

[1] *Sanathana Sarathi*, October 1995, pp. 253-54.

[2] *Sanathana Sarathi*, October 1994, p. 263.

◊ ◊ ◊ ◊ ◊

Students like to worship Ganapathi. They pray to Ganesha to confer on them *buddhi* (intelligence) and *siddhi* (the capacity to realise their aspirations). In the name Ganapathi, G stands for *guna* or virtue and *na* stands for *vijnana* (wisdom). When *ga* and *na* are joined we have the combination of *vijnana* (scientific knowledge) and *prajnana* (spiritual wisdom). It is out of the combination of *vijnana* and *prajnana* that *sujnana* (supreme knowledge) emerges, is the distinguishing mark of a true man. *Agnana* is the sign of ignorance. Ganapathi is the Lord of *vijnana* and *prajnana* (worldly knowledge and spiritual wisdom). Therefore, when a devotee prays to Ganesha, he asks for the conferment of *vijnana, prajnana* and *sujnana*.[1]

◊ ◊ ◊ ◊ ◊

You must emulate Ganesha not in the quantity of food eaten, but in His aspect as Vinayaka, for to become a Vinayaka, a special type of leader, you have to be for long an earnest and enthusiastic servant engaged in selfless, loving service. Service is the best school for training in leadership. You should eliminate in that school all traces of disgust, anger and impatience. Pride and personal prejudices will try to put spokes in the wheel as you go to serve the distressed and the diseased. But you should never give up faith in the right path you have chosen. Remind yourself that you are a *sadaka* (spiritual aspirant) and that *seva* (service) is the spiritual path that you have ventured upon as the easiest and the best.[2]

◊ ◊ ◊ ◊ ◊

---

[1] *Sanathana Sarathi*, September 1992, p. 224.

[2] *Sathya Sai Speaks*, Vol. 13, p. 111.

It is only when a man is pure that the intelligence blossoms. It is only with the blossoming of intelligence that the spiritual goal is attained (*siddhi*). Vinayaka presides over the intellect and spiritual realisation (*buddhi* and *siddhi*). *Siddhi* signifies the realisation of wisdom. The scriptures say that *siddhi* and *buddhi* are the consorts of Vinayaka, and *Kshema* and *Ananda* are his two sons. *Siddhi* and *buddhi* symbolise the powers of attraction of Ganapathi.

The Ganapathi festival is an occasion for people to purify their minds. People generally tend to see in others the faults which they themselves have. Thereby they try to cover up their own defects by attributing the same defects to others. This is a bad quality. A man can improve only by recognising his faults, not by seeing the same faults in others. You must see what is good in others and look at your own defects. Only such a person can improve. Man does violence to his human nature by ignoring his defects and magnifying the faults in others.[1]

◊ ◊ ◊ ◊ ◊

2.
Vigneswara: The Remover of Obstacles and Promoter of Wealth

Worshipping *Vinayaka* or Vigneswara or Ganapathi, as he is also called, endows man with the courage and confidence needed to enter upon and carry through any undertaking in the world. The elephant is the largest animal of the forest. It is very intelligent and has a powerful memory. When it marches through the thick jungle, it clears

---

[1] *Sanathana Sarathi*, September 1992, p. 222.

a path for all other animals to pass. The elephant–headed God confers intelligence and memory and the power to subdue evil and vice. Thus he is also a path–maker. So it is only appropriate that every rite, ceremony or project should be started with the worship of this God.[1]

◊ ◊ ◊ ◊ ◊

Another name for Vinayaka is Vigneswara. Easwara (Shiva) is one who is endowed with every conceivable form of wealth: riches, knowledge, health, Bliss, beauty, etc. Vigneswara is the promoter of all these forms of wealth and removes all obstacles to their enjoyment. He confers all these forms of wealth on those who worship him. Vinayaka is described as *Pratama Vandana* (the first deity who should be worshipped). As everyone in the world desires wealth and prosperity, everyone offers the first place for worship to Vigneswara.

The Vinayaka–principle, however, has only one meaning, which is relevant to everyone irrespective of whether he is a believer or a non–believer. *Vinayaka* means that he is totally master of himself. He has no master above him, He does not depend on anyone.

Vinayaka is the deity who removes all bad qualities, instills good qualities and confers peace on the devotee who meditates on him.[2]

◊ ◊ ◊ ◊ ◊

Vinayaka is also called Vigneswara as he removes all obstacles coming in the way of devotees who pray to Him sincerely. He is worshipped by students with books so that all that is contained in the books may get into their heads.[3]

---

[1] *Sathya Sai Speaks*, Vol. 13, pp. 136–37.

[2] *Sanathana Sarathi*, October 1991, p. 275.

[3] *Sanathana Sarathi*, October 1994, p. 265.

◊ ◊ ◊ ◊ ◊

There is special significance in placing Vigneswara in the forefront before embarking on any undertaking. In a forest, when an elephant moves through the jungle, it clears the way for others to follow. Likewise, by invoking Ganesha, the path is cleared for our undertakings. The elephant's foot is so large that when it moves it can stamp out the footprints of any other animal. Here, again, the symbolic meaning is that all obstacles in the way will be removed when Ganesha is accorded the place of honour. The journey of life is made smoother and happier by the grace of Ganesha.[1]

◊ ◊ ◊ ◊ ◊

Vinayaka is one who drives away all sorrows, difficulties and miseries. He is the enemy of all obstacles. He will not allow any obstacles to come in the way. He is the destroyer of obstacles. He confers happiness and peace (on his devotees). He is the master of all these powers (*buddhi* and *siddhi*). What is this *siddhi* (fulfilment)? When there is purity of mind you achieve peace (which is *siddhi*). Vinayaka is thus the Lord of *buddhi* and *siddhi* (the Intellect and Self–Realisation). Hence, every human being should acquire control over the mind.[2]

◊ ◊ ◊ ◊ ◊

---

[1] *Sanathana Sarathi*, October 1989, p. 263.

[2] *Sanathana Sarathi*, October 1995, p. 225.

3.

Ganesha, Vinayaka, and Ganapathi- Promoter of Buddhi or Intellect and Detachment

People are ignoring the very beacons which illuminate the darkness and reveal the path of liberation from the bonds of incessant struggle, endless pursuit, bewildering agony and ceaseless activity to gain the ungainable! What is the reason? The mind guides him, not the faculty of the intellect. The intellect discriminates; it probes, it analyses. But the mind follows blindly every whim or fancy. The intellect helps one to identify one's duties and responsibilities. Slavishly bound to the vagaries of the mind, man hops from one spot to another, without rest or peace. He runs to catch a bus, rushes to the office, to the cinema hall, to the club and has no moment of calm silence. Peace has to be attained through spiritual efforts, that is to say, through spiritualising every thought, word and deed. What has to be planned today to set the world aright is not a new spiritual order or institution but men and women with pure hearts. They alone can uplift this land from the morass.[1]

◊ ◊ ◊ ◊ ◊

Dwell always on high thoughts. When air fills a football, it takes the form of the ball. When it fills a balloon, it takes the form of the balloon, oval, sausage shaped, spherical or spheroid. The mind

---

[1] *Sathya Sai Speaks*, Vol. 15, p. 34.

assumes the form of the objects with which it is attached. If it gets fixed on small things, it becomes small; if on grand things, it becomes grand. The camera takes a picture of whatever it is pointed at: so take care before you click. Discriminate before you develop attachment. If you have attachment towards wife and children, land and buildings, bank accounts and balances and when these decline, you will come to grief. Develop attachment towards the Universal and you too will grow in Love and Splendour. That attachment must be sincere and steady.[1]

◊ ◊ ◊ ◊ ◊

India has been very fortunate. It has had seers and sages throughout the centuries who have held forth the value of high ideals. It has had the examples of *Avatars* of Godhead. The emphasis has all along been on the *Atma* that is the core of every being — a teaching that can confer courage, contentment, peace and harmony. It is indeed pathetic to see people following the vagaries of the mind and courting disaster, instead of using the intellect to discriminate between the transient and the permanent.

The mind should be checked by the intellect (Ganesha). Or else, evil resolutions will result in sorrow. Resolve on good actions and reap joy. Of course, if one can desist from desires and the tendency to pursue them, one can have unshaken peace. If the mind is set loose and given the mastery, man is driven from one inequity to another. He loses his self–respect. He sets at naught law and justice, rules of conduct and regulations of social behavior. His life becomes a frantic rush from place to place and object to object.

Detachment alone can give happiness. *Thyaga* (renunciation) is the real *yoga*. Three evil qualities have to be renounced before man can rise to his real role. Anger which smothers wisdom (*jnana*), lust which pollutes the deed (*karma*) and greed, which destroys one's Love

---

[1] *Sathya Sai Speaks*, Vol. 5, p. 20.

(*Prema*) for God and man. The touchstone which pronounces an act as meritorious is "renunciation." If an act is self–directed, if it helps to inflate the ego, it is a sin.[1]

◊ ◊ ◊ ◊ ◊

Know the *Atma* which is your Reality; know that it is the same Inner Force of this Universe. Let your intelligence penetrate into the Truth (Ganesha). Analyse yourself and discover the several layers of Consciousness — the physical, the sensory, the nervous, the mental, the intellectual — and arrive at the very core of even the last layer, the layer of joy. The five sheaths have to be transcended, so that you may attain your Truth, which is *Atma*.

The *Atma* can be grasped only by a sharpened intellect and a pure mind (Ganesha). How to purify the mind? By starving it of the bad food it runs after, namely, objective pleasures, and feeding it on the wholesome food, namely, thought of God. The intellect too will be sharp if it is devoted to discrimination between the transient and the eternal. Let your thoughts be concentrated on God, His Name and His Form; you will then find that you are always with the Pure and Permanent; you will then derive pure and permanent joy. That is the reason why I attach so much importance to *namasmarana* as a *sadhana*.[2]

◊ ◊ ◊ ◊ ◊

The first requisite for the seeker is the quality of detachment, of *Vairagya*, a quality that is the product of deep discrimination on the nature and characteristics of the senses, the mind and the intellect, besides the nature of the objects around us. Think deeply of the relative validity of experiences during the waking, the dream and the

---

[1] *Sathya Sai Speaks*, Vol. 15, pp. 29–30.

[2] *Sathya Sai Speaks*, Vol. 4, p. 296.

deep sleep stages and of the "I" or Self that is the witness of these experiences.

That witness is you, the real you, a spark of the Eternal Universal Witness. How then can you, with such a grand heritage and such a grand destiny, run after mean ends and short–lived successes? It is by such discrimination that you get established in detachment (Ganesha). When you know that the "diamond" which you treasured so carefully is just a piece of glass, you need no persuasion to cast it out. Employ yourself usefully; earn, but do not clasp the riches with fanatic zeal. Be like a trustee, holding things on trust, on behalf of God, for purposes which He likes and approves.[1]

◊ ◊ ◊ ◊ ◊

The urge in the mind that animates the senses is stronger than the sense organs themselves. The eyes, for instance, are merely instruments for seeing, but "seeing" itself is a power that is superior to them. Similarly, hearing power is higher than the mere ear. The mind is superior to the sense organs and superior to the mind is *buddhi* (intellect), the power of discrimination (Ganesha). Above the *buddhi* is the animating Life Principle, the *Jeeva*. Above the *Jeevatma* (the individual soul) is the *Paramatma* (Supreme Soul). Between the individual and the Divine, there is an attractive deluding veil, *maya* (illusory power). When this veil falls, the individualised Self and the Universal Omni–self become one.

When the mind turns away from the senses to the *Buddhi* (Ganesha) for enlightenment, *Ananda* (Divine Bliss) starts to flow and the glory of *Atma* (Divine Soul) is revealed. *Buddhi* promotes the search inward. While the sense organs — the eye, the ear, the nose, the tongue and the skin — all open out towards external objects, true *sadhana* (spiritual discipline) consists in turning the vision inwards, in fact, to swim against the on rushing current. It is seldom realised how

---

[1] *Sathya Sai Speaks*, Vol. 4, pp. 298–99.

near is the goal of self–realisation when once the sense organs are turned inwards.[1]

◊ ◊ ◊ ◊ ◊

Reason (Ganesha) seeks to know the unity of the universe, the origin and goal of it all, the laws that govern the *anu* (microcosm) and *bruhath* (macrocosm); and it peeps behind the ever–receding curtain to get a glimpse of the *Sutradhara* (puppeteer), who pulls the strings.[2]

◊ ◊ ◊ ◊ ◊

Buddhi (intellect) revels in discussion and disputation; once you yield to the temptation of dialectics, it takes a long time for you to escape from its shackles and efface it and enjoy the Bliss which comes from its nullification. You must all the while be aware of the limitation of reason. *Logic* must give way to *Logos* and Deduction must yield place to Devotion. *Buddhi* can help you only some distance along the Godward path; the rest is illuminated by intuition. Your feelings and emotions warp even your thought processes; and reason is made by them into an untamed bull. Very often, egoism tends to encourage and justify the wildness, for a person is led along the wrong path by his very reason, if that is the path he likes! You very often come to the conclusion you want to reach!

Unless you are extra careful to examine the very process of reasoning, even while the process is going on, there is the danger that you may be following only the trail you yourself have laid down. Reason can be tamed only by discipline, by systematic application of the yoke, the nose–string, the whip, etc. That is to say, by means of *dhyana, shantam, kshama, sahana* (meditation, calmness, forbearance,

---

[1] *Sathya Sai Speaks*, Vol. 16, pp. 101–102.

[2] *Sathya Sai Speaks*, Vol. 1, p. 121.

endurance), etc. Train it to talk quietly along small stretches of road at first and then, after you have become sure of its docility, you can take it along the tortuous road of the sixfold temptations: the road of lust, anger, greed, delusion, pride and jealousy.[1]

◊ ◊ ◊ ◊ ◊

Develop the power of discrimination and find out which is permanent and which is not, which is beneficial and which is not (Ganesha). Even in selecting a *Guru*, you should use your *viveka* (discrimination). Not all clouds are rain–bearing. A real teacher will be able to attract seekers from afar merely by his personality. He need not be talked about in glowing terms; his presence will be felt and aspirants will hurry towards him, like bees towards a lotus in full bloom.[2]

◊ ◊ ◊ ◊ ◊

Man is essentially a discriminating animal, endowed with *viveka* (discrimination) (Ganesha). He is not content with the satisfaction of mere animal needs; he feels some void, some deep discontent, some unslaked thirst, for he is a child of Immortality and he feels that death is not and should not be the end. This *viveka* urges man to discover answers to the problems that haunt him: "Where did I come from, whither am I journeying, which is the journey's end?" So, *buddhi* (intellect) has to be kept sharp and clear.

There are three types of *buddhi*, according to the predominance of one or other of the three *gunas*: the *tamas*, which confuses *Satyam* (Truth) as the *asatyam* (untruth) and takes the *asatyam* as the *Satyam*; the *rajasic* which like a pendulum swings from one to the other,

---

[1] *Sathya Sai Speaks*, Vol. 1, p. 119.

[2] *Sathya Sai Speaks*, Vol. 1, p. 71.

hovering between the two, unable to distinguish between them; and the *satwa*, which knows which is *satyam* and which is *asatyam*.

The world today is suffering from *rajobuddhi* (passionate intellect) rather than *tamas* (inertia); people have violent likes and dislikes; they have become fanatical and factious. They are carried away by pomp and noise, show and propaganda; that is why discrimination has become necessary. To reach the goal, *satwabuddhi* (equanimous intellect) is essential; it will seek the Truth calmly and stick to it whatever the consequence.[1]

Remember, the sword of *Prema* (Love) has to be kept in the sheath of *viveka* (wisdom). The *indriyas* (senses) have to be rigorously controlled by *viveka* and *vairagya* (discrimination and detachment), the twin talents given exclusively to man. *Viveka* instructs you how to choose your avocations and your associates. It tells you the relative importance of objects and ideals. *Vairagya* saves you from too much of attachment and injects a sense of relief, at times of elation or despair. They are the two wings that lift the bird into the air. They hold before you the impermanence of the world and permanence of the Bliss of Reality. They prompt you to direct your lives towards spiritual *sadhana* and the never failing contemplation of the glory of the Lord.[2]

◊ ◊ ◊ ◊ ◊

The greatest obstacle on the path of surrender is *ahamkara* (egoism) and *mamakara* (mineness or possessiveness). It is something that has been adhering to our personality since ages, sending its tentacles deeper and deeper with the experience of every succeeding life. It can be removed only by the twin detergents of discrimination and renunciation. *Bhakti* (devotion) is the water to wash away this dirt

[1] *Sathya Sai Speaks*, Vol. 1, p. 62.

[2] *Sathya Sai Speaks*, Vol. 1, p. 260.

of ages and the soap of *japam, dhyanam* and *yoga* (repetition of God's name, meditation and communion) will help to remove it quicker and more effectively. The slow and the steady will surely win this race; walking is the safest method of travel, though it may be condemned as slow. Quicker means of travel mean disaster; the quicker the means, the greater the risk of disaster. You should eat only as much as you feel hunger for, more will cause disorder. So proceed step by step in *sadhana* (spiritual effort), making sure of one step before you take another.[1]

◊ ◊ ◊ ◊ ◊

The world is today in deep distress because the common man and his leaders are all distracted by lower desires and lower motives, which require only the lower skills and meaner impulses of man. This is what I call "devaluation." Though man is inherently Divine, he lives only at the animal level. Very few live even in the native human level.

Instead of transforming his hearth, his home, his village, his state and this world into a *Prashanti Nilayam*, the Abode of the Peace that passeth understanding, man has made the world an arena for the wild passions of anger, hate and greed. Instead of making the senses (which are after all very poor guides and informants) his servants, he has made them his masters; he has become a slave of external beauty, evanescent melody, exterior softness, tickling taste; fragrance. He spends all his energies and the fruits of all his toil in the satisfaction of the trivial demands of these untamed underlings.

When the mind is controlling the senses, you have lasting joy; when the senses are masters, you are dragged in the dust. This is the most tragic result of devaluation. Every act which lowers the authority of *viveka* and honours the siren–call of the senses devalues man. Intelligence must be the Lord, the Master (Ganesha). Whenever the senses demand anything, intelligence must start discriminating, asking

---

[1] *Sathya Sai Speaks*, Vol. 1, p. 19.

the question, "Is this an act in keeping with the Divinity immanent in me?" That will prevent devaluation.[1]

◊ ◊ ◊ ◊ ◊

Man is endowed with the capacity to separate himself from his body and the senses and the mind and the intelligence. He feels and says, My eyes, my ears, my feet, my hands, my mind, my reason, etc. He knows, deep down in his consciousness, that he is apart from all these; that he is their user, owner and master. No animal feels itself different from the body; for them, they are the body. They do not know that they are occupants of the physical frames. Man can, by a simple exercise in silent reasoning, discover that the physical frame is unreal and temporary. This should lead to *vairagya* (detachment), achieved through *vichakshana* (analysis), the result of *viveka* (discrimination) (Ganesha).

Once man is free from undue attachment to the body and its appurtenances, he is liberated also from the pulls of joy–grief, good–bad, pleasure–pain, etc. He is firmly established in equanimity, fortitude, undisturbed balance. Then man discovers that the world is one kin, in God; that all is Joy, Love, Bliss. He realises that he himself is all this apparent world, that all the multifarious manifestations are the fantasies of the Divine Will, which is his own reality. This expansion of one's individuality to cover the ends of the Universe is the highest leap of man. It gives supreme *Ananda* (Bliss), an experience for which sages and saints spent years of prayer and asceticism.[2]

◊ ◊ ◊ ◊ ◊

---

[1] *Sathya Sai Speaks*, Vol. 6, pp. 218–19.

[2] *Sathya Sai Speaks*, Vol. 7, p. 217.

One has to practise detachment at every step, or else, greed and miserliness will overpower the finer natures of man (Ganesha). That nature is Divine, because, God is the very substance of which man is but a name and form. To realise it, one has to possess and develop the discrimination between the unchanging and the changing, the permanent and the temporary (Ganesha). *Sadhana–Chatushtaya: Nithyanithya Viveka*, i.e., knowing that the Universe is constantly subject to change and modification and the *Brahman* alone is unmodified; *Iha amuthra–phala–bhoga–vairagya* — detachment from the pleasures of this world as well as the pleasures obtainable in Heaven after attaining the conviction that they are evanescent and fraught with grief; *Sama damadi–shatka sampathti* — attaining the six desirable qualifications: the control of external and internal senses and sensory promptings, fortitude in the midst of grief and pain, of joy and victory, *uparathi* — withdrawal from all activity that brings about consequences that bind, *shradda* — firm faith in the Teacher and the Texts that he expounds; *samadanam* — even contemplation on the basic *Brahman*, without being disturbed by other waves of thought. Though milk is under formation throughout the body of the cow, you have to resort to the four teats, in order to get it; so also these four *sadhanas* or teats have to be pressed (into service) if spiritual knowledge is to be gained.[1]

◊ ◊ ◊ ◊ ◊

Man is endowed with two special gifts: *Viveka* (the faculty of reasoning) and *vignana* (the faculty of analysis and synthesis). Use these gifts for discovering the Truth of yourself, which is the Truth of every one else, of everything else. All countries are borne and sustained by this earth; all are warmed by the same Sun; all "bodies"

---

[1] *Sathya Sai Speaks*, Vol. 5, pp. 196–97.

are inspired by the same Divine Principle; all are urged by the same inner motivator.[1]

◊ ◊ ◊ ◊ ◊

Man has been endowed with *buddhi* (intellect) (Ganesha), so that he might at every turn decide what is beneficent for observance and what is detrimental. Gandhi while going through hate–ridden regions, prayed, "*Sabko sanmathi dho Bhagavan!*" (O Lord! Give everyone a good mind!): The intellect has to be kept sharp, clear and straight.

There are four directions in which the intellect guides man: (1) *Swartha–sukha–buddhi*. This indicates the fully egoistic nature, where the individual does not care for even his wife and children, but, is eager to fulfill his own needs first and foremost. Then we have (2), the *Swartha–parartha–sukha–buddhi*, this allows some consideration for the happiness of others also. Birds feed their young and undergo great exertion to bring them up. The next variety is (3) *Parartha–buddhi*. Those who have this, seek for others as much happiness as they seek for themselves. They are prepared to undergo any trouble to secure for others too what they feel will grant them happiness. The next is (4) *Adyathmic–buddhi* (spiritual intellect). This leads man ever on the path of renunciation and service, for, they alone lead to Spiritual advancement. ...

... The *Adhyatmic* intellect recognises the Unity of creation and so, what the other person feels is felt by the individual too, to the same degree. This vast gathering of people will appear to the *Adhyathmic* intellect as a garland of multi–coloured flowers strung on the one single thread, God. Develop this vision; see the One behind the many; see the *Brahmasutra* — the string that runs through each flower.[2]

---

[1] *Sathya Sai Speaks*, Vol. 8, pp. 114–15.

[2] *Sathya Sai Speaks*, Vol. 13, pp. 45–46.

◊ ◊ ◊ ◊ ◊

4.

The Inner Meaning of Aspects and Equipments of Ganesha

The Single-Tusked (Eka Danta)

When Vinayaka was writing the *Mahabharata* to the dictation of Sage Vyasa, the latter laid down the condition that Vinayaka should go on writing non-stop whatever Vyasa said. But Vinayaka also stipulated a condition that Vyasa should never stop his dictation but should go on without a break. While he was writing, Vinayaka's pen broke and he did not hesitate to break one of his tusks to use it as a pen. That is why he is called *eka danta* or one with a single tusk. This is a shining example of the spirit of sacrifice that Vinayaka exhibited for the welfare of humanity. That is why the *Vedas* proclaim that it is only by sacrifice one can attain immortality.[1]

◊ ◊ ◊ ◊ ◊

An elephant normally has two tusks. The mind, too, frequently comes up with two alternatives: the good and the bad, the excellent and the expedient, the works of the hand and the worries in the head, the fact which lives in the mind and the fantasy which lures it away, etc. However, in order to achieve anything, the mind must become

---

[1] *Sanathana Sarathi*, October 1994, p. 7.

single–pointed.... The elephant head of Ganesha, therefore, has one tusk only, the Ganesha is called *eka danta*, meaning "the single tusked," to remind everyone that one's mind should have single–pointedness.[1]

◊ ◊ ◊ ◊ ◊

Mooshika, the Mouse, Ganesha's Vehicle

Some people, out of ignorance, comment upon the big animal form of this Master Deity and question how one with such a huge form can ride on a small mouse (*mooshika*) which is depicted as His vehicle. *Mooshika* is symbolic of the darkness of ignorance, while Ganesha signifies the effulgence of Wisdom that dispels the darkness of ignorance.[2]

◊ ◊ ◊ ◊ ◊

The mouse is the vehicle of Vinayaka. What is the inner significance of this mouse? The mouse is considered as the embodiment of the sense of smell. The mouse is a symbol of the attachment to worldly tendencies (*vasanas*). It is well known that if you want to catch a mouse you place a strong–smelling edible inside the mouse–trap. The mouse also symbolises the darkness of night. The mouse can see well in the dark. As Vinayaka's vehicle the mouse signifies an object that leads man from darkness to light. The Vinayaka–principle, thus, means that which removes all the bad qualities, bad practices and bad thoughts in men and inculcates good qualities, good conduct and good thoughts.[3]

[1] Sathya Sai Baba's Words in *Life is a Dream, Realize It*, Joy Thomas, p. 133.

[2] *Sanathana Sarathi*, October 1994, p. 5.

[3] *Sanathana Sarathi*, October, 1991, p. 275.

◊ ◊ ◊ ◊ ◊

For his vehicle he has only a mouse. The mouse delights in destroying palm–leaf books (the symbol of knowledge). So the mouse is the symbol of ignorance which derogates and destroys the influence of knowledge through vile and vicious criticism. Ganesha, Lord of Knowledge and Wisdom, has to use the mouse, symbol of ignorance, to carry him around. Likewise, the worshippers of Knowledge and Wisdom may have to use the very criticisms and critics of their knowledge as vehicles to transport that knowledge ....[1]

◊ ◊ ◊ ◊ ◊

The mouse is Ganesha's vehicle. The mouse is a clever and lively creature. As a symbol it means that we should be clever and diligent in our actions.[2]

◊ ◊ ◊ ◊ ◊

How does it happen that Vinayaka has the head of an elephant and has a mouse as his vehicle? The mouse is called *mooshika* (in Sanskrit). It is a sign of night, which signifies darkness. The mouse is a symbol of darkness. Because Vinayaka has control over darkness, he is described as the rider on a *mooshika*. He is the one who dispels darkness and sheds light on the world.

The mouse (*mooshika*) is also a symbol of the sense of smell. The mouse moves about following the direction of the smell (*vasana*). Vinayaka is the one who has mastery over *vasanas*, that is, desires and ignorance (represented by *mooshika*).

---

[1] *The Words of Sathya Sai Baba: Life is a Dream, Realize It,* Joy Thomas, p. 132–33.

[2] *Sanathana Sarathi,* October 1989, p. 263.

◊ ◊ ◊ ◊ ◊

Significance of the elephant-head of Ganesha

Ganesha is depicted as having the head of an elephant. An elephant is by nature whimsical, willful, and powerful. When trained, however, its very strength helps man to overcome the obstacles of nature. Similarly, the mind is whimsical, willful, and powerful but, when trained, attains supranormal powers to help man conquer his nature. The elephant often moves its trunk, ears, tongue, and eyes. So, too, the mind restlessly seeks the enjoyment of the senses. Therefore, Puranic lore depicted the mind as an elephant. The intellect spearheads its activities through the mind; therefore, Ganesha, Lord of the Intellect, is pictured as having the head of an elephant ....[1]

◊ ◊ ◊ ◊ ◊

What is the esoteric meaning of Ganesha's elephant head? The elephant is noted for its acute intelligence. Ganesha's elephant head symbolises sharpness of intellect and the highest power of discrimination. Because of the purity of his intellect, Vinayaka is also called the giver of *buddhi* (intellect). He responds to the prayers of devotees and hence he is known as *Siddhi* Vinayaka (the Vinayaka who grants what is sought).[2]

---

[1] *The Words of Sathya Sai Baba: Life is a Dream, Realize It*, Joy Thomas, p. 132.

[2] *Sanathana Sarathi*, October 1989, p. 263.

◊ ◊ ◊ ◊ ◊

Vigneswara is also regarded as one endowed with the wisdom of the elephant (*gaja thelivi*). The elephant is noted for its supreme intelligence. It is also known for its absolute loyalty to its master. It is ready to sacrifice its life itself for the sake of its master. The direct proof of this is Sai Geetha (Sai Baba's elephant). Ordinarily hundreds of cars will be passing on the road. Sai Geeta will take no notice of them. But when Swami's car happens to pass that way, it will instinctively notice it. It will rush to the road raising its familiar cry. What love for Swami! It will be no exaggeration if faith is equated with the elephant.[1]

◊ ◊ ◊ ◊ ◊

The elephant is proverbially the most intelligent among the mammals and it is vegetarian, indicating its *satwic* (balanced or pure) nature. Ganapathi has the head of the elephant, for, it indicates the intelligence through which obstacles in the path of achievement, secular as well as spiritual, can be overcome.[2]

◊ ◊ ◊ ◊ ◊

The symbolic significance of Ganesha's elephant head has to be properly understood. The elephant has profound intelligence. For example, yesterday Sai Geetha (Bhagavan's elephant) came running when it heard the sound of Swami's car approaching. Though many cars were following Swami's car, Sai–Geetha could unmistakably

---

[1] *Sanathana Sarathi*, October 1991, p. 276.

[2] *Sathya Sai Speaks*, Vol. 11, p. 211.

identify Swami's car from an uncanny recognition of the sound of the car. That is why it is termed *Gaja Thelivi* (elephantine intelligence). One having a sharp brain is described as having the intelligence of an elephant. It has *Medha Shakti*. Moreover, the elephant has large ears and it can hear even minute sounds. *Sravanam* or hearing the glory of the Lord is the first step in spiritual *sadhana* for which ears should be sharp. After hearing one has to ruminate over this and put it into practice (which are termed as *sravana, manana and nidhidyasana*). The elephant takes the praise and blame equally (*dooshana* and *bhooshana*). When it hears something bad, it moves its body this way and that way and shakes off the unwanted things while it retains good things quietly.[1]

◊ ◊ ◊ ◊ ◊

Palmleaf book and rosary

Ganesha is sometimes depicted as holding a palmleaf book in one hand and a *japamala* (rosary) in another. The book represents knowledge and wisdom. The rosary indicates concentration upon the chosen Form and repetition of the chosen Name.[2]

◊ ◊ ◊ ◊ ◊

Ganesha's big belly

No one should regard Ganesha as uncouth because of his elephant head and his immense belly. Vinayaka is a deity who

---

[1] *Sanathana Sarathi*, October 1994, p. 265.

[2] *The Words of Sathya Sai Baba: Life is a Dream, Realize It*, Joy Thomas, p. 133.

encompasses the universe within himself. He is a deity of infinite potency.[1]

◊ ◊ ◊ ◊ ◊

Ganesha's ash-grey body (shasivarnam), white cloth (suklambaradaram), and graceful countenance (prasannavadanam)

Vigneswara is described as one wearing a white cloth. His body is ash–grey. He is depicted as having four arms and cheerful countenance. The white cloth signifies purity of mind and heart. By worshipping him, you must endeavour to achieve similar purity. Vinayaka always appears serene and calm. By his grace the devotee must seek to achieve similar equanimity, whatever may be the ups and downs in life.[2]

◊ ◊ ◊ ◊ ◊

Ganesha is bathed in His Divine Glory; that is the significance of the attribute, *shashivarnam. Chathur–bhuja* (four–handed) is the next denotation. This means that apart from two visible hands, He has two invisible hands, that are available for the two Divine uses of (1) Blessing the devotee, and (2) Guarding him from danger. The last of the descriptive word is: *Prasannavadanam* (of graceful countenance). The countenance depicts the inner calm, happiness and balance, inner grace and mercy, the consciousness of strength and sovereignty.

---

[1] *Sanathana Sarathi*, October 1989, p. 264.

[2] *Sanathana Sarathi*, October 1989, p. 264.

There is a popular verse, used on most occasions when Ganapathi is invoked. It mentions various attributes of this God: *Suklambaradaram* (wearing white vesture) is the first; this is the symbol of purity, for, *ambara* means also the sky, the *akasha* of the heart. Ganapathi is pure, having universal Love and Compassion. *Vishnum* is the second attribute, ascribed to Him. Vishnu means that He is present everywhere, at all times. *Shashivarnam* is the third adjective used: of the complexion of ash or *vibhuti*; that is to say, glowing with spiritual splendour, with the majesty of spiritual attainments, achievements and potentialities. These are also called *vibhutis*, for, in the Geetha, we find Krishna saying, wherever you see Power, Glory, Majesty (*vibhuti*), know that it is Mine![1]

◊ ◊ ◊ ◊ ◊

Food offering made to Ganesha (modaka)

Even the offering that is made to Ganesha has great significance because it is prepared with gram flour and jaggery or pepper and enclosed in an outer covering made from rice flour paste and then cooked in steam without using oil. This is supposed to be a healthy and delicious food item according to the Ayurvedic system. Modern doctors also recognise the importance of such steam–cooked *idlis* (rice cakes) which they recommend as post–operative diet for patients as it is easily digestible. Jaggery too has the property of controlling gas formation and this food item gives relief from eye troubles and prevents gastric disorders.

In the ancient traditional mode of observing these festivals, great emphasis was laid on good health as the pre–requisite for spiritual pursuits with a healthy mind. For achieving the four goals of human life, *Dharma, Artha, Kama* and *Moksha* (Righteousness, Wealth, Desire

---

[1] *Sathya Sai Speaks*, Vol. 16, p. 211.

and Liberation), one should have basically a healthy body. If you want to earn wealth by righteous means and cherish desires which lead to liberation, you should have sound health.[1]

◊ ◊ ◊ ◊ ◊

In connection with the Ganesha festival, *prasadam* is offered to the deity in the form of *Kudumulu* and *Undrallu*. What are the kinds of edibles that should be offered to the deity? The preparations should not involve the use of oil or fire. They have to be cooked by the use of steam. Using rice flour and some pulses and til, one kind of offering is made for Ganesha. In this preparation no oil or fire is used. The significance of this offering is: During the month of *Bhadrapada*, the farmers bring home the harvest of til seeds. Til seeds have medicinal properties for curing lung and eye diseases. When the til seeds and pulses are cooked by steam, the preparation becomes easily digestible. In offering such food to the deity two purposes are served. The offerings are tasty and wholesome (giving pleasure and promoting good health). These were the reasons for the observance of various festivals by our ancients.[2]

◊ ◊ ◊ ◊ ◊

Ganesha as Lambodhara

He is also called *Lambodara*, which means "Guardian of Wealth" (*Lakshmi Swarupa*). Here Lakshmi represents all wealth and prosperity and not only *Dhanam* (money) for which there is a separate deity called Dhanalakshmi, one of the eight Lakshmis. Here wealth means

---

[1] *Sanathana Sarathi*, October 1994, pp. 264-65.

[2] *Sanathana Sarathi*, September 1992, p. 222.

Sukha (pleasure) and *Ananda* (Bliss). What is the use of having all other things when one has no pleasure or Bliss?[1]

◊ ◊ ◊ ◊ ◊

5.

Ganesha as the remover of the obstacles for Self-realisation in the form of individual self-effort through spiritual practices (sadhana)

A. Control and purification of the senses and mind for Self-realisation

Without the control of the senses, man is like a horse without blinkers, he is like a bull that refuses to yield to the yoke; his *sadhana* (spiritual practices) are a waste of time and energy. The special feature of man's composition is that he has discrimination, detachment and synoptic intellect (Ganesha); he can discover Truth and be fixed in it, and gain unshakable Peace.[2]

---

[1] *Sanathana Sarathi*, October 1994, p. 264.

[2] *Sathya Sai Speaks*, Vol. 5, p. 90.

◊ ◊ ◊ ◊ ◊

The mind is the villain; it is another name for desire; the texture
of the mind is just desire; both warp and woof are desire and nothing
else. If desire goes, the mind disappears. When you pull out all the
yarn from a piece of cloth, you have no more cloth. So too, pull out
desires from the mind; it disappears, and you are free.[1]

◊ ◊ ◊ ◊ ◊

The mind is the monarch in man (Ganesha); the senses are the
ministers. It is the slave of its servants and so, the realm has no peace.
Every *sadhak* (spiritual aspirant) who aspires to achieve the expression
and expansion of the Divine in him has therefore to earn mastery over
the senses. That is the first step. The next one is the conquest of the
mind, its elimination. The third is uprooting the *vasanas* (innate
tendencies), and the fourth, attainment of *Jnana* (Spiritual Wisdom).
The branches are the senses; the trunk is the mind; the roots are the
innate tendencies. All three have to be overcome and destroyed, so
that the awareness of the *Atmic* (Divine) Reality can be gained.[2]

◊ ◊ ◊ ◊ ◊

The sages of India had laid down various rites, ceremonies,
disciplines, modes of behaviour, conventions and festivals to help
cleanse the emotions and confirm faith. I shall speak today of the
importance of one of these — of the disciplines that they laid down for
food. Take in only simple pure clean food — what is called *satwic* food
by the sages. That is to say, food which will not arouse the impulses
and emotions, sharpen the passions, upset the equanimity, hamper

---

[1] Sathya Sai Speaks, Vol. 6, p. 158.

[2] *Sathya Sai Speaks*, Vol. 16, pp. 64–65.

health. Food offered to God is free from the evil vibrations that injure the individual in subtle ways. Food offered to the hungry and then eaten has also the same beneficial quality. Since food has a subtle impact on the feelings and thoughts of man, you have to be vigilant ever.[1]

◊ ◊ ◊ ◊ ◊

Dhyana (meditation) is the discipline by which the mind is trained to inner analysis and synthesis. The goal of *dhyana* is the one in which all I's are synthesised, in their purest forms. That One is described in the Geetha as having eight attributes. They are: *kavi* (aware of the past, present and future), *puranam* (timeless in its origin), *anushasitharam* (it lays down the norms), *anoraneeya* (it is more minute than the minutest), *sarvasya dhatha* (at the basis of all), *achinthyaruupa* (of inexplicable form) *adhithya varna* (effulgence) and *tamasa parastat* (beyond darkness). This is a task which can be carried out only by unremitting *dhyana*.

Again, *dhyana* and the control of the senses must go together. The senses block the road to heaven's gate. No sense should be given free rein.[2]

◊ ◊ ◊ ◊ ◊

Dhyana should not be vacillating or wavering from one ideal to another. It should not be reduced to a mere mechanical text–book formula, a rigid time–table of breathing through alternate nostrils, a meaningless stare at the tip of the nose. It is a rigorous discipline of the senses, the nervous current, and the wings of imagination. That is why it is said, the *dhyana* is the valley of peace that lies on the other

---

[1] *Sathya Sai Speaks*, Vol. 10, pp. 37–38.

[2] *Sathya Sai Speaks*, Vol. 16, p. 81.

side of a huge mountain range, with the peaks named the Six Foes. These are lust, anger, greed, attachment, pride and envy. One has to climb over the range and reach the plain beyond. One has to rent the veils, before the light can shine on the path. One has to remove the cataract from the eye, so that the Truth can be seen. *Maya* is the name of that mist of ignorance, that torments the mind which seeks to plunge in the depths of the Self.[1]

◊ ◊ ◊ ◊ ◊

To get *santhosa* and *shanti* (happiness and peace) you must develop a pure unsullied mind, unsullied by egoism and its progeny — lust, greed, envy, anger, hatred and the rest. For this, you must seek *sat sangh* (good company), perform *sat karma* (good deeds), entertain only *sat alochana* (good thoughts) and read *sat granamas* (good books) (aspects of Ganesha to remove obstacles).

You may see a thousand good things or listen to a thousand good words or read a thousand good books — but, unless you put at least one into practice, the blemishes in the mirror of your heart will not be wiped off. The Lord cannot be reflected therein.[2]

◊ ◊ ◊ ◊ ◊

If the *manas* (mind) is neglected and allowed to run wild, *tamas* or "dullness and delusion" will hold sway. Some persons advise you to watch each step of the mind and note down all the false steps and evil intentions it encountered. No, that is a dangerous practice. Do not pay attention to its vagaries; strive for what you need and not for what

---

[1] *Sathya Sai Speaks*, Vol. 10, p. 79.

[2] *Sathya Sai Speaks*, Vol. 10, p. 172.

you have to avoid. Count the false steps and you will be led to commit them again. Resolve to walk right and your steps will not falter or fail.[1]

◊ ◊ ◊ ◊ ◊

Man's progress depends on strength of mind and purity of feelings (aspects of Ganesha). His mental condition and the actions which rise from his feelings, these two decide whether he will be bound or free, happy or miserable, rising or falling. The mind is the framer of all man's intentions and resolutions, his wills and wont's. These *sankalpas* motivate the senses and initiate activities that reveal their real nature. When a pebble is dropped into a well, the ripple causes further ripples and the entire surface is affected. So too, when an intention enters the mind, the waves it causes envelop the body and prompt many activities.

When the will is pure (an aspect of Ganesha), activities are also pure. When it is impure, the activities through which it expresses itself are also impure. So, one has to be vigilant. As soon as an intention is formed in the mind, examine it to find out whether it deserves to be put into action or whether it is unworthy to be acted upon. The intellect must be called in to conduct this examination.

Intentions that arise in the mind have a great potency and vitality. Even after the death of the person, they can shape events, produce good or inflict evil. Why? They are the cause for the person getting embodied again and going through further lives! Therefore, one has to cultivate beneficial resolutions and maintain them. These are like swords. They can cut to pieces (Ganesha) the weeds of evil thoughts, evil feelings and evil habits. As a consequence, good thoughts, good plans, good acts and good lines of action can grow freely.[2]

---

[1] *Sathya Sai Speaks*, Vol. 2, p. 183.

[2] *Sathya Sai Speaks*, Vol. 15, p. 196.

◊ ◊ ◊ ◊ ◊

Do not keep the *manas*, *buddhi* and *chitta* (mind, intellect and thought) hungry or underfed; then they will run after all kinds of foul food. Give them proper nourishment and they will perform their functions well. Their function is to illumine the *Atma* within and help you to discover that the *Atma* is all. Until the auspicious moment, everything will be in disarray; do not worry. ... The Grace of the Lord will overwhelm all obstacles (Ganesha) and the fruit of *sadhana* will be vouchsafed. Once you secure the Grace, you can fulfil all your wishes with it....[1]

◊ ◊ ◊ ◊ ◊

Do not condemn the mind as a monkey, etc. It is a fine instrument with which you can win either liberation or bondage. It all depends on how you manipulate it (Ganesha). It will carry out your orders to the minutest detail. It will lead you, if you so desire, along the royal road, right up to the door of Realisation. Or it will make you wander about in the blind alleys, where every step lands you in dirt.[2]

◊ ◊ ◊ ◊ ◊

The education of the emotions and the control of passions are both included in the definition of *yoga*, the spiritual discipline that purifies the intelligence. To penetrate the thick fog that ignorance spreads over Reality, the intelligence must be built on the basis of virtue. When *karma* (action) is done as dedication and *upasana* (worship) is done as the essential for every life, the intelligence is clarified so much that the fog disappears and the Truth is revealed.

---

[1] *Sathya Sai Speaks*, Vol. 2, p. 189.

[2] *Sathya Sai Speaks*, Vol. 2, p. 224.

Karma, when engaged in as dedicated to God, loses its deleterious effects for the doer.[1]

◊ ◊ ◊ ◊ ◊

Japa and *thapas* (pious repetition of Lord's Name and penance) ánd *puja* and *vratams* (ritual worship and vow–keeping austerities) — all train and subdue the senses. ¯hey cleanse the mind so that God can be reflected therein. Just as thé sugar that your eyes can see and your hands can put into water becomes so dissolved in it that neither eye nor hand can cognise it again, the senses and intelligence cannot cognise that immanent God; *chittasuddi* (cleansing of mind) alone can recognise God, just as the tongue alone can recognise the sugar that has dissolved in the water. ... What exactly are we doing with our minds? In how many different ways are we harmed by the activities of the mind? How does that mind itself get modified and transformed? One has to study these and free oneself from the sovereignty of the mind. One should endeavour, on the other hand, to establish one's sovereignty over the mind (Ganesha). Then alone is the life worth while. Else, it is a colossal waste.[2]

◊ ◊ ◊ ◊ ◊

B. Spiritual disciplines act as Ganesha to remove the obstacles to Self-realization

Spiritual discipline is very necessary; it is not enough if you place charcoal over the cinders; you must fan vigorously, so that the

---

[1] *Sathya Sai Speaks*, Vol. 7, p. 82.

[2] *Sathya Sai Speaks*, Vol. 7, pp. 156–57.

charcoal too is changed into burning cinders. It is not enough if you are at Puttaparthi. You have to engage in *sadhana* to win My *Sankalpa* (resolution). You may ask why the burden of the consequences of acts done in previous births cannot be easily brushed away; no, they can be destroyed, as a heap of cotton is burnt by a spark of fire. *Jnanagni dagdha karmanam* — the spark of *jnana* (wisdom) will destroy the effect of *karma* (actions) in a trice. These consequences are like the cloud of dust that follows a bus, when it runs on a fair–weather road; when the bus reaches the gravel road or the metalled road, the dust is less, but it is still there. When at last it enters the tarred road there is no dust. The mud track is *karma* (action); the metalled road is *upasana* (worship); the tarred dust–free road is *jnana* (wisdom). By human skill and effort it is possible to reduce the burden of past *karma* (actions) (Ganesha).

You do not wait with folded hands for the cup of coffee to cool down to the required warmth; you ask for an extra cup and you start pouring the coffee from one cup to the other, is it not? The same anxiety, the same *sadhana* has to be shown in spiritual matters also, to take in the beverage of Divine Grace. Jesus was great because He showed the value of *sadhana* and the equanimity that can come through spiritual discipline.[1]

◊ ◊ ◊ ◊ ◊

Only Vinayaka teaches the lessons that are essential for mankind. You should not stop with installing the idol and doing *pooja* for a few days. You should make efforts to become a *Nayaka* or Master over yourself (Ganesha). You have the nine–fold path of devotion. *Sravanam* (Hearing), *Keerthanam* (Singing His Glory), *Vishnusmaranam* (thinking of and chanting the name), *Pada Sevanam* (Serving at His feet), *Vandanam* (Obeisance), *Archanam* (Worship), *Dasyam* (Serving Him as a servant serves the Master), *Sakhyam* (befriending God),

---

[1] *Sathya Sai Speaks*, Vol. 5, p. 93.

Atmanivedanam (Surrendering body, mind and soul). The elephant signifies combining of the first and the last, that is, *Sravanam* and *Atmanivedanam*, so that all the other paths in between are covered fully.[1]

◊ ◊ ◊ ◊ ◊

People have specialised in the various methods of worshipping God; there is a host of rites, ceremonials, hymns, festivals, fasts, vows, pilgrimages; but, the best form of worship, the one that will bring the Grace of God in ample measure, is to obey the commands of God. Adulation is poor adoration! Placing God at a great distance from you and praising Him as Omniscient, Omnipotent and Omnipresent will not please Him. Develop nearness, proximity, kinship with God. Win Him by obedience, loyalty, humility and purity.[2]

◊ ◊ ◊ ◊ ◊

The effulgent Sun can be seen only with his own light. Similarly, only by the grace of the Divine (Ganesha) can one obtain a vision of the Divine. No skill, intellectual effort or scholarship is required to experience the Divine. Just as clouds may obscure the Sun, the clouds of egoism, attachment and hatred prevent one from seeing the Divine. Prayer and *sadhana* are the means by which these clouds are dispersed. *Sadhana* (spiritual discipline) is the royal road to reach the Divine.[3]

◊ ◊ ◊ ◊ ◊

---

[1] *Sanathana Sarathi*, October 1994, p. 266.

[2] *Sathya Sai Speaks*, Vol. 10, p. 42.

[3] Sathya Sai Speaks, Vol. —, pp. 29–30.

There is a definite technique by which that Immortal spark can be discovered. Though it may appear difficult, each step forward makes the next one easier and a mind made ready by discipline is able to discover the Divine basis of man and of Creation in a flash. There is no short–cut to this consummation. One has to give up all the impediments (Ganesha) which one has accumulated so far and become light for the journey. Lust, greed, anger, malice, conceit, envy, hate, all these pet tendencies have to be shed. It is not enough if you hear the discourses of Sai Baba and count the number that you have listened to. Thousands are here before Me now; but, that figure has no significance. Only those who practise at least one of the things I emphasise, count.[1]

◊ ◊ ◊ ◊ ◊

It is the experience and practice of the citizens of *Bharat* (India) that they generally worship God with flowers, offer *puja* (ritual adoration) and make obeisance to God. But there is something which is more sacred than this. There is a distinctive type of devotion by which you worship God with a good, clean mind and good conduct. This has been given the name of *Para Bhakti*. By worshipping God always with *puja* and flowers, the *sadaka* (spiritual aspirant) will remain stationary in his place. This is good in a way but to remain in one place all the time and failing to rise to a higher position is not good. It is a superior type of worship — to worship God through good qualities, good conduct, good thoughts and good company. The *Srutis* (scriptures) have described this kind of worship as worship through good qualities. By offering what kind of good qualities do we please God?

The first flower with which we can worship God is *ahimsa* — non–violence. The second flower is *dama* (control of senses). The third flower is *dhaya* (compassion to all living beings). The fourth one is

---

[1] *Sathya Sai Speaks*, Vol. 4, pp. 295–296.

kshama (forbearance). The fifth flower is *shanti* (peace). The sixth flower is *thapas* (penance). The seventh one is the flower of *Dhyana* (meditation). The eighth is the flower of *Satya* (Truth). The inner meaning of this statement is that God will shower grace on you if you worship him through these eight flowers (Ganesha).[1]

◊ ◊ ◊ ◊ ◊

You come to Puttaparthi, secure a picture, and taking it home, begin worshipping it every day or every Thursday; but, all that is simply *satkarma* (good activity). They won't take you far. You must also develop *sat–guna*, virtues, good habits, good attitudes, good characteristics, a good character. Otherwise your life is a chain of pluses and minuses, one cancelling the other out, totalling up to a mere zero. When you say, *Thath thwam asi* (Thou art that), you must have the traits of that which you claim to be. You say, "that and this" are the same; then, reviling that or revering "that" is the same as reviling "this" or revering this.[2]

◊ ◊ ◊ ◊ ◊

---

[1] *Sathya Sai Speaks*, Vol. 15, pp. 47–48.

[2] *Sathya Sai Speaks*, Vol. 5, p. 69.

C. Skill, capacity, will, courage, self-confidence, perseverance and wisdom will remove the obstacles to Self-realization and are therefore qualities of Ganesha

What is wanted now is *utsaha, dairya* and *vishwasa* (effort, courage and faith). In effort, you must follow a regulated routine learnt from some adept in the field. For courage, you must feel your own importance for your uplift; never call yourself a sinner born in sin, bred in sin and engaged in sin. No; that kind of self–condemnation ill becomes a child of God, an *Amrithaputhra.*

In every one of you, God is the moving spirit, the very Soul; how then can you be evil, when you are here for fulfilling God's purpose, according to his Will, His plan, His law? He has endowed you with many faculties so that you may seek Him and reach Him. You are not therefore a helpless neglected individual undergoing a sentence of death. You are *Anandaswarupa* (embodiment of Bliss), born to a rich heritage, which is yours for the asking. Only you do not ask. Have faith in your destiny and work gladly and steadily to attain it.[1]

◊ ◊ ◊ ◊ ◊

I do not like people wasting the precious moments of their limited years of life in idle talk of vain pursuits. Nor do I like cowardly hesitation. Act; act with all your might and with all your mind; make full use of the skill, capacity, courage and confidence that you are endowed with. Then God will bless you. You must have heard of a *Ramabhakta* (devotee of Rama) who sat on the road side by his

---

[1] *Sathya Sai Speaks*, Vol. 1, p. 162.

upturned cart, wailing his bad luck and calling on Rama to lift the cart into position. Rama did not appear to raise the cart and fix the wheel. He therefore began chiding his faith itself and to doubt the experience of the sages who describe Him as the Ocean of Mercy. Rama came into his presence then; but only to tell him, "You fool, I have entrusted you with some intelligence and strength. Use them. Put your shoulder to the task now before you. When you have done your best and that best is found not enough, then call on Me; I am ever ready to reinforce your exertions with My Grace."[1]

◊ ◊ ◊ ◊ ◊

Faith in God should never waver. In no circumstance should anyone go against the injunctions of the Divine. Whatever worship one may offer, however intensely one may meditate, if one transgresses the commands of the Lord, these devotional practices become futile. The reason is that the Divine has no selfish objective or aim. It is out of small–minded selfish motives that people act against the sacred commands of the Lord. Even small acts of transgression may in due course assume dangerous proportions.

Like the clouds in the sky which are brought together or dispersed by the winds, the passage of time brings about for man the union or separation of associates and happiness or sorrow. Time is the form of God. It should not be wasted. It is to understand such sacred Truths that festivals like Ganesha Chathurthi are celebrated.[2]

◊ ◊ ◊ ◊ ◊

Seek the light always; be full of confidence and zest. Do not yield to despair, for it can never produce results. It only worsens the

---

[1] *Sathya Sai Speaks*, Vol. 2, p. 145.

[2] *Sanathana Sarathi*, October 1991, p. 276.

problem, for it darkens the intellect and plunges you in doubt. You must take up the path of *sadhana* (spiritual practice), very enthusiastically. Half–hearted halting steps will not yield fruit. It is like cleaning a slushy area by a stream of water. If the current of the stream is slow, the slush cannot be cleared. The stream must flow full and fast, driving everything before it, so that the slush might be scoured clean.

I shall talk to you of these first steps only, for they are the most important for the *sadakas* (spiritual aspirants); and you are all *sadakas* or are bound to be *sadakas*. "*Moksha* lies in the *sukshma*" they say — "Liberation can be achieved by subtle means." Treat the others in the same way as you would like them to treat you. Never brood over the past; when grief over–powers you, do not recollect similar incidents in your past experience and add to the sum of your grief; recollect, rather, incidents when grief did not knock at your door, but you were happy instead. Draw consolation and strength from such memories and raise yourself above the surging waters of sorrow.[1]

◊ ◊ ◊ ◊ ◊

Will power motivated by God is the active force available for your uplift. This is called *Sankalpa Bala*. Develop it by concentration and *japa*. The mind must be compelled to submit to the dictates of the will. Now, you are easily led astray by the vagaries of the mind. That is why, I say, WATCH! W is for watch your Words; A is for watch your Actions; T is for watch your thoughts; C is for watch your Character; H is for watch your Heart. If the watch reminds you every second of the need to watch these five, you can be quite happy.[2]

◊ ◊ ◊ ◊ ◊

---

[1] *Sathya Sai Speaks*, Vol. 1, p. 71.

[2] *Sathya Sai Speaks*, Vol. 7, p. 184.

Of course, the majority of persons get glimpses of discrimination and detachment off and on; but they soon forget the call and ignore it and cover it up by excess or excuses. One step forward and one step back — the journey does not take them far. Even if some do take up *sadhana*, steadiness is absent. Like a ball of thread which slips out of the hand onto the floor, it all comes off because the grasp is not firm. Steady effort alone will bring success here, as in every other case. How can you expect quick success in the control of the mind? It is very difficult to overcome its vagaries, for it is many–faced and very adamant.

You are unable to understand *Prakriti* (Nature), which is a reflection, a shadow of God; how then can you understand God Himself? No. Steady perseverance alone will tame your mind; and it is only through a tamed mind that you can experience God. In this case, you must become your own tutor; train yourself by using the spark of wisdom that has been implanted in you. Once you try with all your might, the Lord's Grace will be there to help you forward. The first step in the spiritual discipline is the cleansing of the speech. Talk sweet without anger. Do not boast of your scholarship or attainments. Be humble, eager to serve; conserve your speech. Practise silence. That will save you from squabbles, idle thoughts and factions.[1]

◊ ◊ ◊ ◊ ◊

Courage is the tonic for getting both physical as well as mental health and strength. Give up doubt, hesitation and fear. Do not give any chance for these to strike root in your mind. Man, by means of the inner Divine strength with which he is equipped, can achieve anything; he can even become *Madava* (God).[2]

---

[1] *Sathya Sai Speaks*, Vol. 2, p. 24.

[2] *Sathya Sai Speaks*, Vol. 1, p. 80.

◊ ◊ ◊ ◊ ◊

To help you to give up fear and doubt, keep the Name of the Lord always on your tongue and in your mind. Dwell on the endless forms of the Lord, His limitless Glory, while you repeat the Name. Attach yourself to Him; then your attachment for these temporary objects will fall off; or at least, you will start seeing them in their proper proportion as having only relative reality. When the tiny little ego assumes enormous importance, it causes all this bother! That is the root of all the travail.[1]

◊ ◊ ◊ ◊ ◊

D. Self-inquiry as an aspect of Ganesha to remove obstacles to Self-realization

A mere five–minute inquiry will convince you that you are not the body, or the senses, the mind or the intelligence, the name or the form, but that you are the *Atma* Itself, the same *Atma* that appears as all this variety. Once you get a glimpse of this Truth, hold on to it; do not allow it to slip. Make it your permanent possession.[2]

◊ ◊ ◊ ◊ ◊

You must strive to diagnose your own character and discover the faults that are infesting it; do not try to analyse the character of others and seek to spot their defects. This self–examination is very necessary to bring to light the defects that might undermine one's spiritual

---

[1] *Sathya Sai Speaks*, Vol. 1, p. 81.

[2] *Sathya Sai Speaks*, Vol. 1, p. 25.

career. People buy clothes with deep colour, so that they may not reveal dust or dirt; they do not prefer white clothes, for they show plainly their soiled condition. But, do not try to hide your dirt in darkness; be ashamed of soiled natures and endeavour to cleanse them fast.[1]

◊ ◊ ◊ ◊ ◊

The mind too will disappear as soon as the inquiry starts, for it is like cloth composed of the warp and woof of yarn. Each yarn is a desire, a wish, an attachment. Remove them and the cloth vanishes. Delusion is the cotton, desire is the yarn, mind is the cloth. Through *vairagya* (detachment), the warp and the woof can be pulled out. The *sadaka* (spiritual aspirant) must have as his security personnel, *viveka* (wisdom) and *vairagya*, then he can move through the world unharmed.[2]

◊ ◊ ◊ ◊ ◊

E. Pure actions (Karma) as Ganesha to purify the heart for Self-realization

The consequence of *karma* can be wiped out only through *karma*, as a thorn can be removed only by means of another. Do good *karma* to assuage the pain of the bad *karma* which you have done and from which you suffer now. The best and the simplest *karma* is the repetition of the Name of the Lord; be ever engaged in it. It will keep

---

[1] *Sathya Sai Speaks*, Vol. 6, p. 37.

[2] *Sathya Sai Speaks*, Vol. 6, p. 180.

out evil tendencies and wicked thoughts. It will help you radiate Love all round you.

The sages of ancient times divided *karma* into *vikarma* (that is, intentionally done) and *akarma* (that is done without any intention to gain the consequence). Follow the latter and you will save yourselves from suffering. All other activities — the earning of wealth, of reputation, of fame and publicity — result in suffering. Gain internal peace, internal joy; that can be done only when you act without an eye on the gain. The act must be its own reward; or rather, the act must be according to the prompting of the God within, so that its consequence is left to Him. Practise this attitude consistently and you will find great Peace welling within you and around you.[1]

◊ ◊ ◊ ◊ ◊

Sadhana is essential because the effects of *karma* have to be removed by *karma* alone, as thorn is removable only by another thorn. You cannot remove it by a knife or a hammer, or even a sword.

The knowledge that the world is unreal was itself spread by Sankaracharya by means of activity in the unreal world, the establishment of *mutts* (monasteries) and the writing of books, the partaking in disputations.

You cannot desist from *karma*; only, you have got to take care that it is saturated with *Prema* and promotes the welfare of the world.[2]

◊ ◊ ◊ ◊ ◊

The Law of *Karma* holds out hope for you; as the *karma*, so the consequence. Do not bind yourself further by seeking the fruit of *karma*; offer the *karma* at the Feet of God; let it glorify Him; let it

---

[1] *Sathya Sai Speaks*, Vol. 5, p. 97.

[2] *Sathya Sai Speaks*, source unknown.

further His splendour. Be unconcerned with the success or failure of the endeavour. Then, death can have no noose to bind you with. Death will come as a liberator, not a jailor.[1]

◊ ◊ ◊ ◊ ◊

You can yourself judge whether your Love is narrow or broad, whether your Devotion is shallow or deep. Are you content with your achievement? Examine it yourself — pronounce the verdict on yourself, by your own discrimination. Purity of motive is the best guarantee that you will have peace. An uneasy conscience is a tormenting companion. Righteous action will leave no bad effects, to disturb your sleep or health.

> If there is righteousness in the heart,
> There will be beauty in character;
> If there is beauty in character
> There will be harmony in the home.
> When there is harmony in the home,
> There will be order in the nation.
> When there is order in the nation,
> There will be peace in the world.

So, be righteous; avoid all prejudices against others on the basis of caste, creed, colour, mode of worship, status, or degree of affluence. Do not look down on any one; look upon all as Divine as you really are.[2]

◊ ◊ ◊ ◊ ◊

---

[1] *Sathya Sai Speaks*, Vol. 10, p. 11.

[2] *Sathya Sai Speaks*, Vol. 10, p. 5.

God or Guru's Grace as Ganesha to remove all obstacles

God's Grace is as the shower of rain, as the sunlight. You have to do some *sadhana* (spiritual practice) to acquire it, the *sadhana* of keeping a pot upright to receive the rain, the *sadhana* of opening the door of your heart, so that the Sun may illumine it. Like the music that is broadcast over the radio, it is all round you; but you must switch on your receiver and tune the identical wave–length so that you can hear it and enjoy it. Pray for Grace; but do at least this little *sadhana*. Grace will set everything right. Its main consequence is *Atmasakshatkara* (Self–realisation); but there are other incidental benefits too, like a happy contented life here below, and a cool courageous temper, established in unruffled *shanti* (peace). ...

When you have no faith in God, you cannot gauge the efficacy of Grace. If you discard Rama and Krishna, they cannot stand by you in your hour of need. You do not attach yourself to Sai Baba and so you do not receive His Grace. If you start with cynicism and doubt and try to criticise and discover faults, the result is deeper ignorance and confusion. Unholy thoughts fog the mind with foul fumes. How can clarity come to the vision then?[1]

◊ ◊ ◊ ◊ ◊

There is need for a *Guru*, some one who can guide and lead, who has covered the road and knows its ups and downs. You may have the lamp, wick and oil; but, someone must light it. There may be some convolute drawn on the board, but, some one who knows that it is the letter *G*, the letter *O* and the letter *D* must teach the child to identify

---

[1] *Sathya Sai Speaks*, Vol. 8, pp. 70–71.

them as *Jee, O* and *Dee.* That is not enough. Some one must tell him that it has to be read, not as *Jeodee*, but as *God*, and that the sound God represents the concretised Divine principle that is immanent in the Universe, that moves the dew to drop, the lotus to bloom, the butterfly to flit and the sun to rise, that is all the power, all the wisdom, all the love, all the miracle that ever was, is and will be.

Those who teach about Nature and its laws, matter and its properties, forces.and their pulls, teach to bind, not to liberate; it is a burden, not Bliss. It provides a stone boat for you to cross the sea, with waves of grief and crests of joy. It cannot float you along; it is certain to sink. What you need to cross the sea is the bark of *bhakti*, of assurance of Grace, of surrender to His Will. Throw off all burdens, become light, and you can trip across, with one step on one crest and another on the next. God will take you through. You have no need to bother at all. For, when He does everything, who is concerned about what?[1]

◊ ◊ ◊ ◊ ◊

Surrender the ego, dedicate every moment and every movement to Him; he has assured mankind that he will ensure liberation from pain and evil. When asked where God is, people point towards the sky or some far distant region; that is why He is not manifesting Himself. Realise that He is in you, with you, behind you, before you and all around you; and He can be seen and felt everywhere. Realise also that He is all mercy, eager and anxious to fulfil your prayers, if they arise from a pure heart.

He who tells you of this all–pervasive God is the real *Guru*, not he who promises you salvation if you place a purse at His feet. Do not be misled by such worldly men full of greed and egoism. Pray to God to illumine your mind, awaken your intelligence and be your *Guru*. He will surely guide you all right, from the altar of your own heart. For

---

[1] *Sathya Sai Speaks*, Vol. 10, pp. 86–87.

many a *Guru* today, the fence is more essential than the crop; so he emphasises the restrictions and rules, to the detriment of the *sadhana*, which they were designed to protect. So they insist fanatically on the observance of out–dated regulations and checks, while the very purpose of the regulations is allowed to decay. They magnify the role of Fate, and of the consequence of *karma*, without at the same time, consoling man by describing the overpowering might of God's grace.

If there is an iron law of *karma* which binds man hand and foot, why do the *Sruthi* and the *Smithi* (scriptures) extol the earnest efforts and penance of aspirants? Those efforts and that penance can surely transmute the evil consequence of *karma*, and save man from the fate that he has woven for himself. The story of Markandeya, whose date with Death was cancelled, is an instance in point. His *thapas* (renunciation) achieved that victory, by drawing down the Grace of God. There are countless instances in the earthly careers of all *Avatars* to show that Grace is greater than garnered *karma*.

Whatever God grants is for your good, for your liberation, not for your fall or bondage. A God who does evil is not God at all. God has no likes and dislikes; he is above and beyond all traits and characteristics. He is *Gunatheetha* (beyond all *gunas*). So, how can He be hating or revengeful? He is Love. He is Mercy. He is Goodness, He is Wisdom, He is Power. He gives you what you ask (so be careful what you ask) (Ganesha). Learn to ask the really beneficial boons. Do not go to the Wish–fulfilling tree and come back in glee, with a towel that you asked and got![1]

◊ ◊ ◊ ◊ ◊

The Teacher sharpens your intellect, broadens your vision, endows you with discrimination, and helps you to attain higher levels of consciousness and wider horizons of Love (Ganesha). Therefore, one has to offer gratitude to the *Guru* also. The mother leads you to

---

[1] *Sathya Sai Speaks*, Vol. 4, pp. 300–301.

the father, the father leads you to the *Guru* and the *Guru* leads you to God. Today, we have mothers who place the children under the care of the father and many fathers who place children under the care of *Gurus*, but few *Gurus* lead the pupils to God. The parents promote the health and strength of the body; the *Guru* reveals the Resident, the Inner Reality in the body.[1]

◊ ◊ ◊ ◊ ◊

Like underground water, the Divine is there, in everyone, remember. The Lord is *Sarvabhuutha antharAtma* (Indweller in all beings), *Sarvavyapi* (All–pervading). He is the *Atma* (Soul) of every being. He is in you as much as in every one else. He is not more in a rich being or bigger in a fat being; His spark illumines the cave of the heart of every one. The Sun shines equally on all; His Grace is falling equally on all. It is only you that erect obstacles that prevent the rays of His Grace from warming you. Do not blame the Lord for your ignorance or foolishness or perversity. Just as underground water wells up in a gushy spring when a bore is sunk down to that depth, by constant Ram Ram Ram Ram Ram, touch the spring of Divinity and one day it will gush out in cool plenty and bring unending joy.[2]

◊ ◊ ◊ ◊ ◊

The Lord is as the *Kalpatharu* (the Divine wish–fulfilling Tree) that gives whatever is asked. But you have to go near the tree and wish for the thing you want. The atheist is the person who keeps far away from the tree; the theist is the one who has come near; that is the difference. The tree does not make any distinction; it grants boons to all. The Lord will not punish or take revenge if you do not recognise

---

[1] *Sathya Sai Speaks*, Vol. 16, pp. 60–61.

[2] *Sathya Sai Speaks*, Vol. 1, pp. 108–109.

Him or revere Him. He has no special type of worship which alone can please him.

...

Earn the right to approach the Lord without fear and the right to ask for your heritage. You must become so free that praise will not emanate from you when you approach the Lord. Praise is a sign of distance and fear. You must have heard the Kalidhasa story. He said that he would get liberation "as soon as I go," that is to say, as soon as the ego disappears, for then he shines in his native splendour, as *Brahman* (as the indestructible *Atma*). The "I" when crossed out becomes the symbol of a cross; so, what is crucified is the ego, remember. Then, the Divine nature manifests itself unhampered.[1]

◊ ◊ ◊ ◊ ◊

That path is beset with hardships. They help, they do not hinder your forward steps. They serve as the shears that trim a growing bush. No one can escape these ups and downs while on the journey. Fix attention on the goal, that is the means to be happy and peaceful. Whatever the obstacle, God's Grace can transform it into a help for you (Ganesha). Educate your mind to view hardships as helps. The mind it is that binds or liberates. What is the mind ultimately? It is a web of desires and wishes; this handkerchief here is, if you ask Me, only apparently, a handkerchief. Really speaking, it is just yarn; remove the yarn, all the yarns in the warp and woof, and what remains? Why multiply desires and get bound by the mind? Use it for liberation instead.[2]

◊ ◊ ◊ ◊ ◊

---

[1] *Sathya Sai Speaks*, Vol. 1, pp. 55–56.

[2] *Sathya Sai Speaks*, Vol. 6, pp. 226.

So also, the Lord is everyone's Father, in whose property everyone can claim a share. But in order to get it, you must reach a certain age, a certain standard of intelligence and discrimination. The infirm and the idiotic, He will not consider fit to receive property. His property is Grace, *Prema* (Love). But if you have Discrimination and Renunciation, you can claim your share, as of right (Ganesha).

Bring "*Bhakti*" (Devotion) and lay it here and take from here spiritual strength! The more such business is done, the more pleased am I. Bring what you have; namely, your sorrows and griefs, worries and anxieties, and take from Me joy and peace, courage and confidence. In My view, there is no seniority or juniority among devotees. The mother spends more time tending the sickly child; she just asks the older children to look after themselves; she feeds with her own hand the infant. That does not mean that she has no love towards the grown–ups. So too, do not think that because I do not ostensibly pay more attention to one person, he is beyond the ken of my *Prema*.[1]

◊ ◊ ◊ ◊ ◊

God draws the individual towards Himself; it is the nature of both to have this affinity, for they are the same. They are like the iron and the magnet. But if the iron is rusty covered with layers of dirt, the magnet is unable to attract. Remove the impediment; that is all you have to do. Shine forth in your real nature and the Lord will draw you into His Bosom. Trials and tribulations are the means by which this cleansing is done. That is why Kunthi prayed to Krishna, "Give us always grief, so that we may never forget Thee." They are like the dietary and other restrictions that the doctor prescribes to supplement the effect of the drug of *namasmarana* (remembrance of God).[2]

---

[1] *Sathya Sai Speaks*, Vol. 1, p. 15.

[2] *Sathya Sai Speaks*, Vol. 1, p. 6.

◊ ◊ ◊ ◊ ◊

Man, according to this ancient teaching, is not simply a co-ordinated collection of limbs, senses and sensations. He is all these, governed by intelligence, sharpened by the modes and memories earned through many births. That intelligence itself is an instrument with a limited range of efficiency; there are many goals which it cannot achieve. These can be reached only by the descent of Grace and Power from above. Complete surrender of the ego to that Power will bring it down, fill you with Itself.[1]

◊ ◊ ◊ ◊ ◊

It is always preferable to approach God for the fulfilment of wants, rather than cringe before men, who themselves are but tools in the hands of God. In His own silent way, God will transform the mind and turn it towards *sadhana* and successful spiritual pilgrimage. He cannot allow his children to lose their way and suffer in the jungle. When you approach God and seek his help and guidance, you have taken the first step to save yourself. You are then led to accept His Will as your own. Thus, you achieve *Shanti* (Absolute Peace).[2]

◊ ◊ ◊ ◊ ◊

Above all, try to win Grace by reforming your habits, reducing your desires, and refining your higher nature. One step makes the next one easier; that is the excellence of the spiritual journey. At each step, your strength and confidence increase and you get bigger and bigger instalments of Grace.[3]

---

[1] *Sathya Sai Speaks*, Vol. 6, p. 41.

[2] *Sathya Sai Speaks*, Vol. 13, p. 96.

[3] *Sathya Sai Speaks*, Vol. 5, p. 197.

◊ ◊ ◊ ◊ ◊

Without intelligent discrimination, no skill or strength can be profitably used One must know how fire, for example, or the electric current, has to be used and how far one can deal with it as an instrument for our needs. The senses of man are also like fire; they have to be kept under constant vigilance and control.

No worship can succeed unless the heart is pure and the senses are mastered. Ganesha is the God who helps overcome obstacles; but, He will create obstacles when good endeavour is obstructed by bad influences; He will clear the path for the sincere *sadaka* (spiritual aspirant). He is *prasannavadhanam* (of beneficial looks) when you pray to Him for good ends; but, He will not be that, when you seek His help for nefarious stratagems! He is *Pranava–swarupa*, the *Om* personified; so, He is auspiciousness itself.[1]

◊ ◊ ◊ ◊ ◊

The Gayatri Mantra as Ganesha to Remove Obstacles for Self-Realization

Om bhoorbhuvaha swaha
Thath savithur varenyam
Bhargo dhevasya dheemahi
Dhiyo yonaha prachodhayath

The *Gayatri* (*Vedic* prayer to illuminate the intellect) is the Universal prayer enshrined in the *Vedas* (Divine Knowledge), the most ancient

---

[1] *Sathya Sai Speaks*, Vol. 11, p. 212.

scriptures of man. It is addressed to the Immanent and Transcendent Divine which has been given the name "Savitha," meaning "that from which all this is born." The *Gayatri* may be considered as having three parts — (i) Praise (ii) Meditation (iii) Prayer. First the Divine is praised, then It is meditated upon in reverence and finally an appeal is made to the Divine to awaken and strengthen the intellect, the discriminating faculty of man.

The *Gayatri* is considered as *Vedasara* —"the essence of the *Vedas*." *Veda* means knowledge, and this prayer fosters and sharpens the knowledge-yielding faculty. As a matter of fact the four *Mahavakyas* or "core-declarations" enshrined in the four *Vedas* are implied in this *Gayatri mantra*.[1]

◊ ◊ ◊ ◊ ◊

Intelligence is a double-edged weapon. It can cut the chain and liberate you; it can cause fatal wounds and kill. That is why the great *mantra* which the seekers chant, called *Gayatri* (since it saves those who recite it), prays to God to preside over the intelligence and render it beneficial to the individual and to society.[2]

◊ ◊ ◊ ◊ ◊

The sage Vishwamithra devised the *Gayatri mantra* as a fine drug for the spiritual aspirant; he is also to be revered, for the drug awakens your *buddhi* and confers upon you *viveka*, *vichakshana* and *vairagya* — wisdom, discrimination, and non-attachment — the three distinguishing marks of humans, elevating them far above other animals. ... Man is Divine; he has the Lord dwelling in his heart, but yet he is bound, miserable, limited, weak, agitated. Why? He is ignorant of his reality. He imagines himself weak, limited, bound and he is so shaped by the mind, which is the source of that imagination. How then can you be freed? How are you to overcome this *bhrama* or delusion? If you desire to overtake a train, you must speed in a car or board a plane. No vehicle slower than the train

[1] *Sathya Sai Speaks*, Vol. 13, p. 224.

[2] *Sathya Sai Speaks*, Vol. 7, p. 82.

will help. So too, if you intend to overcome the delusion, you must establish yourself in God; the delusion of *Manavashakti* (man–power) can be overcome only by the attainment of *Daivashakti* (God–power). The *Gayatri* promotes the acquisition of *Daivashakti*.[1]

◊ ◊ ◊ ◊ ◊

Never give up the *Gayatri*; you may give up or ignore any other *mantra* but you should recite the *Gayatri* at least a few times a day. It will protect you from harm wherever you are — travelling, working or at home. Westerners have investigated the vibrations produced by this *mantra* and have found that when it is recited with the correct accent as laid down in the *Vedas*, the atmosphere around becomes visibly illumined. So *Brahmaprakasha*, the effulgence of Divine will descend on you and illumine your intellect and light your path when this *mantra* is chanted. *Gayatri* is *Annapoorna*, the Mother, the sustaining Force that animates all life so do not neglect it.[2]

◊ ◊ ◊ ◊ ◊

Summary

The elephant-headed God Ganesha (Ganapathi, Vinayaka, Vigneswara) is a symbol which represents many Divine aspects (powers) or *siddhis* in the human being, as well as in the Supreme Divinity Itself.

Ganesha is the purified intellect that enables man to realize his Divinity, through reasoning, discrimination,

---

[1] *Sathya Sai Speaks*, Vol. 5, p. 46.

[2] *Sathya Sai Speaks*, Vol. 13, p. 226.

and intuition, to gain Immortality. The pure mind, intellect and *Atma* (spirit) merge together into one to reveal that the Man–of–Perfection is Himself the Lord of obstacles, *Vigneshwara.*

Ganesha is the Divine capacity of man to be Master of himself, of his body, senses, mind, emotions; to lead them to support Truth, Peace, Righteousness, Divine Love, resulting in Spiritual Liberation and Immortality.

The Divine power that Ganesha represents embodies strong will that is in line with Divine Will; self–confidence based on one's innate Divinity; courage and perseverance to overcome obstacles and reach the goal of life (liberation); innate skills and capacities to overcome obstacles; and innate wisdom.

Spiritual practices such as devotional singing, repetition of God's name and *mantras,* meditation, self–inquiry into one's nature, performance of pure, dedicated actions, and other practices to purify mind and emotions and develop sense control can be considered as representative of the Ganesha principle, as they remove obstacles in the path of God realization.

God's Grace and the Guru's Grace (which are the same) to remove obstacles are an important aspect of the Divinity represented symbolically by Ganesha.

Ganesha is the Divinity within and all around the human being, and all beings need only have faith and do spiritual practice to invoke this Divine power to aid them in removing obstacles and reaching the goal of life.

Chapter 3

Lord Shiva

SHIVA PARVATI LORD NATRAJ LORD SHIVA

Chapter 3

Lord Shiva

Introduction

"Shiva is the deity responsible for the dissolution of the universe .... Literally, Shiva is one in whom the Universe sleeps after destruction and before the next cycle of creation. All that is born must die. All that is produced, must disintegrate and be destroyed.... The principle that brings about this disintegration, the power behind this destruction, is Shiva.

Shiva is much more than that. Disintegration of the Universe ends in the ultimate thinning out, into a boundless void. This boundless void, the substratum of all existence from which springs out again and again this apparently limitless universe, is Shiva. So, though Shiva is described as responsible for destruction, He is equally responsible for creation and existence. In this sense, Brahma and Vishnu are also Shiva.

Shiva is snow–white in colour, the white representing light that dispels darkness, knowledge that dispels ignorance. He is the very personification of cosmic consciousness ....

Shiva is the Lord of Yoga and Yogis. He is often shown as sitting in deep meditation emersed in the enjoyment of the Bliss of His own Self. The water of the river *Ganga* (Ganges) represents this. Or it can represent *Gnana*, knowledge. Since the *Ganga* River is highly adored as a great purifying agent, it goes without saying that He whom it adorns, is the very personification of purifying or redeeming power.

The crescent moon stands for time, since measurement of time as days or months depends on the waxing and waning of the moon. By wearing a diadem, Shiva is showing that even the all–powerful time is only an ornament for Him.

The venomous cobras which symbolize death for us adorn His frame. He alone, to whom the symbol of death is a decoration, can gulp down the deadly poison, *halahala*, to save the worlds. He is *mrtyunjaya*, the conqueror of death. Coiled serpents may also represent cycles of time in the macrocosm and the basic energy of living beings in the microcosm. So, Shiva is the master of time and energy.

The *trisula* (trident), being an important weapon of offence and defence, indicates that Shiva is the supreme ruler. The *damaru* in His hands represents the alphabets, grammar or language itself. It also represents sound, *logos*, from which the entire creation has proceeded. By holding it in His hand, Shiva is demonstrating the fact that the entire creation, including its various arts and sciences, has proceeded out of His Will, His play.

The Shivalingam is a symbol of the great God of the universe (*Mahadeva*) who is all–auspiciousness."[1]

In the upper right hand corner of the illustration is Dancing Shiva, Nataraja, Lord of the Dance. "The upper right hand holds aloft the *damaru* (drum) representing *Nada*, the sound, the evolution of the universe. From sound came all language, all music, all knowledge. The drum, with its two triangles, tells us of nature and energy which combine together for all creation. The upper left hand in the half

---

[1] Swami Harshananda, *Hindu Gods and Goddesses*, pp. 57-66.

moon gesture, holds a tongue of flames. Why does Shiva hold the hope of creation in one hand, and the flame, the fire that destroys, in the other? For, creation and destruction are the counterparts of His own Being. They are the two aspects of our life, for as we are surely born, so do we surely die. What then is the answer? The right hand, held in front, in the wondrous gesture of protection and peace tells us, "Look, for God's grace is ever with you." The left hand points the way. It lies across the body, directing the gaze to the foot.... This is the hand depicting the trunk of the elephant ... the trunk is discriminating. It can pick up and break the heaviest of objects, as well as handle the most delicate. It can choose between the two. So, too, we should choose between the higher and the lower, and be discriminating. And to help us, He who owns the trunk, Ganesha, remover of obstacles, is ever–present.

The left foot is raised, telling man that as the dancer raises his foot, so can man raise himself and attain salvation. While one foot is raised, the right foot, upon which balances the whole body of the universe, that which at this eternal moment of dance, precariously balances the fate of the world, that foot is not on the firm ground, but upon the body of a struggling dwarf, a man who is the embodiment of all that veils truth from falsehood, the *apasmara purusha*, made up of ignorance and forgetfulness. This is the *purusha* within us which prevents us from realizing our own essential Divinity. It is for us to firmly crush out the ignorance if we are to attain the supreme joy which is our true nature, the eternal bliss that man calls God. Around *Nataraja* is a ring of flames, the *prabhamandala*, the dance of nature, all initiated by the Self in the center, all emanating from Him and all dissolving within Him ...

What is perhaps most significant of all is the combination of this God ascetic, the Solitary One, Master of Meditation, with the frenzied dance of the Yogi and artist. A dancer becomes the being that he impersonates on the stage. In the dance are aroused the entire energy of body, mind, intellect, and soul. It is a complete surrender to God. Thus, a dancer is similar to the Yogi, who gives his all to the Lord.

This is a dramatic and vivid comparison. But look at the face of Nataraja. It is serene, the epitome of inward absorption. While the body moves in a frenzy like the world with its tumult, Shiva Himself is undisturbed by the activity, depicting most wonderfully, the mortal life and Divine Self ...."[1]

In the upper left hand corner of the illustration is depicted Shiva and Parvati. "Parvati is the power and consort of Shiva. She has two main aspects: the mild and the terrible. As Parvati or Uma she represents the mild aspect as depicted in the illustration. Shiva considered as *Mahadeva*, the Supreme God, Parvati represents His power by which the universe is created, sustained and destroyed. Parvati represents the conscious substance of the universe so is called Uma, which means light, and "the bright one." She also represents spiritual wisdom, by which union with Shiva or God is attained.[2] Another concept of Shiva is that of *Ardhanareswara*, half male and half female.... The latest research in psychology reveals that every man has a woman in his mind and each woman has a man inherent in her constitution. This is known as the principle of *animus* and *anima*. Nature has made every individual as an *Ardhanareswara*."[3]

◊ ◊ ◊ ◊ ◊

The following words of Sai Baba explain the deep inner meaning of the names Sankara, Easwara, Ardanareswara, Shiva–Parvati, and Sambashiva, as inner aspects of one's Divine Self.

---

[1] Mrinalini V. Sarabhai, *Symbolism in Hindusim*, compiled by R. S. Nathan, pp. 165-169.

[2] Swami Harshananda, *Hindu Gods and Goddesses*, pp. 91-94.

[3] Anjani K. R. Srivastava, *Symbolism in Hinduism*, compiled by R. S. Nathan, p. 217.

Other aspects of Shiva such as *halahala* (poison), *sadashivalingam* (elliptical symbol of Shiva), *damaru* (drum), *trisula* (trident), *tri–netra* (three–eyed) *Nandi* (Bull), *bhasma* (holy ash or vibuthi), moon on Shiva's brow, elephant skin on which Shiva sits and the Tandava Dance, are explained by Sai Baba in the following excerpts from His Discourses.

◊ ◊ ◊ ◊ ◊

The journey of every man is towards the cemetery; every day brings you nearer to the moment of death. So, do not delay the duty you must carry out for your own lasting good. Recognise that you are Shiva (God), before you become a *shava* (corpse); that will save you from further deaths.[1]

◊ ◊ ◊ ◊ ◊

Birth is the consequence of *kama* (desire, lust): Death is the consequence of *kala* (time, the lapse of time). The god of desire (*kama*) was reduced to ashes by Shiva; the God of Time is *kala* or *yama*. He was subdued by Shiva. So, one has to surrender to Shiva (God) if one has to escape the consequences of these two frightfully fatal forces.[2]

◊ ◊ ◊ ◊ ◊

Whether one does good or bad acts, there is no escape from their consequences. Knowing this, our ancients always sought what was good and auspicious. This is the meaning of the worship of Shiva.

---

[1] *Sathya Sai Speaks*, Vol. 1, p. 211.

[2] *Sathya Sai Speaks*, Vol. 7, p. 179.

When we speak of *Shivaratri*, we refer to the night that is associated with Shiva, that is, an auspicious night. *Shivam* means that which is auspicious. The Shiva principle is totally free from anything that is inauspicious or unholy in any circumstance. When incarnations like Rama and Krishna appear in human bodies, they have some inauspicious associations related to their bodies. Although they incarnate for the purpose of saving the world, protecting the devotees and uplifting humanity, they have to shed their bodies sometime or other. Hence in the name of such *Avatars*, the honorific "Sri" is prefixed to indicate the sacredness of their advent. But for Shiva no such appellation is needed because Shiva transcends corporeal limitations. Unlike Sri Rama or Sri Krishna there is no "Sri Shiva" or "Sri Sankara." Shiva or Sankara is always auspicious. The realisation of oneness with Shiva means the attainment of immortality.[1]

◊ ◊ ◊ ◊ ◊

Shiva is the supreme exemplar of serenity! Shiva, according to the *Puranas* has a curious assortment of family members. Yet, each one is so calm and without agitation, that the Divine Family exists in peace and concord. Shiva has snakes on His arms, round His neck, on His head, around His waist! One of his sons, Kumara (*Subramanyam*), rides on a peacock, which attacks snakes; another (*Ganesha*) rides on a mouse, which the snakes feed on! One son (*Ganesha*) has the head of the elephant, which whets the appetite of the lion, which is the vehicle used by Durga (*Parvati*), the Consort of Shiva, who is so inseparable that she is the left half of the body of Shiva Himself (*Ardanareswara*). Nor is the Lion friendly by nature to the Bull, which Lord Shiva Himself has as His vehicle! Shiva has Fire on the Central Point of His Brow (third eye), and water, the river (Ganga) on His head,

---

[1] *Sathya Sai Speaks*, Vol. 16, p. 30.

incompatibles both! Imagine how loving, how co–operative the various components have to be, to render life in Kailash smooth and happy![1]

◊ ◊ ◊ ◊ ◊

When you realise Sivoham, I am Shiva, then, you have all the happiness, all the auspiciousness that there is. Shiva is not to be sought on the peak of a distant range of mountains, or in some other special place. You must have heard that sin and merit are inherent in the acts that men do; so too Shiva is inherent in every thought, word and deed, for He is the Energy, the Power and the Intelligence that is behind each of them.

All Energy, Power and Intelligence are in you; you need not search for them outside yourselves. God who is manifesting as Time, Space and Causation is in you; why then do you feel weak and helpless? Man is tossed about by his ambitions and the craving to fulfil them. But, he must first know where he stands and where he should will to reach. Now, his efforts are wanton and wasteful.[2]

◊ ◊ ◊ ◊ ◊

Every man is engaged in searching for something lost. Life is the chance afforded to him to recover the peace and the joy that he had lost, when last he was here. If he recovers them now, he need not come again. But, he loses them through ignorance of their value and of the means of retaining them. If only he would stay in the consciousness of *Shivoham* — "I am Shiva; I am immortal, I am the source and spring of Bliss" — he would be supremely content; but, instead of this correct evaluation of himself, this recognition of his innate reality, man goes about weeping at his helplessness, his

---

[1] *Sathya Sai Speaks*, Vol. 11, p. 155.

[2] *Sathya Sai Speaks*, exact volume and page number unknown.

inadequacy, his poverty, his evanescence. This is the tragic fate from which man has to be rescued.[1]

◊ ◊ ◊ ◊ ◊

The *Upanishads* say that thunder teaches *Da, Da, Dha* ... *Daya* (compassion) to the ogres, *Dama* (self–control) to the gods and *Dharma* to men. Now, since man is all three — part ogre, part God, part man — he must practise all three himself; *daya* (to be kind to all), *dama* (be the master of your mind and the senses) and *Dharma* (be constantly alert on the path of right); that is the advice given from the sky in the voice of thunder. The journey of every man is towards the cemetery; every day brings you nearer to the moment of death. So, do not delay the duty you must carry out for your own lasting good. Recognise that you are Shiva (God), ere you become a *shava* (corpse); that will save you from further deaths.[2]

◊ ◊ ◊ ◊ ◊

1.

Shiva – Parvati (Shakti) and Ardanareswara

Both in the *Vishnupurana* and the *Shivapurana*, Parvati is described as the most beautiful goddess. Conscious of her own exceptional charms, Parvati desired to win Shiva as her spouse. But all her efforts

---

[1] *Sathya Sai Speaks*, Vol. 5, p. 302.

[2] *Sathya Sai Speaks*, Vol. 5, p. 80.

proved·fruitless. Learning a lesson from this experience and shedding her ego, she embarked on a severe penance. Facing the rigours of heat and cold, wind and rain, she allowed her body to waste away by her penance. Her mind was solely concentrated on Shiva. Seeing that she had completely got rid of her ego, Shiva agreed to accept Parvati as one half of himself (*Ardanareswara*).

What is the inner meaning of this episode? Nature is symbolic of Parvati. It is exceptionally beautiful. Feeling proud about its charms, it seeks to attract everybody. As it succeeds in its attractions, its ego grows. Man, who is a child of Nature, also develops the ego and leads a life filled with egoism. The ego gets puffed up on the basis of knowledge, physical strength, power and position, handsome looks and such other accomplishments. Even the pride of scholarship takes one away from God. Persons filled with such conceit can never realise God. Only those free from self–conceit can be God–realised souls. Valmiki, Nanda, Kuchela, Sabari, Vidura, and Hanuman are examples of devotees who realised God, but who could boast of no great lineage, wealth or scholarship. Their supreme quality was freedom from ego. Hanuman, for instance, was content to describe himself as a servant of Rama, despite his great prowess and knowledge.

All the accomplishments and acquisitions in this world are transient and impermanent; lured by them, men get inflated and ultimately court ruin. Hence, giving up the notions of one's own doership, man must regard God alone as the doer. He is the giver, He is the recipient and He is also the object that is given.[1]

◊ ◊ ◊ ◊ ◊

In this age of science and technology, students should try to understand the inner meaning of the concept of Ardanareswara (the combination of the male and female principles in Easwara). No scientist has attempted to explain this concept. Consider the similarity

[1] *Sanathana Sarathi*, February 1991, p. 31.

between the ancient sages' concept of Ardanareswara and the ideas of modern science regarding the atom. There are many such ancient concepts which have contemporary validity. Every object is composed of atoms and in every atom (*anu* in Sanskrit) there is a proton and an electron. The electron is described in Sanskrit as the *vebaga* (the left half) of the atom. The *vebaga* represents the female principle and the *danabaga* (the right half) the male principle. The coming together of these two constitutes the material base of each object. This process of coming together is represented in the concept of "*Ardanareswara*" — the coming together of the female and male aspects. "*Ardanareswara*" means half–feminine and half–masculine. The electron represents the feminine aspect. The proton represents the male aspect. The atom is formed when they come together. Every object in the universe is made up of atoms. Hence, the ancients regarded the entire cosmos as an embodiment of the *Ardanareswara* principle.[1]

◊ ◊ ◊ ◊ ◊

The Truth is that Divinity is all–pervading. After profound enquiry, the *rishis* discovered that God is the source of everything in creation. The *rishis* compared *jagat* (the cosmos) to a seed. Every seed is covered by husk. It is only when the grain and the husk are together that the seed can germinate. Likewise, in the cosmos, the inner grain is God, the outer husk is Nature (*Prakriti*). The cosmos demonstrates the unity of God and Nature. Nature is dependent on God and God is the basis for Nature. Likewise, when we seek refuge in God, He provides the protecting cover for us. Dependence of the devotee (*dasatvam*) and protection by God (*daivatvam*) together constitute Divinity at work. This is also described as *Shiva–Shakti–Atmaka–Swarupam* — the union of Shiva and Shakti.

---

[1] *Sanathana Sarathi*, October 1991, p. 260.

The Cosmos, thus, is not apart from God. It is one with God. The scientists are saying the same thing in their own language when they say matter is energy and energy is matter.[1]

◊ ◊ ◊ ◊ ◊

Shiva–Shakti is the conjunction of *jada* (inert matter) and *Chit* (Consciousness), the conjunction of the wire with the current, which activates all the instruments — fan, stove, bulb and radio. Shiva–Shakti is in all, not only in Me; there is only the difference in power and capacity to manifest. The fire–fly has some power of illumination; it also emits light. We have oil lamp, the electric bulb, the petromax lamp, the moon, the sun — all emanate light; that is the common quality.[2]

◊ ◊ ◊ ◊ ◊

In the Divine family of Lord Shiva, we should understand that Shiva represents energy, *Parvati* represents Nature (or *Prakriti*). *Buddhi* (intellect) and *siddhi* (fulfilment) are symbolic of Ganapati and Subramanya, their sons. They are all one, though conceived in different forms. All the five fingers in the hands are not alike but different in size and shape. But when you do any work, they join together to give maximum effect. If all are of equal size, it will not be conducive to effective functioning. This is one of the secrets of God's creation.[3]

◊ ◊ ◊ ◊ ◊

---

[1] *Sai Baba Discourses*, Vol. 1, p. 57.

[2] *Sathya Sai Speaks*, Vol. 3, p. 31.

[3] *Sanathana Sarathi*, September 1993, p. 297.

2.

Sankara

The sages found that Shiva is also the protector of those who seek refuge in Him. Hence, He was called Sankara — one who confers protection and grace. His will (*Sankalpa*) and grace have no bound and are not dependent on any person, condition or qualification. Hence He was described as *Swayambhu* (Self–created). The sages conceived of Him as one Who could incarnate at will for the protection and rescue of man and the safeguarding of *Dharma*. In view of this transcendental power, He was described as *Sambhavah* the one Who incarnates whenever *Dharma* (the reign of Righteousness) is in danger and the good need protection.[1]

◊ ◊ ◊ ◊ ◊

Sankara is made up of the two words, *sam* and *kara*. What does *Sam* mean? *Sam* is that which is all–pervading like air. The air is filled with Bliss. *Sankara* is one who offers this Bliss to all. *Nithyananda*, everlasting Bliss, *Brahmananda*, Supreme Bliss, and every kind of Bliss is conferred by *Sankara*.[2]

◊ ◊ ◊ ◊ ◊

---

[1] *Sai Baba Discourses*, Vol. 1, p. 52.

[2] *Sanathana Sarathi*, March 1995, p. 60.

3.

Samba-Shiva

Shiva is addressed as *Samba–Shiva, Sa–Amba–Shiva, Amba* meaning Mother and *Shiva* meaning Father, and *Sa* indicating *Sathya, Sarvavyap* (Omni–presence), *Sarvajna* (Omniscient) and *Saksathkara* (Self-Realisation).[1]

◊ ◊ ◊ ◊ ◊

"*Samba Sadashiva.*" *Sa* + *Amba* + *Sada–shiva* represent the union of the Universal Divine Mother and the Universal Divine Father, who are eternally auspicious. *Sambashiva* is the embodiment of the *Shiva–Shakti* union. The world may change, but the Shiva principle is unchanging. The same union of the Universal Divine Mother and Father is represented by the name and form of "Sai Baba."[2]

◊ ◊ ◊ ◊ ◊

4.

Sadashivalingam

Lingam means that in which this *jagat* (world) attains *laya* (dissolution) — *leeyathe*; that into which this *jagat* goes — *gamyathe*. Examine the *Lingam*; the three *gunas* (primordial qualities) are represented by the three–tiered *peetha* (platform); the *Lingam* above symbolises the goal of life. *Lingam* means "a symbol," the symbol of creation, the result of the activity of the three *gunas* and of the

---

[1] *Sathya Sai Speaks*, Vol. 9, p. 25.

[2] *Sathya Sai Speaks*, Vol. 16, p. 31.

Brahman (Supreme Reality) which permeates and gives it meaning and value. When you worship the *Lingam*, you should do so with faith in this symbolic significance.[1]

◊ ◊ ◊ ◊ ◊

The *Lingam* is just a symbol, a sign, an illustration, of the beginningless, the endless, the limitless — for it has no limbs, no face, no feet, no front or back, no beginning or end. Its shape is like the picture one imagines the *Nirakara* (Formless) to be. As a matter of fact, *lingam* means — *leeyathe* (that in which all forms and names merge) and *gamyathe* (that towards which all names and forms are proceeding, to attain fulfilment). It is the fittest symbol of the All–pervasive, the All–knowing, the All–powerful. Everything is subsumed in it; everything starts from it; from the *Lingam* arises *Jangam* (Universe), from the *Jangam* arises *sangam* (association, attachment, activity), and as a result of the *sangam*, one realises the *Lingam* (attributeless *Atma*). Thus, the circle is completed — from the beginningless to the beginningless! This is the lesson that *Lingodbavam* (emergence of the *Lingam*) teaches. The *lingashareera* (the physical body) that is inhabited by the *Atma* is but a vesture worn for this particular sojourn! Many a vesture has this soul worn, though its reality is eternal![2]

◊ ◊ ◊ ◊ ◊

You consider *Shivaratri* to be a great event, a sacred festival, because of the emergence of the *Lingam* from this body. The *Lingam* emerged this day from the embodied Shiva, and the *Sastras* (ancient scriptures) say, Brahma and Vishnu who sought to measure its Glory could not succeed in their venture! Some superficial scholars say that Shiva was born this day, as if the *Sath–Chit–Ananda Swarupa* has either

---

[1] *Sathya Sai Speaks*, Vol. 1, p. 113.

[2] *Sathya Sai Speaks*, Vol. 11, p. 86.

beginning or end! Some say that He started *thapas* (penance) today, and some others that today marks the conclusion of His *thapas!* Even this is due to attempt to drag Divinity down to human level, so that man can peer into the face of God and move as His servant or slave! The affinity should elevate both, not degrade the outer and the inner Divine. No low desire or vulgar ambition should be ascribed to Godhead by the meanness of man.

God is all–powerful; God is everywhere; God is all–knowing. To adore such a Formidable Limitless Principle, man spends a few minutes out of the 24 hours, and uses a minute before an idol or image or picture! It is indeed ridiculous, it is practically futile. ...

Adore Him so long as you have breath, so long as you are conscious. Have no other thought than God, no other aim than knowing His command, no other activity than translating that command into action. That is what is meant by surrender. Render yourself unto Him.[1]

◊ ◊ ◊ ◊ ◊

The *Sada–Shivalingam* represents the ever–auspicious *Atma*, which is beyond all dual aspects and concepts, immanent in all beings and everywhere. It is not negated by time; it is *Sada* (always) *Shivam* (beneficial and auspicious).[2]

◊ ◊ ◊ ◊ ◊

Contemplate the *Atma–lingam* (spirit or the soul), the *Jyothi–lingam* (the effulgent form), which this day emerges from Me; be convinced that the *Lingam* is in every one of you, for it is a mark of the Shiva that resides in the *shava* (body shell). Allow the vision of the *Atmalingam* to

---

[1] *Sathya Sai Speaks*, Vol. 11, p. 79–80.

[2] *Sathya Sai Speaks*, Vol. 2, p. 95.

enter into your inner consciousness and elevate it into Divine heights
...[1]

◊ ◊ ◊ ◊ ◊

Just as *Om* is the verbal symbol of God, the *Lingam* is the symbolic form of the Godhead. It is just a form. Everything is *maya* (delusion) and to grasp it, you must deal with *maya*. Otherwise you cannot realise the *Maya Shakti* (Deluding Power). God is as immanent in the Universe as life is immanent in the egg. The chicken is in every part of the egg; so too, God is in every part of the world. I prefer the description *Sarvantharyami* (inner ruler of all) to the description, *Sarvabhutha antharatma* (Inmost soul of all beings). All are in this Hall, each one has no Hall in him, is it not? In the same way, all are in Him; which is better than saying, He is in all.[2]

◊ ◊ ◊ ◊ ◊

Sadashivalingam indicates the person who is ever of the *Swarupa* (form) of Shiva. Here and everywhere, night and day, in joy and grief, he is Shivam: happy, auspicious, graceful; *Anandam* is his breath, his motive force, his demeanour, his inner and outer expression; *Sada* — always and for ever, *Shivam* — auspicious. There is no room here for controversy or intellectual rivalry and competition, like the ones indulged in by *Pandits* and scholars, misusing the valuable paper manufactured by the mills of this country. Instal *Sadashivalingam* in the consciousness and all things will be revealed to you, step by step, by the Grace of the Divine Indweller.[3]

---

[1] *Sathya Sai Speaks*, Vol. 5, p. 53.

[2] *Sathya Sai Speaks*, Vol. 1, p. 114.

[3] *Sathya Sai Speaks*, Vol. 2, p. 87.

◊ ◊ ◊ ◊ ◊

5.

Shiva — The Embodiment of Jnana (Wisdom)

Take the word *hrudayam* used for "the heart." It means *hrudi* (in the heart) *ayam* (He). That is to say, it means not the organ that pumps blood to all parts of the body, but the seat of the God, the altar where Shiva is installed, the niche where the lamp of *jnana* is lit.[1]

◊ ◊ ◊ ◊ ◊

Shiva is known also as Easwara, the repository of all the resources essential for prosperity. The most important resource is *jnana* (wisdom). Three kinds of *jnana* are demarcated: *jivaprajna* (concerning the individualised Divine), *Easwaraprajna* (concerning the Name–Form–Manifestations of the Divine) and the *Atmaprajna* (concerning the Universal Absolute of which the individual is the temporary particular).[2]

◊ ◊ ◊ ◊ ◊

Through *bhakti* (devotion), the *jeeva* (individual soul) is transformed into Shiva or rather, it knows it is Shiva and the *jeeva* idea

---

[1] *Sathya Sai Speaks*, Vol. 1, p. 113.

[2] *Sathya Sai Speaks*, exact volume and page number unknown.

disappears. To posit oneself as *jeeva*, that is *ajnana* (ignorance); to know oneself as Shiva, that is *jnana* (wisdom).

A white cloth that has become dirty is dipped in water, soaked in soap, warmed and beaten on a slab, in order that it may be restored to its colour and condition. So too, to remove the dirt of *ajnana* that has attached itself to the pure *Sath–Chit–Ananda–Atma* (Being, Awareness, Bliss), the water of unblemished conduct and behaviour, the soap of *Brahman* — reflection, the warming of; *japam* (repetition of God's name) and *dhyanam* (meditation), and the slab of renunciation are all necessary. Then only can the fundamental *Brahman*–hood of the *Atma* shine forth.[1]

◊ ◊ ◊ ◊ ◊

Shivaratri is the day on which Maheswara ((Shiva as Dissolver) takes up the *Lingam* form for the benefit of spiritual seekers; what they have to seek from Maheswara is *Jnana* (spiritual wisdom). "*Jnanam Maheswara dhichched.*" — It is *Jnana* that makes manifest the Divinity latent in man. It is the final achievement of all *thapas* (penance), all *yoga* and *yagna* (ritual worship as sacrifice). You cannot get that joy or even a fraction of that joy, pursuing earthly pleasures. To cure you of the bite of a cobra in a dream, you have to be awakened, that is all. "Waking" is the acquisition of *jnana*. That *jnana* (knowledge) is got by ceaseless *dhyana* (meditation) on the glory and potence of the Almighty.[2]

◊ ◊ ◊ ◊ ◊

Shivaratri is a word that connotes the dual nature of man and his duty to discriminate between the higher and the lower. *Shiva* means *Jnana* (the Higher Wisdom, the Unifying Universal Vision); it also

---

[1] *Jnana Vahini*, p. 33.

[2] *Sathya Sai Speaks*, Vol. 5, p. 54.

means the lasting, the timeless, and the beneficial, the holy, the auspicious. And the second word, *ratri*, means darkness of ignorance, the blind pursuit of tawdry pleasures, the bewildering will–o'–the–wisp of sensory joys. It also means the transitory, the fleeting; it connotes the maleficent, the inauspicious, the sacrilegious. So, the message of *Shivaratri* is: discriminate between *Shiva* and *ratri* — the *Prana* (life energy) and the Body, the *dehi* (indwelling spirit) and the *deha* (body), the spiritual and the material, the *Kshethrajna* and *Kshethra*, called in the Geetha as *Vibhaga–yoga* (the *yoga* of discrimination between matter and spirit).

Relying on the merely literal meaning of the words, people wait a whole year for this particular holy day to come, in order to miss a meal and call it a fast, to miss a night's sleep and call it a vigil! The fast is called in Sanskrit as *Upavasa* and it means something far more significant than missing a meal! It means (*Upa*–near; *Vasa*–living) Living with, or Living near. With whom? Near whom? Near and with God. *Upavasa* means living in the unbroken constant presence of the Lord, by *namansmarana* (remembrance of Divinity); that is the real fast, holding fast to Him.[1]

◊ ◊ ◊ ◊ ◊

The *Jnanalingam* is the sign of the attainment of *Jnana* (spiritual wisdom), when the last vestige of the delusion of "I" is wiped off; even the feeling "I know" is gone; then you are the *Atma*, pure and whole, entire and enduring — then your condition is best represented by the symbol of the *Atmalingam*.

You have, each one, the tremendous *Shakti* (Power) of the *Atma* (Infinite consciousness) in you. Some are able to draw upon it; others just know it is there; others are unaware of the methods of tapping it or even of its existence. It all comes in time, through steady *sadana*. ...

---

[1] *Sathya Sai Speaks*, Vol. 9, pp. 17–18.

When a house is to be certified as habitable, the engineer tests the foundations. The Lord too tests the foundations whether faith is true and deep. Shiruthondar, a devotee of Shiva was also similarly tested by Shiva who came as a *jangama* (ascetic). When Shiruthondar showed that he had no attachment to the world, Shiva revealed Himself and said, "Worship Me as your own Self." Then Shiruthondar demanded, "Reveal to me your Immanence in all Creation and then I shall worship Me, for then I can know that I am really You." Shiva blessed him and he saw all as Light. The vision was the finale of his career in *maya*. He merged as light merges in Light, without noise and without announcement. Even his body became a streak of light which rose up into the depths of space.[1]

◊ ◊ ◊ ◊ ◊

6.

Halahala (Poison)

Poison is man's daily food today. His eye delights in poison; his mouth spouts poison; his ears wag when poison is proclaimed; his feet carry him to dens of poison; his mind cogitates plans to poison another's mind! God alone can swallow the poison and rid the world from the holocaust, as Shiva did when the *halahala* (the dreadful poison that emanated from churning the Primal Ocean) threatened to destroy the world. Meditate on Shiva, the God whose throat is blue as a result of the poison he drank; poison will then be powerless to harm you. I call upon you to bring and offer to Me all the poison in you; take from Me health, happiness, Heaven itself.[2]

---

[1] *Sathya Sai Speaks*, Vol. 2, p. 101.

[2] *Sathya Sai Speaks*, Vol. 8, p. 51.

◊ ◊ ◊ ◊ ◊

From the Ocean of milk when it was churned by the *devas* and *asuras* (celestial beings and demons), there emanated the *Kamadenu* (Cow of Plenty), *Kalpatharu* (the Tree that grants all wishes), the Goddess of Wealth, the four–tusked elephant of Indra and also *Halahala* (the deadliest of poisons). Similarly, the mind of man is churned by the forces of good and evil every day and there emanates from the same mind both good and bad. The bad comes because the mind flows towards sensory pleasures and is lost in the swamps of greed and envy, of lust and pride.[1]

◊ ◊ ◊ ◊ ◊

Take the ideal of Shiva. When the devastating *Halahala* poison emerged from the ocean, life on earth was threatened with immediate and total destruction. Shiva offered to drink the poison and save the world. His throat is blue ever since, for the poison has pervaded the area. Be eager to serve, to help, to come to the rescue of others. For this, one must cultivate *Sahana* (Fortitude, Equanimity). Otherwise, life will be as miserable as resting in the thick shade of a tree infested with red ants! If impatience, anger, hatred, and pride overcome a person, of what avail are other accomplishments? In the firmament of the heart, the Names of God must shine as stars and the confidence arising out of the knowledge of *Atma* must shine like the Moon when it is full and bright.

But, the fiery, ferocious poison, Shiva hides behind the blue patch on His throat. That is a lesson for man: keep under restraint, within you, the qualities and tendencies that are anti–social, the poisonous hatreds and competitive greeds.[2]

---

[1] *Sathya Sai Speaks*, Vol. 1, p. 163.

[2] *Sathya Sai Speaks*, Vol. 7, p. 41.

◊ ◊ ◊ ◊ ◊

7.

Shiva – The Embodiment of Compassion and Beneficence

The Grace of the Lord is as the Ocean: vast; by your *sadana* (spiritual practices), your *japam* (repetition of God's name), *dhyanam* (meditation), and systematic cultivation of virtue, this Grace is converted into clouds of Truth; and they rain on humanity as *Prema* (Love) showers, which collect and flow as the flood of *Ananda* (Bliss), back again into the Ocean — the Ocean of the Lord's Grace. When *Prema* embraces humanity, we call it *daya* (compassion), the quality not of pity but of sympathy; sympathy which makes one happy when others are happy, and miserable when others are unhappy.[1]

◊ ◊ ◊ ◊ ◊

Look at Lord Shiva. The poison which will ruin the world ruthlessly, He has hidden in His throat! The Moon that can shower cool calm comfort, He wears on His Head, for all the worlds to benefit from! That is a lesson for you. Why render others miserable, because you are too weak to suppress the bandits your heart has welcomed?[2]

◊ ◊ ◊ ◊ ◊

---

[1] *Sathya Sai Speaks*, Vol. 1, pp. 46–47.

[2] *Sathya Sai Speaks*, Vol. 2, p. 198.

... through the rituals the "terrific" nature of Rudhra is calmed and He becomes Shiva, the beneficent and compassionate. God is above all *gunas* (qualities); He has no *Agraha* (anger). He is ever the embodiment of Love. He is in *gunas*, but *gunas* are not in Him. There is clay in pots, but there is no pot in clay. One should not fear God; One must love Him so much that all acts He disapproves are discarded. Fear to do wrong; fear to hate another; fear to lose Grace.[1]

◊ ◊ ◊ ◊ ◊

8.
Shiva — The Embodiment of Auspiciousness (Mangalam)

The Night of Shiva is the Night that grants *Mangala* — the boon of blessedness. And, the *Mangala is Maha*, great, unlimited. *Maha* or limitless blessedness can be conferred only by the Divine Source; it cannot be acquired from worldly achievements and triumphs. It is dependent on the Immutable Triad, on *Sathyam, Shivam, Sundaram.*

It assumes all forms, this Shantam!
It assumes all names, this Shivam!
It is Sath–Chit–Ananda, this Only One!
It is Sathyam–Shivam–Sundaram![2]

---

[1] *Sathya Sai Speaks,* Vol. 8, p. 65.

[2] *Sathya Sai Speaks,* Vol. 15, p. 207.

◊ ◊ ◊ ◊ ◊

Probing further into the mystery of the Divine, they described Him as *Shiva*. *Shiva* means the One who is free from the three *gunas* (*satwa, rajas, tamas*). He transcends these three qualities. As one who is without qualities, He was also called *Sudda–Satwa*. *Shiva* is that pure untainted *Satwa* quality. It represents the principle of Auspiciousness (*Mangala*). This means that only when the *gunas* are absent, auspiciousness appears. When qualities are present, it is inauspicious. Hence, Shiva is the embodiment of Auspiciousness (*Mangala–Swarupa*).[1]

◊ ◊ ◊ ◊ ◊

9.
Tri-netra (Thryambakam) Three-eyed

The three eyes of Shiva are the eyes which reveal the Past, Present and the Future. Shiva alone has all three.[2]

◊ ◊ ◊ ◊ ◊

Shiva is praised as *Thryambakam*, that is, three–eyed; the eyes are held to be eyes that see into the past and the future, as well as the present; but, they represent also the three urges namely, desire, activity and knowledge — thirsts that move man and decide his fate. These three urges make all beings kin in the Divine bond; those who

---

[1] *Sanathana Sarathi*, 1991, p. 143.

[2] *Sathya Sai Speaks*, Vol. 1, p. 113.

serve beings with love and reverence can contact this core of being and save themselves. They will see in all, the unmistakable reflections and images of the God whom they have enshrined in their hearts.[1]

◊ ◊ ◊ ◊ ◊

The three–eyed Shiva can see the Past, the Present and the Future. A boy of ten whom you have seen, you can recall his picture as he was when you saw him; but you can't see him as he is now or as he will be ten years hence. But, if you earn the *Tri–netra*, capable of seeing the Past, Present and Future, you can see all three. You become master of Time and Space.[2]

◊ ◊ ◊ ◊ ◊

10.
Trident or Trishula, and Damaru

Vairagya (detachment), *bhakti* (devotion and surrender) and *jnana* (realisation of the Supreme Reality) to which they lead — these three are represented by the *Trisula* in Shiva's Hands. Develop *Jnanam* through the stages of *vairagya* and *bhakti*, then, you can yourself be identified as *Shiva–swarupam*. The mind has to be melted out of shape in the fire of *Jnana* (*Jnanagni dagdha karmanam*), in order to manifest *Shiva thatwa* (essential nature of Shiva).[3]

◊ ◊ ◊ ◊ ◊

---

[1] *Sathya Sai Speaks*, Vol. 10, p. 242–43.

[2] *Sathya Sai Speaks*, Vol. 3, p. 16.

[3] *Sathya Sai Speaks*, Vol. 7, p. 128.

We think that God Shiva has got the *damaru* or the drum in one hand and *trisula* in the other hand and we visualise His Form in that way. ... *damaru* or the drum represents sound and *trisula* is *tri–kala*, the symbol of time past, present and future. ... What Shiva has in His hands is sound and time.[1]

◊ ◊ ◊ ◊ ◊

11.
Easwara

Another name given to this Divine entity was *Easwara*. That is, the Divine was regarded as the possessor of infinite and inexhaustible wealth. What is this wealth? Health is one kind of wealth. Material riches are one kind of wealth. Knowledge, virtues, wisdom, are all included in the term wealth (*Easwaryam* or *Aiswaryam*). They realised the Truth that Easwara is the embodiment of every kind of wealth.[2]

◊ ◊ ◊ ◊ ◊

He was regarded as eternal, omnipotent, all–pervading and the possessor of all that is great and glorious — the six indices of the Divine: *Aiswarya, Dharma*, Fame, Sacrifice, Wisdom and Reputation. And for this reason, He was given another appellation — *Easwara*. *Easwara* is one who is endowed with all conceivable kinds of wealth.[3]

---

[1] *Summer Showers in Brindavan*, 1972, p. 175.

[2] *Sai Baba* — source unknown.

[3] *Sathya Sai Speaks*, Vol. 1, p. 52.

◊ ◊ ◊ ◊ ◊

12.

Nandi (Bull)

Every form conceived in the *Sastras* and scriptures has a deep significance. Shiva does not ride an animal called in human language, a bull. The bull is the symbol of stability standing on four legs, *Sathya, Dharma, Shanti* and *Prema* (Truth, Virtue, Peace and Love).[1]

◊ ◊ ◊ ◊ ◊

In temples of Easwara (or Shiva), you find *nandi* (image of bull) in front of the deity. What is the inner significance of this? The usual reply you get is that *nandi* is the *vahanam* (vehicle) of Easwara; as if He could not afford to have a better vehicle than that. This is a wrong idea. The Truth is that just as *Lingam* is the symbol of the Lord (Easwara), *nandi* (bull) is the symbol for *jiva* (individual soul). Therefore, just like the *nandi*, man should turn away from *prakriti* (the world) and direct all his attention towards Easwara (God) only.

There are some more meanings for this symbolism. For instance, it is said that no one should stand between Easwara and *nandi*. One should have the vision of Easwara by looking through the space in between the two ears of *nandi*. The underlying idea is that through their *sadana* of using its ears to listen about Easwara only, and its eyes to see Easwara alone, the animality in the bull becomes transformed into divinity and because of its merger with Easwara it is called *nandeswara* (bull–God). Thus the lesson of the symbolism is that man

---

[1] *Sathya Sai Speaks*, Vol. 9, p. 14.

should also try to merge with God, by following the example of the *nandi*.[1]

◊ ◊ ◊ ◊ ◊

The *nandi* (Bull) is the lower nature of man; when it is used as the vehicle of God it secures a place in front of the central shrine of God and it shares some of the adoration offered to God. It is only association with the Divine that can confer value and significance. The mind too gets illuminated, and feels joy, peace or calm, only because the peace, joy and calm, which are the native characteristics of the *Atma* (God) within are reflected on it.[2]

◊ ◊ ◊ ◊ ◊

13.

Bhasma (Holy Ash) Shiva is Said to Wear on His Body

When *Bhasma* (holy ash) is given, doubt haunts some people whether Swami is wishing that the recipient should be a *Shaivite* (devotee of Shiva)! It is a symbol of the indestructible basic substance which every being is. All things become ash; but ash remains ash, however much you may burn it. It is also a sign of renunciation, of sacrifice, of *jnana* which burns all *karma*–consequence into ineffective ash. It is a sign of *Easwara*, and I apply it on your brow, to remind you that you too are Divine. It is a valuable *Upadesha* (instruction) about

---

[1] *Sanathana Sarathi*, July 1992, p. 153.

[2] *Sathya Sai Speaks*, Vol. 7, p. 217.

your identity. It also reminds you that the body is liable any moment to be reduced into a handful of ash. Ash will be a lesson in detachment and renunciation.[1]

◊ ◊ ◊ ◊ ◊

14.
Shiva Living on the Himalayan Mountains

Lord Shiva resides on the Himalayas, as the *Puranas* (mythological legends) declare. The inner meaning of this declaration is: Lord Shiva lives in hearts that are as pure, as white and as cool as the snow (*hima*) and also as steady and unmoved (*achal*) as these mountains.[2]

◊ ◊ ◊ ◊ ◊

---

[1] *Sathya Sai Speaks*, Vol. 7, p. 87.

[2] *Sathya Sai Speaks*, Vol. 13, p. 44.

15.
Crescent Moon on Shiva's Forehead

Shiva wears the crescent on His crown so that the soft moonlight might mark out the pilgrim route to God, and make the journey less toilsome. He spreads joy and peace.[1]

◊ ◊ ◊ ◊ ◊

16.
Shiva Sits on an Elephant Skin

The elephant skin which forms His cloak is just a symbol for the elemental bestial primitive traits which His Grace destroys; He makes them powerless and harmless; in fact, he tears them to pieces, skins them so to say, and makes them ineffective. His four Faces symbolise *Shantam, Roudram, Mangalam* and *Utsaham* (Peace, Fierceness, Auspiciousness, Determination). In this way, realise while worshipping the *Lingam*, the inner sense of the many attributes of Shiva [2]

◊ ◊ ◊ ◊ ◊

---

[1] *Sathya Sai Speaks*, Vol. 11, p. 319.

[2] *Sathya Sai Speaks*, Vol. 1, p. 113.

17.

The Tandava Dance

Shiva, or the *Paramapurusha*, the Eternal Absolute Person, in His Desire to attract *Prakriti* (nature), engages Himself in the *tandava*, the Cosmic Dance. The Dance is a Divine plan to attract the material creation, for all Divine miracles like those of *Rama* (He who pleases and delights) and *Krishna* (He who attracts), are for drawing people to the Divine Presence for the purpose of correcting or cleansing them, or for confirming their faith and then leading them on to the *sadana* of service so that they may merge in ecstasy, in the source of all ecstasy. The *tandava* dance is so fast that fire emanates from Shiva's body because of the heat generated by activity. In order to cool Shiva and comfort him, Parvati, his consort, places the Ganges on his head, makes the crescent moon rest amidst the coils of his hair, applies cold sandalwood paste all over his body, winds round the joints of his hands and feet cold–blooded snakes, and finally, being herself the daughter of the Himalayas (the mountains with eternal snow), she sits on his lap and becomes a part of him. At this Shiva rises, and both *Purusha* and *Prakriti* dance together to the immense delight of the Gods and of all creation. This happens, according to the Puranas, on the *Shivaratri* day.

The significance of this myth lies in the secret taught by it of pleasing the Lord and winning His Grace ....[1]

◊ ◊ ◊ ◊ ◊

---

[1] *Sathya Sai Speaks*, Vol. 14, pp. 4-5.

18.

Shiva

The sages believed that the Divine principle was present in and outside of everything and that it could be experienced directly as well as indirectly. They pursued their penances further, for the benefit of mankind. They realised the Truth that the Divine Effulgent Person was beyond the outer darkness and, experiencing this Reality, they called upon all to seek and experience it. This Effulgent *Purusha* is utterly selfless, full of light, the embodiment of all auspicious qualities and free from attributes. He was described as "Shiva" meaning one who is beyond the three *gunas (satwa, rajas, tamas)* and hence absolutely pure and untainted.[1]

◊ ◊ ◊ ◊ ◊

Resolve on this Holy *Shivaratri*, in the Presence of Shiva Sai (Baba), to visualize the Shiva as the inner power of all. With each breath, you are even now, asserting *soham,* "I am He," not only you, but, every being that breathes, every being that lives, everything that exists. It is a fact which you have ignored so long. Believe it from now on. When you watch your breath and meditate on that magnificent Truth, slowly, the I and the He (the *Sah* and the *Aham*) will draw nearer and closer, until the feeling of separateness will fade away — and the *Soham* will be transformed into *Om*, the *Pranava*, the Primal Sound, the Fundamental Formula for God. That *Om* is the *Swaswarupa* — the Reality behind this "relative reality."[2]

---

[1] *Sai Baba Discourses*, Vol. 1, p. 52.

[2] *Sathya Sai Speaks*, Vol. 9, p. 16.

◊ ◊ ◊ ◊ ◊

Summary

Shiva is the immortal, Divine source and spring of Bliss within man. The human body and all of creation comprise Shiva–Parvati (Shiva–Shakti) which is the conjunction of matter (*jada*) and consciousness/energy (*chit*). *Ardanareswara* means the coming together of the male and female principles (animus and anima as well as proton and electron in the atom) that constitutes the material base of each object, and is one meaning of the interrelationship of Shiva and Parvati.

Within and around the human frame is *Sankara* — the one who is all–pervading like air, of the nature of Bliss, conferring protection and grace.

Man is in, from, and of *Lingam*. *Lingam* is that consciousness-energy (Shiva) from which all names and forms have emerged, and into which they merge. *Lingam* is always beneficial, auspicious, blissful and immortal.

Meditating on Shiva, one's inner Divinity, one attains *jnana* — the unifying universal wisdom or immortality.

Halahala symbolises the negative, antisocial poisonous hatreds and competitive greeds, etc., within man. Man can curb and eliminate this poison through meditation and acquisition of wisdom (*jnana*) and knowledge of *Lingam*, whereby his true Divine nature of compassion and service manifests.

The moon on Shiva's brow is the cool, comforting, Divine consciousness within each human that confers grace and beneficence on all.

Man as God has the Divine capacity to experience the past, present and future — to become master of time and space (*trisula* or trident). Man is capable of realising that he is the embodiment of Aum (Om) — the primordial consciousness/energy that is continuously creating, sustaining and dissolving the universe, including one's own body–mind complex (*damaru*).

When one lives in the stability of the Atma or Shiva consciousness, and Truth, Righteousness, Peace, and Love are his intrinsic nature, he is riding on *nandi*, the bull. He has conquered his primitive animal nature.

When one realizes that the end of one's body, as well as all material forms is ash and that one is pure consciousness, one becomes Shiva, of the nature of detachment and renunciation. This is the meaning of Shiva wearing ash on his body.

Shiva is to be contemplated upon as one's own Divine nature. Through listening to, and singing devotional songs about Shiva or chanting the sacred *mantra*, "Om Namah Shivaya," remembering all of the aspects and equipments of Shiva, one realises that he himself is Shiva.

Chapter 4

Rama

LAKSHMANA RAMA SEETA HANUMAN

Chapter 4

Rama

Introduction

Rama is the Divine Name for the eternal, formless, attributeless, Principle of Existence, Knowledge, Bliss, that assumed a human form as an *Avatar* of God around 5000 BC, in India. *Rama* is the *Atma* or Spirit living in the hearts of all beings, omnipresent, omniscient, omnipotent, conferring Bliss on all. The Divine Name *Rama* has the potency of a *mantra* to transform and liberate mankind from ignorance and bondage, when chanted constantly with sincere devotion coupled with selfless service to the Divine.

Rama is the embodiment of all types of *Dharma*. *Dharma* refers to righteous, moral, virtuous conduct that is based on Divine Love, Truth, Peace and non–violence.

Dharma is that which sustains, saves, and sanctifies. *Dharma*, Truth and God are synonymous. *Rama* embodies the ideal behaviour for mankind in all of the roles one may play (such as, father, daughter, businessman, etc.), as well as for governments. *Rama* is the ideal of uncompromising goodness and idealistic perfections, as a perfect son, ideal King, true husband, devoted brother, noble enemy, etc. The wielding of the bow and arrow symbolizes His preparedness and strength to maintain peace and justice both within and without. He is the ideal of aggressive goodness as opposed to weak and passive goodness. He stands for righteousness and opposes and destroys all that is unrighteous.

Seeta, the consort of *Rama* (Lord or *Purusha*) is *Rama's Shakti* (energy) for the creation of the universe; she is the embodiment of all of nature (*Prakriti*). She also symbolizes the wisdom and self–realization that comes when the *Atma* knows itself as *Paramatma*. *Ravana* symbolizes one who craves for material things, does not care for the *Atma* (*Rama*) or spiritual life, develops evil tendencies, and thus faces death rather than spiritual liberation.

Ayodhya means the spiritual heart, or *Atma*, no enemy can penetrate. *Rama* and his three brothers embody the four goals of human life: *Dharma* (*Rama*); *Artha* (wealth); *Lakshmana*: *Lakshmana* represents one who has completely surrendered the desire for worldly wealth and has desire only for the *Prema* (Love) of *Rama* and *Moksha* or

Liberation; *Kama* (Desire, *Bharata*): *Bharata* has desire for *Sathya* (Truth) and *Dharma*, and thus, for *Rama* or Liberation (*Moksha*), *Moksha* (Liberation, *Satrughna*), he symbolizes *Shanti* or the Peace of *Moksha*.

Rama's father, *Dasarata*, means "one who rides in a chariot (body) of ten entities"; that is, the five sense organs and the five organs of action. *Dasarata* marrying three wives is symbolic of the human being governed by three attributes, or *gunas* — *satwa, rajas,* and *tamas.*

Hanuman, the great devotee of *Rama*, though a monkey, symbolizes the courageous mind of the *jeeva* (embodied spirit or soul) who through faith and service can penetrate the darkness of ignorance to bring about *Moksha* or spiritual liberation, that is, the realization that *Rama*, or *Atma*, is one's own true Self.

The following excerpts from Sathya Sai Baba's *Divine Discourses* elaborate on the deep inner meaning of *Rama* and those characters who closely interacted with Him in the epic *Ramayana.*

◊ ◊ ◊ ◊ ◊

1.

Rama is Atma, The Embodiment of Existence, Knowledge, Bliss

The Ramayana is the very life–blood of the *Bharathiyas* (Indians). Down to a few years ago, it was difficult to find throughout the length and breadth of India a village without a temple for the worship of Rama, a home where a picture of Rama was not adored, or a tongue whereon the name Rama did not dance. The entire country was saturated with the fragrance of Rama. Such a fortunate land has degenerated in recent times into a region fouled from top to bottom with the contagion of *kama* (lust). Seek to be filled with Rama; you will be saved. Seek, on the other hand, to be fouled by *kama*; you will be damned.

In the *Threta* Age of human history, the Formless, Attributeless Principle of Existence–Knowledge–Bliss was so overcome with compassion that It assumed the human form, as the very embodiment of *Dharma (Ramo vigrahavan Dharmah)*, manifested various examples for man of correct righteous conduct, re–established the supremacy of *Dharma* and its inherent might, and merged again in the Absolute, from which It had appeared.

The *Vedas* describe the Divine entity as *Madava: Ma* meaning *maya* and *dava* meaning Lord. That is to say, He is the Master of all that is born and therefore dies, changes and is therefore, false! Life and death are a part of *maya* (delusion), of which He is sovereign. So, all who are bound by this dual chain have to be loyal to God, and pay homage to Him and obey His order. That is the path to happiness ....

To meet a person living on the tenth floor, you have to go up nine floors. To experience the joy of being with *Madava* (God), you have to rise to that purity, that Love, that Truth, that Peace. Become full of compassion; love all; serve all; do your duty sincerely and with joy; be good, do good, and thus deserve God. Rama will be pleased when you tread the path of Truth, for, that is the path laid down by Him.[1]

◊ ◊ ◊ ◊ ◊

The fame of Divine personalities grows with every word they speak and every deed they condescend to enact. Rama's glory shines brilliantly even after all these centuries. It will shine as resplendently for ages to come. Rama means He who pleases. Nothing pleases man more than his *Atma*, which is an eternal unfailing source of joy. One must prefer the awareness of the *Atma* and the Bliss that the awareness confers, to all other minor momentary joys. The *Upanishad* says, "*Thyagenike Amruthathvam Anasu*" — "By renunciation alone can the Bliss of Immortality be won."[2]

◊ ◊ ◊ ◊ ◊

Rama is the eternal, unchanging *Purusha* (Spirit). The *Atma* in every being is Rama; hence the name *Atmarama*. Rama is eternal and so the *Ramamantram* is said to have been taken by Shiva Himself. Rama means that which showers *Ananda* (Bliss), that is all. Now, what can give greater *Ananda* than the *Atma*? Rama is *Anandam* and He is *Atmarama*, the *Anandam* in your Inner Consciousness. You can understand Ramayana only if you keep this aspect in view.[3]

◊ ◊ ◊ ◊ ◊

---

[1] *Sathya Sai Speaks*, Vol. 11, pp. 110–111.

[2] *Sathya Sai Speaks*, Vol. 5, p. 32.

[3] *Sathya Sai Speaks*, exact source unknown.

The Rama Principle is the Principle of Love, that descended from Heaven, as the gift of the Gods, as a result of the great sacrifice. *Rama* means Delight! Nothing delights more than one's own innate self, and so, *Rama* is also known as *Atma–Rama.*[1]

◊ ◊ ◊ ◊ ◊

Rama is the name for *Ananda* that is inherent in every heart; recite His name, let the *Ananda* respond and upsurge. Do not pretend and get charged with hypocrisy. Be genuine, sincere and true inheritors of *Bharathiya* (Indian) culture! You have to outgrow the idol, picture and image; they are the kindergarten materials in spiritual schools; seek to know the Divine Energy, that is burdened with no Name and no Form. Rise higher into the empryean heights of the Pure, Attributeless, Transcendent One.[2]

◊ ◊ ◊ ◊ ◊

What pleases man most is sweetness — in thought, word and deed. This mysterious component that evokes joy in the human heart is the genuine Rama principle. Rama means "that which causes delight." A stomachful of food, an eyeful of sleep, a home full of children's laughter — these, according to most people, are the highest levels of happiness. But this refers only to the interval between birth and death. What of the before and after? The body is something separate from you. You own it for some years and you feed it and foster it and struggle with it, to tame it to do your will. "You" or the "I" in the body, the "*Atma,*" is the One, without a second. When identification with the body weakens, the effulgence of the *Atma* (Divine Self) will be patent. ...

---

[1] *Sathya Sai Speaks*, Vol. 9, p. 129.

[2] *Sathya Sai Speaks*, Vol. 10, p. 184.

The wisdom to recognize that the body he believes is himself is only an instrument wielded by him, has to dawn in man. That is the first step to the higher spiritual consciousness. There is in every person the ever–free, ever–unattached, ever–pure *Atma*. That is the *Brahman* (Absolute Reality), the Cosmic Awareness latent and patent in every one. *Yoga* (Divine Communion) awakens when the world is viewed with glorious unconcern. This is the source of supreme *Ananda* (Divine Bliss).[1]

◊ ◊ ◊ ◊ ◊

Rama is *Atma*–Rama, the Voice of God within. Do not disobey it or circumvent its directives. Pray that the Voice alerts you ever, pray with humility and surrender to the advice. Then Rama will guide you right with compassion.[2]

◊ ◊ ◊ ◊ ◊

The sun has two properties: Light and Heat. The *Atma* too can be viewed in two aspects: *Swarupa* and *Swabhava* — its "It–ness" and "the effect of Its Itness." The innate Truth or *swarupa* is known as *dharmi* and its effect or quality or *swabhava* is known as *Dharma*. When one is aware of the *Dharma*, he can be said to have attained the *Dharma–bhootha–jnana* (the transformation resulting from the knowledge of the *Atma Swabhava* or *Dharma*). The sublimation resulting from the knowledge of the essence or Itness or *swarupa* of the *Atma* is *Dharmi–bhootha–jnana*. The *swarupa* of the *Atma* is *Anu* or *atomic*. Its *Dharma* or quality is splendour. The *Atma* is described as *Vibhu*. Subtler than the subtle *anu* (atom), Vaster than the vastest, witnessing all everywhere, *Atma* is Brahman, Brahman is *Atma*.

---

[1] *Sathya Sai Speaks*, Vol. 16, p. 55.

[2] *Sathya Sai Speaks*, Vol. 16, p. 58.

This subtlest *anu*, *Atma*, is in all things and its quality is therefore evident everywhere. It occupies all, but it cannot be occupied by any other. The *Atma*–principle, the *Brahman*–principle, is immanent in all things in the Universe, but nothing can penetrate it. Since the *anu* or the *Atma* which has that form is-in all things, it is clear that all things are *Atma*!

There is nothing in the Universe devoid of this *anu* force. This quality of the *anu* is cognisable in all things as the *Dharma*. So, the *Dharma* or *Atma* is omnipresent. The human body too is no exception to this. The atom or *anu* is immanent in it and so, we are the embodiments of *Atma*, of *Atmic* energy.[1]

◊ ◊ ◊ ◊ ◊

The word Rama itself indicates *Anandam*. Rama is *Anandaswarupa*. In every being, He is the *Ananda* in the innermost core, the *Atmarama*. How then are you being affected by grief? Because you ignore the core, you identify yourselves with the shell, the body. Today, the holy day of *Ramanavami*, you should immerse yourself in the *Atma* as *Dharmaswarupa*, as the motivator of the moral life. There is no place where Rama is not; no being to whom He denies Grace. He does not arrive or depart; He is immanent, eternal.[2]

◊ ◊ ◊ ◊ ◊

There are two predominant *rasas* or streams of feeling or mood in the Rama story, the stream of compassion (*karuna*) as Rama and the stream of Love (*Prema*) as Lakshmana. It is the mergence of the two that evokes *Ananda* (Bliss). *Ananda* is the very nature (*swabhava*) of Rama. He is *Bhagavan* Himself, though Valmeeki has not explicitly declared it anywhere. He refers to Rama as "equal in valour to

---

[1] *Sathya Sai Speaks*, Vol. 15, p. 191.

[2] *Sathya Sai Speaks*, Vol. 5, p. 159.

Vishnu," but not as Vishnu Himself. It is only through the mouths of Rama's own sons that the mystery is revealed. *Bhagavan* means: *Bha* (effulgence) *ga* (manifestation) *van* (he who is capable) — he who has the power to manifest *Jyothi* (Effulgence) — the Divine *Jyothi*, the *Atma Jyothi*. He is also *Sambhartha* — He from whom this Created Universe has emerged and He who is intent on fostering it. All who adore Rama as manifesting and protecting the Universe and projecting the Cosmic Effulgence and Intelligence are entitled to be known as *Bhaktas* (Devotees).

But, most seekers are but part–time devotees today. They are not *sathatam yoginah* (always in union with the Lord). They are *yogis* in the morning, *bhogis* (epicures) at noon and *rogis* (sick patients) at night![1]

◊ ◊ ◊ ◊ ◊

The consequence of avoiding the knowledge and practice of *Vedanta* is the increase of three tragedies: *Papam, Thapam, Ajnanam* (Sin, Suffering and Ignorance). The Name usually given to the Reality that you are, namely, Rama, is the cure for all three. *Atma* is known as *Atmarama* because Rama means that which pleases and nothing confers such vast inexhaustible joy as the *Atma*. So, the word Rama means the *Atma*. That word consists of three components: *Ra, a* and *ma*. "*Ra*" is the mystic representative of *Agni* (Fire) principle; it burns sin into ash; "*a*" is the symbol of *Surya* (Sun) principle; it destroys the darkness of ignorance. "*Ma*" is the symbol of *Chandra* (Moon) principle; it cools the *Thapam* or heat of suffering. So, "*Rama*" overcomes all the three tragedies and reveals the Truth, the Beauty and Goodness. Repeat the Name, Rama with significance in mind and you can feel its effect very soon.[2]

◊ ◊ ◊ ◊ ◊

[1] *Sathya Sai Speaks*, Vol. 15, pp. 30–31.

[2] *Sathya Sai Speaks*, Vol. 7, p. 107.

The name "Rama" is not confined only to the son of Dasarata. The *Atma* that confers Bliss is known as Rama. The sage Vasishta gave the name "Rama" to Emperor Dasarata's son. The name Rama symbolises the universal attributes of the Divine such as omniscience, omnipotence and omnifelicity.[1]

◊ ◊ ◊ ◊ ◊

The greatest formula that can liberate, cleanse and elevate the mind is *Ramanama* (the Name of Rama). Rama is not to be identified with the hero of the Ramayana, the Divine offspring of Emperor Dasarata. He was named Rama by the Court Preceptor because it was a Name which was already current. Vashishta, the preceptor, said that he had chosen that Name since it meant, "He who pleases." While every one else pleases the self, nothing pleases the caged individualised self more than the free universal Self. The Self is therefore referred to as *Atma–Rama*, the Self that confers unending joy.

...

Rama is the bee that sucks the honey of devotion from the lotus of the heart. The bee loosens the petals of the flower it sits upon; but Rama adds to its beauty and fragrance. He is like the Sun, which draws the water to itself by its rays and accumulating it as cloud, sends it back as rain to quench the thirst of earth. Rama, the mystic potent sound, is born in the navel and it rises up to the tongue and dances gladly thereon.

The *Vedic* declaration, *Tat–thwam–asi* (That–thou–art) is enshrined in the word Rama, which consists of three sounds: "*Ra*,"*a*," and *ma*. Of these, *Ra* is the symbol of Tat (That; *Brahman*, God) *Ma* is the symbol of *Thwam* (Thou; *jeevi*; individual) and *a* that connects the two is the symbol of the identity of the two.

The word Rama has also a numerological significance: *Ra* counts as two, *a* counts as zero, and *ma* counts as five — so that, Rama adds

---

[1] *Sanathana Sarathi*, April 1992, p. 60.

up to seven, which is an auspicious number. We have the seven *swaras* of music, the seven heavenly sages, and reciting Rama for seven days continuously is considered specially fruitful.[1]

◊ ◊ ◊ ◊ ◊

2.
The Potency of the Name Rama

In the name "Rama," the three deities — *Agni*, Sun and Moon — are present. From where have these three deities originated? The Sun has the power to scorch the earth from millions of miles away. Who are the parents of the Sun? Should they not be even more powerful than the Sun? There is, then the Fire principle. Fire can destroy anything. Who are the parents of *Agni*? The Moon is the source of coolness and light. Who are the parents of the Moon? If the enquiry is made regarding the parents of these three powerful entities it will be found that God is the parent.

Everything has come from God. The common people do not make this basic enquiry into the root cause of all things. Nothing can exist without a basis. Even scientists are now engaged in trying to discover this basis.

In fact, the Name is the basis and the entire cosmos rests on it. The name is the easiest means to identify anything or any person. Hence, the best way to recognise God and envisage His form is through the name. The Name is always auspicious.[2]

◊ ◊ ◊ ◊ ◊

---

[1] *Sathya Sai Speaks*, Vol. 8, pp. 84–85.

[2] *Sanathana Sarathi*, April 1992, p. 62.

For *namasmarana* (repetition of God's name), no expense is involved; no materials are needed; there is no special place or time to be provided. No qualification of scholarship or taste or sex has to be proved. When a bit of iron is rubbed to and fro on a slab of stone, heat is generated; only, the rubbing has to be vigorous and continuous. When you do so at intervals and with poor pressure, the iron will not get hot. So, too, in order to get sufficient heat to melt the soft heart of the Lord, rub the name Ram Ram Ram Ram vigorously and unintermittently. Then, the Lord will shower His Grace. If you devote but two minutes and a half in the morning and another two minutes and a half in the evening, the little heat will cool off twice a day and His heart will not melt.[1]

◊ ◊ ◊ ◊ ◊

In your heart, there is the *Atmarama*, the Rama that confers eternal joy. So repeat the name Rama, the Sun which can make the lotus in the heart bloom. Rama is not the son of Emperor *Dasarata* but the ruler of the *dasa indhriyas* (the ten senses). The recital of the *Ramanama* must become as automatic as breathing, as frequent and as essential. Rama has in it the *beeja–akshara* (seed letters) of both the *Shiva mantra* as well as the *Narayana mantra*, for it is composed of the second letters of both; Na–ra–yana and Na–mah–Shivaya. This name is acceptable, therefore, to all sects; it also endows you with power and all the spiritual capital you need.

Real *Ananda* (Bliss) can be won only by means of the transformation of the impulses which agitate the mind. It is not to be found in wealth. You think that the rich man is happy; ask Me, and I shall reveal to you that they are full of grief, for they come to Me in large numbers for relief. They have no *Shanti* (Peace) at all. A strong physique does not by itself give *Shanti*; nor does scholarship, or asceticism or rituals. Only constant dwelling with the Name of the

---

[1] *Sathya Sai Speaks*, Vol. 5, p. 249.

Lord gives that unshakeable Peace, unaffected by the ups and downs of life. It makes man a *dheera* (a hero).

Sai Baba was till today a formless Name to you, but now it has come with Form and you can keep the *rupa* (form) in your mind. So too, the name "Rama" has a form and you should picture the form also when you repeat the Name; then the name becomes concrete and *japam* is easier. Live always in the presence of that form–filled *nama*. Then life becomes one continuous worship of the Lord.[1]

◊ ◊ ◊ ◊ ◊

The wrong notion that the world is real and that you are the body has been so deeply implanted in you through birth after birth, that it can be removed only by means of a very potent drug, administered continuously. The drug, Ram Ram Ram, is to be swallowed and assimilated *ad infinitum*. Its curative essence will travel into every limb, every sense, every nerve and every drop of blood. Every particle of you will be transmuted into Ram. You must melt in the crucible and be poured into the Ram mould and become Ram. That is the fruition of *jnana*. *Ramanama* or any other Name if chanted and absorbed in the mind, will help control the vagaries of the senses which drag you away into vanities.[2]

◊ ◊ ◊ ◊ ◊

The world is based on three entities: Fire, the Sun and the Moon. No one can deny the existence of these three. *Hethu Krisanu Bhanu Himakara the. Krisanu* means the Fire principle. *Bhanu* refers to the Sun and *Himakara* refers to the Moon. The combination of these three attracts and sustains all beings in the world. They give pleasure, provoke wonder and also delude men. Because they give pleasure, the

[1] *Sathya Sai Speaks*, Vol. 1, pp. 81–82.

[2] *Sathya Sai Speaks*, Vol. 7, p. 4.

three are called *Rama*. In the word *Rama* there are three sounds: *Ra, A, Ma. Ra* refers to Fire (*Agni*), *A* refers to the Sun and *Ma* refers to the Moon. The combination of these three entities represents the *Rama Principle*.

All objects in the world can be cognised by name and form and nothing else. All objects are identified by their names. The form is derived from the name. Hence, for everything in the world, the name is primary and fundamental.

The Divine Name is highly potent. Even the wishfulfilling celestial cow, *Kamadenu*, when it is tethered to the post, comes under control. Likewise, when the Supreme Lord, the Indweller in all hearts, is bound by the rope of *bhakti* (devotion) and tethered to the post of the tongue, He gets bound to the devotee. There are only two means by which the Lord can be bound or enjoyed, namely, through the name and through Love. The Name can be *Rama, Hari* or *Hara* or any other name, because the All–pervading Divine bears all names.[1]

◊ ◊ ◊ ◊ ◊

The Name, Rama, was once indicated by Rama Himself (the son of Dasarata, hero of the Ramayana, the incarnation of the Lord in the *Threta yuga*) as a potent liberator. When Rama was passing through the forests, with Seeta and Lakshmana, the hermits who recognised Him as Divine gathered around Him with a prayer that they be initiated by Him and given some *mantra* (sacred formula) which they could repeat for spiritual uplift and victory. Rama replied that He was a prince in exile, wandering in the forests, and so He could not presume any authority to initiate hermits into the spiritual path. He moved on along the jungle tracks.

Watching Him walking fast, with Seeta immediately behind Him and Lakshmana following in the rear, an aged hermit exclaimed, "Friends! See! Rama is initiating us! He is awarding us the *mantra*! God

---

[1] *Sanathana Sarathi*, April 1992, pp. 59–60.

is leading. Nature (His constant companion, His shadow) is following (Seeta). The *jeevi* (individual), part of the Lord, the wave of the ocean, is in the rear (Lakshmana). He can see the Lord only if the deluding Nature is propitiated or by–passed. This is indeed a silent lesson in *sadana* (spiritual discipline). *Ra* is God; *ma* is the individual, who has fallen behind. *A* is *Prakriti* (Nature); Rama Rama is the *mantra* He is vouchsafing so graciously. Take it and save yourselves. For me, there is no other course," he said.[1]

◊ ◊ ◊ ◊ ◊

3.
Rama as Avatar: Descent of God to Earth

The essence of the religion of *Bharatiyas* as proclaimed in the *Rig, Yajur, Sama* and *Atharvana Vedas,* is the attainment of the unity of the individual with the Divine by the recognition of his inherent Divinity. The *Avatars* come to teach humanity this principle of oneness so that they may get rid of the idea of diversity and manifest their inherent Divinity, realising their basic spiritual nature.

The descent of the *Avatar* means the Divine coming down to the level of the human. No blemish attaches to the Divine as a result of this descent. There is no diminution in His puissance. Here is the example of a child–playing on the ground. If the mother feels it is beneath her dignity to bend and calls upon the child to leap into her arms, the child cannot do so. But out of her love for the child, the mother herself stoops and picks up the baby. By bending down to take

---

[1] *Sathya Sai Speaks*, Vol. 8, pp. 93–94.

the child, does the mother bow to the child? Likewise, the Avatar descends to the level of the human to bless and rescue those who cannot rise to the level of the Divine. The ignorant assume that because the Divine has descended with a human form God has lowered Himself to the human level. This is a case of bending and not kneeling down. It is an act of benediction and not of submission. The attributes and powers of the Divine remain unaltered in their pristine amplitude. The Divine manifests His powers according to the needs, the circumstances and the conditions prevailing at the particular time or place. Take, for example, the case of a Chief Justice of the Supreme Court. He has the power to inflict the supreme penalty on any number of persons, according to the law. He has also the power to protect the rights of citizens. He has both the power to protect and to punish. These powers can be exercised only when he sits in his judicial chair. The same Chief Justice, when he is at home, confers joy on his grandson by letting him ride on his back! By allowing this grandchild to play in this manner, does he forfeit his powers as a Chief Justice? Similarly, the Avatar does not forgo any of His supreme powers merely because He lives and moves among human beings as a man. Narrow–minded persons view these things differently.

This phenomenon could be noticed in several instances in the case of the Rama Avatar. In the Ramayana, Rama is depicted as one who, like other ordinary human beings, experienced the pangs of separation from Seeta. For what reason did Rama exhibit such feelings? Rama behaved in this manner to serve as an example to the common people how individuals should behave in similar circumstances.[1]

◊ ◊ ◊ ◊ ◊

The sun and the moon are shining in the world. People imagine that each of them is shining by its own luminosity. They do not realise that there is an effulgence which transcends the light of the sun and

---

[1] *Sanathana Sarathi*, April 1991, p. 87.

the moon and accounts for their brilliance. The moon shines because of the reflected light of the sun. The moon is not self–luminous; it derives its light from the sun. Likewise, people imagine that wisdom (*viveka*) and intelligence (*buddhi*) in man are *sui generis*. But the light of wisdom is derived from the *buddhi*. The illumination of the *buddhi* is due to the *Atma* (the Indwelling Spirit). Human beings in their ignorance consider only the illumination emanating from wisdom and intelligence, forgetting the basic source of their effulgence, the *Atma*; as a consequence they forfeit their essential human quality. That *Atma* is the foundation. It is *Brahman*. It is the Supreme Cosmic Principle (*Paratatwa*). It is the Omni–Self (*Paramatma*). It is the Avataric Principle.

The common people can derive no benefit if the Formless Absolute remains in *Kailasa* or *Vaikunta* (Heaven). It is not possible to worship the formless Absolute. Hence, the *Rama Avatar* appeared in human form to enable humanity to experience the Formless in a form which is accessible to them and helpful to them. An *Avatar* assumes the form that is beneficial to and within the reach of human beings. Men cannot comprehend the Formless and Attributeless Absolute. Unfortunately, even when the Formless Absolute assumes a form, there are persons, who impelled by their own attitudes, attribute their own human foibles to the Avatar. "When he has the same form as ours, the same physical features, and eats, talks and moves about like any of us, what is the difference between the Avatar and ourselves?" they ask. Because of this narrow–minded approach, these persons are distancing themselves from the Divine.

An effort must be made to understand the nature of Divinity. "*Daivam manusharupena*," declares the scripture ("God in human form"). It is only when God comes in human form can human beings have the full opportunity to experience and enjoy the divine. When human life is sublimated, it gets divinised. Life x Infinity is God. *Virata Swarupa* (the Cosmic Form) is: Body x Infinity. Mind x Infinity is *Hiranyagarbha* (the Cosmic Consciousness). God, *Virata Swarupa* and *Hiranyagarbha* are not distinct entities located in specific places. They are immanent in

man. All religions have come into existence to make man realise the
source from which he has come and to which he should return.[1]

◊ ◊ ◊ ◊ ◊

4.

Rama: The Embodiment of Dharma (Righteousness or Virtue) and an Ideal Man

Rama, whose birthday, *Ramanavami*, you are celebrating today was
the exponent of the means of saving the Self in this perilous journey
from birth to birthlessness. Rama is the embodiment of *Dharma*; that
is why He was able to re–establish *Dharma*. Today is a sacred day
because you get the chance to recapitulate the Glory of God and His
relationship with Man. As a matter of fact, if you go deeper into the
Ramayana, you will find that Rama is the universal *Atma*, the *Atma* in
every being. He did not come down to kill the *Rakshasa* ruler, Ravana;
he is not the son of Dasarata or of Kausalya; nor is He the husband of
Seeta, weeping for her loss and gladdened by reunion.[2]

◊ ◊ ◊ ◊ ◊

Rama was the embodiment of steady adherence to *Sathya* (Truth)
and *Dharma* (Righteousness). Only those who are saturated in
Rama–bhakti (devotion) can dive into that glory. He is the grand ideal,

---

[1] *Sanathana Sarathi*, April 1991, p. 86.

[2] *Sathya Sai Speaks*, Vol. 2, pp. 27–28.

upon whom you can contemplate. By doing so, you can imbibe and develop his virtues, slowly and silently. A tree grows silently for years before it yields fruits. It does not produce them on the spot or in an instant.[1]

◊ ◊ ◊ ◊ ◊

Real and lasting joy can be won only by a life led along the path of *Dharma*. *Dharma* makes the inherent Divinity of Man shine forth; that illumination is the purpose of life, of the recurring sequence of birth and death. Man has in him the spark of Divinity, which is omnipresent, omniscient, omnipotent and immanent in the entire Universe; in order to become ever aware of this innate Reality, man must learn the technique laid down by the scriptures, revealed by the same Divinity.[2]

◊ ◊ ◊ ◊ ◊

It is often said that Rama followed *Dharma* at all times. This is not the correct way of describing Him. He did not follow *Dharma*; He was *Dharma*. What He thought, spoke and did was *Dharma*, is the *Dharma* forever.[3]

◊ ◊ ◊ ◊ ◊

Rama for you should mean the Path He trod, the Ideal He held aloft, the Ordinance He laid down. The path, the ideal and the ordinance are eternal, timeless. Follow the Path, stick to the Ideal, obey the Ordinance — that is the true celebration. Then alone does your life

---

[1] *Sathya Sai Speaks*, Vol. 15, p. 32.

[2] *Sathya Sai Speaks*, Vol. 5, p. 146.

[3] *Sai Baba Discourses*, Vol. 1, p. 90.

become fruitful. Now, you worship His Form, you repeat His Name; but, you ignore His Orders. This is no real *Prema* (Love) at all. Without actual practice of the discipline laid down by the Lord to purify the mind so that He may be reflected therein, all else is mere show, empty ritual.[1]

◊ ◊ ◊ ◊ ◊

Rama strove to uphold *Sathya* as the main plank of *Dharma.* Whatever the trial, however hard the travail, He did not give up Truth. *Sathyam* is *Dharmam. Dharmam* is *Sathyam* — the two are irrevocably intertwined. Sathyam *Vadha, Dharmam Chara,* say the *Upanishads.* Rama will be remembered so long as mountains raise their heads and the oceans exist, because of this strict adherence to *Sathyam* and *Dharmam.* If he had argued, "Why should I be bound by the word of my father?" He would not have earned this Immortality. The Immortal had come in the form of Rama to show the way to Immortality.[2]

◊ ◊ ◊ ◊ ◊

Sathyam nasthi paro Dharmah — "There is no higher *Dharma* than Truth." Be true; that is the acme of Righteousness, the essence of all morality, the Truth of the One–ness of all involves Love, Service, Peace and so, it is the basis of moral living. All distinctions are temporary walls erected by ambition or hate.

Now, *Hindu Dharma* or Christian *Dharma* or Muslim *Dharma* is identified with external conformities like dress, coiffure, hair–styles, rosaries and caste marks, and other attitudes like whom one can touch and yet remain ceremonially pure, when one can pray, where one has

---

[1] *Sathya Sai Speaks,* Vol. 5, p. 160.

[2] *Sathya Sai Speaks,* Vol. 5, pp. 161–62.

to eat and what, and such trivial, transitory marks. It is mostly superstition and mumblery, don't touch this, don't touch that!

Dharma must be surging from the heart as the cool energising water of *Prema* and *Shanti* (Love and Peace). You can learn what exactly *Dharma* is from the Ramayana. Rama is the very embodiment of *Dharma*; every word and every deed is resonant with its message.[1]

◊ ◊ ◊ ◊ ◊

The river of life has four causeways. ... The causeways are *brahmacharya, grihastha, vanaprastha* and *sanyasa* (celibate, householder, recluse, and monk). Of these the *grihastha* (householder) causeway has sunk and become impassable. Repair it and become good *grihasthas*; then the path of life is smooth for the journey. ...

When *Dharma* has gone into disrepair, He who laid down the *Dharma* has come again to get it repaired. The four bridges were laid by the Lord, and He has come to rebuild them now.[2]

◊ ◊ ◊ ◊ ◊

Dharma-sthapana, as the restoration of Righteousness is called, consists of two operations: the removal of wrong and the establishment of right. At the present time, the one means by which both these can be attained is — *namasmarana* (recital of God's Name). *Dharma* is capable of conferring all that man wishes for, here and hereafter. It is the *Kamadenu* (the celestial cow) that grants all boons. With the *nama* (Name of God) as a rope, you can tie her to the post — the tongue; then, you can get from that *Kamadenu* all the good that you crave for. She will rest in your heart-stall.[3]

---

[1] *Sathya Sai Speaks*, Vol. 10, p. 45.

[2] *Sathya Sai Speaks*, Vol. 4, p. 199.

[3] *Sathya Sai Speaks*, Vol. 8, p. 103.

◊ ◊ ◊ ◊ ◊

Dharma is the moral code, the experience of sages, the controlling discipline which checks the mind and the senses. There are many such brakes operating on man: *Vyakti Dharma* (controls affecting the individual, as such), *Sahaja Dharma* (controls affecting the nature of man, as man), *Ashrama Dharma* (controls affecting the stage of life, like student, householder, ascetic), *Varna Dharma* (controls pertaining to the duties cast upon man as a limb of the community, etc.) All these brakes are complementary, they do not cause confusion, they help progress, each in its own way.[1]

◊ ◊ ◊ ◊ ◊

Now, how are you to decide in any particular case what is *Dharma* and what is not? I shall tell you some principles which you can use on such occasions. That which does not inflict pain on you and on others — that is right, that is *Dharma*. So act in such a way that you get joy and others too get joy. Or, take another standard for your actions; make the *manas*, the *vak* and the *kayam* (thought, word and deed) agree in harmony. That is to say, act as you speak, speak as you feel; do not play false to your own conscience; do not cover your thoughts in a cloak of falsehood; do not suppress your conscience by forcibly enslaving it and embarking on actions not approved by it. That is the *Dharmic* way of life. Frequently doing right makes it easier and easier, habit grows into conscience. If you are once established in right conduct, you will automatically follow the right. What you do depends on what you are; what you are depends on what you do. The two are interdependent to a great degree.

Or, there is another principle. *Dharma* trains you to be calm, level–headed, secure in equanimity. You know the transitory nature of success or failure, riches or poverty, joy or grief, appointment or

---

[1] *Sathya Sai Speaks*, Vol. 5, p. 79.

disappointment. You are not elated or deflated. You are serene, unmoved. Anything that helps you to maintain this unruffled stability is Dharma.

To cut it short: sensual life is *adharma*; the spiritual life is *Dharma. Dharma* is that which sustains, saves and sanctifies. Man is born and is given a lease of life so that he may earn the knowledge of His identity with the Infinite.[1]

◊ ◊ ◊ ◊ ◊

Dharma is the *maryadha* (the boundary), the limit that the intelligence lays down for the passion, emotions, impulses of man. ... *Mañava* (man) means "one who observes *mana* (measure or limit)." He does not run wild and untrimmed; he submits willingly to control, regulation and discipline.[2]

◊ ◊ ◊ ◊ ◊

Speak softly, kindly; that is *Dharma* (Righteousness). Give generously, wisely; wipe the tear and assuage the sigh and the groan; that is *Dharma*. Do not simply throw money at the needy; give with respect and reverence; give with grace. Give also with humility. Try to live with others harmoniously.[3]

◊ ◊ ◊ ◊ ◊

Kausalya (mother) counselled Rama at the start of his exile in the forest, "The *Dharma* which you are so scrupulously observing will guard you." That was the farewell she gave, not a banquet of tasty

[1] *Sathya Sai Speaks*, Vol. 2, p. 251.

[2] *Sathya Sai Speaks*, Vol. 8, p. 57.

[3] *Sathya Sai Speaks*, Vol. 8, p. 209.

dishes. The ten–headed Ravana who held the Gods in chains could not stand up to Rama, who had *Dharma* as His sword and shield. Rama was happy when others were happy. He grieved when others were in grief. That is the trait which He wanted man to learn. So, while avoiding pain from others, be vigilant not to cause pain to others, too. Then, you attract the Grace of the Lord, not when you contrive by tricks to harm others, or revel in the misery of others, or concentrate on your own happiness and progress, irrespective of the injury you cause to others.[1]

◊ ◊ ◊ ◊ ◊

Knowledge bereft of noble qualities and virtues becomes only bookish knowledge which is of no use to society. What is it that made Rama God? It is imbibing of the six qualities, namely: character, compassion, non–violence, control of the mind, control of the senses and fame. Students should imbibe these six qualities which make man God. Students should never indulge in violence. Hurting or harming any person essentially means hurting and harming oneself. It is in this context Vyasa stated that the essence of the eighteen *Puranas* is "Help ever, Hurt never."[2]

◊ ◊ ◊ ◊ ◊

Rama is the supreme exemplar of how people should conduct themselves in the world, how a country should be governed, how the integrity and morality of human beings should be protected. High–minded actions, ideal qualities and sacred thoughts are basic foundations of character. Rama is the very embodiment of these three attributes. This means that every human being should cultivate sacred thoughts, right actions and good qualities. Rama demonstrated by his

---

[1] *Sathya Sai Speaks*, Vol. 5, p. 162.

[2] *Sanathana Sarathi*, December 1994, p. 335.

words, thoughts and actions how such a life can be lived. Rama acted up to the ancient injunction: "Speak the Truth. Practice Righteousness." Eschewing harsh words, Rama pleased everyone by His sweet speech. He countered harsh speech by others with His composure, patience, sweetness and smile. He never pried into the affairs of others, never took notice of their faults, never indulged in ridicule, and never caused any pain to others by the way He spoke to them. It is essential for everyone to follow the example set by Rama and cultivate His many noble qualities and do righteous actions. People should entertain sacred thoughts.

Man is an image of the Divine. The Lord has declared in the Geetha: "My Spirit is in all beings." God is the indweller in all human beings. Today, in the pursuit of power, men are prepared to commit any kind of crime and to inflict any kind of harm on people to achieve their ends. Rama, on the contrary, gave up the kingdom and, to honour the pledge given by His father, chose to face the ordeals of life in the forest as an exile. He demonstrated to the world that one should never go back on his plighted word. Rama gave up the throne and became a denizen of the forest. In life, it is not difficulties and calamities that are important. The supreme importance of Truth was what Rama wanted to hold forth to the world. One should never go back on one's pledge even at the cost of one's life.

Today, however, men go back on their words from moment to moment. They indulge in falsehood at every step. Promises are forgotten. How can the Rama Principle flourish in such a human environment? The Rama Principle is remote from such an atmosphere.

God will be in proximity only to those persons whose thoughts, ideals and deeds are in accord with Rama's. Rama was a man of his word, but man is the very reverse. It may be asked: In this situation how is it possible to say that in human beings there is Divinity? Not at all. In such human beings there is either animality or demonic nature. Whatever *sadanas* (practices) one may perform or however much one may recite the Lord's name, God will not judge one by these criteria. What is the transformation in one's heart? If there is no transformation of the heart, of what avail are spiritual *sadanas* (practices)?[1]

Man is not a mere creature of flesh and blood. He is the embodiment of the Spirit (*Atma*). It is only when man recognises this Truth that true spirituality will be evident to him. Concentrating all the time on the physical body as the only reality, time is wasted on external observances. The body should be regarded as a temple of God. To consider it otherwise is a sign of foolishness. Only he is a true human being who recognises the indwelling Divinity within the shrine of his body. The scriptures have declared: "In the temple of the human body dwells the individual Self which is the eternal Self."[1]

◊ ◊ ◊ ◊ ◊

Rama taught Bharata (His brother) how government should be carried on. "Have as your ministers only persons of character and virtue, who are tranquil in mind and devoted to Truth. Don't have as ministers anyone lacking in these four qualities. Moreover, they should possess self–confidence, practise righteous conduct, and be capable of giving proper advice. These are essential prerequisites for wise administrators. Give no place for selfish persons. There should be no room in the government for persons animated by self–interest. Nor is that all. Don't allow anyone given to vices like gambling and drink to wield authority. Entertain only those who command the esteem of the people and who are respected and loved by the people. You must have daily conferences with three or four such ministers. Your talks should be in private and no outsider should know anything about them. It is only when such secrecy is observed that the nation will prosper. You will then be able to ensure peace and prosperity to the nation. Moreover, you must send out as envoys to other countries ambassadors who are totally loyal to the king and not time–servers

---

[1] *Sanathana Sarathi*, May 1995, pp. 114–115.

who practise duplicity. Only such men can convey to the king Truthful information."

Rama did not stop with that. (Swami said that the women devotees should not take it amiss.) Rama told Bharata that he should not permit women to take part in affairs of state. Women have their estimable role in household affairs, but they should be kept out of state politics. "Don't employ women as ministers. The reason is: a nation's honour is based upon its women. It is only when women maintain their respect and honour that the nation will be respected. It is not proper for women to cheapen themselves by roaming in public places."

Such were the sacred precepts of good administration which Rama taught to Bharata. How does the situation in the country today compare with Rama's conception of an ideal government? The state of things today is 100 percent contrary to the ideas and ideals of Rama. How, then, can Rama *Raja* (reign) be established here?

If we desire to establish Rama *Raja* there should be harmony in thought, word and deed. This applies not only to *Bharat* (India) but to the entire world. All countries should have governments which conform to this principle of triple purity. Only then, the people also will reflect the character of the rulers.

Today, the people reflect the vices of the rulers. If a minister prefers one bottle, the man in the streets asks for two (drinks). How can such citizens establish Rama *Raja*? They can do so only if there is a complete transformation in their mental attitudes. Despite all the teachings they have listened to, their minds remain in the same state. Without a mental change, they are not entitled even to utter the name "Rama." What, then is the meaning of talking about Rama *Raja*? It will be only Rama *Raja* in name, but in reality it will only be Ravana *Raja*.

If you really value Rama's ideals, you should practise them. You may say that the high ideals of Rama are beyond your competence. But there is one thing which you can do: Rama carried out the words of his father (*Pithruvakya paripalana*). How many today respect the words of the parent? If the father asks the son, "Son, where are you going?" the son replies: "Shut up and keep quiet in your place." Few have any respect for the words of the father. There is no need to speak about respect for the mother. Such unworthy sons are ruining the world. Mothers are shedding tears over the behaviour of such sons.

This state of things should change. The sacredness of parents should be restored. Young people should cultivate pure thoughts and lead unselfish lives.

Children who disregard their parents will be treated likewise by their children in due course. Partly the parents are to blame for the way they pamper the children. The children of today are worse than even Ravana's children, who obeyed him to some extent. People who acquire knowledge or wealth are making no use of it to help others. They are following a dog–in–the–manger policy. This is not the way to follow Rama's example.

Today people celebrate Rama's birthday as a festival, but do not practise Rama's ideals. Enshrine Rama's ideals in your heart. Without it, there is no meaning in celebrating Rama's birthday. You must follow the example of a noble and ideal person. This is the right meaning of devotion.

People talk about devotion. Does mere participation in *bhajans* (devotional singing) constitute devotion? No. It is all a stunt. True devotion calls for the practice of at least one of the teachings that you learn. By following at least one good lesson, a man should lead an ideal existence.

Remember that the lessons taught to Bharata by Rama are ideal lessons. After instructing Bharata regarding the principles of good government, Rama told Bharata: "You must revere the parents, the preceptors and all elders. If any person misbehaves within your kingdom, do not punish him. Banish him. That will be punishment enough."

Here I wish to explain what is meant by punishment. There is no need to beat or abuse the erring person. Stop talking to him. What is the use of talking to a person who is going astray? I do not want to waste my words on such a person. I attach great value to my words. They may not know it, but I know their value. None of my words has any selfish motive. Everything is for the welfare of all. If one has no such broad outlook and is only concerned about his personal interests, what is the use in talking to such a person? As long as one remains self–centered, he cannot understand the Divine.

At the outset, understand what is *Rama Raja*. It is the reign of morality, of Truth and virtues. *Rama Raja* means that which engenders happiness (*Ramayathi*). There should be no ill–will towards anybody. No one should be harmed. That is Rama *Raja*. When such feelings arise among the people Rama *Raja* will come into existence of its own accord.[1]

◊ ◊ ◊ ◊ ◊

Rama was prepared to honour a boon given by his father to his step–mother in fulfilment of an old promise. He renounced the throne at the moment of coronation and elected to go to the forest as an exile. Eminently qualified as he was to become the ruler, nevertheless he chose to go to the forest to honour his father's plighted word. This is a glorious example of an ideal life. Today people would set at nought promises given by the father and place their self–interest in the forefront. Rama demonstrated to the world that men born in the *Ikshvaku* dynasty were unflinching in honouring the pledges of the fathers. Rama was prepared to face any ordeals and troubles in upholding this sacred principle. Rama was ever active in fulfilling the wishes and responding to the opinions of the people. Highly sensitive even to the remarks of a petty washerman, Rama sent away Seeta to the forest out of a feeling that the washerman's comment might be an indication of the unspoken feelings of many others among his subjects.

Rama stands out as an ideal ruler intensely responsive to the wishes of the people. *Today persons who are incompetent and unworthy are aspiring for positions of power. This is utterly wrong. This is the reason for the nation finding itself in the doldrums today. The disastrous decline of Bharat (India) is entirely due to the incompetence of those in power. Men of*

---

[1] *Sanathana Sarathi*, May 1995, pp. 117–119.

character, who are totally free from self–interest should occupy the seats of power. Rama demonstrated the ideal relations that should exist between the ruler and the ruled.[1]

◊ ◊ ◊ ◊ ◊

Rama is closest to mankind. Wherever they may be, to whatever land or clime they may belong, people everywhere have to understand the Rama principle. Rama was an ideal son. Every family requires an ideal son. On the eve of the coronation he chose to go to the forest as an exile in accordance with the command of his royal father. In carrying out the injunctions of the father, Rama stands out as the supreme exemplar.

Rama, moreover, was an ideal brother. He exemplified harmony and love among brothers. He treated his brothers as his own life–breath and showered his love equally on all of them. Thus Rama is an example of fraternal love for every family.

Rama was an ideal husband. Rama's adherence to the principle of monogamy has to be properly understood. Valmiki understood it very well. One word, one arrow, one wife was the rule for Rama. What is the reason? In the body there are many organs. But all of them are animated, nourished and sustained by the heart alone. In the same manner the wife, for the husband is only one and the husband for the wife is only one. To demonstrate to the world this ideal of monogamy, Rama set the example.

Rama was an ideal friend. There cannot be a greater friend than Rama. There are in the world fair–weather friends who display their friendship when one is wealthy or wielding power. But if wealth and position are gone, not a single friend will show his face. Rama, however, was not such a friend. He was loving, considerate and affectionate equally in weal and woe, in times of joy or sorrow. Guha was an ordinary boatman. Rama hailed him as his fourth brother and

---

[1] *Sanathana Sarathi*, April 1991, p. 88.

showered his love on Guha. Rama treated in the same friendly spirit everyone who came to him for any help or to find an asylum. He thus stood out to the world as an ideal friend.

Rama was not only an ideal friend; he was also an ideal enemy. In the world, it is common to see men resorting to all kinds of deceitful devices to foil their enemies. But Rama never stooped to such unworthy practices. Rama adhered to the noble heroic path even in dealing with his enemies. For example, when Rama was engaged in battle with Ravana, Ravana could not stand up to the arrows of Rama. All the weapons of Ravana were destroyed. Rama noticed that Ravana was tired and weaponless. In such a situation it was not proper to kill the enemy. There is no heroism in killing a weak or powerless man. The enemy should be destroyed when he is strong and powerful. Recognizing the plight of Ravana, Rama laid down his arms and told Ravana, "O, Ravana! You are tired and without weapons. You are not in a fit condition to carry on the fight. Go home, take rest and return to battle tomorrow. We shall resume the fight tomorrow." By displaying this kind of magnanimity towards his enemy, Rama demonstrated that he was an ideal enemy.

Rama was, first of all, an ideal son. In any country, anywhere in the world, every family needs an ideal son. Hence Rama's story does not have a message for the Bharatiyas (Indians) alone. It has a lesson for all countries and for all mankind.

Rama was an ideal husband. When Seeta was abducted, Rama felt the loss as if he had lost half his body. He looked upon his wife as *ardhangini*, one half of himself. When Rama appeared grief–stricken over the absence of Seeta he wanted to merely show to the world what the loss of a wife means. He never thought of a second wife. Rama felt, "It is my duty to protect my wife." Every husband in the world should have a similar conviction.[1]

◊ ◊ ◊ ◊ ◊

---

[1] *Sanathana Sarathi*, June 1994, pp. 141-43.

The effulgence of the Lord is equal to that of one *crore* (10 million) Suns. The Lord's face is beaming with the brilliance of the Sun. On being struck by the radiant effulgence in Rama's face, Sabari became ecstatic and described it as that of the blemishless full moon. (Swami jocularly remarked that the faces of present–day men look like a jungle with dense growth of beards and sideburns. Brilliance is absent.) Rama's face was spotless because His heart was pure and was filled with feelings of sacrifice. He never did anything for Himself. Whatever He did was only for the welfare of the world (*Lokasamrakshana*). *Ramo Vigrahavan Dharmaha*. Rama was the embodiment of *Dharma*. If one follows *Dharma*, He is protected by the same *Dharma*. Rama sacrificed all His comforts and enjoyments of royal life and endured the privations of forest life. Rama is to be taken as the ideal for the students. They should respect and obey their parents' words. The Guru, teacher, comes only after the parents.[1]

◊ ◊ ◊ ◊ ◊

The reign of Rama was marked by concern for justice and morality. Today the people are bedevilled by distrust and suspicion at every step. "Why should God do like this?" Such questions are asked out of narrow–minded doubts. There will be no room for such doubts if the infinite nature of the Divine is properly understood. The petty–minded folk who cannot grasp the omnicompetence of the Divine raise such questions. Their entire life is wasted in this matter. Hence, people should get rid of such pettiness.[2]

◊ ◊ ◊ ◊ ◊

---

[1] *Sanathana Sarathi*, July 1994, p. 176.

[2] *Sanathana Sarathi*, April 1991, p. 85.

5.

The Inner Meaning of Rama-Seeta

Rama, the *Purusha*, accepts *Prakriti*, Seeta, and enacts the play, Ramayana. Seeta ... as *Prakriti* or *Maya* activates the Pure Existence of *Brahman*. Now see what happens! *Brahmajnana* (knowledge of Supreme Reality) is lost and Rama wanders about in the jungle, wailing for Her. Of course, Lakshmana or *manas* (mind) is always with Him, for *manas* is the instrument with which Liberation has to be achieved. Vali is the spirit of despair and he has to be overcome with the help of discriminatory wisdom or *viveka*, viz., Sugreeva.[1]

◊ ◊ ◊ ◊ ◊

Rama was verily the Over–Self itself. Seeta was Rama's *Shakti* (energy, power). She was the daughter of Mother Earth. She was the embodiment of Nature. Ravana developed enmity towards Rama and wanted to abduct Seeta. What was the result of all this? Hating God and going after Nature, how did he end? At the end of it all, not only himself, and kingdom, his entire brood was destroyed. In spite of all his knowledge and powers, he ruined himself because of his moral lapses. He did not recognise the Divinity within him.

What is the lesson to be learned from Ravana's fate? It is this: However much of worldly knowledge you may have, you should seek *Atma* Vidya, knowledge of the *Atma*. Your parents or relations may be distant from you. But God is not distant from you. God is always with you, in you, behind you and around you and He will protect you.

---

[1] *Sathya Sai Speaks*, Vol. 2, p. 29.

Giving up the Divine, which is so close to you, and going after worldly happiness, is fraught with danger. Ravana made all efforts to satisfy his own desires, became an enemy of His and was ultimately destroyed.[1]

◊ ◊ ◊ ◊ ◊

Seeta is the daughter of earth, of *Prakriti* (Nature), seeking the eternal comradeship of *Purusha*. She weds the *Purusha*, the Lord come as Rama. When Rama agrees to go into exile and proceeds to the forest for a stay of fourteen long years, Seeta too gives up all the luxuries she was accustomed to; she braves the perils of jungle life, for the sake of being in the presence of Rama. She renounced desire from her heart for the sole goal of Rama.

Thirteen years she spent with the Lord, in perfect Bliss, as a consequence of the sacrifice she dared to make. Then, quite suddenly, desire sprouted in her mind, and carried her away, far away from the Lord! She saw a golden deer, and she coveted it! She who had renounced huge treasures of gold and diamond was attracted by a fantasy and this led to the agonising separation.

So too, for those long attached to Me, there arises some desire — for lands, jobs, family life, fame, position, possessions — and they move away! But Seeta repented for her mistake, and her mind suffered extreme anguish at the separation. She called on her Lord to redeem her, calling out in contrition, Rama, Rama, Rama, Rama, with every breath. And, finally, Rama Himself moved towards her and restored Himself to the devotee! So too, if you are agonisingly repentant and aware of the loss and anxious to rejoin, craving for the presence, this Sairam too will move towards you and grant you Grace.[2]

◊ ◊ ◊ ◊ ◊

---

[1] *Sanathana Sarathi*, October 1992, p. 236.

[2] *Sathya Sai Speaks*, Vol. 11, p. 87.

The whole world seemed to rejoice at the wedding of Rama and Seeta because it had its cosmic significance. It represented the union of *Prakriti* (Seeta) with *Purusha*, the Supreme Absolute: Every being in the cosmos, whatever may be the gender, in external form, is essentially feminine. She represents one–half of the Lord — Ardangini. The *Paramatma* (the Overself) is the Purusha (the Supreme Godhead). Together, *Prakriti* and *Purusha* represent the concept of *Ardanareeswara*, the Divine conceived as half–male and half–female. This union of male and female is found in every human being. Everyone should understand this aspect of the Ramayana story.

Ramayana should not be considered as a sacred epic for Bharatiyas (Indians) alone. The term *Rama* means "One who delights the heart" ("*Ramayati iti Ramah*"). Whomsoever you may worship, it is the one Divine Who delights the heart. There is only one God and one Goal.[1]

◊ ◊ ◊ ◊ ◊

The *Ramayana* teaches also another lesson. The search for Seeta is symbolic of the secret of Self–realisation, in the field of experience. Rama, when she was recovered, recovered the wisdom of Self–realisation, now confirmed by experience. *Jnana* (Wisdom) had become *Anubhava–jnana* (knowledge derived from experience). The *Ramayana* teaches that, when a person is yearning for the precious goal of Self–realisation, all the forces of Nature and all Creation will help him and render all assistance. Monkeys, birds, squirrels, and even boulders and rocks were his comrades in the task. Aim high, resolve on the supremest adventure — everything will be set right to lead you on to the goal.[2]

◊ ◊ ◊ ◊ ◊

---

[1] *Sanathana Sarathi*, June 1994, p. 146.

[2] *Sathya Sai Speaks*, Vol. 9, p. 134.

Believe that *Dharma* or Moral Rectitude will never play false; it will ensure greater joy than can be gained through all other means. Rama destroyed Ravana; it was victory of one head over ten; concentration over distraction. Ravana craved for *Prakriti* (Seeta) discarding the *Purusha* (Spirit) which gave it values and meaning, viz., Rama. If you crave for *Prakriti*, the objective world, you degrade yourself, you deny your reality, and you join Ravana's brood. Do not also imagine that the Lord is outside *Prakriti*, or even of you, who are really a part of the objective world. He is in you, behind you, beside you, before you. He is the eye of your eye; the I of your I. Yearn for the *yoga* or union with Him, through the unwavering awareness of His being the real you. Yearn for *yoga*; and whatever *bhoga* (pleasure) you really need will be offered to you in due course. If on the other hand, you yearn for *bhoga* itself, you are gone! You are blessed only with *roga* (disease), remember!

Live in the consuming conviction that you are the *Atma*. That is the hard core of the Eternal Teaching. The *Atma* it is that sees through the eyes, hears through the ears, handles through the fingers, moves through the feet. That is the basic "you." When some one carps at you, reason out thus within yourself: "Is he casting aspersions on my body? Well. Why should I be worried? He is doing just what I should myself do, casting out the attachment to the flesh, to this paltry prison. Or, is he throwing them at the *Atma*? Nothing can affect its purity; or tarnish its glory. So remain calm and unperturbed!" You may ask, what happens then to the strings of abuse? Like the letter sent by post and refused by the addressee, it returns to the sender![1]

◊ ◊ ◊ ◊ ◊

On the day when Rama was crowned Emperor at Ayodha, every personage got some present or other before leaving the city. Hanuman alone refused any material gift. He asked Rama to explain to him the

---

[1] *Sathya Sai Speaks*, Vol. 4, pp. 49–50.

mystery of His Life, which he had failed to understand inspite of the length and loyalty of his service. Rama then asked Seeta to slake the thirst of Hanuman and reveal to him the secret of their careers. Seeta announced that she was the *Mula Prakriti* (the Primal Nature), the *Maya Shakti* (the Energy which agitates in all Matter), which transforms and transmutes it into all this variety that binds and blinds; the Ramayana, she said, was nothing but the play she designed.[1]

◊ ◊ ◊ ◊ ◊

Ravana had vast knowledge of spiritual texts. His ten heads represent the learning he had earned from the six *Sastras* and the four *Vedas*. But, he never put that knowledge to any use. He craved for the possession of *Prakriti* (material objects), only; he wanted to master the world of matter, the objective world. He was a master of the material sciences. But, he was not tamed by the Spirit. He discarded the Spirit, *Purusha*–Rama; he was content with the possession at Lanka, of *Prakriti* (Matter) represented by Seeta. That was why he fell.[2]

◊ ◊ ◊ ◊ ◊

---

[1] *Sathya Sai Speaks*, exact volume and page unknown.

[2] *Sathya Sai Speaks*, Vol. 4, p. 74.

6.

The Inner Meaning of Dasaratha (Rama's Father), Baratha (Rama's Brother), Lakshmana (Rama's Brother), Ayodhya (Rama's City), and others

It is stated, "Dasarata had four sons: Rama, Lakshmana, Bharata and Sathrughna." Well. Who is Dasaratha? Which kingdom was he ruling over? If in some City called Ayodhya, there was once a ruler named Dasaratha and he had a son called Rama, how are we related to that episode? Why should we celebrated that event, at this distance of time and space?

Go a little deep into the story and you will realise that Dasaratha is not the ruler of a far–off land, that his capital city is not on the map of Northern India, and that the four brothers are not people who lived and passed away! Ayodhya means a city that is unconquerable, into which the enemy cannot penetrate, an impregnable fortress. It represents the *Atma*, the heart where the Lord resides, which is proof against temptations, the subtle foes of passion and emotion, impulse and instinct. And, Dasaratha? The person who has as his *rata* (chariot) the ten entities, namely, the body with the five senses of action and the five senses of knowledge! This individual, who is the symbol of all individuals, married three brides.

Now, though each married man may have a wife with a physical existence of her own, he has also wedded to him, inseparable from him, till death "do separate," three attributes: *satwa, rajas* and *tamas,* the three natures — balanced, passionate and dull. The three queens represent these *gunas* — Koushalya, the *satwic* (balanced) *guna,* Sumithra, the *rajas* (the passionate, active) and Kaikeyi, the *tamasic* (ignorant, undiscriminating). No one can escape living with these three *gunas,* and experiencing the varied reactions which that contact involves. In due course, the yearning arose in the mind that it must have a Master whom it can obey and revere. The agony became so acute that the transcendent Divine actualised Itself in Grace that took the form of *payasam* (rice pudding), brought by a messenger of God from the sacrificial fire. That gift of Grace was shared by the three *gunas* (qualities) and four sons were born, representing *Dharma, artha, kama* and *moksha* (virtue, wealth, desire–fulfilment and liberation), the four prime ends of man. Rama, the eldest, is *Dharma* and the other three stand for the rest (*Lakshmana, Bharata and Sathrughna*).

You will have to sacrifice a great deal, if *Dharma* must be born in your heart. That is why Dasaratha had to do the *Puthrakameshtiyaga* (a great sacrifice for obtaining sons). The Divine is the very embodiment of *Dharma* and it is only by means of *Dharma* that He can be worshipped. And *Dharma* is a garland of the flowers of holy deeds, holy words, holy thoughts. Earn the reputation of being good, serviceable and efficient in doing good. Children who do not render their parents happy by such good conduct are remembered by their mothers only through the pain they gave them at birth.[1]

◊ ◊ ◊ ◊ ◊

Who was Dasaratha? Dasaratha was the emperor of Ayodhya. The word *Dasaratha* signifies the body endowed with the senses. These ten senses are five *karmendriyas* and five *jnanendriyas.* Dasaratha is the

[1] *Sathya Sai Speaks,* Vol. 1, p. 112–13.

chariot drawn by the ten senses. The three wives of Dasaratha represent the three qualities, *Kaushalya*, symbolising *satwic* quality, *Sumitra*, *rajasic* quality, and *Kaikeyi*, the *tamasic* quality.

Who was Ravana? Ravana is described as a demon with ten heads. These ten heads are the six vices, namely, desire, anger, greed, infatuation, pride and jealousy, *manas* (mind), *buddhi* (intellect), *chitta* (conditioned consciousness) and *ahamkara* (ego). Since these ten are present in every human being, all men are Ravana indeed! Whoever beheads all these ten heads in fact becomes a Rama. It is God alone who can behead these ten heads! When a man surrenders himself to God, all these ten heads will go and he will merge in Rama.[1]

◊ ◊ ◊ ◊

Rama had mustered so much spiritual strength through his consistent observance of *Dharma*, that he could wield and bend the mighty bow named *Sivadhanus*. That was the proof of the *Jeeva* (the individual) having overcome delusion. Janaka (father of Seeta), the ruler of *Videha* (knowledge), had the bow in his custody. He was on the lookout for a hero who had mastered the fatal flaw.

The story relates that Janaka, the *Videhi* (ruler of *Videha*, that is to say, without body or body–consciousness), offered his daughter (Seeta) (the awareness of *Brahman*) to Rama. Wedding Seeta is another way of saying "*acquiring Supreme Wisdom*," for, from where was Seeta gained? The story says, "*from a furrow on the Earth*," that is to say, from *Prakriti*, from Nature. This statement reveals that *Brahmajnana* (Supreme Wisdom) can be won by meaningful involvement with *Prakriti*.

The next stage in the career of Rama finds him in the thick jungle of life. The jungle was infested with attractions and aversions. The Supreme Wisdom cannot co–exist with duality. It insists on the renunciation of both aspects. Rama pursued the golden deer, which

---

[1] *Sanathana Sarathi*, August 1992, p. 186.

Seeta longed to possess. *Brahmajnana* disappeared as a consequence of this lapse.

Rama (the representative of *Jeeva*) had to undergo many spiritual austerities to regain the abode of total detachment. There he secured two allies, Sugriva (discrimination) and Hanuman (courage). The alliance was sealed by an act of service from Rama, which indicated his loyalty to *Dharma* under all conditions. He slew Vali, the vicious victim of wickedness. Vali had dethroned his father, forced him to take refuge in the jungles, associated with Ravana, of evil fame, and ill-treated his brother Sugriva for no reason at all. Vali succumbed so low because of the company he preferred to be in. He serves as a warning to everyone. Einstein said, *"Tell me your company; I can tell you what you are."*

Rama installed *Viveka* (discrimination) on the throne of Vali. With his allies, he entered on the quest for the Wisdom that he had lost. He found across his path a wide ocean of delusion (*moha*). His ally, Hanuman (courage) had a vision, unclouded by desire or ignorance. His only desire was fixed on the Name of Rama and the Form of Rama. So he was able to leap across the ocean, smooth and safe.

Rama reached the other shore. He slew Ravana (the embodiment of the *rajasic*, passionate, impulsive, possessive traits) and his brother, Kumbhakarna (the embodiment of the *thamasic*, dull, self–destructive, lethargic, traits). Rama recovered Seeta (*Brahmajnana*) now confirmed by striving and struggling, and more convincingly precious as a result of constant meditation. And, Rama returned with Her to Ayodhya (the Impregnable city, the Source and Spring of Wisdom). The consummation of the soul's journey is the Coronation, the *Maha Pattabhishekam*.

This is the *Ramayana* which needs to be gone through, during the life of every aspirant. The heart is the Ayodhya. Dasaratha is the body, the *gunas* are the consorts, the *Purusharthas* are the sons, Seeta is wisdom. Attempt and attain this Realisation by purifying the three tools — body, speech and mind.[1]

◊ ◊ ◊ ◊ ◊

Bharata's (brother of Rama) name itself signifies that he is saturated with love of Rama. (*Bha* — means *Bhagavan*, the Lord Rama; *rata* — means pleased by, happy over, attached to).

Let the Love for the Lord grow in you, as it did in *Bharata*. Let that sense of adoration, which discarded even a throne, flourish in you. Then, you can be of great use to your country, your culture, your society, your religion and your community. Or else, all this bother that you have undergone, to attend *sathsang*, to listen to spiritual discourses, to meet spiritual masters, study spiritual texts, etc., will be a colossal exercise in futility.[2]

◊ ◊ ◊ ◊ ◊

The allegorical meaning of the Ramayana story should be properly understood. Rama stands for *Yajur Veda*, as he was the embodiment of *Dharma*. Lakshmana esteemed Rama's words as law and followed him. He was always chanting the name of Rama. He represents *Rig Veda*. Bharata represents *Sama Veda*, as he was always singing the glory of Rama. Sathrughna represents *Atharva Veda*. Thus the four sons of Emperor Dasaratha of Ayodhya represent the four *Vedas*. Dasaratha's capital, Ayodhya, symbolises a place where no enemy can enter. Dasaratha symbolises the five organs of action (*karmendriyas*) and the five organs of cognition (*jnanendriyas*). The three queens of Dasaratha, Kausalya, Sumithra and Kaikeyi, represent the *satwic*, *rajasic* and

---

[1] *Sai Baba Discourses*, Vol. 1, p. 88–89.

[2] *Sathya Sai Speaks*, Vol. 9, p. 130.

tamasic gunas. If the inner significance of the Ramayana is properly understood, it will serve as a manual of ideal living for all mankind.[1]

◊ ◊ ◊ ◊ ◊

Out of the basic sound Omkara, we get so many different sounds. Those sounds are mere transformations of the shape of Omkara. It is only in this context that the Maharishis addressed Rama by saying *Ramo Vigrahavan Dharmaha* — which means Rama is the embodiment of *Dharma* or Righteousness. Just as for this Omkara, there are three principal sounds which go to make it up, namely A, U, M, Rama who is the embodiment of *Dharma* also has three supporting characters who are Lakshmana, Bharata and Satrughna. The analogy is that Lakshmana, Bharata and Satrughna together make up Rama, the Embodiment of *Dharma.* The sound A can be compared to Lakshmana, U can be compared to Bharata and M can be compared to Satrughna. The combination of all these three is the Omkara and that is Rama Himself. So we have to recognise the inner meaning that Rama who is no other than Omkara, took birth on this earth in order to establish *Dharma* or Righteousness.[2]

◊ ◊ ◊ ◊ ◊

Hanuman is courage, courage won through unflinching faith, that alone can penetrate the darkness and bring the good news of the Dawn. Then Rama crosses the sea of illusion; He destroys the demon of *tamoguna* (quality of inertia), namely, Kumbhakarna; the demon of *rajoguna* (emotional quality), namely, Ravana; and He instals on the throne, the *satwaguna* (quality of goodness), Vibheeshana. After this, Rama meets and receives Seeta, who has become now *Anubhavajnana*

---

[1] *Sanathana Sarathi,* January 1994, p. 13.

[2] *Summer Showers in Brindavan* (1982), pp. 120–21.

(knowledge derived from experience), not merely *Brahmajnana*. That is represented by the *Pattabhisheka* (Coronation).[1]

◊ ◊ ◊ ◊ ◊

Rama is the personification of *viveka*, the discriminating faculty of the intellect. Seeta and Lakshmana are the higher levels of consciousness — *sujnana* and *prajnana*. Rama puts an end to evil feelings and promotes good thoughts. Rama is the Emperor of Ayodhya. That name means "Impregnable," "with no enemy," that is to say, no injurious or demeaning feeling or thought, can invade the heart when Rama is installed therein. Thyagaraja sang, "*Thelisi Rama chinthana cheyave manasa*" (Oh! Mind! Meditate on Rama with the full knowledge of what He represents).[2]

◊ ◊ ◊ ◊ ◊

The Ramayana has a deep undercurrent of significant meaning. Dasaratha means, he who rides in a chariot of ten, that is to say man. He is tied up with three *gunas* (qualities), or three wives, as in the Ramayana. He has four sons, the *Purusharthas* — *Dharma* (Rama) *Artha* (Lakshmana), *Kama* (Bharata), and *Moksha* (Sathrughna). These four aims of man have to be systematically realised, always with the last one, *Moksha*, clearly before the eye. Lakshmana represents the *buddhi* (Intellect) and Seeta is Truth. Hanuman is the Mind, and it is the repository, if controlled and trained, of courage. Sugreeva, the master of Hanuman is Discrimination. With these to help him Rama seeks Truth and succeeds. That is the lesson of the Epic to everyman.[3]

---

[1] *Sathya Sai Speaks*, Vol. 2, p. 29.

[2] *Sathya Sai Speaks*, Vol. 15, p. 130.

[3] *Sathya Sai Speaks*, Vol. 13, p. 59.

◊ ◊ ◊ ◊ ◊

You talk glibly of *Ramaraja* but how can it be established, if you do not emulate Rama? He was *Vigrahavan Dharma* — the very embodiment of virtue. He never deviated from it. *Dasaratha* means he who is master of his ten senses, the five *karmendriyas* (senses of action) and the five *jnanandriyas* (senses of perception): that is to say, the successful *sadaka*. Such a person can have the holy progeny of the four *Purushartas: Dharma* (Rama), *artha* (Lakshmana), *kama* (Bharata) and *moksha* (Sathrughna). Become a Dasharatha and have that holy progeny, as a gift from God.[1]

◊ ◊ ◊ ◊ ◊

Who are Rama, Lakshmana, Bharata and Shatrughna? The four *Vedas* came in the form of the four brothers to the abode of Dasaratha and sported there. Rama was *Rig Veda* and Lakshmana, who closely followed Rama, was *Yajur Veda*. Bharata, who always delighted in chanting Rama's name, was *Sama Veda*, and Shatrughna, who obeyed the commands of the three brothers and surrendered himself completely to them, was *Atharvana Veda*. Hence the four brothers were the embodiments of the four *Vedas*.

Lord Rama was *Pranava* itself (*A, U, M*). The three brothers are the syllables of *A, U* and *M* in *Omkara*. Lakshmana was *A*, Bharata was *U*, Shatrughna was *Ma*, and the Lord was the *Pranava*.[2]

◊ ◊ ◊ ◊ ◊

Contemplate on Rama, the Ideal lived by God for man. Rama is virtue personified (*Vigrahavan Dharma*). Rama is the supreme exemplar of the virtues that man must cultivate so that he might live as a

---

[1] *Sathya Sai Speaks*, Vol. 6, p. 100.

[2] *Sanathana Sarathi*, August 1992, p. 186.

master, as a husband, son, brother, friend, or even as a foe. The other three brothers of Rama personify the other three ideals: Bharata is the embodiment of *Sathya*, Sathrughna of *Shanti* and Lakshmana of *Prema*. Study the Ramayana with the aim of imbibing from it the ideals for happy living, for making this life worth while, and you will be amply rewarded. Then you can deservedly style yourselves devotees of the Lord.[1]

◊ ◊ ◊ ◊ ◊

There are many who spend much time in mechanically reciting the name Rama or systematically reading the entire Ramayana according to a fixed time–table, or who worship the images of Rama, Seeta, Lakshmana, and Hanuman, as a daily ritual, with pomp and pedantry; but, like the person who puts a foot forward only to draw it back again, these persons do not progress at all, though years might elapse. Without gaining purity of thoughts and intentions, compassion and the urge to serve, these outward expressions and exhibitions are but ways of cheating the society which applauds you as a great devotee. Your sight must become insight; it must be turned within and used to purify and clarify.[2]

◊ ◊ ◊ ◊ ◊

The ideal of brotherhood as depicted in the Ramayana is without parallel in any other epic anywhere in world literature. When, ,during the battle with the *rakshasa* (demon) hordes in Lanka, Lakshmana fell unconscious and could not be revived, Rama lamented the calamity, saying, "Alas! Lakshmana is the source of my breath; there is no brother like him on the whole earth." Lakshmana's life and relationship with his brother Rama are shining examples for mankind.

---

[1] *Sathya Sai Speaks*, Vol. 6, p. 50.

[2] *Sathya Sai Speaks*, Vol. 13, pp. 60–61.

It can be said that Lakshmana is the A in the sacred syllable *AUM;* Bharata, the second brother, is the U; Sathrughna, the third, is the M and Rama, the eldest, is the full *AUM.* Rama is the concretisation of the *Brahman* (Universal Absolute) that first emanated as the Primeval Sound, *AUM.* When Rama and Lakshmana were wading through the jungle after the loss of Seeta, the sages who saw them described them as the "Sun and Moon," so majestic and magnificent was their mein. They shone with the splendour of courage and determination. When strength of body and steadfastness of mind reinforce each other, one's mein becomes attractive. Youth today has neither physical strength nor mental steadfastness, so young people appear old very early in life. When the body is weak, the mind, too, gets weak. You must try to develop physical well–being and health, for a gem has to be treasured in a safe, strong box. The gem of Divinity that is your reality also has to be kept in a strong box, namely, the body.[1]

◊ ◊ ◊ ◊ ◊

The path of direct realisation of the Divine consists in total surrender to the Divine, as exemplified by Lakshmana in his surrender to Rama. He told Rama that after his surrender he had nothing that he could call his own and he existed only to carry out Rama's will in every matter.

Thyagaraja (saint, musician and poet), who once for a brief while entertained doubts about Rama's capacity to relieve him of his troubles, later extolled the limitless power of Rama, which enabled Hanuman to leap across the ocean and which accounted for Lakshmana's total surrender to Rama.[2]

◊ ◊ ◊ ◊ ◊

---

[1] *Sathya Sai Speaks,* Vol. 13, p. 212.

[2] *Sanathana Sarathi,* April 1995, p. —.

Lakshmana had a pure heart from his very birth. As he grew up he was able to overcome the urges of his senses and establish himself as their master. His character was above reproach. He eagerly welcomed any order from Rama and enjoyed fulfilling it to the best of his ability. Lakshmana spent the first two days of his life wailing aloud in the lap of Sumithra, his mother. She tried all remedies, magical and ritual, to console him, but the baby would not be consoled or persuaded to eat or to sleep. She consulted Vashishta, the Royal Preceptor, who advised that Lakshmana be laid beside Rama in the palace of Kausalya. She did as directed, and in the company of Rama, Sumithra's child slept soundly and played most happily. He could not tolerate separation from Rama. His greatest desire was to be in Rama's presence. He followed Rama like his shadow, never residing in a place where Rama was not present. Rama was all that he wanted, all that he cared for.

When Rama started out into exile in the forest wearing garments of bark, Lakshmana, too, did the same. For fourteen years he watched over his brother and his wife, guarding them day and night without any regard for his own comfort or even for sleep or food. Thulsi Dhas pays great tribute to Lakshmana for this devoted service. According to him, when Rama returned to Ayodhya after his period of exile, the citizens in *lakhs* (100,000) cheered at the distant sight of the flag on top of the chariot which was bringing him. But they did not know, he says, that the pole which carried the flag of Rama's triumph was Lakshmana, the devoted brother. How could the flag fly so splendidly without the dedicated service, the undaunted courage and the steadfast loyalty of the brother who gladly shared the travails of exile with Rama?

In the course of Narayana's enactment as a *nara* (man) named Rama on earth, He had a crucial role to play. Lakshmana laid down his life for the purpose of realising the Mission of the *Avatar* (Divine incarnation). He never transgressed by as much as a step, the boundary laid down by Rama. When Rama ordered him to raise a fire into which Seeta was advised to step as part of the fire–ordeal to prove her chastity to the world (symbolic), Lakshmana obeyed with a bleeding heart. When Rama ordered him to take Seeta out into the forest and leave her alone and unguarded there, Lakshmana obeyed, though his heart was wrung with pain. ...

Lakshmana decided every act of his on the touch–stone of either Rama's wish or the general good. He gave up everything — his wife Urmila, his mother Sumithra and the princely life at Ayodhya — for the chance of serving Rama and furthering His mission. When he killed Indhrajith in battle, Rama embraced him with unbounded joy, and exclaimed, "Ah, dear brother! What a great victory you have achieved today. Now I feel as if I have already got Seeta back."

Between Rama and Lakshmana there was never any trace of envy or suspicion. Lakshmana was supremely indifferent to what was happening around him if it did not affect Rama. His greatness is immeasurable. He served Seeta every day for fourteen years, but never once raised his eyes to her face. His conduct was the height of Righteousness. ...

When Lakshmana fainted during the battle with Indhrajith, the latter wanted to lift his unconscious body and carry him into Lanka as a hostage. But since Lakshmana was the incarnation of the cosmic serpent, Sesha, he was tremendously heavy and could not be moved. So Indhrajith gave up the idea and went away. Meanwhile Hanuman arrived there, and on his uttering the name of Rama, Lakshmana's weight was reduced to that of a feather, so responsive was he to *Ramanama* (Rama's name) even in his unconsciousness. This is a measure of the humility and the heroism of this great brother of Rama.[1]

◊ ◊ ◊ ◊ ◊

The Ramayana exemplifies the amity and harmony which should prevail among the members of a family. It extols the glory of ideal brotherhood, noble friendship and the greatness of love and affection.

---

[1] *Sathya Sai Speaks*, Vol. 13, pp. 213–217.

Rama was an ideal ruler who ruled his people with due regard to their likes and dislikes, having their welfare as his primary concern. As a ruler Rama has no equals. He was a veritable mine of strength, virtue and love. Hence it is essential that every student should take Rama as an ideal to be emulated and derive happiness by practising the ideal of Sri Rama.

The first canto in the Ramayana is called *Balakanda* (the canto describing boyhood of Sri Rama). Sage Viswamitra came to Dasaratha and sought the help of his two sons, Rama and Lakshmana, for protecting his *Yagna* (sacrificial rite). Rama and Lakshmana were fourteen years old when the Sage sought their help. When Dasaratha was hesitating to send his sons in view of their tender age, Viswamitra remarked, "O! Dasaratha! Swayed by paternal affection, you have mistaken them to be mere mortals, of flesh and blood, whereas in fact they are Divine incarnations. Do not give vent to sadness. They are the embodiment of Divinity. Send your sons with me without any hesitation."

Rama, while going with the Sage, encountered three women of three different temperaments. The first woman he confronted was Tataki of *tamasic* temperament. The *tamasic* nature makes a person mistake Truth for untruth. It robs one of the capacity for discrimination. Rama killed Tataki while keeping guard over the performance of Viswamitra's *yagna*. The two brothers saw to it that the *yagna* was performed without any obstruction. After the successful completion of the *yagna* Viswamitra proceeded to Mithila, accompanied by Rama and Lakshmana. On the way Rama came to the hermitage of Sage Gautama. There he absolved Ahalya of the curse which had turned her into a stone. Ahalya might be deemed a woman of *rajasic* temperament. After imparting moral advice to Ahalya, Rama went to Mithila with Viswamitra.

It was in Mithila that Rama encountered Seeta, representing the *satwic* quality. Having killed Tataki of the *tamasic* temperament and redeemed Ahalya representing the *rajasic* temperament, He accepted Seeta, who represented the *satwic* quality. The marriage of Seeta and Rama is symbolic of the union between *prakriti* and *Paramatma*. The citizens of Mithila greatly rejoiced hearing about the prospective marriage of Rama and Seeta. (Swami recited in His own mellifluous voice a ballad in praise of the wedding of Rama and Seeta.)

One of the rites in the marriage ceremony in India is "Talambralu," the act of pouring rice on the head of the bridegroom by the bride. Since Janaka, the father of Seeta, was immensely rich, he arranged for the pouring of pearls instead of rice. Seeta held a palmful of pearls in her hand over Rama's head. The white pearls in the palms of Seeta shone with reddish splendour as her palms were of reddish hue. When she poured the pearls on the white turban which Rama wore for the occasion, the pearls shone with the white hue of the turban. The pearls, rolling down the body of Sri Rama assumed a dark blue colour reflecting the bluish colour of Sri Rama. The pearls shining with reddish hue in the hands of Seeta are symbolic of the *rajo–guna*, conveying the message that one who is *rajasic* is in the company of *prakriti*. The pearls shining with whitish splendour are symbolic of the *satwa–guna*, indicating the fact that one acquires the *satwic* nature in the company of God. The nature of persons who belonged neither to *prakriti* nor God will be *tamasic* persons like the colour of the pearls that rolled down from Rama's head. People of divine orientation shine with *satwic* serenity and purity. People with a worldly outlook display *rajasic* quality while those who are neither worldly nor Godly are *tamasic*.

As Sri Rama was a king, His friends too were kings. Jambavan, the king of the forest, was a *satwic* friend. He became a friend of Rama out of sheer love for Him. Sugriva, the king of the monkeys, was a *rajasic* friend of Rama, who sought Rama's friendship for securing his help. It is out of desire for getting relief from his trouble and tribulations that he sought the help of Rama. Sugriva wanted his kingdom and wife to be restored to him. The third friend was Vibhishana, the brother of Ravana. He represents the *tamasic* quality, as he belonged to a *rakshasa* family.

Rama had three enemies, whose qualities represent the three *gunas*. The first enemy was Vali, a *satwic* enemy; he was a *satwic* enemy because, at the end, he acknowledged his mistakes and accepted the punishment meted out to him by Rama. Ravana was the second enemy, who harboured hatred for Rama. He refused to acknowledge his mistake and was responsible for the downfall of his country. He was a *rajasic* enemy because a *rajasic* enemy never acknowledges his mistakes. The third enemy, Kumbakarna was a *tamasic* enemy. A *tamasic* person is one who mistakes good to be bad and bad to be good. Rama put an end to all these three enemies.

Rama was the redeemer of the fallen *Pathita–pavana* (distressed, suffering ones). He redeemed and gave salvation to three characters in the Ramayana. They are Sabari, Guha and Jatayu. Sabari was a helpless and hapless old woman with no one to look after her. Her preceptor told her about Lord Rama. She was yearning for the arrival of Ramachandra whom she considered to be her saviour. She was deeply absorbed in the contemplation of Rama's name at all times and in all places. One day sage Matanga said to her, "O, Sabari, Lord Narayana has descended on the earth in the form of Rama. He is living in the garb of an ascetic. He will be soon arriving here, but I will not be alive at the time of his arrival. He is an embodiment of immaculate purity. Greet him and honour him with devotion." From that day, Sabari started preparing herself for the arrival of Sri Rama. Since she thought that Rama might ask her to give him something to eat, she would gather all sorts of fruits, and to satisfy herself that the fruits were sweet, she would taste them first and keep only the sweetest ones for her Lord. That was how Sabari transformed herself into a *satwic* devotee. Rama responded to her inmost prayers and Sabari in the end merged herself in Rama.[1]

◊ ◊ ◊ ◊ ◊

People talk glibly of *Sakshatkara* (Vision of the Divine), the vision that liberates. The See–er and the Seen have to merge and become One and experienced as One only, without a second. That is the

---

[1] *Sanathana Sarathi*, August 1992, pp. 184–86.

Sakshatkara that is worthwhile. You may have fruit. You may earn the
fruit of *thapas* (penance) in your hand. But, unless you eat it, digest it,
and make it part of your own nature and derive strength therefrom,
you are not saved at all. Merge into the Divine which you really are;
that is the consummation.

In order to reach this goal, you have to proceed far. First examine
your present equipment; find out its defects, for example, whether it
is damaged by egotism, greed, insincerity, waywardness and sloth. For,
with these faults, it is difficult to concentrate on thoughts of God,
either within or without. You must also cultivate the positive quality
of *Prema* (Love) for the Embodiment of *Prema* can be realised only
through *Prema*. That is the message the Ramayana gives all those who
study it with sincere desire to learn. That is the message I wish to give
you today.[1]

◊ ◊ ◊ ◊ ◊

7.

Hanuman: An Example of Dedicated Service and Devotion

Dhasya Bhakti ... highlights the attitude of the servant to the
master. Hanuman is the classic example of a devotee embodying this
type of devotion. He was at the service of Rama at all times. Though
encased in the form of a monkey, he had mastered the sixty–four
branches of learning and the meaning of the four *Vedas*; he could
recite the six *Sastras*. He was physically mentally and spiritually a
redoubtable hero. Nevertheless, he served Rama with no trace of ego
in thought, word and deed. He had achieved purity of all three.

---

[1] *Sathya Sai Speaks*, Vol. 13, pp. 60–61.

But, the *Dhasya Bhakti* of Hanuman was not free from defects. His service was steadfast and total to God as Rama. He was not attached to God as Krishna or as bearing any other name. The *Vedas* declare that God has a thousand names and He can assume a thousand forms. Hanuman's allegiance was limited to only one name and one form. *Dhasya Bhakti*, therefore, leads to a partial vision of the Universal Absolute.[1]

◊ ◊ ◊ ◊ ◊

Hanuman was a servant. He exemplified the idea of a servant. Rama embraced Hanuman and said: "Dear friend, Hanuman! You in your physical form belong to a different species. You are a monkey and I am a man. But the Love Principle is one and the same in both of us." Caste and creed may vary. But the Love principle is one. In all beings, in all countries, in all individuals love animates everyone. Today the reign of this Love Principle has to be established all over the world. God is the indweller in the heart. The heart is full of Love. That Love must be shared with others. It is only when the Love is shared that the old saying about equal–mindedness in joy and sorrow, in gain and loss, will be realised.[2]

◊ ◊ ◊ ◊ ◊

Hanuman is pictured as a monkey, and monkeys are by nature, wayward and frolicsome. "Monkeyish" has become a synonym of fickleness. But Hanuman did not have any trace of this fickleness. He was of Divine descent and distinguished with the Divine qualities mentioned in the Geetha. He derived Bliss in the contemplation of Rama. He had full mastery over physical and sensual cravings. He was shining in *Atmic* splendour. He had established his life on the

---

[1] *Sathya Sai Speaks*, Vol. 15, pp. 230–31.

[2] *Sanathana Sarathi*, June 1994, p. 143.

foundations of *Sathya* (Truth) and *Dharma* (Righteousness) and led his companions also on the same path, exercising the force of his example on them.[1]

◊ ◊ ◊ ◊ ◊

Hanuman became the messenger of Rama. There are three classes of messengers: those who do not understand the orders of the master or do not care to understand, and who operate to the detriment of the work assigned them; those who do only just as much as the order literally communicates; and those who grasp the purpose and significance of the orders and carry them out unflinchingly till the purpose is achieved. Hanuman belonged to the last category. He never flinched in his efforts, whatever the obstacle, and reported back only after he was satisfied with the result of his assignment. He could delve into the commands of Rama and know what his order meant.

As soon as Hanuman received the order, he felt a thrust of power inside him and a new confidence that since he had been so ordered, the strength and intelligence, the courage and the adventurous spirit needed, would be granted by Rama himself. So he never had any qualms about his capacity or capability. His body and spirit were vitalised by the very fact that Rama asked him to do something. An electric cable has a copper wire inside its plastic coating; for good operation, both must be of high quality. So, too, the body and the spirit within, have both to be in good trim, and Rama's words made them both efficient and active. The *darshan* (sight) of Rama conferred on Hanuman an enormous reinforcement of power, even physical power. ...[2]

◊ ◊ ◊ ◊ ◊

---

[1] *Sathya Sai Speaks*, Vol. 13, p. 184.

[2] *Sathya Sai Speaks*, Vol. 13, p. 182.

There are in the world today millions of people who recite the Lord's name. But while reciting the name, they do not realise the greatness and glory of the Divine name.

When Hanuman entered Lanka, the land of *rakshasas*, the first friendly person he encountered was *Vibheeshana*. All the *rakshasas* in Lanka, who had not seen a monkey, were curious to know all about the simian visitor. They asked him: "Who are you? Wherefrom have you come and at whose behest? How did you enter Lanka?" Hanuman was unruffled. He told them, "I am the servant of the Lord Kosala, Sri Rama," though he was very powerful. This means also that in any situation one should remain calm and unperturbed.

How is this tranquility to be secured? When the heart is pure, peace is assured. Without purity of the heart peace is unattainable. Even if one appears to be at peace, it is only a pretence. When one has both purity of heart and peace of mind, one can achieve anything. There are three P's. The first P stands for purity. The second P for patience. The third P stands for perseverance. When these are present, one can acquire the grace of Sri Rama. This was amply demonstrated by Hanuman.

But Vibheeshana was full of anguish. He told Hanuman: "Oh Hanuman! How lucky you are, how meteriorous to earn the company of Ramachandra! I have not had that good fortune. I have been meditating on Rama's name for many years. But so far I have not got the *darshan* of Rama. You have not only enjoyed the company of the Lord, but you are privileged to carry out the commands of Rama. Please tell me how I can secure such a blessing." Hanuman replied: "Vibheeshana! It is not enough if you merely recite the name of Rama. You have to carry out the injunctions of Rama and engage yourself in the service of Rama. Only then you will experience the power of Rama within you." From that moment, Vibheeshana resolved to participate in the service of Rama.

Today in the Kaliyuga, there are any number of persons chanting Rama's name. Chanting the name (*nama–japa*) is not enough. Whatever name you recite, you must also be active in the service of the form associated with the name. What is implied by the term, "*Rama–Karya*" (service to Rama)? Rama is immanent in the entire cosmos. Rama is present everywhere. Hence, you have to take part in social service. By rendering service to one's fellow beings, rendering help to the helpless, and performing sacred acts of dedicated service, one becomes eligible for Sri Rama's grace. Although Hanuman was highly intelligent in matters relating to the Divine, he made no distinction between good and bad. He carried out implicitly whatever he was ordered to do. He did not care to enquire whether it was right or wrong. Why? Because he regarded whatever Rama said as Gospel Truth (*Vedo–Vakya*). God's word is beyond question. Hanuman felt that he was not competent to stand in judgement on the Lord's words. "My duty is to carry out whatever Rama says, "*Karthyavyam Yogam Uchyathe*".[1]

◊ ◊ ◊ ◊ ◊

The name of the Lord is like a precious jewel which must be considered valuable and cherished as a gem. Tulsidas sang in praise of the Lord's Name (Rama's name) as the most invaluable gift given to him by his guru. The Lord's name should be recited with deep feeling so that it gets firmly entrenched in the heart. Hanuman is the supreme exemplar of true devotion. At the time of Rama's coronation in Ayodhya after his return from Lanka, Rama gave presents to all those who had helped him in the battle against Ravana. When it came to Hanuman, Rama could not find anything that was worthy of the unparalleled devotion of Hanuman. Praising Hanuman's unexcelled services, Rama said that the only fitting reward for such a devotee was to give Himself to Hanuman. He embraced Hanuman most lovingly. Seeta saw this and felt Hanuman should not be left unrewarded for his great services. She took out from her neck the pearl necklace she had received from her father Janaka at the time of her wedding and gave it to Hanuman. Immediately after receiving the necklace,

---

[1] *Sanathana Sarathi*, December 1995, p. 326.

Hanuman removed one pearl after another from the necklace, crushed it between his teeth, placed it close to his ear and then threw it away. Surprised at his strange behaviour, Seeta asked him why he was treating the pearls in that manner. Hanuman explained that he had no use for any object that did not chant Rama's Name. Seeta asked him how he could expect to hear Rama's name from an inert object like a pearl. Hanuman immediately pulled out a hair from his arm and kept it close to Seeta's ear. The hair was chanting Rama's name! "Ram! Ram!"

True devotion means that even the blood stream should proclaim the Lord's name. Because Hanuman was such a devotee he could be the foremost servant of Rama. He was totally free from egoism, pride and envy. In Lanka, he did not boast of his prowess, but was content to declare himself a humble servant of Rama. This humility is the true mark of a devotee.

When a person is asked, "Where do you live?" the correct answer is: "I am dwelling in the *Atma* (The Indwelling Spirit)." This is the Truth to be learnt from all the scriptures and epics. Everyone should realise the oneness in spirit of all mankind, which is proclaimed equally by all religions.[1]

◊ ◊ ◊ ◊ ◊

Hanuman was ordered to discover the whereabouts of Seeta and he obeyed implicitly, without question, and succeeded. He did not calculate the dangers of the journey and hesitate; he did not feel proud that he was chosen for the high adventure and enthuse. He listened, he understood, he obeyed, he won. The name *Ramadhutha* (Messenger, servant of Rama) that he earned thereby has made him immortal. You must earn the name, *Sai Rama Dhutha*. Have fortitude and self–control, use good and sweet words; examine each act of yours on the touch–stone of My Preference. "Will Swami approve of it?" you

---

[1] *Sanathana Sarathi*, January 1995, p. 15.

should ask yourselves; that is the *thapas* (penance) in which you are being initiated. It is a life–long *thapas*, not for these ten days of Dhasara alone.[1]

◊ ◊ ◊ ◊ ◊

Hanuman succeeded in co–ordinating his thought, word and act. Therefore he had the unique distinction of being great in physical strength, mental stability and virtuous character. He shines as an invaluable gem among the personalities of the Ramayana. He was also a great scholar who has mastered, of all things, the nine schools of grammar! He knew the four *Vedas* (sacred scriptures of the Hindus) and the six *Sastras* (spiritual sciences). The Geetha says that a scholar is "one who sees the same Divine force motivating everyone" — *Panditha Samadarsina.*

Hanuman was a good example of this outlook. He did not pride himself that he knew so much. He was the very picture of humility, born out of genuine sincerity and wisdom. He realised that the Rama–principle, *Atmarama*, was illumining every being, and he adored it above all else.[2]

◊ ◊ ◊ ◊ ◊

Of Hanuman too it is said, "*roma romamu Rama Namame*" — every single hair recited "*Rama Nama.*" His tail was a formidable flail, for it was suffused with the might of the Name. He is also called *Sundara*, the charming, the beautiful. Why? Because, he had Rama installed in his heart; since the splendour of Rama reflected on his face, he was charming to behold. He was a charming companion because he spoke of Rama only, sang of Rama alone.[1]

◊ ◊ ◊ ◊ ◊

A *sevak* must be neither elated nor dejected; he must adhere to the middle path. When Rama asked Hanuman to proceed towards the Southern region and described the dangers of the route, he was not dejected; when He gave him the ring to be handed over to Seeta, he was not elated that he had been chosen for the supreme task and given the glorious chance. He just obeyed. Sufficient unto him was the order of his Master, "Go." Hanuman is the ideal volunteer; efficient, humble, silent, serviceable, intelligent, eager, devoted.

Develop *bhakti* (devotion) and *shraddha* (faithful practice) by means of *namasmarana* and *japam*. Practise silence and sweetness. Serve all as *Saiswarupa* (embodiments of Sai); that is the best plan to realise the Sai in you.[2]

◊ ◊ ◊ ◊ ◊

Take Hanuman as your example in *seva*. He served Rama, the Prince of Righteousness, regardless of obstacles of all types. Though he was strong, learned and virtuous, he had no trace of pride. When asked who he was by the *rakshasas* (demons) in Lanka into which he had entered so daringly, he described himself, in all humility, as the "servant of Rama." That is a fine example of uprooting of the ego which *seva* must bring about in us. No one can serve another while his ego is rampant. The attitudes of mutual help and selfless service develop the "humanness" of man and help the enfoldment of the Divinity latent in him. ...

---

[1] *Sathya Sai Speaks*, Vol. 5, p. 250.

[2] *Sathya Sai Speaks*, Vol. 7, p. 75.

The Lord sets the example for the devotees to follow. He teaches that service done to any living being is offered to Him only and is accepted by Him most joyfully. Service rendered to cattle, to beasts, to men is laudable *sadana*.[1]

◊ ◊ ◊ ◊ ◊

Hanuman was intoxicated by his devotion to Rama and was always in a state of ecstasy in chanting Rama's name. He was all humility in the presence of Rama. He was utterly fearless before Ravana. Before the Divine he was a suppliant. Before a *rakshasa* he was a hero. Hanuman knew how to conduct himself in any situation. He was supremely intelligent. He stands out as an ideal for mankind.

People today lead meaningless mechanical lives with no ideals to inspire them. The purpose of life is to experience the Divine that is subtle and invisible like the roots that sustain a tree. Men today want fruits without considering the roots. The ancient sages searched for the roots to realise the fruits. *Bharatiya* culture was based on this concern for what is fundamental and primal. Today people forget the basic Truths and pursue the ephemeral. Worldly life is inescapable. But it should be lived with the ultimate goal in view. Human action and Divine aim should go together. To forget the Divine is to descend to the level of the animal. A hero becomes a zero if he forgets God.

All over the world men are perpetually haunted by fears of every kind because they have not secured the freedom from fear which God alone can give. ... God's grace alone can free men from fear. All should strive to secure Divine grace by developing firm faith in God. You may worship any form, chant any name, but have firm faith in God. Call the Divine by any name — Rama, Krishna, Allah, Jesus or Buddha — all names are the same. The one Lord is adored by different names.[2]

---

[1] *Sathya Sai Speaks*, Vol. 15, pp. 164–65.

[2] *Sanathana Sarathi*, December 1995, p. 328.

◊ ◊ ◊ ◊ ◊

For all the mighty deeds done by Hanuman and great help rendered by him, Rama asked him: "Hanuman! What reward can I give you? Apart from expressing My gratitude to you I cannot give you any fitting recompense. The only way I can show my gratitude to you is that whenever you think of Me at any time in your life, I shall appear before you." Rama was showing His gratitude to Hanuman in this manner.

This indicates that the primary duty of man is to be grateful all his life to the person who has done him a good turn.

Man has to realise his Divinity and look at all Nature from the Divine point of view. Instead, man looks at everything only from the mundane point of view. The body is indeed perishable. But it is also the means for realising the imperishable Truth. This means all speech should be about the Divine. All actions should be Godly. Every thought should be about God.[1]

◊ ◊ ◊ ◊ ◊

---

[1] *Sanathana Sarathi*, May 1995, p. 114.

8.

Hanuman: Symbol of Bhakti (Devotion)

Anjaneya (Hanuman) demonstrates the might of the Name. With the Name imprinted on his heart and rolling on his tongue, he leaped across the sea; temptations called on him to halt on the way; terrors pleaded with him to turn back; but the Name urged him on and carried him forward, through space, to distant Lanka where Seeta was. He had no space in his mind for anything other than the Name of his master.[1]

◊ ◊ ◊ ◊ ◊

Bhakti (devotion) is something sweet, soothing, refreshing and restoring. It must confer patience and fortitude. The *bhakta* will not be perturbed if another gets the interview first or if another is given greater consideration. He is humble and bides his time: he knows that there is a higher power that knows more and that it is just and impartial. In the light of that knowledge, the *bhakta* (devotee) will communicate his troubles and problems only to his Lord; he will not humiliate himself by talking about them to all and sundry, for what can a man, who is as helpless as himself, do to relieve him? It is only those who have that implicit faith in God, who will deign to communicate only with the Lord and none else, who deserve *Amritha* (Nectar of Immortality).[2]

---

[1] *Sathya Sai Speaks*, Vol. 5, p. 247.

[2] *Sathya Sai Speaks*, Vol. 5, p. 224.

◊ ◊ ◊ ◊ ◊

Bhakti or devotion to God is not to be judged or measured by rosaries or candles, daubings on the forehead or matted hair or jingles on the ankles; purity of motives and intentions is essential, so that *Prema* (Love) which is the one component of *bhakti* (devotion) does not leak out of the heart.[1]

◊ ◊ ◊ ◊ ◊

There are no short–cuts in the spiritual field. As a matter of fact, *bhakti* (devotion) is even more difficult than *jnana* (wisdom); for, to get the attitude of "Thou," not "I," one has to surrender completely to the Higher Power, personified as the Lord. The ego has to be fully curbed; the faith that "not even a blade of grass can shake in the wind without His being aware of it and thus having caused it" has to be implanted in the mind. *Bhakti* is not a leisure time job. Erase sensual desire; clear the heart of all blemish; then, the Lord will be reflected therein as in a mirror.[2]

◊ ◊ ◊ ◊ ◊

Bhakti is the state of mind in which one has no separate existence apart from God. The *bhakta*'s very breath is God; his every act is God, for God; his thoughts are of God; his words are uttered by God, about God. For, like the fish which can live only in water, man can live only in God — in peace and happiness.[3]

◊ ◊ ◊ ◊ ◊

---

[1] *Sathya Sai Speaks*, Vol. 9, p. 132.

[2] *Sathya Sai Speaks*, Vol. 5, p. 92.

[3] *Sathya Sai Speaks*, exact page and volume unknown.

You are called *sevaks* (servants), because you are engaged in *seva* (service). What exactly is *Seva*? Is it the way in which *bhakti* (devotion) manifests itself, a consequence of devotion? Or is it the cause of *bhakti*, one of the methods by which *bhakti* is expressed and developed? It is neither. It is not the *sine qua non* of *bhakti*, nor is it the result. It is the very essence of *bhakti*, the very breath of a *bhakta* (devotee), his very nature. It springs from the actual experience of the *bhakta* — an experience that convinces him that all beings are God's children, that all bodies are altars where God is installed, that all places are His Residences.

Consider *seva* as the best *sadana* (spiritual discipline). This is a great chance that you have secured. Your work among these large gatherings is more beneficial for your spiritual development than days of *japa* or meditation.[1]

◊ ◊ ◊ ◊ ◊

Devotion to God is not to be calculated on the basis of the institutions one has started or helped, the temples one has built or renovated, the donations one has given away, nor does it depend on the number of times one has written the Name of the Lord or on the time and energy one has spent in the worship of the Lord. These are not vital at all, no, not even secondary. Devotion is Divine Love, unsullied by any tinge of desire for the benefit that flows from it or the fruit or consequence of that Love. It is Love that knows no particular reason for its manifestation. It is of the nature of the Love of the soul for the Oversoul; the river for the sea; the creeper for the tree, the star for the sky, the spring for the cliff down which it flows. It is sweet, in bad times as well as good. It is not like pepper or salt with which you savour your dishes; it is the very bread and butter, the essential substance itself. It is not the pickle, which only lends a twang to the tongue and helps you to consume little more of the food. It is

---

[1] *Sathya Sai Speaks*, Vol. 7, p. 69.

an unchanging attitude, a desirable bent of the mind, standing steady through joy and grief. For, Divine Bliss comes through knowledge of the Self; the devotee is the true witness. ...[1]

◊ ◊ ◊ ◊ ◊

Through devotion to God alone can that knowledge be attained. *Bhakti* purifies the heart, elevates the feelings and universalises the vision. It also brings down the Grace of God; for, the clouds have to come over the fields and pour rain; the plants cannot rise up to drink the life–giving fluid. The mother has to bend to the cradle to fondle the child. *Bhakti* has that power, to bring the Lord down. Once Narada was asked to name the most noteworthy among the things of the world. He answered that the earth was the biggest. But, he was told water has occupied three–fourths of the earth; it threatens to swallow up the balance too, bit by bit. So, water, he had to agree, was more powerful. However, water too was drunk up by the sage Agasthya and the oceans were rendered dry by him, and he, in turn, is now just a star in the sky! Is the sky the biggest, then? No. For, it was covered by one single foot of the *Vamana–avatar* of the Lord (Vishnu's Incarnation as *Vamana*, the Dwarf). And, the Lord? O, He enters the hearts of the devotees and is imprisoned there. So, Narada had to conclude that the hearts of devotees are the grandest things in Creation!

That is why I condemn all signs of weakness and call the sense of weakness itself a sin, an unpardonable sin. It is an insult to the heritage of Immortality, the title *Amrithasya Puthra*, which mankind deserves and must earn. Weakness, vacillation, despair, all these bring dishonour on Him who conferred on you the honour of child Immortality; you are *bala–swarupa* (of the nature of strength). Whenever accosted, you must declare yourself so, and not otherwise. Do not bend and cringe and barter your self–respect. Do not believe that you are this little lump of body. You are the indestructible,

---

[1] *Sathya Sai Speaks*, Vol. 4, pp. 67–68.

immortal *Atma*, of the same nature as the Absolute Reality, *Brahman* itself.[1]

◊ ◊ ◊ ◊ ◊

Bhakti is also a *yoga*, a process of eliminating the mind or transforming the mind into an instrument for realising God. *Bhakti*, however, has been watered down into a routine ritual — like turning the beads of a rosary, squatting a specified number of hours before an image, offering incense, waving of lights, ringing of bells, dipping in holy waters, or climbing hills to reach shrines. These are acts that quieten some urges and quicken others, which may or may not be congenial.

Bhakti is not a penitential uniform that can be put on or off, as occasion demands. The constables on duty here wear uniforms, complete with ribbons and medals; but, when they reach home after their hours of duty, they take it off and wear other dresses. Devotion cannot come upon you during stated hours and fall off when you relapse into normalcy. It is a continuous, constant condition of the mind, a confirmed attitude, a way chosen and adhered to with avid attention.

Today, man dabbles in *yoga* (devotional practices) in the morning hours, revels in *bhoga* (festivity and luxury, catering to the senses) during the day, and tosses about in *roga* (disease) during the night! *Bhakti* is not to be "performed" during certain periods every day and superseded by other fashionable attractions. *Bhakti* is a constant, continuous bent of mind, a habit of thought, a way of life. It must be loyally adhered to whatever may happen — dishonour, distress, despair, deprivation, pleasure, prosperity, power and pomp.

The true devotee is deeply aware of the transitoriness of earthly triumphs. He knows that death is the final arbiter, that God is the only dispenser, and so, he is firm and calm, whether it is foul or fair. He

---

[1] *Sathya Sai Speaks*, Vol. 4, pp. 69–70.

will not slide or climb whatever happens. He knows that the God whom he adores is the indweller in the blade of grass and in the most distant star. God gives ear to the prayers that rise in all languages and even from the silence of the dumb. He has no trace of anger or worry. You too have no reason to develop anger and anxiety.[1]

◊ ◊ ◊ ◊ ◊

Dedication is different from service; in service, there is the element of ego. "I serve, He is the master, He acquires my service, I am necessary for Him."

But, in dedication, the I is wiped out. There is no desire for the fruit; the joy consists in the act being done.

To cultivate that attitude of dedication, every one must think of God, remember the Name of God and deepen faith in God.[2]

◊ ◊ ◊ ◊ ◊

Summary

It is evident through Sathya Sai Baba's teachings that all of the characters mentioned in the life of Lord Rama, including Lord Rama Himself, are integral aspects of the human being, manifest or unmanifest. Rama is his innermost core, his Soul, which manifests as righteous, moral thoughts, words and actions. Seeta symbolizes one's own body, mind and intellect, that is *Prakriti* or

---

[1] *Sathya Sai Speaks*, Vol. 8, pp. 126–127.

[2] *Sathya Sai Speaks*, Vol. 15, p. 27.

Nature. The individual consciousness can be infatuated by the material world or turned toward the *Atma* through wisdom, relying with awareness on the *Atma* (Rama), in every aspect of living. Hanuman is each one's own courageous, devoted, pure, surrendered mind, or consciousness, that is always in union with the Supreme Consciousness, or Rama. Ayodhya is the impregnable heart of man, filled with Atmic Light, capable of radiating Light and Love to the world.

Chapter 5

Lord Krishna

RADHA KRISHNA

Chapter 5

Lord Krishna

Introduction

Lord Krishna is the eternal Spirit (*Atma*) residing in the hearts of all beings, omnipresent, omnipotent, omniscient as the Soul (*Paramatma*) of the Universe. He descended to the earth in a human form, around 3000 BC, as a *Poorna Avatar*, a full incarnation of Divinity. His advent had the purpose of restoring *Dharma* (Righteousness) based on Truth (Divinity) as well as liberating willing souls who had surrendered, having no thought other than that of Divinity. Krishna, the embodiment of Divine Love, Bliss, and Infinite Wisdom, attracted many to Him through His charm, Love, eyes, speech, and sportive actions.

Krishna was widely known as *Gopala* because He protects, guides, feeds and fosters the go's (literally, "cows"), that is, the *jeevis* or living beings, and helps to purify their hearts and lead them to God realization. The *gopikas* are devotees who, being highly evolved, purified *jeevis*, and intensely loving Krishna, seek union with Paramatma. *Radha* and *Meera* were examples of devotees who completely surrendered their lives, to merge with the Krishna Principle.

The Divine eternal *Atma* (Soul), within each being, is Krishna. Every human can become an Arjuna (friend of Krishna) by purifying his mind, developing confidence and courage, turning his entire being toward the Divine, listening to Krishna's guidance from his heart and thereby attain spiritual liberation (*moksha*). Krishna dwells within every one of us. It is up to oneself to make this *Atmic* power bright. To invoke Him is only to claim Him. He alone gains Krishna who chooses him.

The following excerpts from Sathya Sai Baba's Discourses explain the deep inner meaning of the main aspects of Lord Krishna's life and mission.

◊ ◊ ◊ ◊ ◊

1.

Lord Krishna: Advent of the Avatar

The ever auspicious Lord
The manifest form of *Om*, the one who has come to teach,
The One who churns for butter, the hearts and minds of men,
The Friend, the charmer, the liberator from blinding bondage,
The Comforter of those who clamour and pray, the Destroyer of currents that drag,
The Consoler of torn hearts, like the moon so cool,
The Derider of Pride, the Healer, curing birth and death,
The Lotus–eyed, the Negator of Time, Himself the process and the play of Time,
The Thief who steals for Himself the pure minds of the good,
Beauty embodied, the child of Devaki, Vasudeva, Son of Vasudev,
The glory of the Yadhu race, is here, with you, beside you.[1]

◊ ◊ ◊ ◊ ◊

What sort of personality is Krishna? Although He moved amongst all kinds of persons, sported and played with all, He was not attached to anyone. He was ever content, ever blissful. He transcended all qualities. He was free from egoism. He was a sovereign without a crown. Though He conquered many kingdoms He did not rule over any of them. He enjoyed witnessing others rule over the kingdoms.

---

[1] *Sathya Sai Speaks*, Vol. 16, p. 26.

He was totally free from any desires. Whatever he sought was for the sake of others. In this way He revealed His Divinity.[1]

◊ ◊ ◊ ◊ ◊

Krishna was born in prison, a fact that teaches us that God has to incarnate or present himself in the dark and narrow prison–house of our hearts, so that we may derive light and earn freedom. *Maya* is the delusion that hides the Truth of Being; it tends to identify one's Truth as the physical body with its appurtenances, and prompts us to cater to the cravings of the body. Man thus forgets the Divine and instead listens to the call of the animal in him, consequently falling from his high ideal. But when Krishna is born in the cellar of his mind, man is saved. Man must therefore become aware of God within the cavity of his heart. ...

Sri Krishna was born as the eighth child of Devaki. This is significant, for *Samadi* is the eighth stage of spiritual effort, coming after *yama, niyama, asana, pranayama, prathyahara, dharana* and *dhyana*. These are known as *ashtanaga–yoga*, the eight–fold discipline (abstention from evildoing, observance, control of breath, posture, withdrawal of mind from sense objects, concentration, meditation and absorption in the *Atma*. The Lord can be visualised only after the seven steps are successfully negotiated and the mind purified in the process. ...

Samadi combines *sama* (equal) and *di* (intelligence), that is to say, intelligence grasping the fundamental equality of every being. Not only will all feeling of difference and distinction disappear, but even notions such as heat and cold, grief and joy, good and bad, will become meaningless. When man reaches that state, the Lord is automatically born in his consciousness.[2]

---

[1] *Sanathana Sarathi*, September 1989, p. 230.

[2] *Sathya Sai Speaks*, Vol. 13, pp. 248–250.

◊ ◊ ◊ ◊ ◊

The *Avatar* (Divine Incarnation) comes to reveal man to himself, to restore to him his birthright of *Atmic* Bliss. He does not come to found a new creed, to breed a new faction, to instil a new God. If such a thing happens, it is the consequence of the evil in man. The *Avatar* comes as man in order to demonstrate that Man is Divine, in order to be within reach of Man. The human mind cannot grasp the absolute, attributeless principle; it is abstract and beyond the reach of speech, mind and intellect.

Fire is inherent in the match–stick but it is only when it is struck as a flame that we can benefit by it. The *Nirguna* (attributeless) has to manifest as *Saguna* (with qualities); the *Nirakara* (Formless) has to appear with Form. Then only can man listen, learn, understand, follow and be saved, through the Bliss of that experience. The *Avatar* lights the flame of Realisation in each; and the age–old ignorance is destroyed in an instant.

...

Krishna, like all *Avatars*, attracts not only seekers, saints and sages but the simple, the innocent and the good. He draws also the curious, the critics, the sceptics and those who suffer from atheism. He draws them towards Himself by the irresistible charm of His person, by His invincible look, His voice, His flute, His counsel and His undaunted heroism. He is ever in a state of Bliss, spreading harmony, melody and beauty around Him. ...

Why does He attract all to His Presence? To plough the heart, prepare it for receiving the shower of Grace, to grow the seeds of Love, weed it of all evil thoughts which smother the crops of joy and to enable it to gather the harvest of Wisdom. That wisdom finds its fulfilment in Krishna Himself, for Krishna also means the Pure Essence, the Supreme Principle, the *Sat–Chit–Ananda*.[1]

---

[1] *Sathya Sai Speaks*, Vol. 11, pp. 290–92.

◊ ◊ ◊ ◊ ◊

Krishna–avatar is a *Sampurna Avatar*, the Lord appearing with all the 16 *kalas* (distinctive marks); whereas Rama shared the *kalas* with other brothers. Rama appeared as if He was associated with *gunas* (qualities), or as having qualitative behaviour, whereas Krishna was above and beyond such. Krishna never prayed, even in the direct crisis! But, Rama does so, to *Aditya* (Sun God), for instance; the intent of that *Avatar* was different. Krishna was unaffected by the *gunas*. ...
When the *gopees* pleaded, "Krishna! is it *Dharma* for you to treat us thus?" Krishna replied, "My act is not *adharma*; but yours is, for body–consciousness is against the highest spiritual *Dharma*."[1]

◊ ◊ ◊ ◊ ◊

All *Avatars* are *Purna Avatars*, have all the attributes of the Divine. But the *Sastras* (revealed scriptures) have held that the *Krishna Avatar* alone is the complete incarnation, with all the sixteen aspects. Despite His Omnipotence, Krishna was easily accessible to the devotee. He submitted Himself to the devotee. When we are filled with devotion, the Lord is ready to serve us as our servant. The Lord is ever prepared to subject Himself to any kind of difficulty or ordeal to protect or help His devotee. Many a devotee has sung songs in praise of Krishna and lamented the fact that he had not been fortunate enough to be born during His advent and enjoyed His divine music and witnessed His divine exploits.[2]

◊ ◊ ◊ ◊ ◊

Krishna declared in the *Geetha* that when men forget their *Dharma* and unrighteousness becomes rampant, the Divine makes His advent.

---

[1] *Sathya Sai Speaks*, Vol. 4, p. 235.

[2] *Sathya Sai Speaks*, Vol. 16, p. 125.

The purpose of the advent is to promote *satwic* qualities, eradicate evil tendencies, propagate Love and to install in the hearts of humanity the Divine who is the very embodiment of Righteousness (*Dharma*). God's advent on Earth is for spreading Divine Love which is the fountain–source of Righteousness (*Dharma*). There is no gulf between love and Love. Love is one. Krishna declared: "I incarnate to propagate this Love." The various expounders of *Bhagavad Geetha*, however, have given different interpretations to the message of the *Geetha* and created confusion.[1]

◊ ◊ ◊ ◊ ◊

When the formless transforms itself, it may appear as *Vibhavakara* or as *Swakara* (endowed with some particular glory or power or as the full manifestation of itself). That is to say, the *avatara* might manifest only that part of the Divine glory as was essential for the task which brought the Form, or it might exceed the limited purpose for which it came and shine in full grandeur. Rama is a good example of the first and Krishna of the second.[2]

◊ ◊ ◊ ◊ ◊

Become the ruler of the senses, not their slave. *Krishieksa*, an appellation of Krishna, means Master of the senses; *Gudakesa*, an appellation of Arjuna, also conveys the same sense. That is the reason why these two became comrades.[3]

◊ ◊ ◊ ◊ ◊

---

[1] *Sanathana Sarathi*, November 1991, p. 284.

[2] *Sathya Sai Speaks*, Vol. 4, p. 202.

[3] *Sathya Sai Speaks*, Vol. 5, p. 29.

The *Avatar* of Krishna was a full incarnation, with all the sixteen facets of glory. In the *Avatar* of Rama, out of the sixteen, the three brothers had one each and Parashurama, the contemporary, had one, until Rama met Him and overpowered Him and drew within Himself the fraction of the Divine power that He had. Other incarnations were for ad hoc purposes, the suppression of evil represented by one evil person or group of persons. The Rama and Krishna *Avatars* were, however, for more general purposes, the mission of restoring *Dharma* and fostering virtuous living, besides punishing the wicked and teaching the world that vice will not succeed. ...

Before every incarnation, two collaborators for the task on which the incarnation comes, also appear — the *Mayashakti* (deluding power) and *Yogashakti* (power of communion with the Divine). *Maya* comes as the elder sister to warn the wicked; *Yoga* comes as the elder brother, to enthuse and keep constant company.[1]

◊ ◊ ◊ ◊ ◊

Avatars are of two kinds: One, *Amsavatar;* two, *Purnavatar.* All human beings are *Amsavatar* (partial incarnation of the Divine). *Mamaivamso jeevalike jeevabhuta–sanatanah* ("A part of My eternal Self has become the *jeeva* — individual soul — in the world of living beings," says Krishna in the *Geetha*). These partial incarnations, caught up in *maya*, develop egoism and possessiveness and lead worldly lives. The *Purnavatars*, however, subduing and transcending *maya*, manifest their full Divinity to the world in their lives. The *Purnavatar* may behave, according to the circumstances, as if He were subject to *maya*, but in fact He is free from *maya* at all times.

In the *Rama Avatar*, for instance, Rama conducted himself as if he was subject to *maya*, but upheld *Dharma* for promoting the welfare of the world. The *Krishna Avatar* was different. Keeping *maya* under control, He manifested His *Leelas* (miraculous deeds). This was why

---

[1] *Sathya Sai Speaks*, Vol. 7, pp. 38–39.

Vyasa, in his *Bhagavatha*, characterised Krishna as *Leelamanusha Vigrahah* (The Divine manifesting as man for performing His *Leelas*). The *Bhagavatha* has described in detail the *Leelas* of Krishna and proclaimed His glory to the world.

In the *Krishna Avatar*, Krishna not only performed many marvellous deeds, but also taught the Supreme Wisdom to the world. He was one who had transcended the *gunas*, but, for the sake of regeneration of the world, behaved as if He was influenced by the *gunas*, and delighted the world by His deeds ... Krishna did everything, whatever He spoke or whatever action He did, for the good and well–being of the world. But some people, not understanding this Truth owing to their own limitations, attributed wrong motives for some of Krishna's actions. In this they reflected their own feelings.[1]

◊ ◊ ◊ ◊ ◊

When Krishna made His advent on earth, He also had to play His part according to His role. While Sisupala was railing at Krishna, He allowed him a long rope and destroyed him when the appropriate time came. The *Bhagavatam* relates the story of how Krishna retreated repeatedly in His encounters with Jarasanda. How can the All–knowing, All–powerful, Omni–present Lord flee from anywhere? Where can He hide Himself? This is utterly fanciful.

When one has faith in the ways of the Lord and abides by the will of the Lord, the Lord can be understood and experienced.

For instance, there is the example of Draupadi in the *Mahabharata*. In the court of Duryodhana, although she was humiliated and dishonoured by Duryodhana and Dussasana, Krishna, in accordance with the role He had to play, did not intervene, as both of them were destined to meet with their death at the hands of Bhima.

---

[1] *Sanathana Sarathi*, September 1990, pp. 225–226.

During Krishna's life-time, he was the target of attacks and accusations by many wicked persons. But the Divine has no likes or dislikes. The wicked persons suffer from the consequences of their own actions according to their deserts.

What one gets in life is dependent partly on what he has earned by his actions. This is called *Prarabdam*. This is by its nature temporary. What is got as the fruit of past action will not last long. Forgetting this fact and forgetting also his true nature (*Swabhavam*) man is carried away by the transient and acts according to his whims.

When an actor in a play is assigned a certain role, he studies the entire play, but while acting his role, he has to play his part alone in each scene as required in the play and not all the roles that he knows. He has to suit his actions to the demands of his role in each scene in the play. Likewise, the Lord, when He has assumed a role in the Cosmic play, has to act in each situation according to what is appropriate to it and according to the rules of the game.[1]

◊ ◊ ◊ ◊ ◊

Krishna was a *Paripurna–Jnani* (One who possessed the Supreme Wisdom). Why did he take on a human body? "*Parithranaya sadhunam*" (to protect the good). Krishna incarnated in human form to teach the highest Truth to the pious and the godly persons who were filled with good thoughts and performed good deeds.[2]

◊ ◊ ◊ ◊ ◊

---

[1] *Sanathana Sarathi*, December 1994, p. 310.

[2] *Sanathana Sarathi*, November/December 1995, p. 324.

2.

The Birth of Lord Krishna During the Dark Fortnight

Embodiments of the Divine! Do not think that celebration of the birth of Krishna relates to what happened some millennia ago in the Dwapara Yuga. Everyone has to cherish the Krishna consciousness in one's heart every moment ceaselessly. Who is Krishna? When was He born? Krishna was born in the month of *Sravana*, in the dark fortnight (Krishna *paksha*), on *Ashtami* day, in a dark room. ...

The effulgence of the Lord is seen with greater effect when it is dark. In a world of disorder, Krishna was born to establish order. He was born on *Ashtami* day. *Ashtami* is associated with troubles and difficulties. When do troubles arise? When Righteousness is forgotten. Krishna's advent signifies the dispelling of darkness, the removal of troubles, banishing of ignorance and teaching mankind the Supreme Wisdom.

Krishna's primary role was that of teacher. He taught the *Geetha* to Arjuna. He told Arjuna: "Be only My instrument!" Krishna thereby declared: "Using you as an instrument, I am reforming the whole world." All the teachings of the Divine are related to *Dharma* and *Prema* (Divine Love).[1]

◊ ◊ ◊ ◊ ◊

God can protect as well as punish. He may impose trials or confer joy. Krishna destroyed Dantavakra and Sisupala. He protected the Pandavas all through. God (in His earlier *Avatars*) destroyed

---

[1] *Sanathana Sarathi*, September 1990, pp. 227–28.

Hiranyaksha and Hiranyakasipu and protected Prahlada. In the *Rama Avatar*, He punished Ravana and Kumbhakarna and crowned Vibhishana as King. As Krishna, He teased the *gopikas* and made them weep. He gave delight to His *gopala* companions. All these are different aspects of the Lord's *Leelas* (sport). "Why should He do this and why should He behave differently?" Such questions are irrelevant in the context of the Lord's utterly selfless actions. God's deeds are free from blemish. There is not an iota of selfishness in the Lord.[1]

◊ ◊ ◊ ◊ ◊

3.

The Meaning of the Name Krishna

The word *Krishna* has three meanings. One is: "*Krishyathi iti Krishnah*" (The one who cultivates is Krishna). What is it that has to be cultivated? The field of the heart (*Hridaya kshetra*). Krishna cultivates the field of our hearts by removing the weeds of bad qualities, watering it with Love, ploughing it with the use of *sadana*, and sowing the seeds of devotion. This is how Krishna cultivates our hearts.

The second meaning of the word is: *Karshathi iti Krishnah* ("The one who attracts is Krishna"). Krishna attracts you by His eyes, His speech, His sports, and by every action of His. By His words, he softens and calms the hearts of even those filled with hatred and makes them rejoice. ...

A third meaning of the word Krishna is one who is always blissful (*Kushyathi iti Krishnah*). Krishna was always in a state of bliss.

---

[1] *Sanathana Sarathi*, April 1991, p. 90.

It was because He had these various qualities, the sage Garga named Him Krishna. The ordinary meaning of the word Krishna is "one who is dark." But people think only of this meaning and forget the deeper and truer meanings of the Lord's name.

The essence of Krishna's life is He proclaimed the Truth to the world, propagated the eternal verities and delighted the world by His *Leelas.* ...

Nor was that all. Krishna, in fulfilling the pledge He had given to Mother Earth, rid the world of many wicked rulers and sought to establish the reign of Righteousness for the protection of the good.

The Divine incarnates from age to age for the purpose of protecting the virtuous, punishing the wicked and establishing *Dharma.* Krishna is said to have destroyed many wicked persons. But this is not quite correct. It is their own wickedness which destroyed these evil persons.

Today if the Divine wants to punish the wicked and protect the righteous, there will not be even one wholly righteous person. All will qualify for punishment. It is not a question of destroying the wicked. The task today is to transform unrighteousness (*adharma*) into Righteousness (*Dharma*). How is this to be done? Through Love alone.

Krishna also changed the hearts of many people through Love. It may be asked: Is it not Krishna who killed Kamsa? Not at all. This is the text–book version. In Truth, it was his own heated imagination (*bhrama*) which killed him.[1]

◊ ◊ ◊ ◊ ◊

---

[1] *Sanathana Sarathi,* October 1994, pp. 259–260.

4.

Lord Krishna as Yogeswara

Krishna is named *Yogeswara* in the *Geetha*. What does that mean? *Yoga* is defined by *Pathanjali* as the *nirodha* (control) of the *vrittis* (agitations) of the *chitta* (mind–stuff). If the mind is stilled and free from waves produced by the wind of desire, then he becomes a *Yogi* and the Lord is the highest *Yogi*, for He is the ocean that is unaffected by the waves which agitate the surface. Krishna danced on the hood of the serpent Kaliya and forced it to vomit its poison, it is said. This is only another way of saying that he forced sensual desires to divest themselves of pernicious effects. *Yoga* of this type is the best means of attaining the *Yogiswara* (the Lord of *yogis*); not breath control, but sense control is the prescription.

Transcend *anekathwa bhava* (the consciousness of the many) and cultivate *ekathwa bhava* (the consciousness of the One), that will end strife, grief, pain and pride. See all as but expressions of the same God, as appearances on the same screen, as bulbs lit by the same current, though of manifold colours and wattage.[1]

◊ ◊ ◊ ◊ ◊

---

[1] *Sathya Sai Speaks*, Vol. 9, pp. 27–28.

5.

Lord Krishna is the Embodiment of Prema (Divine Love)

Live with *Prema*, in *Prema*, for *Prema*. Then the Lord who is *Premaswarupa* (Divine Love personified) will grant you all that you need in spite of your not asking for anything. He knows; He is the Mother who does not wait to hear the moan of the child to feed it. His *Prema* is so vast and deep; He anticipates every need and rushes with the help you must have. You are all waiting anxiously to know, from when I am granting you the "interviews" so that you can place before Me the long lists of "*korikas*" (wishes), which you have brought. These wishes go on multiplying; they never end. The fulfilment of one leads to a new series. Strive to arrive at the stage when His Wish alone will count and you are an instrument of His Hands. The *gopees* desired to listen only to Krishna's Glory, Krishna's charm, Krishna's Words, Krishna's Pranks, Plays, Pastimes, Krishna's Achievements, His Attainments.

When you fill yourselves with Love for Krishna (*Krishna Prema*), you achieve *sarupya* and *sayujya* (likeness of form and absorption into Krishna). Strive for that consummation, not for lesser victories.[1]

◊ ◊ ◊ ◊ ◊

As a lump of sugar sweetens every drop of water in the cup, the eye of Love makes every person in the world friendly and attractive.

---

[1] *Sathya Sai Speaks*, Vol. 5, p. 193.

The simple milkmaids of Gokul saw each other as Krishna; such was their overwhelming Love for the Divine Incarnation.[1]

◊ ◊ ◊ ◊ ◊

The supreme message of the life of Krishna is the uniqueness of the Love Principle (*Prema Tathwa*). This message is all that the world needs. Krishna is the embodiment of Love. This Love can be understood only through Love. This Love is strong, brilliant and unbreakable like diamond. It is extremely precious. If you want to secure such Divine Love your Love (for God) must be equally strong. You can cut diamond only with diamond. If there is any defect in your Love, it should be removed only through Love. Love begets Love. Jealousy begets jealously. Anger breeds anger. Therefore, if you want to foster Love, you have to get rid of hatred, jealousy and anger.

To attain Krishna, the very embodiment of Love, Love is the only way.[2]

◊ ◊ ◊ ◊ ◊

With or without Form, It is *Ananda* (Bliss). Welcome It into the heart, as Rama — He who is joy and grants joy — or as Krishna — He who draws you by means of the joy He imparts — and live all your moments with It, offering It your *dhyana*, your *puja*, your *japa*. That will open the doors of *jnana* (wisdom) and of Liberation.[3]

◊ ◊ ◊ ◊ ◊

---

[1] *Sathya Sai Speaks*, Vol. 7, p. 133.

[2] *Sanathana Sarathi*, September 1989, p. 232.

[3] Sathya Sai Speaks, exact volume and page not known.

6.
Lord Krishna as Sanathana Sarathi (Eternal Charioteer)

He is the *Sanathana Sarathi*, come to be the *Sarathi* (Charioteer) of all. He is the Lord, for all who seek a Master, a Support. The *Atma* is the Master in every one and Krishna is the Universal *Atma*, personified.

There are two birds sitting on one tree, the *Upanishad* says, the *Jivatma* (Individual Soul) and the *Paramatma* (Supreme Soul), on the tree of this Body, this World. One bird eats the fruits of that tree, while the other simply looks on, as a witness. But, the wonder is, the two birds are really one, though they appear as two; they cannot be separated, since they are two aspects of the same entity. Steam in the air cannot be seen; it has no shape or form; but, it is the same as ice, which is hard and heavy and cold. *Nirakara* (formless) and *Sakara* (formful) are just two ways in which the One manifests itself.

The minute hand of the clock is the *Jivatma*, the bird that eats the fruits. It goes round and round but, the hour hand moves silently and slowly, with a certain dignity. The hour hand can be said to be the *Paramatma*. Once an hour the two meet, but, the *Jivatma* does not get that consummation fixed for ever. It loses the precious chance and so has to go round and round again and again. Liberation is when the two merge, and only one remains.

When the obstacles in the path of Truth are laid low, deliverance is achieved. That is why *moksha* is something that can be won, here and now; one need not wait for the dissolution of the physical body for that. *Karma* must not be felt as a burden, for that feeling is a sure sign, indicating that it is against the grain. No *karma* which helps your progress will weigh heavily on you. It is only when you go counter to your innermost nature that you feel it a burden. A time comes when you look back on your achievement and sigh at the futility of it all. Entrust to the Lord, before it is too late, your mind and let Him shape it as he likes.[1]

◊ ◊ ◊ ◊ ◊

7.

Lord Krishna as Gopala

If you take Krishna to be a *Gopala* (cowherd), a man of the world like others, then for you he will be just a cowherd! You too climb only up to that stage. You have to take it in the *yogic* sense that "*Go*" in *Gopala* means "*jeeva*" (living being) and therefore, *Gopala* means "He who protects, guides, feeds and fosters the *jeevis*"; that is to say, "He who is the protector and preserver of beings." You will have noticed that Udava, who looked upon Krishna as his *Guru*, benefitted more than Arjuna who looked upon Him as a *sakha* (a friend). If you have faith that He is God, He will be God to you; if you dismiss Him as mere man, He takes on that role and becomes useless for you. Search for Him with the heart, not with the eye for externals. The superpower has to be sought in the super–state itself, not in the lower states. Then, if you have the eyes that are fit to see and the wisdom to understand, you will find Him.[2]

◊ ◊ ◊ ◊ ◊

Go (cow) also means, beings, souls, individuals. So that, *Gopala* is He who tends the souls, keeps them away from harm, encourages them to graze in peace, and drives them back into the sheds when

---

[1] *Sathya Sai Speaks*, Vol. 3, pp. 146–47.

[2] *Sathya Sai Speaks*, Vol. 1, p. 185.

evening falls on earth. Individual beings too are under the loving care
of God, who knows what is good for them and saves from ruin.[1]

◊ ◊ ◊ ◊ ◊

... *Raso vai sah* — "He is sweetness." So, the *jagat* (the Universe),
which is His creation cannot but be sweet for those who recognise it
as His handiwork. The *jagat* (world) has to be used to instruct you on
the glory and the power of God, so that you may seek Him and reach
Him. There are four stages in the journey towards this goal; each one
is called a *loka*, a region which you reach. The first is *A–vidhya loka* (the
region of ignorance and delusion) from which you start, prompted by
the chain of grief and pain it inflicts on you. The second is the
Vidhyaloka, where you penetrate into the *Vijnanamayakosha* (the
intellectual plane) and are able to distinguish between the true and
false, the kernel and the husk. The third is the *Anandaloka*, where you
are immersed in Bliss, at the glimpse of the eternal source of power
and peace. And, lastly, you have the *Go–loka*, where the *Go–pala* reigns,
and all the *go's* (*jeevas*, sparks from the Divine), waves of the
Premasagara (the ocean of Love) are One in ecstasy and enlightenment!

Unless you have Love, you cannot claim kinship with the votaries
of God; mere ritualistic exactitude or pompous adoration, or loud
acclamation will not entitle you to enter the portals of *Go–loka*! They
are as tin and trash before the treasure–chest of Love. Love is the
bridge which helps passage from birth to death to deathlessness, from
death to birthlessness. When you rise from the *jeeva*–sense to the
Deva–sense (human–ness to God–ness), then, there is no more birth or
death. Liberation happens when you love every being so intensely that
you are aware of only ONE. Soak your heart in Love, soak your acts
in Righteousness, soak your emotions in compassion; then you attain
God soonest.[2]

---

[1] *Sathya Sai Speaks*, Vol. 11, p. 38.

[2] *Sathya Sai Speaks*, Vol. 11, pp. 203–204.

◊ ◊ ◊ ◊ ◊

"*Go*" means "*indriya*" or the senses; so, the word "*Go–pala*" means, he who controls the senses. And, why should they be controlled? So that they may not stand in the way of *thyaga* or sacrifice. All the senses are self–centred, egoistic. They must be educated to be "inward–directed," towards the *Atma* which is Universal. That is gained by trusting to *Go–pala*, by entrusting the senses to Him. Every one must pass through *sat–karma* or good deeds, into the realm of expanding Love and from Love he learns the lessons of sacrifice, of dedication, of surrender to the One Overlord. This takes him on to faith in the supremacy of Godhead, everything else being but His shadow, His being the One and Only Reality.[1]

◊ ◊ ◊ ◊ ◊

8.

Lord Krishna had eight wives and 16,000 Gopikas

In the life of Krishna, there are many incidents which have an esoteric meaning, but which have been misunderstood and misinterpreted by scholars and commentators. Such misunderstandings have been caused by stories that Krishna had eight wives and that he dallied with 16,000 *gopikas*. In the spinal column, there are six chakras, of which two are important — the *Sahasrara chakra* in the brain and the *Hridayachakra* in the middle of the spinal column. The *Hridayachakra* is a flower–like *chakra* with eight petals. The eight petals are symbols of the eight parts of the earth, whose master is the Lord Himself. The

---

[1] *Sathya Sai Speaks*, Vol. 5, p. 101.

esoteric meaning of this is that God is the Lord of the eight–petalled lotus of the heart in man. The Lord of the Heart is described as *Madava*. *Ma* means *Lakshmi*, or *maya* or *prakriti*. *Dava* means husband. God is the Lord of *Lakshmi*, or *maya* or *prakriti*. Krishna is thus the Lord of the eight–petalled lotus of the heart.

Sahasrara is the topmost chakra of the spinal column. It is pictured as a thousand–petalled flower. In each petal, God dwells with all His sixteen potencies (*kalas*). Altogether, there are 16,000 potencies, which represent the *gopikas*. *Go* means sound, speech, and life–breath. God is the Lord of this thousand–petalled *Sahasrara*. The inner significance of the reference to 16,000 *gopikas* should be understood in this manner. Few attempt to understand the spiritual significance of many episodes in the *Bhagavatam*. Young men may easily be misled by references to Krishna's eight wives or His association with 16,000 *gopikas*. The real meaning is that each one should awaken the sixteen thousand potencies within him. This can be done only by implicit obedience to the commands of God.[1]

◊ ◊ ◊ ◊ ◊

In the human body, there are what are called *Shadchakras*, six spiritual centres. Of these, the two most important are: the *Hridayachakra* (the Heart Centre) and the *Sahasrara* (the thousand–petalled centre). The *Hridayachakra* is also known as the Lotus of the Heart (*Hridayakamala*) and the *Sahasrara* is called the Thousand–Petalled Lotus. These eight petals symbolise the eight worlds, the eight directions, the eight guardians of the world, the eight spirits (*bhutas*) and the eight parts of the earth. Because Krishna was the Lord of these eight petals, He was described as the husband of eight queens. The master is called *Pathi* and those under him are described as wives. This is a symbolic relationship and not a husband–wife relationship in the worldly sense. It is because the

---

[1] *Sanathana Sarathi*, October 1991, p. 259.

esoteric significance of these relationships was not properly understood, the *Bhagavatam* came in for misinterpretation.

It is also stated that Krishna was wedded to 16,000 *gopikas*. Who are these *gopikas*? They are not cowherdresses in physical form. In the human head there is a lotus with a thousand petals. Each of these petals has 16 *kalas*. The Lord is described as the embodiment of the 16 *kalas*. As the Lord of the *Sahasrara* (thousand–petalled lotus), He presides over the 16,000 kalas which are present in this lotus. The *Kundalini Shakti*, which starts at the bottom of the spinal column (*Mooladara*), rises and merges with the 16,000 entities in the *Sahasrara*. This is the esoteric significance and the meaning of the role of the Divine within the body. Oblivious to this inner meaning, people indulge in misinterpretation and perverse expositions.[1]

◊ ◊ ◊ ◊ ◊

9.

Lord Krishna, Arjuna, and the Kurukshetra War

The last sloka of the *Geetha* says, "*Yathra Yogeswarah Krishno Yathra Partho Dhanurdharah, Tatra Sreer Vijayo Bhuthir Dhruva Neethir Mathir Mama*" — "Where there is Krishna the Supreme Yogi and where also there is Arjuna bearing his bow, there victory for Truth and justice is assured." This verse assures victory not only when the *Mahabharata Arjuna* wields the bow in the presence of Krishna. Everyone of you can be Arjuna and wield the bow and achieve victory. For the bow is but the symbol of courage and faith, of high resolve and undaunted calibre. And how can you become Arjunas? Arjuna means white, pure,

---

[1] *Sanathana Sarathi*, January 1990, p. 10.

unsullied, without blemish. As soon as you become that and hold the bow (the *Upanishads* declare that the *Pranava* or *Om* is the arrow and God is the target), Krishna is ready with His Presence, for He is everywhere at every moment. There is no need to invite Him or instal Him. He will answer from your very heart.[1]

◊ ◊ ◊ ◊ ◊

One question is often asked. Krishna is the Lord of the universe. He is all–pervading, and yet the same Krishna was responsible for the destruction of forty *lakhs* (one *lakh* = 100,000) of men on the battlefield. Is it violence or non–violence? This is my answer to this question. An individual, let us say, has developed cancer on his back. There are millions of germs in that cancerous boil. Does the doctor pause and ask, "Should I kill so many millions of germs?" Is it not the duty of the doctor to save the life of the patient? Which is of greater importance? Should he protect the life of the patient or should he have consideration for the germs? The doctor comes to the conclusion that these germs are dangerous and kills them and saves the patient's life. In this process, the doctor has taken into consideration quality and not quantity. In the same manner, the world at that time had developed a cancer in the shape of Kauravas. When Krishna found that these Kauravas were like cancer, He became a surgeon, took Arjuna as His assistant and performed the great operation. In that operation, forty *lakhs* of germs were killed.[2]

◊ ◊ ◊ ◊ ◊

Geetha means "song"; Krishna sings at *Brindavan* with the Flute. He sings on the battlefield too; in both places the call is for the Particular to merge with the Infinite, the Universal. For Him, the *Rudhrabhumi*

---

[1] *Sathya Sai Speaks*, Vol. 11, pp. 295–96.

[2] *Summer Showers in Brindavan* (1972), p. 249.

(place of cremation) as well as the *Bhadhrabhumi* (sanctified ground) are the same; they are equally placed for imparting *Upadesh* (spiritual instruction) in the form in which the *bhakta* most likes it, namely, song. And imagine with what concentration Arjuna heard it? His concentration was steady as that of the *gopees* (cowherd girls) who listened to the Message of the Flute in *Brindavan*. He forgot the opposing armies, his own hatreds and enthusiasm for war and he became immersed in the teaching he secured. If you develop that *ekagratha* (one–pointedness) in the Kurukshethra of your own particular "battlefields," you can assuredly also listen to the *Geetha* — the *Bhagavad Geetha* or the *Sai Geetha* or the *Sathya Sai Geetha*, intended for you.

The *Geetha* was spoken to remove the *ajnana sammoha* (the delusion caused by ignorance), and it succeeded in removing it so far as Arjuna was concerned; others like Sanjaya and Dhritharashtra who also heard it did not benefit, because they were still bound by their own particular brand of *ajnana* (ignorance). Dhritharashtra was all the while worried that the battle had not started yet and that his sons' enemies had not been destroyed! So he was not benefitted. Therefore, many read the *Geetha* but few benefit. You must have Arjuna's *Vairagyam* (detachment) and Arjuna's *Ekagratha* (one–pointedness) to derive profit from the *Geetha*. *Nirmala hridhaya* (pure heart) and *Nischala bhava* (firm disposition of mind) are essential.[1]

◊ ◊ ◊ ◊ ◊

It is only when the principle of cohesion and community reigns and resides in the Universe that it can be termed Human. Krishna is the Humanisation of this Universal Eternal. When we picture Him in the midst of the cowherd comrades, sharing and eating His breakfast with them, laughing and joking, playing pranks and spreading joy all around, we feel the pang of kinship, which ultimately lifts us into the

---

[1] *Sathya Sai Speaks*, Vol. 1, pp. 178–79.

beyond. Where this comradeship is evident, there we have a spark of Divine Love. Wherever such thrill is evident, there one has taken a step over the frontiers of our individuality: One step at a time, correct and consolidated — that is the way this pilgrimage should progress.

Arjuna prayed that Krishna should appear to him as a friend and comrade rather than as the Immanent Director, the Transcendent Sovereign, the Innate Substance of all that is, was and will be! He longed for the joy of kinship rather than the Bliss of Mergence. To conceive of the Divine as the inner core and the outer shell of every atom and planet, every speck of dust and every system of nebulae, as well as of oneself is an exercise that overwhelms individuality and so, Ramakrishna Paramahamsa and others have prayed for the role of the adorer, rather than the abolition of roles![1]

◊ ◊ ◊ ◊ ◊

In the body of man, the *Atma* (inner real Self) is the husband and the inclinations are the wives. Every act and word and thought must subserve the needs of the emancipation of the individual, by the recognition of the sovereignty of *Atma*. The Primal, Formless, Absolute wedded Desire and Mind was born. The mind wedded two wives, inner contemplation and outer activity. The first gave birth to five sons, *Sathya, Dharma, Shanti, Prema* and *Ahimsa* (Truth, Virtue, Peace, Love and Non–violence), the five Pandava brothers. Mind was infatuated more with the second wife, and so, she gave birth to a 100, each one with a name indicative of badness and wickedness, the Kauravas. God was on the side of the Pandavas, and they won.[2]

◊ ◊ ◊ ◊ ◊

---

[1] *Sathya Sai Speaks*, Vol. 10, pp. 9–10.

[2] *Sathya Sai Speaks*, Vol. 11, p. 20.

The Pandavas sought from Him only His Grace! The Lord agreed; He came over to their side, alone and unarmed! He held just a whip and drove the horses of Arjuna's chariot! That was all; but, that was all that was needed for victory. The Kauravas were defeated to the uttermost; the Pandavas won the empire and eternal fame.

If God is on your side, you have the world in your hold. This is the lesson driven home by the Hindu scriptures. "Give up all bonds of right and duty, surrender unreservedly to Me; I shall guard you from sin and liberate you from that sad cycle of 'entrances' and 'exits' on the stage of life. You can remain ever in your own Reality of Eternal Calm," the Lord has assured.

Freedom and Light are what man needs more than anything else. He needs them even more than breath. That is why he is miserable when bound and in the dark.[1]

◊ ◊ ◊ ◊ ◊

Krishna moved among men as an ordinary person, and drew them to the observance of His prescriptions by means of His Divine *Prema*. He refrained from parading His Divine Insignia, comprising a Conch, a Wheel, a Mace and a Lotus. He did not wear even a crown. While a boy, He followed the cows into the pastures with just a towel bound round His head. (Here Baba called for a longish towel and wound it round His head to show how Krishna appeared at that time). He said that in those days, as now, there were peacocks in plenty in and around *Brindavan* and *Gokul*, so when He came across a fallen feather, He stuck it between the folds of the towel. It was a moment of rarest and finest delight when Baba stood revealed as the boy *Gopala*, before hundreds of awe–struck and adoring devotees.)

When the Pandavas celebrated the Aswameda and the Rajasuya *yajnas*, Krishna asked for some assignment to be given Him, so that He might be of service. Though He could destroy the entire Kaurava race,

---

[1] *Sathya Sai Speaks*, Vol. 8, p. 128.

He tried His best to instill good sense into them in order to save them. Now, as well as then, the Teaching and the Message are the same: "Know thyself, that is the only way to know Me."

Being associated ardently with all living beings winning their Love through Love, and through a process of correcting their vision and purifying their consciousness, leading them to the realisation of the God which is their core — this is the task before You. Unless the human form is assumed, no one will come near; if the appearance is super–human, people will keep away. So, as the *Sastras* (spiritual sciences) say, *Dhaivam manusha rupena*: "the Divine in human form" has to come to save mankind.

The "five elements" are the products of the Lord's Will, so they obey the Will of Krishna. Whatever Krishna said, came true. In fact the only correct definition of Truth is, "that which Krishna speaks." Believe in that. Be firm in that belief. One day when Krishna went on a stroll with Arjuna, he pointed to a bird perching on the branch of a tree and asked Arjuna, "Do you see that peacock?" Arjuna answered, "Sure, I do." "Oh, Arjuna. It is not a peacock. It is an eagle," said Krishna, and Arjuna promptly agreed that it was an eagle. Then Krishna corrected Himself and pointed to the same bird, said, "I am sorry. It is a dove." Arjuna, too, corrected himself and said, "Yes. I see now it is a dove, all right." Krishna laughed at Arjuna and said, "It is not a dove at all; it is a crow," and Arjuna agreed without demur, "Undoubtedly, it is a crow." Krishna then accused Arjuna of stupidity, because he was blindly agreeing with every observation he made — peacock, eagle, dove or crow. Arjuna replied, "What you say is the Truth for me. You can make a crow a dove, or a peacock an eagle. Why should I differ from that You declare? Your word is the Truth I go by."

You, too, must develop that faith and not be turned away by your egoism or others' cynicism. Develop *viveka* (wisdom) and *vairagya* (detachment) and then your hearts will bloom into fragrant beauty. You have here a picture of Sai standing on a lotus. Sai Krishna will instal Himself in the lotus of your heart. He will be ever with you, as guard and guide, and will shower Grace on you. He will be the

Mother, Father and Preceptor, the nearest kinsman; He will be your All.[1]

◊ ◊ ◊ ◊ ◊

10.

Lord Krishna's Words in the Bhagavad Geetha

The *Geetha* instils this very lesson in you: "Whoever does *upasana* with no thought other than Me, him I shall have with Me; I shall bear his burden now and forever." The *Geetha* says, "Keeping Me ever in memory, engage yourself in the battle of Life."

This "Me" to which Krishna refers is not something outside you or extraneous to you. It is your own Divine Reality which you can cognise in the silence of your own *dhyana* (meditation), when you shut out of your awareness the distraction of the senses, the mind and the ego. You can take refuge in the calm coolness of your heart where He has installed Himself as the Charioteer. You must only engage yourself in work that is purifying, with an attitude that sanctifies.[2]

◊ ◊ ◊ ◊ ◊

This was the first message given to the world by Sri Krishna: "*Those who experience the Truth that the Atma (Spirit) which dwells in all beings is the same as Mine, whether they are full of desires or free from desires, whether they are householders or renunciants, whether they perform*

---

[1] *Sathya Sai Speaks*, Vol. 13, pp. 255–56.

[2] *Sathya Sai Speaks*, Vol. 13, pp. 114–15.

the prescribed duties (Karma) or not, they will abide in Me." This message was given to all mankind five thousand years ago.[1]

◊ ◊ ◊ ◊ ◊

Krishna says in the *Geetha* that He will release you from bondage, the moment you renounce *Sarvadharma* — all feelings of obligation and responsibilities, of rights and duties, of "from me" and "to me"; that is to say, He requires the renunciation of the identity of the individual with the body.

That is the *Dharma*, the Supreme Duty which Krishna had come to teach. Man has a duty to himself — recognising that he is Divine, and nothing else. When he neglects this, and strays into the bypaths, God incarnates and brings him on the right path again.[2]

◊ ◊ ◊ ◊ ◊

11.
The Lord Has no Favourites or Foes

God is not drawn into desire; He has no wants; He is full, free and ever content. He has no aversions or attractions. He has no bonds of kith or kin. One poet has sung, "O *Krishna*! O *Gopala*! I do not count on Your being kind to me, or being moved by my appeals for mercy. Don't I know that You killed with Your own hands Your maternal uncle? You killed the very nurse who came endearingly to You in

---

[1] *Sanathana Sarathi*, October 1994, p. 253.

[2] *Sathya Sai Speaks*, Vol. 9, p. 155.

order to feed You at her breast! With no iota of compassion towards the father of Your dearest devotee, You tortured him and killed him while the son, Prahlada, was looking on! You approached Bali as if for alms, and when he gladly placed all he had at Your Feet, You trampled on his head and pressed him down into the nether regions! How can a heart that has no tenderness, melt at my misery?" Yes! the Lord is above all attachments; He has no favourites or foes. You decide the distance between Him and yourselves. *Moksha* is the stage when *moha* (attachment) attains *kshaya* (extinction). How, then, can the Grantor of *moksha* be Himself abridged by attachment?

God has no will or want. He does not confer or withhold. He is the eternal witness. To put it in the language that you can understand, He is like the postman, who is not concerned with the contents of the letters that He hands over to the addressee; one letter might communicate victory, another, defeat; you receive what you have worked for. Do good and have good in return; be bad and accept the bad that comes back to you. That is the law, and there is really no help or hindrance.[1]

◊ ◊ ◊ ◊ ◊

12.

Lord Krishna's Flute

If you have the capacity to draw the Lord to yourself, He will Himself come to you and be with you. Be like the flute, a hollow reed, straight, light, with no substance to hinder His breath. Then, He will come and pick you up from the ground; He will breathe divine music through you, playing upon you with a delicate touch; He will stick the flute into His sash; He will press his lips on it. In His hand, the infinitesimal will be transmuted into the Infinite, the *anu* (light atom) will be transformed into the *ghana* (heavy solid).

---

[1] *Sathya Sai Speaks*, Vol. 9, p. 90.

One day, Krishna pretended to be fast asleep, with the flute carelessly thrown aside by His side when *Radha* approached the fortunate flute and asked it in plaintive terms, "O lucky Murali!" (flute) Tell me how did you earn this great good fortune. What was the vow you observed, the vigil you kept, the pilgrimage you accomplished? What was the *mantra* you recited, the idol you worshipped?" The Flute got a voice through His grace and said: "I rid myself of all sensual desire, of envy, greed, of ego, that is all. I had no feeling of ego left to obstruct the flow of His *Prema* through Me to all creation."[1]

◊ ◊ ◊ ◊ ◊

In fact, you must each one try to become ego–less and then the Lord will accept you as His Flute. Once, when a number of people were asked by Me what they would like to be in the hands of God, I got various answers: some said the Lotus, some the *Shankha* (Conch), some the *Chakra* (Discus) but no one mentioned the *Murali* (Flute). I would advise you to become the *Murali*, for then the Lord will come to you, pick you up, put you to His lips and breathe through you and, out of the hollowness of your heart due to the utter absence of egoism that you have developed, he will create captivating music for all Creation to enjoy. Be straight without any will of your own, merge your will in the Will of God. Inhale only the breath of God. That is Divine Life, that is what I want you all to achieve.[2]

◊ ◊ ◊ ◊ ◊

To realise the Lord in every being, you must cultivate *Prema* and drive out the bats that infest the dark caverns of your heart, the bats of hate, envy and malice. Let the light of *Prema* illumine your thoughts, your words, your movements, your activities, your

---

[1] *Sathya Sai Speaks*, Vol. 4, p. 175.

[2] *Sathya Sai Speaks*, Vol. 1, p. 25.

judgements. When you become transmuted into *Prema*, the Lord who is *Premaswarupa*, will reveal Himself to you, and play on the Flute, awakening your higher consciousness in the flood of Universal Love.[1]

◊ ◊ ◊ ◊ ◊

Narada once asked Krishna the secret of the attraction that His flute–play had on the cowherds of *Brindavan*. "Do they run to You, or do You run to them?" he queried. "Among us, there is neither I nor they; how can a picture be separated from the cloth on which it is painted? I am imprinted on their hearts so inseparably, so inextricably," Krishna replied. Have God imprinted on your hearts; be ever so inextricably established in Him — that is My message to you this day.[2]

◊ ◊ ◊ ◊ ◊

The *gopikas* were examples of true devotion. Krishna was five years old when He did the Rasakreeda — sporting with the *gopikas*. There is nothing sensuous in this; it is the sacred Atmathatwa which the *gopikas* experienced, that is, oneness with the Divine. They enjoyed the music of Krishna's flute as *Nadabrahman* (the Cosmic Absolute in the form of sound). Krishna gave them the essence of the music of the *Vedas* in His music and talked to them in the language they could understand.[3]

◊ ◊ ◊ ◊ ◊

All actions should be done wholeheartedly. This was exemplified by the total devotion of the *gopikas* to Krishna. They were lost in

---

[1] *Sathya Sai Speaks*, Vol. 4, p. 191.

[2] *Sathya Sai Speaks*, Vol. 8, p. 149.

[3] *Sanathana Sarathi*, July 1995, p. 185.

ecstasy over the melodious music of Krishna's flute. They found in that music the essence of all the *Vedas* and the scriptures. ...

What is the significance of the flute? It symbolises the human body. The flute has nine holes. The human body has nine openings. The body should be considered as the flute of God. It should be rendered completely hollow, so that the Divine may blow through it. Today the body is anything but hollow. It is filled with all kinds of desires. Only when the desires are removed, the body will be a fit instrument for the Divine to fill it will nectarine music. This is the process of surrender to the Divine. Then one gets intoxicated with the music of the Divine.

Pomp and pride have to be given up to experience the Divine. People talk about meditation. But how much of it is concentrated on God? Nor is formal meditation necessary when you realise that the Divine is within you. The purpose of meditation is to recognise one's unity.[1]

◊ ◊ ◊ ◊ ◊

13.
Radha: A Great Devotee of Lord Krishna

The *Radha*-thatwam is a deep, inscrutable one. She was ever in the contemplation of the Lord and His Glory. She too saw the child Krishna as the Divine Manifestation, separate from the human form. Yasoda (step–mother of Lord Krishna) one day was searching for Krishna who had strayed away; she sought almost everywhere and at last, she went to the house of *Radha*. *Radha* just closed her eyes and meditated on Krishna for a while and when she called "Krishna,"

---

[1] *Sanathana Sarathi*, December 1995, p. 321.

Krishna was there. Then, Yasoda shed tears of joy. She said, "I love Krishna as a mother; I have a sense of egoism in me that He is *my* son and that I must save Him from harm and seek to give Him guidance and protection. Your *Prema* is pure; it has no egoism prompting it."[1]

◊ ◊ ◊ ◊ ◊

The *Radha thatwam*, the real nature of *Radha* can be understood only by those who have acquired that deep "distressing" thirst for the Formful Aspect of the Lord, and for the Divine Call that resonates in the heart as the entrancing tune of the Flute.[2]

◊ ◊ ◊ ◊ ◊

Udava, when he came among the *gopees*, discovered that Krishna was roaming in their hearts without a moment's respite. They were seen scanning the dust on the roads to discover a foot–print of Krishna, so that they could fall down and worship it! *Radha* was the greatest devotee of all; she saw all foot–prints as Krishna's own, including even hers! Really, is there any one who is not He? Any Form that is not His? Any Name that does not connote Him? Udava exclaimed, "I have no need of Narayana; I am content with this vision of the Glory of the *Bhakta* (Devotee)." ...[3]

◊ ◊ ◊ ◊ ◊

When you sing of *Radha*, as you did just now, "*Radha Madava Nanda lala!*" do not imagine that *Radha* is a woman and Krishna, a man. You can become *Radha*, now, here, if only you know what *Radha*

---

[1] *Sathya Sai Speaks*, Vol. 3, p. 39.

[2] *Sathya Sai Speaks*, Vol. 6, p. 124.

[3] *Sathya Sai Speaks*, Vol. 2, p. 97.

represents. She is the basis (*adhara*), which is worshipped (*ardh*) as ever–flowing stream (*dhara*); she is the very basis of the world, which is another name for God Himself. Have it as a *dhara* (flowing from your tongue), the Name of the Lord; avoid all lesser talk. On the Ocean of Milk (the *Ksheerasagara*) of the Pure Mind, plant the peak of *Mandara*, steady faith, in the unity of creation; take the serpent, Grace of the Lord (*Iswaranugraham*), and use it as a rope to churn the ocean; churn it through meditation and spiritual discipline (*dhyana* and *sadana*); then, you are able to acquire the Nectar — the essence of *Veda*, of spiritual knowledge, of spiritual experience.[1]

◊ ◊ ◊ ◊ ◊

Ramanuja (the exponent of the *Visishtadvaita* philosophy) derived the meaning of *bhakti* from the name of *Radha* and interpreted it as the continuous flow of love for God. The word *Radha* contains four syllables: *Ra, aa, dh* and *aa*. If you read the word starting from *Ra*, you have *Radha*. Starting from the *aa*, you get the word *Adara*. Starting from *dh*, you get the word *Dhara*. Starting from the second *aa*, you get the word *Arada*. *Adara* means "basis." *Dhara* means "continuous flow." *Arada*, means worship. Thus *Radha* signified for Ramanuja the continuous stream of worship of the Divine.[2]

◊ ◊ ◊ ◊ ◊

When you recite *Radheshyama*, you should dwell on the significance of the Name; the deeper mysteries of the word must be present before the mind's eye: then, *namasmarana* will yield quicker results. *Radha* is not an individual. It symbolises *Dha–ra* meaning Earth or *Prakriti*, the *Jada* (creation). Krishna or Shyama is the Creator, the Active Principle: the *Chit* (awareness), the *Purusha* (Supreme Being).

---

[1] *Sathya Sai Speaks,* Vol. 5, p. 113.

[2] *Sanathana Sarathi*, February 1996, p. 38.

Shakti (Supreme Energy) is *Paramatma*; the *Vyakti* (individual) is the *Jeevatma* (individual soul); the Ocean is *Shakti* and the Wave is the *Jeeva*. All the taste and all the forces and roar of the Wave are derived from the Ocean and they disappear into the Ocean itself. The disappearance of the wave form and the wave-name is called *moksha* (liberation): that is, merging of the wave in the ocean from which it seemed to differ. De-individualisation is in other words, *moksha*.[1]

◊ ◊ ◊ ◊ ◊

Two *gopees* were moving about on the sands of the Yamuna, talking about Krishna and lost in the contemplation of His Sports and His Majesty. Of them, Neeraja had a doubt suddenly arising in her mind! It was a metaphysical conundrum! "When I practise identity with Krishna and feel that I am Krishna, I am afraid that I will lose the thrill of being with Him, conversing with Him and hearing His sweet Voice. I long to be distinct from Him, and to taste the Love and glory that He is." Then, Sarala, her companion, consoled her and said, "No! Your fears are baseless. For, Krishna too is contemplating you and your purity. By the time you are transformed into Krishna on account of the *sadana* of identity, Krishna would have become "you," as a result of His longing for you and so, there need not be any apprehension in your mind or frustration!"

Prakriti is *Dhara* (Earth, Creation). Think of it always. Long for it. Pine for *Dhara*, *Dhara*, *Dhara* and you find you are pining for *Radha*, *Radha*. So, *Radha* is the Becoming and Krishna is the Being; the desire of the Being to become, the longing of the Becomed for the Being — this is the Radha–Krishna relationship, which has been sung by seers and poets, calumnied and caricatured by ignorant critics, appreciated and apprehended by aspirants, analysed and realised by sincere scholars of spiritual lore.[2]

---

[1] *Sathya Sai Speaks*, Vol. 1, p. 167.

[2] *Sathya Sai Speaks*, Vol. 10, p. 62.

◊ ◊ ◊ ◊ ◊

The sweetness of Krishna is filling this Nature or objective world and *Radha* is tasting it and being thrilled by it. Who is *Radha*? She is Nature, the *prakriti*, the *maya shakti* (power of delusion), the *hladini shakti* (power of joy) of Krishna Himself, His *Mahabhava* (Great State). She has stolen and treasured in her heart the *Ananda* of Krishna which manifested as *prakriti* and so, like the owner who roams round and round the house of the thief until he gets back his property, Krishna too is ever around *Radha*'s residence, seeking His *Ananda*.[1]

◊ ◊ ◊ ◊ ◊

Know your Reality and the reality of all beings as revealed to you; that very instant you become *Radha* and since *Radha* is Krishna and Krishna is *Radha*, you enter and merge in the *Krishna–thatwa* (the Krishna Principle), the Divine Truth. Whoever adores Krishna unintermittently, without any other thought or feeling to perturb him, is *Radha*. See with the eyes of Love; hear with the ears of Love; work with the hands of Love; think thoughts of Love; feel Love in every nerve. The God of Love, Krishna, will come to you on the wave of Love and fill your hearts with Himself!

Do not cage Him in a picture–frame; do not confine Him in an idol. He is all forms. His is all names. He is the Reality of all beings. Infect yourselves with madness for Him, instead of for the World. Some one has written a song about Me, saying that I cure madness and confer madness, that I wipe tears and cause tears to flow! Yes; madness for visualising God is any way preferable to the madness after riches and reputation.[2]

◊ ◊ ◊ ◊ ◊

---

[1] *Sathya Sai Speaks*, Vol. 4, p. 174.

[2] *Sathya Sai Speaks*, Vol. 11, p. 208.

The Yamuna bank: calmness ... charm ... inspiration ... thrill. The cool breeze brought soft and sweet strains of Divine music from the Flute of Krishna to the ear. Radha came down from the high sand dune towards the waterline, with a big pot on her hip. Half way through she stopped short, for she heard her name wafted on the wind from where Krishna stood, "Radha, Radha." With eyes wide open she looked on all the four sides. No one was to be seen anywhere. And no habitation around. Krishna was ever thus.

Radha went off in a faint and fell down, the pot still in the fold of her arm. Then she suddenly awoke to the Reality: "There is no place where You are not," she said in her heart, addressing Krishna. "The call surely came from You, none else could be so soft and sweet, so sincere and compelling. But let me ask just for one boon of You. You made us all act our roles; we played our parts as best as we could. You urged us to laugh and to weep, and enjoyed both to Your heart's content. I have had enough. Please, please let me go back to where I belong. I addressed myself in desire and in disappointment, in anger and anticipation, in anxiety and aspiration. I fed myself with sensual thrills — melodious sound, smooth touch, ambrosial taste, bewitching sight, and bewildering fragrance. I had on my ankles the jingle of illusion. I met both the applause and the jeering of the world. When I sang, delusion marked time in accompaniment. The *thamasic* (quality of inertia) and *rajasic* (quality of passion) encouraged me to dance with their background melody. Now my limbs fall. I am sick of the whole affair. May the play end. Please, please agree to this my prayer."

But Krishna did not agree. He approached nearer and nearer. The Lord is a clear mirror wherein the pure heart is reflected clearly. Radha was His image, the embodiment of His ecstasy. Radha was the *Ahladini Shakthi* (Gladdening Power) of Krishna, and so the two were inseparable, indivisible. That is why Krishna called out "Radha, Radha," when she made her appearance on the Yamuna bank.

Radha continued, "This is the best chance for me to lay the gem of my devotion at Thy Feet. Alas, it is still uncut and dull. I was misled for so long into the belief that the world is only sweet, but it is bitter as well. I have had enough. I am, as You know, *prakriti dhara* (uninterrupted flow of objective world), called Radha. So I am burdened with three *gunas* (qualities) the *satwa*, *rajas* and *thamas* (goodness, passionate and dullness). Since *Prakriti* (Nature) is feminine, I, too, perforce am feminine."[1]

◊ ◊ ◊ ◊ ◊

14.

Mira: A Great Devotee of Lord Krishna

The potency of the Divine Name is such that it can convert even poison into nectar. This is illustrated by an episode from the life of Mira. She was a queen. But she was so much absorbed in her devotion to Krishna that she would sing and dance with ecstasy unmindful of whether she was in a palace or in a crowded bazar. Her brother–in–law, who was incensed at such conduct in public places by the queen, was not aware of what true devotion meant. Mira had no body–consciousness at all. A true devotee should be totally free from the sense of "I" and "Mine." Feeling that Mira's conduct was casting a slur on the royal family's prestige and reputation, her brother–in–law decided to do away with her by giving her a cup of milk mixed with poison. Having dedicated herself heart and soul to Krishna, Mira used to take any food only after offering it to Krishna. When she offered the milk given to her to Krishna before drinking it, the Lord accepted all the poison in it and made the entire milk pure. In this way, Mira demonstrated to the world the power of the Lord's name and the greatness of devotion to the Lord.

---

[1] *Sathya Sai Speaks*, Vol. 14, pp. 27-29.

Very few in the world try to find out how the Name emerged, how it is to be pronounced and what is its potency. The authority for the exponent of the glory of the Lord's name is the *Bhagavatam*.[1]

◊ ◊ ◊ ◊ ◊

Mira was a devotee who had completely merged herself in Krishna consciousness. After her marriage, she requested her husband to build a temple for Krishna. The Rana built for her a temple in marble. Mira spent all the time in the temple singing *bhajans* oblivious of the outside world. The Rana, who allowed Mira to carry on her worship of Krishna as agreed to by him before the marriage, got vexed with her complete absorption in Krishna and prohibited her from going to the temple and closed its doors to prevent her from going there. Mira felt: "The Rana may bar me from the temple which he has built. But who can bar me from seeking the Krishna who resides in the temple of my heart?"[2]

◊ ◊ ◊ ◊ ◊

15.

The Gopikas and Lord Krishna

You have heard that when the Divine Cowherd boy played on the flute, the men, women and children and even the cattle of *Brindavan* hurried to Him, as if drawn by the irresistible magic of His music, Divine Melody, that stills all the turbid waves which we name as joy and grief. They left off the work they were engaged in; they had no other thought than the attainment of the Divine presence; the

---

[1] *Sanathana Sarathi*, April 1992, p. 60.

[2] *Sanathana Sarathi*, July 1987, p. 196.

cattle stopped grazing, the calves stopped guzzling milk. The story of Krishna and the *gopees* (cowherd–girls) has a deep inner meaning. *Brindavan* is not a specific place on the map; it is the Universe Itself. All men are cowherds; all animals are cows. Every heart is filled with the longing for the Lord; the flute is the call of the Lord; the sport called *Rasakreeda* (the sportive dance; the dance of Krishna in His boyhood with the cowherdess), where Lord Krishna is described as dancing with the milk–maids in the moonlight — every maid has a boy–Krishna holding her hand in the dance — is the symbol of the yearning and the travail borne by those who aim at reaching His presence. The Lord manifests such Grace that each one of you has the Lord all for yourself; you need not be sad that you won't have Him, when others get Him; nor need you be proud that you have Him and no one else can have him at the same time! The Lord is installed in the altar of your heart.

Offer your entire self, your entire life, to Him; then your adoration will transform and transmute you so fast and completely that you and He can be merged into One. He thinks, feels and acts as you do; you think, feel and act as He does. You will be transformed as a rock is transformed by the sculptor, into an idol, deserving the worship of generations of sincere men. In the process you will have to bear many a hammer stroke, many a chisel–wound, for He is the sculptor. He is but releasing you from petrification! Offer your heart to the Lord, let the rest of you suffer transformation at His hands. Do not defile time, or the physical sheath, or this life's chance, using them for paltry ends.[1]

◊ ◊ ◊ ◊ ◊

The *gopees* (milkmaids) of *Brindavan* were inextricably involved in the *Avatar*. They had Him indelibly imprinted on their hearts. He alone was real; the rest were also He. When *Radha*, the most ardent

---

[1] *Sathya Sai Speaks*, Vol. 8, pp. 243–44.

aspirant among them was in agony at what she wailed about as Separation from Krishna (!), the *gopees*, who gathered around her to turn her mind away from the infatuation, could not use any other words of consolation and comfort than *Govinda! Dhamodhara! Madava!* — words that sent pangs of loss through *Radha's* heart! When the *gopees* brought milk, curds and butter for sale, and peddled them along the streets, they used to shout the names of the ware they had for sale. But the words that emerged were the words that had displaced all else — *Govinda! Damodara! Madava!* — the loving Names of the Krishna they adored! When Akrura, the messenger from the wicked uncle of Krisha, took the Lord away from *Brindavan* with him, the *gopees* hurried across the road to stop him but even in their desperate protest, they could not utter any words except, *Govindha, Dhamodhara, Madava!*

God is the sugar that can make the tasteless drink of life into a sweet potion. Stir the sugar well so that each molecule of the water is saturated with its taste. The *gopees* are your guides in this *sadana*. They had, as you have also, the *Avatar* in their midst and so, their salvation was assured when they achieved purity and acquired faith.[1]

◇ ◇ ◇ ◇ ◇

The *gopikas* had that *chittashuddi* (purity of thought), though inferior minds full of gross desires have fouled the clear springs of their *Prema* with their ignorant comments. Narada too thought that the illiterate milkmaids could not have the highest form of devotion; but, when he offered to teach them, he found them so immersed in God–consciousness that they had no thought other than those of Krishna, no words unrelated to His Glory, no act unconnected with his *seva*. They had surrendered their all to the Lord who ruled them from within themselves.[2]

---

[1] *Sathya Sai Speaks*, Vol. 11, pp. 292–93.

[2] *Sathya Sai Speaks*, Vol. 7, p. 154.

◊ ◊ ◊ ◊ ◊

The *Prema* of the *gopees* towards Krishna was super–physical, the Love of the soul for the Over–soul, of the river for the sea. Persons deep in this type of Love see nothing else, hear nothing else; they behave like mad persons, as the world goes. Their joy when they feel His presence is as supreme as their grief when they feel they are deprived of it. That is why among the songs of the saints, you have *Nindhasthuthi* also; that is to say, songs, which blame Him for being cruel, partial, negligent, etc.![1]

◊ ◊ ◊ ◊ ◊

Man aspires for Bliss (*Ananda*) in the world. Vedanta defines Divine *Ananda* as *yoga*. *Yoga* is usually considered as some form of breathing or physical exercise. This is not the true meaning of *yoga*. *Yoga* means *Ananda* or Bliss. Wherefrom can this Bliss be got? Only from the One who is the embodiment of Bliss. It cannot be got from possessions of any kind or from position or power. Bliss can only be got from God, who is the embodiment of Bliss.

How is this Bliss to be got? Srikanth (a student who had spoken earlier) referred to the single–minded devotion of the *gopikas* and *Radha*. The *gopikas* have been misunderstood and misrepresented by commentators. *Gopikas* symbolise thoughts. *Radha* symbolises the combination of all thoughts in the mind. So, thoughts and the mind should merge in Krishna, represented by *prajna* (in a human being). That is the significance of the *Vedantic* declaration: "*Prajnanam Brahma.*" This *prajnanam* pervades every part of the human body, the mind and the intellect. It is constant integrated awareness. All our thoughts, desires and aspirations should be merged in this *prajna*.

When this *prajna* (constant integrated awareness) is present in all beings as the Divine (as *Brahman*), what is the need, it may be asked,

---

[1] *Sathya Sai Speaks*, Vol. 4, pp. 188–89.

for the descent of the *Avatars*? There are reasons for the advent of the *Avatars*. There are two kinds of perception, *viz.*, *pratyaksham* and *paroksham* (direct and indirect). There are also two kinds of potencies: internal and external. For example, there is fire within a piece of firewood. But this fire is latent and invisible. It is only when the fire latent in it is brought out that it can be used for cooking. Likewise, everybody is like a piece of firewood. The *Atmic* principle is latent within it. To make it manifest, some form of Love has to be practised. Just as you have to strike a match–box against a coating of sulphur on the match–box to produce fire, Love has to merge in Love to experience the Divine.

You may consider that the love within you and that the love represented by God are the same. But there is this difference. God's love is totally selfless. It is absolutely pure. It is eternal. It is flawless. Human love is self–centered and tainted. Such a love cannot merge with God's Love. It is only when one is free from egoism, pride, hatred and envy that God will abide in you. Without renunciation (*thyaga*) if a person is immersed in worldly pleasures and leads a mundane life, all his devotion is only artificial and a kind of self–deception. Such devotion will not lead him to God.

Today the world is full of such persons. People claim that they are loving God. I have not seen a single person who really loves God. Everyone loves God for his own sake and not for the sake of God. This is pure selfishness. Man seeks all things in the world for his own reasons. Even God is sought for such a reason. God cannot be got so easily. The heart has only a single seat. There is room in it for only one person. If you install worldly desires on that chair, how can you expect God to sit on it? God will enter that seat only if you empty it of all other things.

Today in the name of Love (*Prema*) men are playing a game of musical chairs with their hearts. The chair of the heart is being used for occupation by different persons at different times. The *gopikas*, however, dedicated their hearts to one person alone. All their thoughts were centered on Krishna. All their senses were dedicated to the Divine. They spoke only about God. Their thoughts were centered on

God. They listened only to the Divine words. Their hands were engaged in Divine work. All their limbs and senses were dedicated to the Divine. They did not consider anything as their own. Krishna was their all.

(*Bhagavan* then related an episode from the life of Krishna to demonstrate the total devotion of the *gopikas* to the Lord. Once Krishna feigned that he was suffering from a head-ache for which the cure was the application of the dust from the feet of a devotee to His head. Sage Narada sought to collect the dust from Sathyabhama, Rukmini and others, whom he regarded as great devotees of the Lord. But all of them declined to give the dust from their feet because they considered it sinful to offer their dust to be placed on the Lord's head Ultimately Narada went to the *gopikas*, who did not have the slightest hesitation to offer the dust from their feet if only it would give immediate relief to the Lord, regardless of the consequences to themselves.)

Bhagavan said: "The *gopikas* did not consider whether it was right or wrong for them to offer the dust of their feet. They were only concerned with giving relief to their Lord by any means. They declared: 'Our entire life is dedicated to Krishna. His joy is ours.' This was the spirit of oneness with which they offered the dust of their feet. And that very moment Krishna was rid of His ailment. By the time Narada reached Krishna, the Lord was found wreathed in smiles. Krishna told the sage: "You are boasting that you are devotees of the Lord. But none of you has the utterly selfless devotion of the *gopikas*."

Today there are many who claim to be devotees of the Lord and close to the Lord. But few can be described as real devotees of God. In each one there is some element of selfishness in his or her devotion. As long as there is an element of selfishness and egoism, the Lord will take no notice of such "devotees." The Love of the Divine is all the time present. But like the cloud that hides the sun from a person, the selfishness and ego of the devotee comes between God's Love and the devotee.

To proceed from the human condition to the Divine in man, the only means is the Love Principle (*Prematatwa*). All other means are of no avail. (Illustrating from the *Mahabharata* the example of the fate of Karna and the destiny of Arjuna as indicating the difference between one who does not have Divine Grace and another who has the benefit of Divine Grace, *Bhagavan* said that while Karna, who was associated with the wicked Kauravas, met with a tragic end, Arjuna, who was a firm devotee of the Lord, was blessed with victory.) All Indian scriptures and *Puranas* demonstrate the power of the Lord's grace to transform the human to the state of the Divine. Although people have been taking birth after birth because of their attachment to worldly pleasures, they have not been able to get rid of their involvement with worldly concerns. Hence they are unable to experience the Bliss of oneness with the Divine. All the bad thoughts and bad actions which they have experienced in previous lives continue to prevent them from experiencing the Divine. It is only when one gets rid of these impure thoughts that he can experience Divine feelings.

The Love Principle is the essence of the Krishna Principle (*Krishna Tatwam*). It is associated with the Divine. Worldly love cannot be equated with Divine Love (*Prema*). The term *Prema* is used in ordinary parlance to describe what is really worldly attachment. People are attached more to names and forms than to the inner spirit of things. To get over this false attachment to external forms and names, it is essential to cultivate Love in its purest form. There is no greater path to the Divine than this Love. To manifest this Love the first requisite is to get rid of selfishness and self–interest.

Dear students, dear devotees! It is not so easy to experience the Divine. You may imagine that you have comprehended the Divine. But this is a delusion. You are immersed in the affairs of the phenomenal world. This cannot lead you to the Eternal Reality. Only those who are dedicated to the realisation of the Eternal can attain it. This is illustrated by the *gopikas'* total dedication of their life to Krishna. They sought the complete mergence of themselves in the Divine.

People today are totally immersed in worldly concerns and do not devote any attention to the spiritual quest. It is true, involvement in worldly affairs cannot be given up totally. But all such actions can be sanctified by performing them in a spirit of dedication to the Divine. The *Bhagavata* demonstrates how this kind of dedicated life can be led by a devotee. It is not enough if you claim to be a devotee of the Lord. The Lord must recognise you as a devotee. Only then does one's devotion acquire value. Arjuna for a long time felt proud about his closeness to Krishna and about his devotion to Him. It was only towards the end he realised that he had to abide by the words of Krishna and completely surrender to the Lord. He then declared: "I shall carry out your words" ("*Karishe Vachanam Tava*").[1]

◊ ◊ ◊ ◊ ◊

His prattle, His pranks, His innocent tricks were all–conquering. He gave the *gopees* a heap of bother and a heap of joy. That was the *thapas* (penance) for them; the bother was *anugraham* (favour); the joy was *prasadam* (grace). You cannot have only one.[2]

◊ ◊ ◊ ◊ ◊

The *gopikas* (cowherdesses) exemplified such deep devotion in their love for the Lord. They offered all they had in the service of the Lord and performed every act as an offering to the Divine. The term *gopee* is derived from the word *gup*. The term *go* means the *Vedas*. It has another meaning, "the earth." It also refers to the cow. The *gopikas* used to chant the *Vedas*. They protected the cows. They sanctified the earth. Not understanding this sublime aspect of their nature, people have misrepresented them in various ways, regarding them as ordinary women. Even their devotion was misconstrued because of the failure to understand the true nature of their love for the Lord. On

---

[1] *Sanathana Sarathi*, September 1992, pp. 216-28.

[2] *Sathya Sai Speaks*, Vol. 4, p. 244.

account of their narrow–mindedness, these critics could not grasp the deep significance of the *gopikas'* devotion.[1]

◊ ◊ ◊ ◊ ◊

You must develop the devotion of the *gopees*, of *Radha*, of Udava, of Hanuman. Ramakrishna Paramahamsa did intense *sadana*, transmitting himself into the attitude of Hanuman and even his physical attributes changed to suit the role. He developed a small tail during the period; such is the tremendous power of mind over body. Many husbands and mothers–in–law tried to scare away the *gopees* from Krishna by spreading scandals about Him but how can any one keep the *Jeeva* (individual soul) and the *Jagadeeswara* (Lord of the Universe) apart? *Vyasa*, the great saint, says that words are inadequate to describe the intensity of that devotion, the devotion of the *gopees* to the Lord. They had no egoism left in them and that is why they became the supreme devotees of the Lord.[2]

◊ ◊ ◊ ◊ ◊

Narada asked Vishnu once: "*The Rishis* (sages) who had attained the purest Wisdom relating to the Universal *Atma* could not win Your Grace; but, the illiterate milkmaids of Gokul who were charmed by Your beauty, Your sport, Your music, Your prattle, Your sweetness, Your inscrutable mystery — they won Your Grace. How did this happen?"

Narada himself came to know later that the *gopees* had Krishna (the Lord) as the very breath of their lives, as the very sight of their eyes, the very sound of their ears, the very taste of their tongues, the very touch of their skin. While tending the cows and calves, attending to their husbands and children, doing the thousand and one chores of

---

Sanathana Sarathi, September 1993, p. 226.

[2] *Sathya Sai Speaks*, Vol. 4, p. 143.

worldly life, they lived in Krishna, with Krishna and by means of Krishna only. *Sarvada sarva kaleshu sarvathra Hari chinthanam* –"Under all conditions, at all times, in all places, their minds dwelt on Hari (Krishna; the Lord)." How then can God deny them Grace?[1]

◊ ◊ ◊ ◊ ◊

The *gopees* had that one–pointed *Prema*, unwavering, clear, pure. The relationship between the *gopees* and Krishna as depicted in the *Bhagavata* has been unfortunately judged by persons who have not regulated and controlled their vrittis. This subject is beyond the comprehension of such people. Only Brahmacharins of the most ardent and ascetic type like Shukamaharshi who described it to Parikshit and in recent years, Ramakrishna Paramahamsa, can appreciate that relationship and pronounce upon its uniqueness. All the rest are apt to see in it only the reflection of their own failings and their own feelings. The language of *samsar* (worldly life) is the only language they know; the regions of *thuriya*, beyond the regions of wakefulness, dream and deep sleep, to which those experiences relate are not within their reach. So, they drag the subject down to their own level and claim that they have mastered their mystery.

As a matter of fact, the inner eye, the inner senses are needed to grasp the meaning of this relationship. Oruganty has shown that it has eluded the grasp of most interpreters, for it is closely allied to the *advaitic* (one without a second) experience of *Nirvikalpa* (formless light) *Samadhi* itself. The mind has to be the master, not the slave, of the senses, if the interpretation has to be just. Thoughts, wishes, deeds and feelings — all have to be purified of the desire for gain: *Ahamkara* (ego) itself must lose all its hold on the interpreter, as it did on the *gopees*. *Prema* towards the Lord such as the *gopees* had, should make a man strong, not weak. In fact, the *gopees* were not weakened by their Love; they were rendered tough. ...

---

[1] *Sathya Sai Speaks*, Vol. 8, pp. 146–47.

And then who are these *gopees*, according to the *Bhagavata* itself? They are the gods who wanted to share in the glory of the *Avatar* and who came down to the world as witnesses and sharers in the Divine *Leela*. They came for a purpose; they are not ordinary village folk, who could be dismissed as a crowd of voluptuous women. They saw in every gesture and gait, every word and phrase of Krishna the Divine, not the human at all. They had no occasion or chance to be agitated by a secular vritti; all vrittis were awakened by Divine promptings and urges. Like the magnifying glass which catches the rays of the sun and directs them all to one spot, thus concentrating the heat on one point and helping it to ignite, the hearts of the *gopees* collected all the Vrittis and concentrated them and caused the illumination and the flame. The flame burnt all dross; the illumination revealed the Truth. All other interpretations are to be laid at the door of either ignorance or scholasticism, the pompous pride of mere book learning, which scorns the exercise of discipline.[1]

◊ ◊ ◊ ◊ ◊

Love (*Prema*) is nectarine in its sweetness. Love for the Lord (*bhakti*) was the highest expression of devotion among the *gopikas* (the cowherdesses of *Gokulam*) because they were saturated with the sweetness of Divine Love. They did not seek liberation or higher knowledge. The ecstasy they derived from merely seeking Krishna, they did not get from any other source. Narada coined the phrase, *Parama Bhakti* (Supreme Devotion) to describe the devotion of the *gopikas*. These supreme devotees regarded the Lord as their companion and most precious treasure. So intense was their devotion that they used to go about as highly intoxicated persons who were unmindful of the world. Leaving their homes, on hearing the music of Krishna's flute, they rushed to the forest in search of Krishna, oblivious to everything. The *gopikas* realised that supreme wisdom (*Jnana*)

---

[1] *Sathya Sai Speaks*, Vol. 3, pp. 39–40.

consisted in experiencing oneness with the Divine and that all other knowledge was only mundane and related to the physical. Krishna was everything for them. In their feeling of oneness with the Divine, they made no distinction between the animate and the inanimate.[1]

◊ ◊ ◊ ◊ ◊

The *gopikas* experienced the presence of Krishna in everything. What joy can be had when God's omnipresence is experienced can be known only to those who have had the experience. Many have treated the *gopikas* as deluded simpletons carried away by their own fancies. This is a grievous mistake. Their hearts were pure and filled with selfless Love. Mundane Love believes only in receiving and not in giving. God's Love revels in giving and not receiving. This is the difference between worldly Love and Divine Love. The *gopikas* were able to experience the Divine by pure .selfless Love. For them there was no difference between Krishna's words, Krishna's music and Krishna's form.

The body had been described as a temple. But when does it become a temple? Only when it is filled with thoughts of God. When there is no thought of God, it becomes a mere dwelling place (*bhavanam*) and in due course becomes a jungle (*vanam*). There is no need to go elsewhere in quest of a temple. When the name of the Lord dances on your tongue, your body itself becomes a temple. Once you regard your body as a temple, you will have to keep it pure and unpolluted to be worthy of God's residence.

This is precisely how the *gopikas* considered themselves. They were totally indifferent to gold and other worldly goods. For them God was everything. They were totally immersed in Krishna Consciousness and were oblivious to everything else. They were aware that Krishna was the omnipresent Divine. But still they were devoted to the particular form of Krishna. This is true of other devotees of God.

---

[1] *Sanathana Sarathi*, September 1990, p. 226.

Mira adored the Lord as *Giridhara Gopala*. Sakkuba worshipped the Lord as "*Ranga! Panduranga!*" and was devoted to that particular name and form. Other than *Gopala* Yasoda was not interested in any other appellation of Krishna. That name alone was sweet and dear to hear. Likewise, the *gopikas*, though they knew that Krishna was the omnipresent Lord, adored Him only in the form of the flute-playing Krishna. The *gopikas* alone fully understood the Krishna Principle because of their intense and unqualified faith in His Divinity.[1]

◊ ◊ ◊ ◊ ◊

However, the *gopees* are a class of devotees by themselves. They reached the highest peak of devotion. They had no consciousness of anything other than the Lord; they had renounced the consciousness of the senses and the body. They were attached only to the Principle of Krishna that was resident in that body. They were eager to know the "other," not to experience "this." When King Parikshit asked Sage Shuka, who was relating to him the wonderful tale of the *gopees* and their Love towards Krishna, about the nature of that Love, Shuka replied that since they had no body-consciousness they were always immersed in God-consciousness only; therefore there was no touch of the gross or material with the body and the slavery to the senses that it breeds that cause all the cruelty, injustice and violence that stalk the world. ...

The *gopees* knew the secret of spiritual surrender. Their worship was not tainted by any bargaining spirit. For those who bargain and crave for profit, reverence is equated with the returns; they sell homage at so much per unit of satisfactory response. They are like paid servants, clamouring for wages, overtime allowance, bonus, etc. They calculate how much they are able to extract for the service rendered. Be, on the other hand, a member of the family, a kinsman, a friend. Feel that you are the Lord's own. Then, the work will not

---

[1] *Sanathana Sarathi*, September 1989, p. 230.

tire; it will be done much better; it will yield more satisfaction; and, the wages? The master will maintain you in bliss. What more can any one aspire for? Leave the rest to Him; He knows best; He is All; the joy of having Him is enough reward. This is the secret of human happiness. Live out your lives on these lines and you will never come to grief. *Na me bhaktah pranashyathi*, says Krishna — "My devotees never suffer sorrow."[1]

◊ ◊ ◊ ◊ ◊

The *Bhagavata* shows how the Lord responds to the yearning of the devotees and assuages their anguish caused by separation from the Lord. When Krishna left for *Mathura*, the *gopees* (cowherdesses) were languishing in grief, unable to bear the separation. They were all the time looking towards *Mathura* to see when Krishna would return. One day, they espied a cloud of dust and imagined that Krishna had at last relented and was returning to *Gokulam*. They saw a chariot and a man seated in it. The chariot stopped but there was no Krishna in it. With their hearts given over to the Supreme Lord, the *gopees* were not inclined even to look at the strange visitor, who was none other than Krishna's very dear friend, Udava. Krishna, who was aware of the agony the *gopikas* were experiencing, had sent Udava to offer them solace and to cheer them up.

The moment Udava got down from the chariot, he started delivering a long exhortation to the *gopikas*. "Oh ye *gopikas*! You are ignorant of the *Sastras*. You have no wisdom. Like silly, dumb persons, you are pining for Krishna. If you know the *Sastras*, you will realise that Krishna is ever with you. He resides in your hearts. Instead of taking delight in the Krishna that dwells within you, you are pining for the physical form of Krishna. This is due to your ignorance. I shall teach you the science of *Yoga* for which Krishna has sent me."

---

[1] *Sathya Sai Speaks*, Vol. 5, pp. 205–206.

The *gopikas* did not consider it proper to speak directly to a stranger. They adopted the device of addressing a bee to give their reply to Udava. The *gopees* said: "Oh bee! These words (of Udava) are adding fuel to the fire that is burning in us because of separation from Krishna. Enough of these words." Udava then held out to the *gopikas* the letter Krishna had sent to them and said: "Here is Krishna's message to you. At least read that." One *gopee* immediately said: "Oh bee! We are illiterate village folk. We are stricken with grief. Show us Krishna." Another *gopee* wailed: "We are being burnt by the fire of agony caused by Krishna's absence. If we touch His letter, it may be burnt to ashes. We dare not touch it." Yet another *gopee* said: "The tears from our eyes will stain the pearl–like letters in Krishna's epistle. We cannot endure seeing His message."

Udava then said: "At least listen to my message. I shall teach you knowledge of *yoga*." A *gopika* answered, addressing the bee, unable to control her grief: "Oh bee, we have only one mind and that has gone with Krishna to *Mathura*. If we had four minds, we could turn one to *yoga*, another to some other subject, and so on. But the only mind we had has been surrendered to Krishna. We have no room for any *yoga* lessons." Udava was stupefied when he realised their single–minded devotion to Krishna.

The essence of all the *Vedas* and *Sastras* (ancient sacred scriptures) is single–mindedness. This single–mindedness results in one–pointed devotion to God. Udava reflected within himself that he had not cultivated the single–minded devotion which the *gopees* had demonstrated. He decided to return to Krishna.

Among the *gopees*, the foremost devotees of Krishna were *Radha* and Jeeraja. Before Udava left, he heard them address Krishna as the Rama–parrot and pleaded for a vision of Krishna to assuage their grief–stricken hearts. Udava asked *Radha*, who was lying unconscious on a sand–dune, whether she had any message for Krishna. Recovering her senses, *Radha* thought only of Krishna. She cried:

Were you a tree, growing upwards,
I would cling to you like a creeper;
Were you a blossoming flower

I would hover over you like a bee;
Were you the mountain Meru
I would cascade like a river;
Were you the boundless sky,
I would be in you like a star;
Were you the bottomless deep
I would merge in you like a river;
Where are you, Oh Krishna?
Whither have you gone, Krishna!
Have you no pity, Krishna! Krishna!

On seeing *Radha* in this piteous state, Udava's heart melted. He realised that Krishna had sent him on this mission to the *gopees* to make him learn what is true *bhakti*. (devotion). Udava realised that Krishna had enacted that episode to show to him that even those well versed in the *Sastras* had to learn the inner Truth about true devotion from the one–pointed, unalloyed devotion shown by the *gopees* towards Krishna. Love of God is the means and the goal. This was the secret revealed by the *gopees*. They saw Love in everything — in the music of Krishna's flute, which filled the world with Love and flooded the parched earth with Love.

The Divine is in every one. But to realise it, there is only one way. It is to cultivate intense Love of God. Only that day when one strives to develop such Love for God is the day of Krishna's birth. Krishna is not born on every *Gokulashtami* day. Krishna is born in us when we try to develop Divine Love as the means to overcome our bonds. To live up to the teachings of Krishna is the true way to celebrate His birthday.[1]

◊ ◊ ◊ ◊ ◊

For the *gopees* and *Gopalakas* (cowherd girls and boys), Krishna was the heart. That is how they appear to us in the *Bhagavata*. They

---

[1] *Sathya Sai Speaks*, Vol. 16, pp. 126–29.

revered Krishna as their *Pathi*, Master, Lord; for, really speaking, the Lord is the only *Purusha* (true strong personality). All the rest are *A–balas*, feminine, weak, the weaker sex. Even the most heroic of men moan and weep while in distress; in silence and solitude. They have moments of helplessness, as much as the others. When they are irresolute and haunted by doubts, they resort to prayer and supplication; they too are weak. It is only the Lord who can be said to be strong under all circumstances, impregnable, imparting strength to all. So, when you read about the *Prema* of the *gopees*, remember that all beings are "feminine" and the Lord alone is the *Purusha*. It is only through *Prema* that God can be persuaded to reveal Himself and *jnana* earned.

Now I must stop; because these devotees from Bangalore have put up a floral *jhoola* (swing) and they are insisting that I should sit in it and swing. I do not appreciate this. How happy I would be to swing in the *jhoola* of your hearts! In the *jhoola* of *Omkara*, to swing to the tune of *Tat–thwam–asi* (that thou art) rising from the hearts of living beings from all the seven worlds — how magnificent that would be! You sit on the *jhoola* set up in your hearts, not *Madava* (God) but *manas*! That is why mankind is denied peace and joy.[1]

◊ ◊ ◊ ◊ ◊

The Love of the *gopees* (milk–maids of Dwaraka) about which so much philosophical speculation and analysis was made before you is, let Me tell you, *Sahaja Prema* — the genuine *Prema* that is beyond physical awareness, that is unaffected by praise or blame. It is not like the thin filament of oil floating on water, which comes off on the finger when it is touched. It is like the lotus stalk, which penetrates deep down through all the layers of water into the soil underneath; but the leaf floats above, unaffected by the water which gives it the essential environment. Man should struggle similarly to rise above the

---

[1] *Sathya Sai Speaks*, Vol. 6, p. 182.

sensory world which is his inevitable environment; the sensory world tempts you to strive for this triviality and that, but like the *gopees*, you should discard the hankering and fix your eye on the vitally precious fountain of joy. The *gopees* had no other goal, no other ideal, no other wish. It was surrender of the self — complete unquestioned.[1]

◊ ◊ ◊ ◊ ◊

Every *gopi* had the highest type of *bhakti* in her heart. They saw only Krishna wherever they turned; they wore on their foreheads blue *kumkum*, in order to remind themselves of Krishna. There were many husbands who protested against the colour of the *kumkum*, but they dared not wipe it off, lest harm should befall them and the sacrilege recoil on them alone. (Here Baba who had filled his hand with petals of Mallika flowers pulled apart by Him from garlands given to Him, showered the petals from one palm to another and they fell in a cascade of blue gems.) Even the gems they preferred were of this type, blue, like Krishna. (He showed the astounded gathering the gems He was referring to. Each gem had Krishna's form in it, beautifully clear.)

There was Neeraja, for example. She was warned against the stratagems of Krishna, when she came to *Brindavan* from a distant village as the bride of a *gopi*. In spite of all warnings, however, she saw Krishna during the *Govardhanagiri* Festival and when she saw Him, she surrendered her heart to the Lord. She passed through great ordeals on account of this spiritual attachment, but she bore it all with courage. She had seen Krishna first at the foot of the *Govardhana* Hill, playing sweetly on the Flute. So, she used to go often to that bower where she first saw Him, to inhale the holy air. Years passed thus; she was the foremost among those *gopees* who tried to curb the horses that drew Akrura's chariot with Krishna in it, away from *Brindavan* to *Mathura*. She suffered silently the separation for years and years, until one day when she was exhausted with the agony and wellnigh spent,

[1] *Sathya Sai Speaks*, Vol. 2, pp. 282–83.

Krishna appeared before her in the self–same bower, where she was. He fondled the *gopi* and consoled her. She had one request to make, however: she longed to hear the Divine Flute, before she died on Krishna's lap. The Lord said, "I have not brought it," but, just to grant her the boon, he broke a length of reed from the bower, made it in a trice into a Flute and played on it a tune that melted Neeraja's heart into tears, which washed her soul away. She passed into the *Krishnathatwa*, the moment the song ended. And, Krishna, too gave up the Flute that He had resumed for her sake. The bower came to be called Vamsikunj, in memory of the Flute that it gave birth to, and which it heard so often.[1]

◊ ◊ ◊ ◊ ◊

The *gopees* were so filled with the highest type of Love that they saw and experienced the Krishna Principle in every speck of dust and every blade of green that they saw. Love of Krishna makes the whole world Krishna. The denial of everything else is the method of visualising Krishna in all. There is only One, the integer I. When it is repeated once again, we have two. The manifold creation is only He and He and He, repeated so often. Dust and blade, drop and spot — each is He, He, and He alone. And you are no exception; you are also He. The realization of this Truth, this identity, this mergence — this is Self–realization.[2]

◊ ◊ ◊ ◊ ◊

The *gopees*, the simple sincere cowherd maids of *Gokula*, sought Krishna within or behind every bush and bower, for He was fascinating them, but ever keeping Himself away! This is only another way of describing the search for the God that we know to be within

---

[1] *Sathya Sai Speaks*, Vol. 3, pp. 42–43.

[2] *Sathya Sai Speaks*, Vol. 7, pp. 473–74.

us, who eludes our efforts to sink into that sweetness. Krishna is hiding in the recesses of your hearts; you have to trace Him there and hold fast. He runs away, but leaves footprints marked by the spilt milk on which He has trodden, in His hurry to be beyond our reach. Yes, the lesson is: recognise His Footprints in everything of beauty, every act of goodness, every tear of gratitude, every sigh of compassion, and discover Him in the bower of your own heart, filled with the fragrance of Love and Light of Virtue.[1]

◊ ◊ ◊ ◊ ◊

The *gopikas* prayed to Krishna that He should never leave their hearts into which they had installed Him. Mira also sang in the same strain. "I dived deep into the ocean and found a pearl. Will You let me slip it out of my hand?" (Swami sang the song in Tamil).

Samsara (worldly life) is a vast ocean. Desires are like the waves. Our feelings constitute the depth of the ocean. In this deep there are crocodiles, whales and sharks in the form of attachments and hatred. It is not easy for ordinary beings to cross this ocean. The *gopikas* declared that only with the help of the Divine name can people save themselves.

People tend to look upon the devotion of the *gopikas* in worldly terms. Their minds never turned towards any sensory objects. They were completely free from sensual desires. All their desires were concentrated on God. They viewed the entire universe as the manifestation of God.

The *gopikas* did not concern themselves with the question whether the Divine was attributeless or full of attributes. They preferred to worship the Divine in the form of Krishna and they wanted their forms to merge in the Divine. "Thereby we shall be formless," they declared.

---

[1] *Sathya Sai Speaks*, Vol. 9, p. 89.

It is when we forget our form that we can merge in the Formless. The Divine cannot be experienced through *dhyana* (meditation) or *japa* (reciting the Lord's name). This is a delusion. These practices may give momentary peace of mind. To experience permanent joy and the Knowledge of the Spirit you have to develop your Divine nature. For this, the environment also must be congenial. Such an environment can be secured only in a place with pure and Divine vibrations. This was the reason why the ancient sages sought the solitude of the forests for their penance in divinely charged atmosphere. They betook themselves to the forests because they felt that the happenings in the villages were not conducive to mental purity. This is a sign of weakness. It is not necessary to go to a forest if you can concentrate on the Divine *Atma* dwelling in the heart. The forest is remote. Here you have "for rest" your heart. The key to inner peace is within you and not outside. In the atmosphere of a sacred Divine Presence, you can promote more effectively your quest for peace.[1]

◊ ◊ ◊ ◊ ◊

16.
Lord Krishna and Yasoda (His Step-Mother)

Krishna, the Lord, was fostered by Yasoda, but, she did not know where He was born! He was loved and treated as if He were her own son; that is to say, her Love was pure and unaffected by selfish considerations. The parable is to be understood thus: Born in the region of the navel, the Divine vitality was later preserved and

---

[1] *Sanathana Sarathi*, September 1990, pp. 228–29.

developed on the tongue (in *Gokula*, by Nanda and Yasoda), by constant repetition of the Name.[1]

◊ ◊ ◊ ◊ ◊

Vatsalya Bhakti advises the *sadaka* (devotee) to adopt the relationship of a mother to her child. The example held before the aspirant is that of Yashoda and her adoration of the child Krishna. She recognised only this one relationship, though others praised Krishna as *Madhurapuri–nivasa* (He who lives in the city of Madhura) and worshipped Him as *Gopeehridaya–vasi* (He who is installed in the hearts of the *gopees*). When *Udava* came from Madhura, Yashoda enquired about her *Gopala*. "I do not know the Krishna who lives in Madhura or in the hearts of *gopees*. I am asking you about my child *Gopala*" she insisted. Thus, the *Vatsalya Bhakti* too leads to a certain amount of exclusiveness.[2]

◊ ◊ ◊ ◊ ◊

Yashoda reached the place where the child Krishna had hidden himself, by following the footprints He had left behind Him, with His curd–besmeared feet. He could not be caught when she attempted to tie a rope round His waist and drag Him to herself. That rope was the rope of ego; how can the Lord be bound by your ego? It was found to be always short, two finger breadths short, every time! What does that indicate? It means that there were two virtues short — and that explains why every rope, however long, was too short. The two virtues were: *Dharmanishta* and *Brahmanishta*, steadiness in rectitude and in aspiration. It is enough if you seek Him, through one–pointed attention and devotion, through His footprints: beauty, strength,

---

[1] *Sathya Sai Speaks*, Vol. 9, p. 129.

[2] *Sathya Sai Speaks*, Vol. 15, p. 231.

Truth, morality, Love, sacrifice, goodness in Nature and in the heart of Man.[1]

◊ ◊ ◊ ◊ ◊

There is a stanza about the child Krishna overturning the pot of curds and running away with the ball of butter and Yashoda the mother discovering His hiding place, by means of the footprints impressed on the floor by the curd–smeared soles.

The butter the Lord covets is the fruit of *yoga*, the final product of the churning of the mind by *viveka*. He loves to feast upon it; and He moves away with it into the solitude of self–realisation. We too can discover the Lord through His Footprints, which can be discovered everywhere, provided sincere search is made with trained eyes. You can find the footprints wherever there is Beauty, Virtue, Humility, Justice, Truth, Love and Peace.[2]

◊ ◊ ◊ ◊ ◊

Yashoda traces Krishna to the place He hides in, by the footprints He leaves, when He has broken the curd–pot, which she was churning. This is the symbolic story to illustrate how the Lord breaks our identification with the body and leads us on to Himself, by signs and signals that He provides all round us. These signs are ever present in the Nature around each one of us, in the beauty of the rising Sun, the ecstasy of the rainbow, the melody of the birds, the lotus–spangled surfaces of lakes, the silence of snowcrowned peaks — in fact, since God is *Rasa* (sweetness, ecstasy), all Nature which is but Himself in action is sweet and ecstatic.[3]

---

[1] *Sathya Sai Speaks*, Vol. 5, p. 19.

[2] *Sathya Sai Speaks*, Vol. 6, p. 183.

[3] *Sathya Sai Speaks*, Vol. 8, p. 144.

◊ ◊ ◊ ◊ ◊

When Balaram told Yasoda that he had found Krishna eating mud, Yasoda questioned Him about it. In reply, Krishna said: "Oh mother, am I a child, a miscreant or a madcap to eat mud? See for yourself whether there is any mud in my mouth." And when He opened His mouth, Yasoda was awe-struck to see the fourteen worlds of the Cosmos in that Divine mouth. She could not believe her eyes and exclaimed: "Is this a dream? Or is it the *maya* of Vishnu? Is it an illusion produced by someone? Is it true? Am I Yasoda or someone else? I am totally bewildered.

Yasoda had no faith in herself and hence could not recognise Krishna's Divinity. Confidence in one's self is the prerequisite for the recognition of Divinity. The reason in Yasoda's case is that she always looked upon Krishna as her son and the maternal attachment clouded her understanding.[1]

◊ ◊ ◊ ◊ ◊

17.

Lord Krishna Steals Butter and Breaks Butter Pots

The *Bhagavata* says that Krishna was stealthily eating the butter that was stored in the houses of the *gopees*. What is the significance of this behaviour? Did he go about stealing butter because he had no butter at home? It is not butter that he coveted; it is the cream of virtue kept in the (heart) pot that he wants. That cream is the genuine *Atma*, secured after vigorous churning. And, was it "stealing" that he did? He is "*Hari*," He who robs, who appropriates. He sees all, Himself

---

[1] *Sanathana Sarathi*, September 1990, p. 230.

unseen. As soon as He enters, you awake, your inner consciousness is alerted. You offer Him the fragrance of your virtue, the courage of your heart, the wisdom of your experience. That is the kind of thief He is! Cultivate Love towards Him. Likes and dislikes are more the products of habit and training. The senses drag you away from Him; but, do not yield; they will lie low soon. Sincere yearning born of steady determination — this alone can help you....[1]

◊ ◊ ◊ ◊ ◊

This *Bhagavta* is so called because it deals with the *Leela, Mahima* and *Upadesha* (divine sport, greatness and instruction) of the Lord, as manifested during His various appearances in history. The career of the Lord, whenever He appears, is made up of two strands, one earthly and the other Divine — one external and the other, inner. You heard just now of the breaking of butter pots by the infant Krishna. The outer meaning is that the child broke the mud pots wherein the milkmaids of *Brindavan* kept the butter they had prepared. The inner meaning is that Krishna broke the material casement in which their souls were imprisoned and liberated them from temporary attachments. He then appropriated to Himself what always belonged to Him — the butter of Faith. This butter is the result of the churning of the mind, the spiritual discipline of self–purification.[2]

◊ ◊ ◊ ◊ ◊

The Name is redolent with Divine Glory; so when it is turned over in the mind it transmutes it into an instrument for liberation from delusion. Take the name, *Navaneethachora* (Butter–thief) that is used for Krishna. It does not mean a person who runs away with the butter that people have stored. It is not the stuff called butter, that is got by

[1] *Sathya Sai Speaks*, Vol. 5, p. 23.

[2] *Sathya Sai Speaks*, Vol. 5, p. 16.

churning curdled milk, that He stole. It is the butter of Faith, won by the churning process called "yearning," from the curdled milk called, "worldly experiences." He covets only this "butter." When Yasodha chided the child Krishna for this "theft," He replied, "But Mother, they like me for stealing it; they are sorry if I do not; they churn it."[1]

◊ ◊ ◊ ◊ ◊

Krishna is slandered by ignorant, prejudiced critics as *"jara"* and *"chora"* and extolled by seekers and sages with the same appellations, *jara* and *chora!* He stole the hearts and the owners were glad of it; he shed light, awakened people and made those whose hearts He stole, richer and happier. He destroyed all craving for sensual pleasure and sensual knowledge and filled the entire being with thoughts of the Divine; how then can He be referred to as *"jara"* and *"chora"*? When the blind lead the blind in this, both have to fall into the pit![2]

◊ ◊ ◊ ◊ ◊

Krishna is condemned as a thief who stole butter from the cowherd maidens; but, the butter represents the *bhakti* of the heart that is got after the process of churning. It is a question of a symbol being taken as literally true. He is *Chittachor*, the stealer of hearts. The thief steals at night, in the darkness, without awakening the master; but, when this thief steals, the master awakens; He wakes him and tells him that He has- come. The victim is left supremely happy and satisfied.[3]

◊ ◊ ◊ ◊ ◊

[1] *Sathya Sai Speaks*, Vol. 7, p. 139.

[2] *Sathya Sai Speaks*, Vol. 8, p. 168.

[3] *Sathya Sai Speaks*, Vol. 3, p. 41.

18.

Gokula, Madhura, Brindavan and Dwaraka

The *Avatar* (Incarnation) in the Krishna Form has vast mysteries enshrined in it. *Brindavan* (the forest of *Brinda*) is the tangled jungle of life. The cows tended by Lord Krishna in *Brindavan* are none other than the humans that are helpless without His care and guidance. *Gokula* (the herds of cows) is the name given in the *Bhagavatam* (Story of the Glory of the Lord) to the region where Krishna tended the cows. "*Go*" means also the individual who is enclosed in the body. So, *Gokula* is the region inhabited by man.[1]

◊ ◊ ◊ ◊ ◊

When you say that Krishna was born in *Gokula*, that He grew up in *Brindavan*, that He ruled over *Mathura* and that He later reigned at *Dwaraka*, what do those statements signify? The *manas* (mind) is the *Gokula* where He was born (where He is born even now to whoever takes the spiritual path); the heart is the *Brindavan* where He grows, where *Prema* (Divine Love) for Him develops; the *Chit* is the *Mathura* which He rules over and the *Nirvikalpa* stage is *Dwararka* where He installs Himself, as the reigning monarch. Make the *Krishna–thrishna* (thirst for Krishna) grow through these stages and you will be saving yourself! You will be joining the ranks of *Radha, Meera* and *Sakkubhai* (devotees of Lord Krishna).[2]

---

[1] *Sathya Sai Speaks*, Vol. 9, pp. 88–89.

[2] *Sathya Sai Speaks*, Vol. 4, p. 128.

◊ ◊ ◊ ◊ ◊

The Krishna whose advent you should celebrate is not the cowherd boy who charmed the village folk with His flute, but the Krishna, the indefinable, inscrutable, Divine Principle, that is born in the navel of the body (*Mathura*) as the product of the Divine Energy (*Devaki*), that is then transported to the mouth (*Gokulam*) and fostered by the tongue (*Yashoda*) as its source of sweetness. Krishna is the visualisation of the *Atma*, that the repetition of the Name grants; the Vision that was gained by *Yashoda*. You must foster that Krishna on your tongue; when He dances on it, the poison of the tongue will be ejected completely, without harming any one as happened when as a child He danced on the hoods of the serpent *Kalinga*.[1]

◊ ◊ ◊ ◊ ◊

Krishna is said to have been born in *Gokula*, He grew up in *Brindavan*, He proceeded to *Mathura* and He established His home finally at *Dwaraka*. The significance of this to the *sadaka* is, "Let Krishna be born in the *Gokula* of your Mind; let Him grow and play prankishly in the *Brindavan* of your Heart; let Him then be fixed in the *Chitta* (inner mind) of *Mathura*; and, finally, let Him rule over the agitationless Consciousness as the Lord and Master of *Dwaraka*." The *Nirvikalpa Anandam* is the final result of His Kingdom established at *Dwaraka*, in the centre of the waves.

Krishna will get born in the mind of man only when three prerequisites are attended to: Make the mind (*manas*), *bhaktimaya* (saturated with *bhakti*). Make the intellect (*buddhi*), full of *jnana deepthi* (illumination of His glory). Make the body (*deha*), the instrument for *Sath–Dharmacharana* (practice of *Dharma*, of moral virtues). *Bhakti* is the Raja; *Jnana* and *Vairagya* are the two Aides–de–camp of this monarch.

---

[1] *Sathya Sai Speaks*, Vol. 8, p. 144.

They are the guards that ensure safety. Unaccompanied by these two, the Raja is not quite secure.[1]

◊ ◊ ◊ ◊ ◊

Yasoda did not know where Balama and Krishna were born. She brought them up as her own children. They were born in *Mathura*, but grew up in *Gokulam*. They grew in the womb of Devaki (the wife of Vasudeva). But they lived and played in Yasoda's house.

When we try to explore the inner meaning of these events, we realise the Divine story unfolded by them. Balarama and Krishna were born in *Mathura*. *Mathura* signifies the navel. Devaki represents the Divine Sakti. The Divine sound (*Nadam*) represented by the names Balarama and Krishna emerging from the womb of the Divine Sakti, proceeding to *Gokulam*, represented by the mouth was playing on the tongue, represented by Yasoda. "Rama" signifies one who gives delight. "Krishna" means one who attracts.

The Divine Name thus has its origin in the navel and its sacredness should be safeguarded when it is uttered by the tongue. Thus *nama–smarana*, remembrance of the Name of the Lord, implies chanting the name from one's inmost being and preserving its sacredness.

What is the significance of the word *Nama*? *Na + A + Ma*, according to the science of numerology, amounts to a total of 7. *Na = 0, A = 2, Ma = 5*. The total is 7. Seven is associated with the saptaswaras in music (*Sa, Ri, Ga, Ma, Pa, Da, Ni*). The Sun's rays are made up of seven colours. There are seven oceans in the world. The supreme sages are seven in number (*Saptarishis*). It is significant that certain religious observances are spread over seven days (*Saptaham*).[2]

◊ ◊ ◊ ◊ ◊

---

[1] *Sathya Sai Speaks*, Vol. 6, pp. 125–27.

[2] *Sanathana Sarathi*, April 1992, pp. 60–61.

19.

Significance of Yellow Sandalpaste (Harichandana), Dot on Forehead (Thilakam), Kowsthuba Gem, Shining Pearl on Nose-ring, Kankara Bangles and the Dark Colour of Lord Krishna

The transcendent can be understood by the common man only through the language of the transitory. The unknowable has to be hinted at through the crude landmarks of the already known. Take the hymn that describes Krishna as, "*Kasthur thilakam.*" Outwardly, it delineates the beautiful form and describes the ornaments and appurtenances of the Lord. But each of these words has a deeper significance which should not be missed.

The *thilakam* or dot of *kasthuri* or musk on the forehead of Krishna is the symbol of the Eye of Wisdom, the Inner Eye, in inward–directed vision, like the third eye on the forehead of Shiva. *Kasthuri* means *jnana* or supersensual knowledge or wisdom. Then the hymn speaks of *kowsthubha* gem on the chest. It indicates the *Ananda* in the heart, the untarnished *Ananda* of the Lord who is *Ananda swarupi* (bliss personified). Next in the poem is the shining pearl on Krishna's nose–ring. Well, the *Navamoukiikam* on His *nasagra* (nose–tip) is indicative of the success that attends one–pointed concentration on His Glory for which the tip of the nose is considered by adepts in *yoga* as a point of help. And, the pearl is, in Hindu mythology, produced out of the rain drop, from the first, pure, unsullied showers that are swallowed by the oyster that has been waiting long for the precious gift from the heavens. It indicates the transforming effect of yearning and the natural thirst for the pure and the true which irks the human heart.[1]

◊ ◊ ◊ ◊ ◊

The poem goes on to another item, the *Harichandana* (yellow sandalpaste) that He has applied over all His limbs. He wears yellow robes and has the fragrant yellow sandal all over. The yellow is the symbol of *Prakriti*, which He wears as His outer apparel and attraction. In fact *Prakriti* or Nature is what He is pleased to wear or appear in; He can don it or doff it at will. It is His *Atma maya*.[2]

◊ ◊ ◊ ◊ ◊

And the *kankana*, in the description, "*kare kankana*." That does not mean "bangles," which is the meaning given in the lexicon. *Kankana* is the word for dedicatory armlet, worn when a person resolves on a vow. You may wonder what the vows are which Krishna took upon Himself! I shall tell you what they are. They are mentioned in the *Bhagavad Geetha*, for all humanity to read, know, and believe. There are three vows in all:

(1) *Parithranaya sadhoonam, vinasayacha dushkritham, Dharma samsthapanarthaya sambhavami yuge yuge* — "For the protection of the good and the punishment of the bad, for the establishment of the Moral Order, I shall concretise Myself, age after age."

(2) *Ananyaschinthayantho mam ye janah paryupasathe, thesham nithya–abhiyukthanam yoga kshemam vehamyaham* — "Whoevever is

---

[1] *Sathya Sai Speaks*, Vol. 5, pp. 24–25.

[2] *Sathya Sai Speaks*, Vol. 5, p. 26.

wholly immersed in My contemplation, with no other thought, I shall be ever with Him: and I shall bear the burden of his welfare."

(3) *Sarvadharman parithyajya mamekam saranam vraja, aham thwa sarva papebhyo mokshayishyami, masucha* — "Surrendered unto Me, giving up all other duties and obligations; I shall liberate you from all sin; do not grieve." These are the three vows that Krishna has taken, and the armlets are reminders of these tasks on which He is set.[1]

◊ ◊ ◊ ◊ ◊

According to the folk–belief, they pierced the ears and nose of Krishna in order to ward off death, which had carried away many children from the family, and put a golden wire on the nose. The nose–ring had a small–sized pearl. The pearl is won by diving into the depths of the sea, so it symbolises the *viveka* (discrimination) that is won after diving into the secrets of the objective world. Also since it marked the tip of the nose, it sought to emphasise the need to concentrate, to meditate on the tip of the nose, the eyes not being fully open (for that would distract the attention), nor being fully closed (for then sleep would intervene and put an end to the process of meditation). They should be half–open, their sight being directed to the tip of the nose, where Krishna wore the pearl.

Krishna's complexion was neither fair nor dark; it was three parts dark and one part fair, an amalgam of both. Since they were of the *Vaishnava* caste, the parents placed the line of musk on the centre of his brow. ...

He says, when promising His Grace to all who adore Him with no other thought, that there is no restriction of caste, creed, colour or country or origin, and no one receives special favour as a result of erudition or age or caste. Krishna was the embodiment of *Prema* (Love); His *Prema* had no bounds. How fortunate you are that you have today the same Krishna, the full *Prema–Avatar*, moving among

[1] *Sathya Sai Speaks*, Vol. 5, p. 26.

you! I shall show you the very *kowsthubha* that I was wearing at that time. (Here Baba waved his hand, and in a trice a brilliant flash of light revealed a unique jewel in his palm — the *kowsthubha*, famed in the *Bhagavata* and the *Puranas* (mythological stories). A large greenish–blue emerald of unexcelled brightness, rectangular in shape and bordered by resplendent diamonds, hung on a gold chain. Then Baba moved among the students, teachers and others, and graciously allowed every one of them to see the sacred jewel from close).[1]

◊ ◊ ◊ ◊ ◊

God is the greatest mystery; the dark blue colour in which He is depicted is a symbol of the depth of that mystery. The sky and the sea are blue on account of their vast depth. Some one described the *Kalingamardhana* (killing of the cobra *Kalinga*) episode of Krishna as the height of mystery, for, in the dark depths of the dark Yamuna (River), where the dark sky was reflected, the dark Krishna was dancing on the dark hoods of the deadly dark cobra called *Kalinga*! And, he blamed his eye which sought to visualise the scene as itself equipped with a dark cornea! Remove from the heart the darkness of vice and ignorance; then, in that white background, the *Megashyama* (He whose colour is that of a rain–cloud) can easily be seen. Instead of this, man is further darkening his consciousness, while blaming God for evading his search. Seeking light, man's steps are moving further and further towards darkness; this is the pity. Better live a moment as *hamsa* (swan) on milk than live for a century as crow, feeding on carrion.[2]

◊ ◊ ◊ ◊ ◊

One *bhakta* sings, "O Krishna! You are dark; the 'Kalindi deeps' in the Yamuna river into which you have descended is also dark with

---

[1] *Sathya Sai Speaks*, Vol. 13, pp. 252–54.

[2] *Sathya Sai Speaks*, Vol. 4, pp. 263–64.

rain clouds; my eyeball is dark; my heart too is darkened with dark thoughts. How then can I discover You? Your secret is beyond me; Your majesty is ever receding before my imagination." Now, the dark colour of the Lord is the colour of the deep sea and the deep sky. It signifies the fathomless, unfathomable.[1]

◊ ◊ ◊ ◊ ◊

Krishna draws the mind away from sensory desires; that is another way in which the draw operates. He pulls the mind towards Him and so, it is pulled away from everything else, for everything else is inferior, less valuable. He satisfies the deepest thirst of man, for peace, joy and wisdom. That is why He is *Megashyama* — dark–blue as the rain cloud. The very sight of the rain–laden cloud is so refreshing. He is lotus–eyed, lotus palmed, lotus–soled; the lotus is reminiscent of cool, calm, deep lakes of limpid water, the water that quenches thirst. When *Krishna–thrishna* is quenched, the highest *Ananda* is attained; there is no more need, no more want, defect or decline. The urge to drink inferior drinks, that only feed the thirst, disappears when once the sweetness of *Krishna nama* and *Krishna bhava* (name and thought of Krishna) are tasted. Sense objects are like sea water and can never allay thirst. *Radha*, Godha, Mira, Chaithanya, Ramakrishna, Surdas — they knew the nectarine taste of that Name.[2]

◊ ◊ ◊ ◊ ◊

You know that in Theluga, *Geetha* means a streak! And, in the *Upanishads* God is described as a "streak of lightening, flashing through a thick blue cloud"; Krishna is "blue," of the blue cloud; the *Vedas* say, *neela thoyadha*; the *Bhagavatam* says, *neela megha*. Both mean that He is

---

[1] *Sathya Sai Speaks*, Vol. 4, p. 229.

[2] *Sathya Sai Speaks*, Vol. 6, p. 124.

as deep as the sky or the sea and so His colour is that of the sea and the sky![1]

◊ ◊ ◊ ◊ ◊

20.
Narakasura: The Demon Slain by Lord Krishna

When we enquire into the significance of the Dipavali festival which we are celebrating today, we find that traditionally it is a joyous festival to celebrate the destruction of the demon Narakasura by Sri Krishna. It is only when we first understand the meaning of the Krishna Principle will we be able to understand the significance of the Naraka Principle. Krishna is the embodiment of the five elements (ether, air, fire, water and earth). He is also the embodiment of the five lifebreaths (*prana, apana, samana, udana* and *vyana*). *Kleem–Krishnaya–Govindaya — Gopijanavallabhaya–Swah*. This mantra contains the essence of the *Bhagavata*. The five names represent the five *pranas* (vital airs). *Kleem* refers to the earth. *Krishnaya* refers to water. *Govindaya* refers to *Agni* (the Fire–God). *Gopijanavallabhaya* refers to *vayu* (air). *Swah* refers to ether (or sky). When we recognise that the Divine is immanent in the five elements, we will realise that there is no place in the cosmos where these five are not present. The human body is composed of the five elements. These elements, because they constitute the body, can affect only the body but cannot affect the *Atma* in any way. ...

Krishna's encounter with the demon Naraka has to be understood against this background. *Nara–ka* means one who is opposed to the *Atma*. *Naraka* does not mean a demon. It is the name of a satellite

---

[1] *Sathya Sai Speaks*, Vol. 9, p. 89.

which revolved round the earth. When people were filled with apprehension about the threat to the earth from this satellite, when it seemed to be approaching the earth, Krishna removed their fear by destroying the satellite. Dangers from the planets are apprehended from time to time. For instance, some years ago, people expected greater danger to the world from the combination of the eight planets (*Ashtagraha*). Five thousand years ago people dreaded the approach of a planet near to the earth. To allay their fears, Krishna came to their rescue and averted the impending danger. The celebration of *Dipavali* as the day of deliverance from *Narakasura* commemorates Krishna's victory. The day is observed as an occasion when the Divine leads mankind from darkness to light.

The legendary version of the *Narakasura* episode describes the demon as master of *Pragjyothishapura*. The symbolic meaning of *Pragjyothishapura* is that it is a place which has forgotten the *Atma*. The inner meaning of this is that demonic forces dwell in any place where the *Atma* is forgotten. All the chaos and evil in the world today are due to the fact that men have forgotten the *Atma* (the Supreme Spirit). Every man is conscious of the body and of the individual soul, but is not conscious of the Divinity (*Paramatma*) within him.

Man is encased in five sheaths (*kosas*): *Annamaya, Pranamaya, Manomaya, Vijnanamaya* and *Anandamaya kosas*. The physical body is the *Annamaya* sheath (the sheath based on food). Man takes good care of the body. Man also takes care of the *Pranamaya kosa* as he cannot exist without the life–breath. Without the *Manomaya kosa* (the mental sheath), man cannot accomplish any of his desires. Man today has progressed up to the stage of caring for the first three sheaths. Up to this stage his vision is turned towards the external. The *Vignanamaya* sheath calls for internal vision. It leads to the understanding of the *Anandamaya kosa* (the sheath of Supreme Bliss). Starting from the sheath of food man should progress towards the sheath of bliss and not get stuck up midway in the mental sheath. This is the reason for men getting filled with demonic qualities, which can only lead him to hell (*Naraka*). The demonic qualities (symbolised by *Narakasura*) have to be destroyed to avoid being thrust into *Naraka* (hell). By taking refuge in Krishna, the destroyer of *Narakasura*, man can get rid of the demonic qualities in him.

On *Dipavali* day, we light numerous lamps with one candle. The light with which other lamps are lit is a symbol of the Divine. The other lamps are *jivana jyothis* (individual lamps). They derive their light from the One Supreme Light. It is to teach this Truth to men that the Festival of Lights is observed.

Thus every festival has an inner meaning and purpose. Forgetting this, the holy days are observed only as occasions for feasts and fun. Holy days in *Bharat* (India) are all full of spiritual significance. Forgetting this, people are lost in meaningless observances.

According to the legend, Krishna killed Narakasura with the help of Sathyabhama. What does this signify? Each of us has to fight and destroy the demonic forces within each by resorting to *Sathya* (Truth). "*Sathaymeva Jayathe*," declares the Upanishad. "Truth alone triumphs." "Speak the Truth" is a *Vedic* injunction. Once the Goddess of the Earth went to Vishnu and lamented that she can bear any kind of burden but not the burden of carrying those indulging in falsehood. One must be prepared to make any kind of sacrifice for upholding Truth.[1]

◊ ◊ ◊ ◊ ◊

Today is described as *Naraka Chathurdasi*. What is *Naraka*? Whatever is associated with suffering is called *Naraka*. *Ka* stands for bad qualities. *Naraka* means human life with bad qualities. That is a hellish life. How did Krishna deal with *Naraka*? Krishna is the Divine, one who attracts by His magnetic vibrations. These vibrations represent the Life Force. The Consciousness that animates the Life Force is known as *Prajnanam*, the source of radiation. When radiation and vibration are active in the body, you have the whole human being.

---

[1] *Sanathana Sarathi*, January 1990, pp. 10–11.

The bad qualities in man, in the form of *Narakasura*, have to be destroyed. Krishna came to destroy these bad qualities. He enlisted the aid of *Sathyabhama*, who represents the bearer of Truth. This means that with the help of Truth, Krishna destroyed the bad qualities. Thyagaraja sang ecstatically about the glorious achievements of the Lord. On *Dipavali* day, people should pledge themselves to get rid of their bad qualities.

"There is no greater virtue than Truth." Truth is not limited to one nation or one people. It belongs to all mankind. Truth sustains the cosmos. Therefore Truth is God. Follow the path of Truth. Speak the Truth. That is the foremost spiritual exercise.

Embodiments of Love! Your duty today is to destroy the demonic qualities in you. Evil thoughts and evil actions are rampant everywhere. You cannot remain a mere witness to these happenings. Placing your faith in God, you have to fight these evil forces as a human being. You have to demonstrate your human estate. You have to earn a name as a good man. That alone counts. All other acquisitions are worthless. Only a good man endures. Every moment of one's life should be devoted to practising Righteousness (*Dharma*) and earning a good name (*Kirthi*). Fill every cell in your body, with the spirit of Truth.

Naraka Chathurdasi is the day on which you resolve to get rid of your bad qualities and follow the path of Righteousness. Dipavali is celebrated today as a festival of lights, with the firing of crackers and display of fireworks. In olden days the ancients rejoiced over the destruction of the demon *Narakasura* and let off fireworks.

There is another meaning in the burning of crackers on Dipavali day. This is the rainy season. All kinds of germs fill the atmosphere. The smoke from the crackers destroy these germs. Thereby infectious diseases are controlled. The joy derived from the burning of crackers should really come from the elimination of bad qualities within one. For this it is essential to meditate on God. Participate in *bhajans*.[1]

◊ ◊ ◊ ◊ ◊

---

[1] *Sanathana Sarathi*, December 1995, p. 318.

Summary

Lord Krishna is the Supreme Spirit, the Supreme Being that became this Universe. Krishna is within the human being and the human being is within Krishna. The goal of man is to realize that he is, in Truth, this Supreme Spirit, through destroying the demonic and animal qualities symbolized by the slaying of the demon Narakasura and through relying on the Supreme attraction and Grace of Krishna.

When man turns his mind and intellect inwards and his eye of wisdom opens, symbolized by the *thilakam* on Krishna's forehead, and when he meditates on his nose–tip with pure yearning for union, symbolized by *navamouktikam*, the shining pearl on Krishna's nose–tip, man achieves union with Krishna, his own innate *Atma*.

Gokula, Madura, Brindavan and *Dwaraka* are with man always: *Gokula* symbolizes both the inner psychological arena as well as the outer world in which man lives as a *jeeva*, where Krishna is always there as the Divine Basis. *Brindavan* is the spiritual heart within man where the knowledge of *Atma* is experienced and Divine Love grows. *Madura* is the *chitta* or mind–stuff that Krishna or *Atma* rules over as the inner knower and controller, and *Dwaraka* symbolizes the *nirvikalpa* stage where *Atma* or Krishna is Master of the entire being and one lives as God consciousness.

The light of *Atma* through spiritual practices and Grace destroys the notion that "I am the body," as well as attachment to worldly objects symbolized by the breaking of the mud pots by Krishna. Through faith in *Atma* and spiritual practices for self–purification, symbolized by churning of the milk to find butter, a devotee becomes awakened, or enlightened, to a state of *Satchidananda* (Being, Awareness, Bliss). Krishna stole the pure soft hearts of the devotees, symbolized by His theft of butter from the *Gopees'* homes, so they could become enlightened through awareness of the unity of the *Atma*.

Every human being is a *gopi* in the making; all will one day turn their minds inward to seek the liberation and bliss of the innate *Atma*. *Gopis* are those human beings who have turned their minds inward with intense yearning and purified Divine Love to experience and merge with the pure, subtle *Atma* within their hearts and everywhere. The goal of every human being is to experience and realize unity with the all pervasive One through one–pointed, unwavering pure Love for the Divine.

Radha, a perfected *gopi*, is potential within every human as the pure mind–soul adoring the *Atma* in any form of God such as Krishna, Jesus or Sai Baba, having no other thought or feeling to disturb the mind. *Radha* is the pure flame of Divinity, the full flowering of the soul, within the individual, whereby *Radha* is Krishna and Krishna is *Radha*. Looked at from a different perspective, *Radha*, as a spark of the Divine embodied in Nature (the human being), represents the Becoming and Krishna is the Being (the eteri.al, changeless). When the Becomed longs to merge back into the Being or *Atma*, it is *Radha*. When the Being has desired to Become, it is Krishna.

One's own body with senses, mind and intellect is Krishna's flute. When it is hollow and empty of ego and evil qualities, the Divine *Atma* will play through it Divine qualities and actions, thus transforming man into Divinity.

Chapter 6

Bhagavan Sri Sathya Sai Baba

Chapter 6

Bhagavan Sri Sathya Sai Baba

Introduction

Bhagavan Sri Sathya Sai Baba is a *Poorna Avatar*, a full
incarnation of Divinity descended in human form. He is
Truth (*Sathya*), Sovereign, the Divine Mother,
embodiment of all powers (Sai), and Divine Father
(Baba). He is at all times the embodiment of the Supreme
Spirit (*Paramatma*), of Supreme Divine Love (*Prema*), and
Supreme Bliss (*Ananda*).

Bhagavan means one who has the six Divine
Excellences in full: 1) *Aisvaryam* (Greatness, Might,
Omniscience, Omnipotence, Omnipresence), 2) *Dharma*

(Virtue, Righteousness, Equity, Impartiality, Propriety), 3) *Yasas* (Fame, Reputation, Splendour), 4) *Sri* (Propriety, Plenty, Majesty, Dignity, Grace, Lustre), 5) *Jnana* (Wisdom, Intelligence), 6) *Vairagya* (Detachment, Tranquility, Balance).

Sathya Sai Baba has come embodied to the earth to illumine the human heart with Divine Light so that man may rid himself of delusion and attain God Realization. He has come to revive the *Vedic Sanathana* (Eternal) *Dharma* for the good of all the peoples of the world, and to protect the virtuous and the devotees.

In the following excerpts from His Divine Discourses, *Bhagavan* Baba talks about His Mission, His characteristics as an *Avatar*, His Grace, the nature of *sadhana* (spiritual practice), and the significance of His birthday and His appearance in dreams.

◊ ◊ ◊ ◊ ◊

1.

The Meaning of the Names Sathya, Sai, and Baba

What exactly is the meaning of Sai Baba? *Sai* means *Sahasrapadma* (thousand lotuses), *Sakshathkara* (Realisation), etc. *Ayi* means Mother and *Baba* means Father; it means He who is both Father and Mother, and the Goal of all *Yogic* endeavour — the ever-merciful Mother, the

All–wise Father and the Goal of spiritual efforts. When you are groping in a dark room, you must seize the chance when some one brings a lamp into the room. Hurriedly collect your belongings scattered there, or discover where they are located, or do whatever else you need. Similarly, make the best of this chance when the Lord has come in human form to your very door and get ready to save yourself from disaster.[1]

◊ ◊ ◊ ◊ ◊

I am neither man nor God nor an aerial spirit; I am neither a *Brahman,* nor a *Kshathriya,* nor a *Vaishya,* nor a *Sudra;* I cannot be described as *Brahmachari* or a house–holder, or a recluse or a monk; describe me as a Teacher of Truth, as *Sathyam* (Truth), *Shivam* (Goodness) and *Sundaram* (Beauty). Your reality too is *Sathyam, Shivam* and *Sundaram.* Without Truth there cannot be Goodness; without Goodness, what does Beauty avail? The effect of Truth on the mind is goodness; the joy that flows from goodness is the genuine Beauty that artists Love. The three are really one and indivisible. Experience this Truth; this Truth as Goodness and this Goodness as Beauty. That gives the highest Bliss.[2]

◊ ◊ ◊ ◊ ◊

Of course, I never deviate from Truth. Since I recline on Truth, I am called Sathya Sai; *Sayi* (as in *Seshashayi*) means reclining. The name is very appropriate, let me assure you. It is only those who fail to follow my instructons and who deviate from the path I have laid down, that fail to get what I hold out before them. Follow my instructions and become soldiers in My army; I will lead you on to victory. When someone asks you, in great earnestness, where the Lord

---

[1] *Sathya Sai Speaks,* Vol. 2, p. 6.

[2] *Sathya Sai Speaks,* Vol. 10, p. 33.

is to be found, do not try to dodge the question. Give them the answer that rises up to your tongue from your heart. Direct them. He is here in the Prashanti Nilayam.[1]

◊ ◊ ◊ ◊ ◊

There is one point that I cannot but bring to your special notice today. At the moment when Jesus was merging in the Supreme Principle of Divinity, He communicated some news to his followers, which has been interpreted in a variety of ways by commentators and those who relish the piling of writings on writings and meanings upon meanings, until it all swells up into a huge mess.

The statement itself has been manipulated and tangled into a conundrum. The statement of Christ is simple: "He who sent me among you will come again!" and he pointed to a Lamb. The Lamb is merely a symbol, a sign. It stands for the Voice — Ba–Ba; the announcement was the Advent of Baba. "His Name will be Truth," Christ declared. *Sathya* means Truth. "He will wear a robe of red, a bloodred robe." (Here Baba pointed to the robe He was wearing!) "He will be short, with a crown (of hair). The Lamb is the sign and symbol of Love.:"

Christ did not declare that he will come again. He said, "He who made me will come again." That Ba–ba is this Baba, and Sai, the short, curly–haired–crowned red–robed Baba, is come. He is not only in this Form, but, he is in every one of you, as the dweller in the Heart. He is there, short, with a robe of the colour of the blood that fills it.[2]

◊ ◊ ◊ ◊ ◊

Having installed Sai in your village, you must grow in *Prema* (Love), for Sai is *Premaswarupam* (Love personified). Sa — means

---

[1] *Sathya Sai Speaks*, Vol. 2, p. 266

[2] *Sathya Sai Speaks*, Vol. 11, p. 346.

Sarvashakti (All–powerful), *Sarvasakshi* (the Witness in All); *Ayi* means mother; *Baba* means Father. The *Prema* of Sai is the *Prema* characteristic of the Father and the Mother; not the earthy Father and Mother but of the Father and Mother who are the Witness of every thought, word, and deed in every being. Respect the Father and Mother who are concrete and then you transfer that type of respect to the Abstract Father or Mother or Guardian — God.[1]

◊ ◊ ◊ ◊ ◊

2.

The Global Mission of Bhagavan Sri Sathya Sai Baba Avatar

It is to clear the path of spiritual progress of Man that the *Avatar* (Divine Incarnation) has come. The *ashanti* (restlessness) in which man is immersed has to be curbed. That is what is meant by *parithranaya sadhoonam* — "the saving of *sadhus*," the saving of all good *jeevis* (individual beings) from the tentacles of *ashanti* (grief) caused by want of knowledge of the relative unimportance of worldly things. All *jeevis* must get *Shanti* (Peace) and *santhosha* (contentment); that is the mission on which the Lord comes again and again on this earth. He selects a place full of *pavithratwam* (holiness) and *Dhivyatwam* (Divinity) and takes on the human form, so that you may meet Him and talk, understand and appreciate, listen and follow, experience and benefit.

The tragedy is that when Godhead is invisible and formless, you concretise it as you like and pray to it and get consolation and strength out of it; but when it is before you, concretised in human form, you doubt and discuss and deny! ...

---

[1] *Sathya Sai Speaks*, Vol. 2, p. 146.

You must dive deep into the sea to get the pearls. What good is it to dabble among the waves near the shore and swear that the sea has no pearls in it and that all tales of its existence are false. So also if you must realise the full fruit of this _Avatar_, dive deep and get immersed in Sai Baba. Half–heartedness, hesitation, doubt, cynicism, listening to tales, all are of no avail. Concentrated complete faith — that alone can bring victory. This is true in any worldly activity, is it not? How much more true must it be, therefore in the spiritual field? But if you have already attached yourselves to some one Name and Form, do not change it, do not choose another in place of the _Prema Swarupam_ (Embodiment of Love).[1]

◊ ◊ ◊ ◊ ◊

Nothing can hold Me up or agitate Me or cast a shadow on Me come in this Human Form; be certain of that. Not even a hair can be touched by forces of calumny or distrust or ignorance. My _sankalpa_ (resolve) must prevail; My tasks must be accomplished. My mission will succeed. I have come to illumine the human heart with the Light Divine and to rid man of the delusion that drags him away from the path of _Shanti_ (Peace), the perfect equanimity born of Realisation.[2]

◊ ◊ ◊ ◊ ◊

Again, how fortunate you are that you can witness all the countries of the world paying homage to _Bharat_ (India); you can hear adoration to Sathya Sai's Name reverberating throughout the world, even while this body is existing — not at some future date, but when it is with you, before you. And again, you can witness very soon the restoration of _Sanathana Dharma_ to its genuine and natural status, the _Dharma_ laid down in the _Vedas_ for the good of all the peoples of the

---

[1] _Sathya Sai Speaks_, Vol. 1, p. 131.

[2] _Sathya Sai Speaks_, Vol. 1, p. 93.

world. The revival of *Vedic Dharma* is the *Sai Sankalpa* (the resolve that Sai has) not only drawing people towards Me, attracting them by the manifestation of My *shakti* (power) and *samarthya* (capability). This is not a *bhrama tatwam* (phenomenon of delusion). This *tatwam* (phenomenon) will sustain Truth, it will uproot unTruth, and in that victory make all of you exult in ecstasy. This is the *Sai Sankalpam*. ...

So utilise the chance of association with Me as much as possible, and endeavour as quickly and as best as you can, to follow the directions that I have been giving. Obeying My instructions is enough; it will benefit you more than the most rigorous asceticism. Practise *Sathya* (Truth), *Dharma* (Righteousness), *Shanti* (Peace) and *Prema* (Love), which are dear to Me; resolve to keep those ideals before you ever, in all your thoughts, words and deeds. That can confer on you the *summum bonum* of mergence in the Supreme Substance of Divinity.[1]

◊ ◊ ◊ ◊ ◊

It is the running after *vishaya vasana* — attachment to sense objects — that produces all this discontent. That *vasana*, that type of desire, has no end. Once you become a slave to the senses, they will not leave hold of you until your death. It is an unquenchable thirst. But I call you to Me and even grant worldly boons, so that you may turn Godward. No *Avatar* has done like this before, going among the people, the masses, the millions, and counselling them, guiding them, consoling them, uplifting them, directing them along the path of *Sathya, Dharma, Shanti* and *Prema*. You must have wondered why I have prohibited you from bringing flowers and fruits and other offerings; you argue that the *Geeta* requires that you must bring at least these when you come to the Lord; that when going to the presence of elders and saints, one should not go empty handed.

---

[1] *Sathya Sai Speaks*, Vol. 8, pp. 101–101.

Here, in this Prashanti Nilayam, *pathram, pushpam, phalam* and *thoyam* (leaf, flower, fruit and water) — all the four should not be brought by devotees. Of course, I accept your offerings, but I take another four: *Sathya, Dharma, Shanti* and *Prema* (Truth, Virtue, Peace and Love). Bring me these or any one of these and I shall most gladly accept the gift. When you demand a thing, you must be prepared to pay the price, the price equal to its value. You cannot bargain a costly Benares sari for one paisa. Give something Divine if you want the Divine. *Prema, Shanti, Dharma* and *Sathya* are Divine. Do not try to get it for a flower that fades, a fruit that rots, a leaf that dries, water that evaporates. There are some who write and speak as if they have known Me, all that is to be known of Me. Well; I can only say this: they can never know Me and My nature, even if they are born and reborn a thousand times. To know Me one has to be like Me, rise to this height. Can ants discover the depth of the Ocean?[1]

◊ ◊ ◊ ◊ ◊

The way in which the *Avatar* has to be used for one's liberation and uplift is: watch His every step, observe His actions and activities, follow the guiding principle of which His life is an elaboration. Mark His Love, His Compassion, His Wisdom, try to bring them into your own life. Man has become artificial, crooked, twisted out of his normal shape. He has left behind the simple natural ways and made his mind a lumber–room for ideas, worries, anxieties and terrors. He can live on very much less, with much greater joy for himself and others. If only he remembers that he is a treasure chest with a Divine spark in it, he will be more loving and more useful.

God incarnates for the revival of *Dharma* (Righteousness) which includes morality, Truth, virtue, Love and a host of other qualities that uphold the communities of man as well as the individual. The other purposes usually given, such as serving the devoted, destroying the

---

[1] *Sathya Sai Speaks*, Vol. 5, pp. 233–235.

wicked, re-establishing the sacred tradition — these are all secondary. For, he who is righteous will be guarded from harm by Righteousness itself; he who is unrighteous will fall into disaster through the evil that he perpetuates. The one task includes all else.

I shall fulfil the task, whatever the comments that others may make. Comment is a natural corollary. I do not pay any attention to it; nor should you. The higher the hill, the deeper the valley. Praise or blame will not affect me in the least. The unshakable foundation on which My work is proceeding is *Ananda* (Bliss). ...

Dedicate your heart to God; God will be one with you, the heart of your heart. Do not exaggerate the creation and the manifestation of the *Linga*; it is only the manifestation of an atom of My majesty. In Me, who can create worlds, and fill the Universe, there are things more worthy of adoration; universal Love, the teaching of *Dharma* (Virtue), the revival of the *Vedas*, the fostering of the good, the benediction on *sadakas* (spiritual aspirants).[1]

◊ ◊ ◊ ◊ ◊

Do not delay any more; take hold of this unique chance, even while you can. Ask me about the *sadhana* (spiritual practice) you should adopt for your liberation; begin practising from this day. Later, it may be difficult to approach Me and ask Me. For, people are coming towards Me in full unending streams, and you may have to take *darshan* (sight) of Me from miles away! This is bound to grow into a *Vishwa-vriksha* (a World-tree), that sheds shade and shelter on all. This has come down in this Form with that very purpose. It knows no halting, no hesitation. My name is *Sathya* (Truth). My teaching is Truth; My path is Truth; I am Truth.

In each *Yuga* (Age), the Divine has incorporated itself as an *Avatar* for some particular task. This Incarnation is different in that It has to deal with the crisis which is world-wide and world-shaking.

---

[1] *Sathya Sai Speaks*, Vol. 8, pp. 34-35.

Intellectual conceit has grown so wild that men have become foolish enough to ask, "What and where is God?" Immorality has put on the garb of morality and is enticing man into the morass of sin. Truth is condemned as a trap; justice is jeered at; saints are harassed as social enemies. Hence this Incarnation has come to uphold the True and suppress the False. I behave like you, moving, singing, laughing, journeying, but watch out for the blow I inflict all of a sudden, to chastise and to warn. I shall scorch the wrong–doer for his wrong and soothe the virtuous for his Righteousness. Justice shall be meted out to all.[1]

◊ ◊ ◊ ◊ ◊

People tell Me that mankind is on the brink of destruction, that the forces of hypocrisy and hate are prevailing fast in all the continents, and that anxiety and fear are stalking the streets of every city and village of the world; there is no need to tell Me this, for, I have come precisely for this very reason. When the world is on the verge of chaos, the *Avatar* comes to still the storm raging in the hearts of men. *Prashanti* (the higher Peace, the calming of perturbations) will be stabilised soon; the demonic deviations from the straight Divine Path will be corrected. *Dharma* will be revived and re–vitalised, in every human community.[2]

◊ ◊ ◊ ◊ ◊

My *Prema* (Love) towards the *Veda* is equalled only by My *Prema* towards humanity. My Mission, remember, is just fourfold: *Veda poshana, Vidwath poshana* (fostering the *Vedas* and *Vedic* Scholars), *Dharma rakshana* and *bhakta rakshana* (Protection of virtue and

---

[1] *Sathya Sai Speaks*, Vol. 8, p. 157.

[2] *Sathya Sai Speaks*, Vol. 11, p. 207.

devotees). Spreading My Grace and My Power along these four directions, I establish Myself in the Centre.[1]

◊ ◊ ◊ ◊ ◊

What exactly has been won by people who have struggled for a hundred years? They have hungered and eaten, slept and awakened, laughed and wept — but what is the result of it all on the personality or on the world? Nil. When humanity flows purposeless and meaningless into the sands, the *Avatar* comes to warn and show the way. The one task has to be fulfilled in various ways; that is the Mission of the *Avatar*. ...

I am determined to correct you only after informing you of My credentials. That is why I am now and then announcing My Nature by means of miracles — that is, acts which are beyond human capacity and human understanding. Not that I am anxious to show off My Powers. The object is to draw you closer to Me, to cement your hearts to Me. ...

As a matter of fact, each one of you has to be saved: you have to escape from this net, when the opportunity comes. I shall not give you up, even if you forsake Me; for it is not in Me to forsake those who deny Me. I have come for all. Those who stray away will come again to Me, do not doubt this. I shall beckon them back to Me. I bless you that you earn the Vision of the Divine in this life itself, with this body itself.[2]

◊ ◊ ◊ ◊ ◊

My acts are the foundations on which I am building My work, the Task for which I have come. All the "miraculous acts" which you observe are to be interpreted so. The foundation for a dam requires a

---

[1] *Sathya Sai Speaks*, Vol. 2, p. 271–72.

[2] *Sathya Sai Speaks*, Vol. 2, pp. 140–41.

variety of materials; without these, it will not last and hold back the waters.

When the Lord has incarnated, He has to be used in various ways by man, for his uplift. Krishna held aloft the Govardhana Giri, not to demonstrate His *siddhi* or attainment, but to protect the *gopas* and *gopees* (cowherd boys and girls) and the cattle they held dear. He had to do something which man could not accomplish. He had no intention to publicise Himself. Only inferior minds will revel in publicity and self–aggrandisement. These have no relevance in the case of *Avatars*. They need no advertisement. Those who decry the superhuman are the ignorant or .the wicked, that is, those who have no authority to judge the spiritual. The establishment of *Dharma* is My aim; the teaching of *Dharma*, the spread of *Dharma* — that is my objective. These "miracles" as you call them are just a few means towards that end.

Some people remark that *Ramakrishna Paramahamsa* said that *siddhis* (acquired powers) are obstructions in the path of the *sadaka* (spiritual aspirant). Of course they are; he may be led astray by *siddhis*; he has to keep straight on without being involved in them. His ego will increase if he yields to the temptation of demonstrating his *siddhis*. This is the correct advice, which every *sadaka* should heed.

The mistake lies in equating Me with the *sadaka* (spiritual aspirant) whom Ramakrishna wanted to help, guide and warn. This is merely the nature of *Avatar*: the creation of things, *ab initio*, with intent to protect, guard and give joy, a creation that is spontaneous and lasting. Creation, Preservation and Dissolution — these three, only the Almighty can accomplish; no one else can. Cynics carp without knowledge. If they learn the *Shastras*, they can understand Me, or they should cultivate direct experience.

Your innate laziness prevents you from the spiritual exercises necessary to discover the nature of Godhead. The *Guru* says, "Through *karma* (action), clarify your intellect." The disciple is lazy; he prefers *dhyana* (mediation), sitting quietly in one place. After a few attempts, he asks that some other path be laid down for him. The laziness should go out of man's nature, in whatever shape it appears. That is

My mission. This is the first step in converting *Manava* into Madava —
man into God.

God alone is eternal, man is a momentary flash, a tiny wavelet,
that rises and falls. So, fill yourselves with vast thoughts, magnificent
ideas, indefinable splendour, by reciting the Names of God, names that
describe Him to your receptive consciousness. That is the main
discipline for this Age.[1]

◊ ◊ ◊ ◊ ◊

India was the home of Peace and prosperity when *Dharma* was
followed by rich and poor alike; but, now, the land is plunged into
darkness and confusion. Therefore, another *Avatar* has come, for
teaching people of *Dharma* they have forgotten. Rama, Krishna and
other *Avatars* had to kill one or more individuals, who could be
identified as enemies of the *Dharmic* way of life, and thus restore the
practice of virtue. But, now, there is no one fully good, and so, who
deserves the protection of God? All are tainted by wickedness, and so,
who will survive if the *Avatar* decided to uproot?

Therefore, I have to correct the *buddhi* (intellect), by various
means; I have to counsel, help, command, condemn and standby as
friend and well–wisher to all, so that they may give up evil
propensities and recognising the straight path, tread it and reach the
goal. I have to reveal to the people the worth of the *Vedas*, the *Shastras*
and the scriptural texts, which lay down the norms.

The easiest path to self–realisation is the surrender of the ego,
sharanagati. Arjuna surrendered and so, the war in which he was
engaged was transformed into a *yajna*, a spiritual exercise! Daksha
performed a *yajna*; but he did not surrender; he was so full of egoism
that he slighted God! So, his *yajna* was transformed into a war reeking

---

[1] *Sathya Sai Speaks*, Vol. 4, pp. 267–68.

with hate. Do not pit your tiny ego against the Almighty; leave it to His Will and you will have lasting Peace.[1]

◊ ◊ ◊ ◊ ◊

Human lives are now passing on and on, filth over filth, bent, broken, diseased, distressed, disheartened. To ennoble these lives and to make the human heritage worth while, I have come. I am evincing all this enthusiasm to teach you the proper attitude to *Seva* (Service), for, Love expresses itself as *Seva*; Love grows through *Seva*; Love is born in the womb of *Seva*, And God is Love. The *Avatar* (Divine incarnation) is a Child to the children, a Boy to the boys, a Man among men, a Woman among women, so that the *Avatar's* message might reach each heart and receive enthusiastic response, as *Ananda* (Bliss). It is the compassion of the *Avatar* that prompts His every activity.

Birds, beasts and trees have not deviated from their Nature; they are still holding it valid. Man alone has disfigured it, in his crude attempt to improve upon it. So, the *Avatar* has to come as man among men, and move as friend, well–wisher, kinsman, guide, teacher, healer and participant among men. He has come to restore *Dharma* (Righteousness, Virtue), and so when man follows *Dharma*, He is pleased and content. Act so that your career as a man is not degraded, desecrated. With hands on chest, assert, "I am man; I am human; I am saturated with shining humanity, humanness." God does not draw you near or keep you far, you go near to Him or keep away from Him. God has no likes or dislikes. You live according to the highest demands of your nature and you are near Him.[2]

◊ ◊ ◊ ◊ ◊

---

[1] *Sathya Sai Speaks*, Vol. 4, pp. 224–25.

[2] *Sathya Sai Speaks*, Vol. 10, pp. 136–37.

"Whenever there is a languishing of *Dharma* or Righteousness and an upheaval of unrighteousness, I create Myself, for it is part of primal resolution or *Sankalpa* to protect the spiritual structure of the Universe. I lay aside My formless essence and assume a name and a form suited to the purpose for which I come. Whenever evil threatens to vanquish good, I have to come and save it from decline." The Lord does not insist on all men following one path and accepting one discipline. There are many doors to His Mansion. The main entrance is, however, *moha–kshaya* (the overcoming of attachment).[1]

◊ ◊ ◊ ◊ ◊

After the song with which Baba opened His discourse, He thrilled everyone by singing the two lines from the *Bhagavad Geeta*, which declare "*Yada yada hi dharmsaya glanir bhavati, Bharat, Abhyuththanam adharmasya tadh atmanam srujamyaham,*" and adding "*Parithranaya sadhunam, vinasayacha dhushkrutam, Dharma samsthapanarthaya sambhavami yuge yuge.*" "Whenever *Dharma* declines, I restore it and put down the forces which cause the decline, by assuming a form" and "I am born again and again in every crisis in order to protect the good, punish the wicked and restore *Dharma*." He began His discourse after this announcement of His Identity with the source of all *Avatars*.[2]

◊ ◊ ◊ ◊ ◊

Make full use of Me, that is all that I ask of you. I have at no time any feeling of separateness. I invite all to come and know and derive benefit from Me. Dive and know the depth; watch and discriminate; eat and know the taste. I long for people who do that.[3]

---

[1] *Sathya Sai Speaks*, Vol. 7, p. 65.

[2] *Sathya Sai Speaks*, Vol. 4, p. 223.

[3] *Sathya Sai Speaks*, Vol. 6, p. 108.

◊ ◊ ◊ ◊ ◊

3.

Sathya Sai Baba as Atma (Supreme Spirit of the Universe), Prema (the Embodiment of Divine Love) and Ananda the Embodiment of Divine Bliss)

Believe that Sai Baba is in your heart, as your *Atma*, unshakable, full of Love. Do not encourage the pretensions of low egoistic men, who claim that I am "possessing" them, or that I need *mandirs* (halls) for which they are collecting donations. I need only one *mandir*, your hearts! Whoever may ask, even if they say that I have authorised them — even if you feel I have asked, do not give even a single paisa. This craze for putting up temples and pulling down temples, raising new ones and razing old ones is only a craze for earning some money or reputation. It should not be encouraged. Preserve the purity of your hearts, so that Sai may reside therein. That will be enough.[1]

◊ ◊ ◊ ◊ ◊

---

[1] *Sathya Sai Speaks*, Vol. 10, pp. 171–72.

I have come to light the lamp of Love in your hearts, to see that it shines day by day with added lustre. I have not come to speak on behalf of any particular *Dharma* (Righteousness), like the *Hindu Dharma*. I have not come on any mission of publicity for any sect or creed or cause; nor have I come to collect followers for any doctrine. I have no plan to attract disciples or devotees into My fold or any fold. I have come to tell you of this Universal unitary faith, this *Atmic* principle, this path of Love, this *Dharma* of *Prema*, this duty of Love, this obligation to Love.[1]

◊ ◊ ◊ ◊ ◊

The goal will near you faster than the pace with which you near the goal. God is as eager to save you as you are eager to be saved; He is *Prema*. He is *karuna* (loving and compassionate), for all who flounder on the road. He is called *bhakta–abheesta–pradha* (He who grants the desires of the devotees). You say that I laugh within Myself, that I roll My hair on My fingers and draw them tight over My face — but let me say why. It is a sign of My *Ananda* over leaping its bounds, *Ananda* at the success of *bhaktas* in capturing My heart.[2]

◊ ◊ ◊ ◊ ◊

Take the Lord to be your father or mother, but only as a first step to your overstepping that relationship and merging in the Absolute. Do not stop on the steps; enter the Mansion to which they lead. The *Atmasambanda* (connection with the Soul) is the everlasting unchanging *sambanda* (association). At a first step, you use the flower, the lamp, the incense, etc., to worship the *Saguna* (attributeful) form. Soon, your *bhakti* (devotion) moves on to newer forms of dedication, newer offerings, purer and more valuable and worthier of your Lord. No one

---

[1] *Sathya Sai Speaks*, Vol. 8, p. 118.

[2] *Sathya Sai Speaks*, Vol. 6, p. 114.

sticks to the slate for long; you feel that you should place before the Lord something more lasting than mere flowers; and something more yours than incense. You feel like purifying yourselves and making your entire life one fragrant flame. That is real worship, real *bhakti*. Do not come to Me with your hands full of trash, for how can I fill them with Grace when they are already full? Come with empty hands and carry away My tieasure, My *Prema*.[1]

◊ ◊ ◊ ◊ ◊

Rely on the Lord and accept whatever is your lot. He is in you, with you. He knows best what to give and when. He is full of *Prema* (Love). That is My uniqueness: *Prema*. *Prema* is the special gift I bring, the special medium through which My Grace operates. That is the basis of all My acts. God is said to reside in every being. Yes; He resides as *Prema*. Devoid of *Prema*, the world becomes a cauldron of misery. It is as water to the fish. Keep a fish in a golden bowl, set with gems; it will struggle in mortal agony to leap back into water.[2]

◊ ◊ ◊ ◊ ◊

Develop *Prema* (Divine Love) towards the Lord, the *Parama–Prema* (Supreme Divine Love) of which He is the embodiment. Never give room for doubts and hesitations, for questions to test the Lord's *Prema*. "My troubles have not ended; why? Why is it that He did not speak to me? How is it I did not get a room for staying here? Why did He not call me?" you whine! Do not think that I do not care for you or that I do not know you. I may not talk to you, but do not be under the impression that I have no *Prema*. As a matter of fact, it is to give you the chance of *darshan* that I move along the verandah from this

---

[1] *Sathya Sai Speaks*, Vol. 2, pp. 122–23.

[2] *Sathya Sai Speaks*, Vol. 8, p. 62.

room to that. Whatever I do, it is for you, not for Me. For, what is it that can be called Mine? Only you.

So, do not get shaken in mind; do not allow faith to decline. That will only add to the grief you already suffer from. Hold fast — that must be your vow. Whoever is your *Ishta devata* (the chosen deity) — Vishnu or Rama or Shiva or Venkateswara — hold fast to Him. Do not lose the contact and the company; for, it is only when the coal is in contact with the live embers that it can also become live ember. Cultivate nearness to Me in the heart and you will be rewarded. Then you too will acquire a fraction of the Supreme *Prema*. This is the great chance. This chance will not come your way again, beware of that. If you cannot, if you do not cross the sea of grief now, taking hold of this chance, when again can you get such a chance? Really you are the fortunate few; out of millions and millions of people you have come, though no one specially invited you to be present here. That is what I call the mark of destiny.[1]

◊ ◊ ◊ ◊ ◊

Strive to become embodiments of *Prema*. Be ready to offer all your capabilities and skills to the Lord of All. It is God's Love that rewards you when you engage yourselves in *japa*, *thapa* or *yaga* (Repetition of God's name, penance, ritual of sacrifice). What greater achievement can you strive for than receiving Love Divine from God?

However, you must understand well the nature and significance of this Love. You are now experiencing and sharing this Love at the level of your awareness of the Principle. This is a mistake. It is too literal an interpretation. The Principle of Love has no trace of ego or blemish. It is fully free from foolish attachments. Whatever Sai does, whatever Sai thinks, whatever Sai says, whatever Sai observes, it is all

---

[1] *Sathya Sai Speaks*, Vol. 4, pp. 182–83.

for your sake, not for Sai's sake. My only desire is your joy, *Ananda*. Your *Ananda* is My *Ananda*. I have no *Ananda* apart from yours.[1]

◊ ◊ ◊ ◊ ◊

I have no sense of distinction between *bhaktas* who worship this Form or that. All can come near, all who crave for heat and light. The heat of this splendour will destroy the chill of sensual pleasure; the light will scatter the darkness of ages. Cultivate *Prema* (Love) towards all; that is the way to gain nearness. I do not measure distance in terms of meters or miles. The range of Love decides distance for Me.

Another point: You desire that I should come to your houses; you pray to Me to do so, you grieve when I do not come, you start reviling yourself that you are poorer than others, that you are less spiritually developed perhaps, and so on. Now, all this is irrelevant. I have no place in My heart for such distinctions and differences. You may believe this or disbelieve. But I must reveal the real response of My Heart. I have no enthusiasm to visit the houses of people; nor have I any disinclination to do the same. I do not care for the brick and mortar structures in which you live; I care to visit and reside in your hearts. This Prashanti Nilayam is not my residence; when your hearts are transformed into Prashanti Nilayams (the abodes of deepest Peace), they are My residence.

When you pray that I should visit your village, I think of the facilities it has — not for Me, I need only standing space — for the thousands, the tens of thousands, the hundreds of thousands that gather to have My *darshan* (sight). How can I tolerate the slightest inconvenience to them, the women, the children, the sick, the aged, the blind, the decrepit, that come for counsel, consolation, courage and cure?[2]

---

[1] *Sathya Sai Speaks*, Vol. 15, pp. 311–12.

[2] *Sathya Sai Speaks*, Vol. 8, pp. 156–57.

◊ ◊ ◊ ◊ ◊

I know the agitations of your heart and its aspirations, but you do not know My Heart. I react to the pain that you undergo, to the joy that you feel; for, I am in every heart. I am the dweller in that temple. You must know Me better, for how can a telegram sent in Morse code be understood by the receiving office, when the receiver does not know Morse? The *Prema* (Love) that you give is of the same Morse Code, as the *Ananda* (Bliss) I give you.[1]

◊ ◊ ◊ ◊ ◊

I am alone on this dais; you are thousands in front of Me. What has brought you all, in this vast number, from your homes and villages to this place? It is the Love you have for Me, and the Love I have for you. The reason for your presence is not any force or authority or temptation to earn material profit or gain. Ponder over the things I have told you out of My Love and try to cleanse your minds through repentance for wrongs done or contemplated and through a firm resolve to shape your lives anew, according to the Divine Plan, by which each can stand revealed as fully Divine.[2]

◊ ◊ ◊ ◊ ◊

Love is the word which indicates the striving to realize the falsehood of the many and the reality of the One. Love identifies; hate separates. Love transposes the self onto another and the two think, speak, and act as one. When Love takes in more and more within its fold, more and more entities are rendered as One. When you Love Me, you Love all, for you begin to feel and know and experience that I am in all. By means of meditation you can realize that I am the

---

[1] *Sathya Sai Speaks*, Vol. 5, pp. 117–18.

[2] *Sathya Sai Speaks*, Vol. 8, p. 228.

resident in all hearts, the urge, the motive, the guide, the goal. Yearn for that vision, that awareness, and make it your priceless possession. Then you have what you so often ask Me for — Self-realization. Your Love has to be as pure, as vast, as free from the taint of ego as Mine in order to merge in Me.[1]

◊ ◊ ◊ ◊ ◊

There is nothing greater than this Love. You have all been drawn to Me by this Love. To give Love and to receive Love. This is My business. No income–tax officer can know the extent of the "income" derived from this "business." There is no limit to My *Ananda* (Divine Bliss). I am always immersed in Bliss. This is because My Bliss is associated with Love and not with any material objects. If you follow this path, you will also derive this ineffable *Ananda*. You will realise Peace of every kind.[2]

◊ ◊ ◊ ◊ ◊

I am *Anandaswarupa* (embodiment of Supreme Bliss); My nature is *Ananda*; *Ananda* is My sign. The *ajna*, the rules of discipline and *sadhana* laid down in *Bhagavata*, the *Ramayana*, the *Bhagavad Geeta*, the *Mahabharata* are not heeded, though they are read and learnt by heart, since centuries. Now that the *Nirakara* (the Formless, attributeless principle) has come in human form, be earnest to observe the orders given for your own Liberation. Do not cast away the nectar of Grace when it is offered.[3]

◊ ◊ ◊ ◊ ◊

---

[1] *Sathya Sai Speaks*, Vol. 7, pp. 473–74.

[2] *Sathya Sai Speaks*, Vol. 16, p. 49.

[3] *Sathya Sai Speaks*, Vol. 8, p. 184.

Reference was made to the bond of *Prema* which binds you to this place. Your *Prema* towards Me and My *vatsalya* (affection of mother to the child), these two are the bonds. I have no desire to keep you here at the *Prashanti Nilayam*; I know you have duties and obligations to individuals and institutions who depend on your service. They are also Mine. I also want to give you the experience of My being everywhere, not restricted by time or space, or causation.[1]

◊ ◊ ◊ ◊ ◊

I am *Ananda–swarupa* (Divine Bliss personified) all the time and so, I am never ill. Nor am I in the least disturbed by either the praise or by the maligning, that people pour. When I am spoken of, either in derision or in adoration, My *Ananda* is the same. ...

This *Prema* is My distinctive mark, not the creation of material objects or of health and happiness, by sheer exercise of Will. You might consider what you call "miracles" as the most direct sign of Divinity; but, the *Prema* that welcomes you all, that blesses all, that makes Me rush to the presence of the seekers, the suffering and the distressed in distant lands or wherever they are, that is the real sign! It is that which declares that I am Sai Baba.[2]

◊ ◊ ◊ ◊ ◊

It is impossible for any one to understand or explain the meaning and significance of Swami. There can be no possible means of approach to this manifestation, from the stage which you can attain. This is an Incarnation, an Embodiment, which is beyond any one's comprehension. Trying to explain Me would be as futile as the attempt of a person who does not know the alphabet to read a learned volume, or the attempt to pour the Ocean into a tiny waterway. You

---

[1] *Sathya Sai Speaks*, Vol. 6, p. 195.

[2] *Sathya Sai Speaks*, Vol. 7, pp. 169–70.

can at best only prepare yourself to receive and benefit by the *Ananda* I confer, the Bliss I grant.

You too have the Sai principle in you, but the difference is a matter of voltage. You have bulbs of zero watt power, and bulbs of vast quantities of wattage giving enormous light. The same electric current passes through them no doubt, but, how incomprehensible must be the "Supreme" for the "molecule."

Krishna in the *Geeta* declared against the worship of low forces. He said those who adore the *devas* attain the *devas*; those who adore the Manes attain the Manes; those who adore the low forces attain them; but, those who adore Me, attain Me. He said, *Manmana Bhava, Madbhakto, madyaji, Mam namaskuru* — "Fill your mind with Me, be devoted to Me, renounce for My sake, surrender to Me." Do not have low desires and seek low deities that cater to the fulfilment of these. Yearn for the highest wisdom, the highest Bliss, the highest Power, the *Atma*. Yearn for nothing less than the Highest; pray to the Sovereign Giver.[1]

◊ ◊ ◊ ◊ ◊

Do not count and calculate what the Puttaparthi Sai Baba gives. I do not give in order to attract you to Me; I give only to fill you with *Ananda*. Showering *Ananda*, that is My task. I do not want you to extol Me; I shall be satisfied if you rely on Me. The mysterious indescribable Super–power has come within reach. It will never engage Itself in any task without fruit.

I bring tears and I wipe tears, someone has sung. Yes, I bring tears of joy into your eyes and I wipe the tears of grief. I am said to make people mad and also to cure madness. Yes, I make them mad about God and about the *sadhana* needed for that. I cure the madness which

[1] *Sathya Sai Speaks*, Vol. 10, pp. 170–71.

makes people run frantically after fleeting pleasures and fall into fits of joy and grief.[1]

◊ ◊ ◊ ◊ ◊

Let me tell you that you cannot understand Me and My Secret without first understanding yourselves. For, if you are too weak to grasp your own Reality, how can you hope to fathom the much grander Reality of My Advent? To grasp My meaning, you have to tear into tatters the doubts and theories you now have and cultivate *Prema*, for the embodiment of *Prema* can be understood only through *Prema*. The "miracles and wonders" which cannot be explained by the categories of science, are so natural to Me that I am amused when you label them as miracles. The Lord had announced that He would come down for the restoration of *Dharma* (Righteousness) and that He would assume human form so that all might gather round Him and feel the thrill of His companionship and conversation. And the Lord has come, as announced.[2]

◊ ◊ ◊ ◊ ◊

I do not know whether you are aware of Swami's nature. When someone comes to Swami and says that he is suffering from an unbearable stomach ache, Swami says: "*Ananda, Ananda*" ("Happy, Happy"). When a woman comes wailing over the loss of her husband, Swami says: "*Chala santosham*" ("Very happy"). Swami is always in a state of Bliss. Happiness is the very nature of the Divine.

What is the use of lamenting over anything? All things are passing clouds. Nothing is lasting. Why, then, bewail over any loss? You should not bother about them. This is the teaching of the *Avatar*. Don't feel distressed over anything that may happen. Every pain is followed

---

[1] *Sathya Sai Speaks*, Vol. 1, p. 188.

[2] *Sathya Sai Speaks*, Vol. 1, p. 154.

by some pleasure. Pleasure is an interval between two pains. It is on
this basis that you should lead your lives.

There is a vast difference between Divine Bliss and momentary
pleasure. What is called happiness is incidental to a situation and is
not permanent. But Bliss (*Ananda*) is different. It is lasting. When you
are hungry, you go to the canteen and feel happy after taking food.
But that does not last long. Permanent happiness can be got only
through devotion to the Divine. *Avatars* make their advent only to
confer Divine Bliss on mankind.

The petty difficulties met with in everyday life can be overcome
by Love. Once you cultivate Love, you can overcome any difficulty.
Strive for God's grace. But do not regard God as different from you.
He is within you. Where there is God, there is victory. That is the
inner meaning of the last stanza in the *Geeta*: "*Yathra Yogeswarah
Krishno yathra—Partho Danurdhara Tatra Sri Vijayo Bhutir–Dhruva
nitir–mathir mama.*" The esoteric meaning of this sloka is: "The heart in
which the Lord of Yoga dwells and where there is the courage and
strength represented by Arjuna, there all prosperity and success are
assured."[1]

◊ ◊ ◊ ◊ ◊

I have been seeing your devotion and enthusiasm ever since I
entered your town this morning; and during the procession through
the streets, I could see the ardour of your *bhakti* (devotion). Even now,
I feel that I could give you joy by merely sitting here and giving
darshan (audience), for I can listen to your silent prayers and you can
sense My *Prema* (Love). That is enough. That gives *Anandam*. You are
born, you grow, you live and you merge, all in *Anandam* (Bliss); that
is the Truth, though very few know it. That is why I remind you of it
by addressing you as *Ananda–swarupulara* (embodiments of Bliss). Your

---

[1] *Sanathana Sarathi*, September 1990, p. 231.

swarupa (natural state) is *Anandam* (Bliss), however much you might have ignored it.[1]

◊ ◊ ◊ ◊ ◊

4.

The Characteristics of Sathya Sai Baba Avatar

This body of mine is named *Sathya* (Truth); the principle that is in this body is also Truth. Truth enclosed in Truth has been rendered the Truth of Truths (*Sathyasya Sathyam*). This Form has been assumed in order to lead mankind from unTruth to Truth.

I eat as you do, move about as you do, talk in your language, and behave as you can recognise and understand, for YOUR sake — not for My sake! I turn you towards the Divine, winning your confidence, your Love, your submission, by being among you, as one of yourselves, one whom you can see, listen to, speak to, touch and treat with reverence and devotion. My plan is to transmute you into seekers of Truth (*Sathya–anveshaks*).

I am present everywhere, at all times; My Will must prevail over every obstacle; I am aware of the past, present and future, of your innermost thought and carefully guarded secrets. I am *sarvantharyami, sarva shakti* and *sarvajnana* (Omnipresent, Omnipotent and Omniscient). Nevertheless, I do not manifest these powers in any capricious manner or merely for display. For, I am an example and an inspiration for whatever I do or omit to do. My life is a commentary on My message.

---

[1] *Sathya Sai Speaks*, Vol. 2, p. 9.

For example, you must have noticed that I never call a woman, alone for the "interview." I call women only in groups of ten or fifteen. I want that you should note this and infer that one has to be extremely cautious in dealing with the other sex. For, though I am above and beyond the *gunas*, since this body is obviously masculine, I want to teach both men and women how they have to regulate their social behaviour and be above the slightest tinge of suspicion, or of small talk.

Again, I am active and busy all the twenty–four hours of the day. Every day, the mail brings me thousands of letters, and you hand over to me personally hundreds more. Yet, I do not take the help of any one else, even to open the envelopes. For, you write to Me intimate details of your personal problems, believing that I alone will read them and having implicit confidence in Me. You write each one only a single letter; that makes for Me a huge bundle a day; and I have to go through all of them. You may ask, how I manage it? Well, I do not waste a single moment.

And, all this I do, not for personal gain, but only because I have come for your sake. I never seek another's help; I offer help, never receive it. My hand always gives; it never takes. Conclude from this that this must be Divine, not human power.

Some of you may be wondering, "How does Swami arrange these elaborate festivals and functions? Whom does He charge with the various items of work?" I do not allot work to this person or that, or consult any one for ideas and suggestions. All this is done by the Divine Will, operating through the force of Love. For example, though there are thousands gathered here, absolute silence prevails. Under what compulsion? Only the compulsion of Love. In other places, where a hundred people collect, a hundred and fifty constables are present to keep them quiet! Here, there is no need for any one to see that silence is maintained. For, here God is the Master, and Creation dances in joy. There is no third entity here. Only *Purusha* and *Prakriti* (God and Nature) are here. A glance from the corner of the eye is enough to get things going towards successful conclusion. Love activates, Love fulfils.[1]

◊ ◊ ◊ ◊ ◊

Sai is ever full of joy. Anxiety, grief and unrest cannot approach Sai, not even as near as millions of miles. Believe it or not, Sai does not have the slightest experience of anxiety, for Sai is ever aware of the formation and transformation of objects and the antics of time and space and of the incidents therein. Those who have no knowledge of these and those who are affected by circumstances are affected by sorrow. Those who are caught in the coils of time and space become the victims of grief. Though Sai is involved in events conditioned by time and space, Sai is ever established in the principle that is beyond both time and space. Sai is not conditioned by time, place or circumstance.

Therefore, you must all recognise the uniqueness of the Will of Sai, the Sai *Sankalpa*. Know that this *sankalpa* is *Vajrasankalpa* — it is irresistible Will. You may ignore its expression as weak and insignificant but, once the will is formed, whatever else undergoes change, it cannot change.[2]

◊ ◊ ◊ ◊ ◊

The chief characteristics of Sathya Sai are, let me tell you, equanimity, forbearance (*sahana*). There are many who are engaged in criticism and calumny. Many papers publish all types of writings. Many pamphlets are printed. All kinds of things happen in the world. My reply to all these is a smile. Such criticisms and distortions are the inevitable accompaniments of everything good and great. Only the

---

[1] *Sathya Sai Speaks*, Vol. 10, p. 184–86.

[2] *Sathya Sai Speaks*, Vol. 15, p. 143.

fruitladen tree is hit by stones thrown by greedy people. No one casts a stone on the tree that bears no fruit!

There are some others who suffer from sheer envy at the increasing number and phenomenal progress of Sathya Sai Seva Organisations and the Sathya Sai Educational Institutions and they try to invent falsehoods and cause agitation.

Embodiments of Love! Even if the entire world opposes Me unitedly, nothing can affect Me. My mission is essentially Mine. I am engaged in doing good. My heart is ever full of benediction. I have no ego. I do not own any thing. This is My Truth. Those who have faith in this, My Truth, will not hesitate to dedicate themselves to it. Those who have doubts and defects react with anger and fear. But the person with no doubt and defect will not react so. I am aware of this and so I am always in *Ananda, Ananda, Ananda* (Bliss).[1]

◊ ◊ ◊ ◊ ◊

I do not need any publicity nor does any other manifestation of the Lord. What are you daring to publicise? What do you know about Me, let Me ask? You speak one thing about Me today and another tomorrow. Your faith has not become unshakable! You praise, when things go well, and blame when things go wrong. You flit from one refuge to another.

And even before your *bhakti* (devotion) ripens, you strive to lead others, you collect donations and subscriptions and plan *mandirs* (halls) and *sanghams* (gatherings); all this is mere show, which brings spiritual loss, rather than spiritual gain. When you start publicity you descend to the level of those who compete in collecting clientele, decrying others and extolling themselves.

---

[1] *Sathya Sai Speaks*, Vol. 15, pp. 179–80.

Where money is calculated and garnered, and exhibited to demonstrate one's achievements, I will not be present. I come only where sincerity, faith and surrender are valued.[1]

◊ ◊ ◊ ◊ ◊

I have come to re-form you: I won't leave you until I do that. Even if you get away before I do that, do not think you can escape Me; I will hold on to you. I am not worried if you leave Me, for I am not anxious that there should be a huge gathering here, around Me. Who invited you all here? There was not even a little notice in print, but you have come here in thousands. You attach yourselves to Me. I am unattached. I am attached only to the Task for which I have come.

But, of one thing, be assured. Whether you come to Me or not, you are all Mine. This *Shivamatha*, this *Sai Matha* (Mother of all) has the Love of a thousand mothers towards Her children; that is why I do so much *lalana* (fondling) and so much *palana* (protecting). Whenever I appear to be angry, remember, it is only Love in another form. For, I have not even an atom of anger in me; I just evince My disappointment that you do not shape as I direct. When I direct you along a line of action, reflect on My advice; you have full liberty to do so; in fact, I shall be happy if you do so; I do not like slavish obedience. If you feel that it will help you to reach the goal, follow it; if not, go to some other place; but, let Me tell you one thing: Wherever you go, you meet only Me. I am everywhere.[2]

◊ ◊ ◊ ◊ ◊

Along the lines already familiar to you, continue the worship of the God of your choice; then you will find that you are coming nearer

---

[1] *Sathya Sai Speaks*, Vol. 4, p. 210.

[2] *Sathya Sai Speaks*, Vol. 4, pp. 24–25.

and nearer to Me; for, all Names are Mine and all Forms are Mine. There is no need to change, after you have seen Me and heard Me. That is what I wanted to tell you, since the Shastri spoke to you of *Avatars* and their significance.[1]

◊ ◊ ◊ ◊ ◊

When God assumes the human form and is behind, before and beside you, speaking to you and moving with you, and allows you to cultivate attachment of various kinds with Him, you do not recognise Him. The Divine cannot be easily recognised, when It is embodied. The Divine proclaims, "I am not a mass of flesh and blood; I am not a bundle of desires, which the mind is; I am not the heap of delusion which the imagination is; I am the *Paramatma* (Supreme Soul), the Origin and the End."

I am the urge within you, the knowledge which you seek as a result of the urge, of your own self. "One word of Swami grants the treasure of all the riches. A single glance of Swami bestows all boons; it is the Paraijatha (wish–fulfilling flower–tree) Glance. The arms of Sai confer the *Hai* (soft comfort) the mother gives, not one mother, no, the *Prema* (Divine Love) of a thousand mothers!" This Sathya Sai is such *Prema Dhayi* (Bestower of Love)."

When the Divine plays and sings with us, meets us and eats with us, we should not be misled into the belief that It is just human and nothing more. We generally forget the Truth.

Embodiments of Divine Love! You must be clear about the distinction between birth in general and the Advent of the *Avatar* (Divine Incarnation). *Karma* (the cumulative consequence of deeds and thoughts) is the cause of ordinary birth. Birth in the human body is the reward for the merit acquired by worthy *karma* (past deeds). What is the *karma* that has caused the Advent? That too must have some *karma* as the antecedent, it may be said. Well! In your case you earn

---

[1] *Sathya Sai Speaks,* Vol. 5, p. 122.

the type of life which the good and bad *karmas* you have done entitle you to have. Unless you go through the mass of consequence, you cannot change the vehicle or instrument. For, it is a role you have been assigned in the Cosmic Drama on the world stage. The role is part of a play for which it is allotted. You may appear in the first scene but you cannot change your make–up.

But, God is not bound or affected by *karma*. He takes on a role, as a consequence not of any *karma*, but to reward good *karma* and impose retribution for bad *karma*. God incarnated as Narasimha as a consequence of the bad deeds of *Hiranyakashipu*, and the good deeds of *Prahlada*. The Truth is, the body that the *Avatar* wears is not a *karma deha*, designed according to the nature of the individual's deeds in past lives. God, as *Avatar*, can mould or change the body in any way He wills. He can develop it or discard it, as and when He wills. No other power or person can affect it. Everything happens as He desires, as He decides. To look upon the *Avatar* as the body it has assumed is not correct. The *Guru* has, as his duty, to teach mankind this great Truth of the *Paramatma* and the *Atma* and of the Glory and Compassion of God.[1]

◊ ◊ ◊ ◊ ◊

God comes with a body, as *Avatar*, and when He moves about, He seems to be only human as far as one can see. But, there is a fundamental inner difference. The incarnate God, the *Avatar*, is unconcerned. He has *upeksha* (indifference to results). The ordinary man with the body has *apeksha* (yearning for the result). *Mamatwa* (mineness–principle) is human; *Brahmatwa* (*Brahman*–principle) is Divine. You cannot discern the distinction, even when you look or listen. You can understand only by experience. The *Avatar* has no wants. He has no egoism. He is ever alone in the *Brahmatwam*. ...

---

[1] *Sathya Sai Speaks*, Vol. 16, pp. 88–89.

The *Avatar* appears as any other human being, equipped with body, senses, mind, etc. But, consider the vast difference in thoughts, feelings, emotions, etc. The *Avatar* is the total, the all–comprehensive, the *Purna* (Full). The human is partial, narrow, negative. But, in the human, the Divine exists as the core and can manifest as Bliss.[1]

◊ ◊ ◊ ◊ ◊

I never exult when I am extolled, nor shrink when I am reviled. Few have realised My purpose and significance; but I am not worried. When things that are not in Me are attributed to Me, why should I worry? When things that are in Me are mentioned, why should I exult? "*Sayeeki Sarvamu* yes, yes, yes," (for Sai it is always yes, yes, yes). If you say, "Yes; You are the Lord," I am the Lord to you; if you say "No," I am No to you.

I am *Ananda, Shantam, Dhairyam* (Bliss, Equanimity and Courage). Take Me as your *Atmatutwum* (Reality of *Atma*); you won't be wrong.[2]

◊ ◊ ◊ ◊ ◊

The Lord has said that, "*madh bhakta yathra gayante thathra thishthami, Narada*" — "Where my devotees sing of Me, there I install Myself, *Narada*." I must tell you that you are luckier than men of previous generations. The accumulated merit of many previous births must have granted you this luck. You have got Me and it is your duty now to develop this relationship that you have achieved by sheer good fortune.

In four or five years time, you will see *Yogis* and *Maharishis* and *Munis* (ascetics and sages) crowding here and you may not have such chances of asking Me questions and getting the answers, of approaching Me and directly speaking to Me. So do not be like frogs

---

[1] *Sathya Sai Speaks*, Vol. 15 p. 255.

[2] *Sathya Sai Speaks*, Vol. 5, pp. 128–29.

around the lotus; be like the bees. Plantains and mangoes are kept, while yet green, in straw or dried grass or in a closed room so that the heat may make them ripe and tasty. The meditation on God gives you too the right temperature to ripen yourselves and become sweet and tasty.[1]

◊ ◊ ◊ ◊ ◊

The snows on the mountain peaks soften during day, as a result of the Sun; they harden during the night, since the Sun is absent. So too, your hard heart hardens Me; your soft heart softens Me. Understand this: Each of you knows the Love of a single mother only. But My affection, My Love towards every one of you is that of a thousand Mothers! Do not deny yourself that affection, that Love, by denying Me your Love![2]

◊ ◊ ◊ ◊ ◊

I am untouched by elation or sadness, or any of the consequences of activity. The ball of butter, floating on buttermilk, though it is in it, is not of it. My nature is unaffected by My movements and activities. I talk and walk among you, I arrange and direct, I advise and admonish, but I am away from any attachment. The Divine is so distinct and distinguished from the mortal and the bound. Train your minds to follow not the devious, but, the Divine path, of which I am revealing to you the trail.[3]

◊ ◊ ◊ ◊ ◊

---

[1] *Sathya Sai Speaks*, Vol. 1, pp. 182–83.

[2] *Sathya Sai Speaks*, Vol. 10, p. 142.

[3] *Sathya Sai Speaks*, Vol. 11, p. 69.

I have not got the slightest intention to utilise the *Seva Samithis* (Service Organisations) for propagating My Name or canvas homage for My Name. No! I am content only when spiritual endeavours and disciplines to elevate and purify man are progressing everywhere. It is only through these that My universal reality will be revealed. So, do not limit Me to the boundaries of any one name and form. Your aim should be to see the self–same God in all the Forms that are worshipped, to picture Him in all the Names, nay, to be conscious of His presence as the inner motivator of every living being, in every particle of matter. Do not fall into the error of considering some to be men worthy of reverence and some unworthy. Sai is in every one; so, all deserve your reverence and service. Propagate this Truth; that is the function I assign to the *Seva Samithis*.

You can observe Me and My activities; note how I adhere to Righteousness, moral order, Truth and universal compassion. That is what I desire you to learn from Me. Many of you plead for a "Message" from Me, to take to the *Samithi* of which you are members. Well. My life is My message. You will be adhering to My message if you so live that your lives are evidence of the dispassionate quiet, the courage, the confidence, the eagerness to serve those who are in distress, that My life inspires you with.

God is immanent in the world. So, treat the world lovingly, as you will treat your Master.... Serve, whatever the obstacle, whatever the cynical ridicule you may attract. Such reactions are inevitable when one is engaged in doing good. Take My example. Praise and calumny have accompanied Me throughout the Ages. Opposition and obstacles only tend to highlight the good and strengthen resolve. ...

Of what avail is it if you simply worship My Name and Form, without attempting to cultivate the *samatwa* (equal Love for all) that I have, My *Shanti* (Unruffled Equanimity), My *Prema* (Love), My *Sahana* (Patience and Fortitude), My *Ananda* (Ever–Blissful Nature)?

You elaborate in your lectures the unique powers of Sai, the incidents that are described as "miracles" in books written on Me by some persons. But I request you not to attach importance to these. Do not exaggerate their significance; the most significant and important power is, let Me tell you, My *Prema* (Love). I may turn the sky into earth, or earth into sky; but that is not the sign of Divine might. It is the *Prema*, the *sahana*, effective, universal, ever–present; that is the unique sign. ...

This is the very first time that a World Conference is held of persons devoted, while the incarnation is present before everyone, with the body assumed for the purpose, bearing the Name that is chosen for it by Itself.

I must tell you this fact, because ninety–nine persons out of a hundred among you do not know My Reality. You have come here drawn by diverse needs, a taste for spiritual matters, eagerness to develop the institutions to which you are attached, admiration or affection ....[1]

◊ ◊ ◊ ◊ ◊

I am emphasising another point today. You are using the name Sai family while addressing devotees, and referring to yourselves as members of the Sai family. This is a narrow, restrictive expression. I have no limits_ or restriction. I am in all, for all. There can be no distinct Sai family. Whatever the Name and Form they address, Rama, Krishna, Sai, etc., they all belong to Me, to God. To assume that God responds to one Name only and can be adored in one Form only, is a sacrilege.[2]

◊ ◊ ◊ ◊ ◊

It is the nature of the world that every person must encounter one opponent or enemy. Sai alone does not have even a single enemy in the whole world. Some people, following their own fantasy, may assume that I dislike them. But, in my view, there is no one I do not

---

[1] *Sathya Sai Speaks*, Vol. 8, pp. 96–98

[2] *Sai Baba Discourses*, Vol. 1, p. 15.

Love. All are dear to me. Let me tell you that no one else in the world today has as much wealth, as much property, as much treasure as I have, not even the World Bank, not even the richest emperors and kings.

What is that wealth, that property, that treasure? It is my selfless, universal Love. That uniquely potent Love has kept this body radiant and young. As the world goes, at the age of 60, the physique becomes weak and the mind loses its alertness. But I skip along as fresh and active as ever. I see and hear, I play and sing as bright and busy as a youth of sixteen. This sacred nature I have assumed will not allow physical or other weakness to hinder me.

Some people are misled by happenings that do not affect my Reality or my Purpose. They observe, with their feeble understanding, that a few have left my Presence and they clamour that thereby, My Works are bound to be affected! Those who have left have done so, not because they do not like Me, but because they did not get from Me what they desired. Or, they could not receive here the status and respect available in the outer world. When they are questioned, they invent other reasons to explain their conduct. They do not realize that being with Me and shaping their lives under My Direction can be the source of even higher status and respect. I am glad, however, that they are contented with their lot, though they impute faults in Me to buttress their action. That, too, is an act of service, a boon from which they draw "benefits."

Does the ocean depend on rivers for its existence or do rivers depend on the ocean for the rains that feed them? My status and success are based on My own Will, My Goodness, My Love. These do not grow or decline, when a few stay or depart. They alone are the beneficiaries or losers.

No one, in fact, has the right or reason to point a finger at any blot in Me. My total selflessness, my compassionate heart full of eagerness to serve and save, My resolve to establish Peace and prosperity, My determination to shower *Ananda* on the world — these are being manifested more and more from day to day, and I am at all times in immeasurable *Ananda*. I am not affected by anxiety even for a moment. Is there anyone in this world who can say this? It is sheer ignorance that induces people to comment otherwise. When they experience My Love and witness the unfolding of My Mission, the comments will cease, and the Reality that Sai is, will be clear to them. That knowledge can bear fruit by transforming your human–ness into Divinity, into Sai. The Knower of *Brahman* becomes *Brahman* Itself.[1]

◊ ◊ ◊ ◊ ◊

You must have observed that I do not mention in any place about your worshipping Sai Baba. On the other hand, I strongly discourage attempts to build temples in My Name. I ask them, instead, to renovate and utilise the temples existing all over the country. This "*Mandir* Construction Scheme" has become a profitable spiritual business. People go about with lists of likely victims and squeeze donations out of them in My Name. In this business, a great deal of back–biting, malice, envy and greed are generated and it ends with factions blaming each other in every place. Why go about doing Sainatha publicity or Meher publicity or Haranath publicity? Pushing your master's name forward easily degenerates into tarnishing the name of the other man's *Guru* or God and this leads to defaming both master and disciple.[2]

◊ ◊ ◊ ◊ ◊

I have no wish to draw people towards Me, away from the worship of My other names and forms. You may infer from what you call My miracles, that I am causing them to attract and to attach you to Me, and Me alone. They are not intended to demonstrate or publicise; they are merely spontaneous and concomitant proofs of Divine Majesty. I am yours; you are Mine, for ever and ever. What

---

[1] *Sai Baba Discourses*, Vol. 1, pp. 3–5.

[2] *Sathya Sai Speaks*, Vol. 5, pp. 91–92.

need is there for attracting and impressing, for demonstrating your Love or My compassion? I am in you; you are in Me. There is no distance or distinction. ...

But Sai wants that the votaries of each religion must cultivate faith in its own excellence and realise their validity by their own intense practice. That is the Sai religion, the religion that feeds and fosters all religions and emphasizes their common Greatness. Take up this religion, boldly and joyfully.[1]

◊ ◊ ◊ ◊ ◊

The Lord is devoid of attachment or hatred. He comes on a Mission and is bent only on that task. It is His nature to support the right and admonish the wrong. His task is to restore vision to man, to turn his footsteps along the path of morality and self-control, so that he may achieve Self-knowledge.[2]

◊ ◊ ◊ ◊ ◊

The *Guru* warns and wakens. He reveals the Truth and encourages you to progress towards it. Unless you have the yearning, the questioning heart, the seeking intelligence, he cannot do much. The hungry can be fed; he who has no hunger will discard food as an infliction. The *Guru* is a gardener, who will tend the plant; but, the sapling must have sprouted before he can take charge. He does not add anything new to the plant; he only helps it to grow according to its own destiny, quicker perhaps, more fully perhaps, but, not against its inner nature. He removes poverty by pointing to the treasure that

---

[1] *Sathya Sai Speaks*, Vol. 8, p. 246.

[2] *Sathya Sai Speaks*, Vol. 13, p. 148.

lies buried in the very habitation of man; he advises the method of recovering it, the vigilance needed to use it to the best advantage, etc.[1]

◊ ◊ ◊ ◊ ◊

Many people who have some questions regarding Swami do not realise the ways of the Divine. They look at all things from the worldly point of view. They should look at things from the Divine point of view. Change the angle of your vision. When you practise seeing the world from the point of view of the omnipresence of the Divine, you will get transformed. You will experience the power of the Divine in everything in creation. You cannot hide anything from God. Many imagine that Swami does not see what they are doing. They do not realise that Swami has a myriad eyes. Even your eyes are Divine. But you are not aware of your true nature. When you have faith in yourself, you will have faith in God. ...[2]

◊ ◊ ◊ ◊ ◊

Some persons have said in their ignorance that I am Divine sometimes and that I become human after that! They say I alternate between *Daivatwam* and *Manavatwam* (Divinity and human). Do not believe this. I am always of one *twam* (reality) only. The Lord will never undergo a fundamental change; only the external form may change, the essence will be the same. There will not be any decline in value, like becoming human for some time, etc. The Lord will be characterised by unbounded *Prema* (Love) and unsullied sweetness.

There are two duties to be done by man; the one along the *Dharmamarga* (path of Righteousness) for this world and the one along the *Brahmamarga* (path of Supreme Reality) for eternal liberation. The *Dharmamarga* is the left hand, and so it can be left. Why, it will leave

---

[1] *Sathya Sai Speaks*, Vol. 5, pp. 195–96.

[2] *Sanathana Sarathi*, March 1995, p. 63.

of itself after the fruit becomes ripe. That is why it is called "left"! Leave it and do not grieve over it. But hold on to the right, the *Brahmamarga;* for it is "right" that you should do so.

Finally, you must know how to use the chance that you have got in this life to come in contact with the Lord. The lamp sheds illumination but it can be used for various purposes, good and bad; the Ganga (Ganges River) is holy but its waters are used for good as well as bad purposes. How you use this chance depends upon your destiny and luck and the amount of Grace that you are able to win. Develop faith; strengthen devotion; and everything will follow. Rama was the representative of *Sathyam,* Krishna of *Prema,* Buddha of *Dharma.* Now it is, of all the four, *Sathya, Dharma, Shanti* and *Prema. Sathya* is the *Dharma, Prema* gives *Shanti.* I command you: never hate others, or wish evil to them or talk ill of them. Then only can you attain the *Shanthaswarupam* (natural form of Peace). ...

You are My treasure, even if you deny Me. I am your treasure, even if you say No. I shall be affectionate to you and attach Myself to you; I shall take all the trouble to keep My property safe in My custody! That is to say, in the custody of the Lord, by whichever name you may be calling upon Him. All the powers I have are for you: I am just the store, keeping them ready to be given to you, whenever you ask for them. I shall give *Prema* even if you do not ask, for it is your right to share in it.

Some complain that I did not give them this or that, but that is because their vision is limited to the immediate future or the present; whereas I know what is in store and so I have to safeguard them from greater grief. They even blame Me and heap abuses but I will not give them up. I am not influenced by anybody, remember. There is no one who can change My course or affect My conduct to the slightest extent. I am the Master over all.

But let Me tell you this. I speak harsh words and "punish" some persons because I have *Prema* towards them and I am eager to correct them and make them better instruments. If they were not Mine, I would have given them up and not cared to take any notice of their lapses. I have a right to chastise those who I feel are Mine. I also know that they still value My Word and that they will feel sad at My being displeased with them. It is due to your wayward mind that you are easily wafted away from Me by some silly persons' irresponsible words.

I sometimes act as if I keep you at a distance; that is done to reform you quicker. When a stretch of road is being repaired, I go by another detour and I do not use that bit of road for some time. The purpose is to let the repair works proceed more quickly so that I may use that road again.

I have come to set the world right and so I have to collect all those who are ill and treat them in My "Hospital" and restore them to sanity, strength and wisdom and send them back to their stations in life. I must intensify your *bhakti*, reinforce your faith and rebuild the foundations of your moral nature, so that you can counter temptations with greater confidence. I have come across people who recite a prayer and believe that they are bringing the world nearer to Peace with every occasion on which they pray. But Peace can be won only the hard way, by eliminating violence and greed from the hearts of individuals.[1]

◊ ◊ ◊ ◊ ◊

In Truth, you cannot understand the nature of my Reality either today, or even after a thousand years of steady austerity or ardent inquiry even if all mankind joins in that effort. But, in a short time, you will become cognisant of the Bliss showered by the Divine Principle, which has taken upon itself this sacred body and this sacred name. Your good fortune which will provide you this chance is greater than what was available for anchorites, monks, sages, saints and even personalities embodying facets of Divine Glory!

Since I move about with you, eat like you, and talk with you, you are deluded into the belief that this is but an instance of common

---

[1] *Sathya Sai Speaks*, Vol. 1, pp. 189–92.

humanity. Be warned against this mistake. I am also deluding you by My singing with you, talking with you, and engaging Myself in activities with you. But, any moment, My Divinity may be revealed to you; you have to be ready, prepared for the moment. Since Divinity is enveloped by human–ness you must endeavour to overcome the *maya* (delusion) that hides it from your eyes.

"This is a human form in which every Divine entity, every Divine Principle, that is to say, all the Names and Forms ascribed by man to God, are manifest — "*Sarvadaivatwa sarvarupalanu dharin–china manavakarame ee akaram.*" Do not allow doubt to distract you; if you only install, in the altar of your heart, steady faith in My Divinity, you can win a Vision of My Reality. Instead, if you swing like the pendulum of a clock, one moment, devotion, another moment, disbelief, you can never succeed in comprehending the Truth and win that Bliss. You are very fortunate that you have a chance to experience the Bliss of the vision of the *sarvadaivatwa swarupam* (the form, which is all forms of all Gods) now, in this life itself.

Let Me draw your attention to another fact. On previous occasions when God incarnated on earth, the Bliss of recognising Him in the incarnation was vouchsafed only after the physical embodiment had left the world, in spite of plenty of patent evidences of His Grace. And the loyalty and devotion they commanded from men arose through fear and awe, at their superhuman powers and skills, or at their imperial and penal authority. But, ponder a moment on this Sathya Sai Manifestation; in this age of rampant materialism, aggressive disbelief and irreverence, what is it that brings to It the adoration of millions from all over the world? You will be convinced that the basic reason for this is the fact that this is the Supra–worldly Divinity in Human form.[1]

◊ ◊ ◊ ◊ ◊

---

[1] *Sathya Sai Speaks*, Vol. 8, pp. 99–100.

Baba here sang a song: "One man's mind prefers Krishna, another's likes Shiva, another prefers the Formless Allah." He said, "My Voice, you have noted, gets lost exactly here because in the song the next line is about some preferring the name of Sai; I never call upon people to worship Me, giving up the Forms they already revere. I have come to establish *Dharma* and so I do not and will not demand or require your homage. Give it to your Lord or *Guru*, whoever He is; I am the Witness, come to set right the vision."[1]

◊ ◊ ◊ ◊ ◊

The beaming joy on the faces of this vast multitude is the food that I live upon; I am refreshed when you are happy and content. My thirst is quenched by the joy which lights up your eyes. Your *Ananda* is My *ahara* (food). I do not feel like talking to you at all, for I desire only to communicate to you My Joy and to get into communion with your Joy. This mutual fulfilment is the essential thing; talking and listening are subsidiary.[2]

◊ ◊ ◊ ◊ ◊

Embodiments of Divine *Atma! Bharat* (India) has been the centre of spiritual progress for ages past and the region where Divine incarnations re–establish *Dharma* for the good of humanity. In order to make known My Majesty and My Glory as the Divine that has Incarnated, miraculous happenings of an amazing nature do take place in certain areas. Taking advantage of the attraction that those happenings draw upon them, many misuse them for personal propaganda and aggrandizement. They trade for money the *Vibhuthi* (sacred ash) that the pictures in their altars shower! They go about pretending that they are "superior devotees" of a higher order and

---

[1] *Sathya Sai Speaks*, Vol. 2, p. 89.

[2] *Sathya Sai Speaks*, Vol. 5, p. 96.

conferring boons and blessings on the innocent folk whom they fleece. Others put forth false claims that *vibhuthi* is emanating from the pictures of Baba in their homes, that *Amrith* (nectar) is dripping from them or that material objects are falling from them, like written answers to questions. *Samithis* and other Units should have no contact with such cheats and crooks. Any one who is attached to such or who encourages such can be immediately removed.

There are others who claim that I am speaking through them, and answering questions put to them. These people must be either insane or hysteria–affected or they are possessed by some ghost or by the greed to earn money thereby. I can only tell you that it is not I that speaks through them. I do not need media; nor do I need substitutes or subsidiaries or representatives. There are some crooks who are publicising that I have allotted them some regions for ministration by them on My behalf, because, they say, My devotees have increased so much that I am unable to attend to all of them, single–handed! On the face of it, this is an absurd lie. Moreover, consider another aspect.

· Even those who cry in pure agonising yearning, Sai Sai Sai, and lead pure unselfish virtuous lives, even these find it hard to realise Me; how then can these low scheming vulgar men who know no *sadhana*, sincerity, Truth and humility, how can these people claim that they have been blessed by Me? They may wear the same style of dress, imitate gestures and style of speech but these will only bring their falsehood into greater prominence. That I am supposed to "possess" such people or speak through them or shower My Grace on them is an assumption of which one ought to be ashamed! How then can anyone believe it, I wonder.

Evil forces which design to damage or diminish the faith and devotion of the simple and the sincere do emerge into action and try to attract attention by devious means. They try to draw away aspirants from the spiritual path into worldly paths of avarice and malice. There is a big chasm of difference between the *Sai Shakti* (Sai Power) and these inferior *shaktis*. Since the opportunity has now offered itself, this has to be said.

There can be no limit for *Sai Shakti*, no hindrance, no opposition or obstacle. You may believe it or you may not, but *Sai Shakti* can transform earth into sky, the sky into earth. Only, there is no call for that transformation. This Divine Behaviour is far distinct from the mean exhibitionistic tricks of the inferior *shaktis*. This is spontaneous manifestation; those are calculated to collect customers and exploit the ignorant. The inferior *shaktis* may imitate the dress or the gestures, for imitation cannot be prevented. But you have to ask yourselves the question: "Can all green feathered birds be parrots? Or, can all worms on petals turn into butterflies? Or, can a donkey wearing a tiger–skin become a tiger or can an overgrown boar be honoured as an elephant?" Beware of being cheated by dress or speech or by tricks. Nor need you feel angry or upset by these.

For Truth is ever Truth. Falsehood can never become Truth, whatever its tactics. This is the very embodiment of Truth. It has no unreality or falsehood in Its composition.

But, those afflicted with jaundice can see all things only as yellow. Those who have no appetite or digestion find even delicious food, bitter. Such men may proclaim this in their own manner, as different from what it is; but I am not in the least perturbed nor will I change.

Others who are taken to be elders have posed certain problems, to confuse the mind. Krishna, they say, showed many wonders, with amazing disregard of the Laws of Nature and therefore, according to them, Krishna had to meet his death from the arrow of a hunter. Jesus, they say, suffered crucifixion for, he too manifested many miracles. Their argument is that since I am defying the laws of nature, I too will suffer likewise. They plan to create panic and spread false alarm. But, these are the prattlings of weakness, helplessness and envy. These can never be Truth. They only plan to decry and diminish the glory they cannot understand or tolerate.

Whoever may join in this campaign, whatever tactics they employ, even if all the "fourteen–worlds" unite as one, they cannot succeed; they cannot affect Me in the least. And, even if ten more worlds, say 24 in all, lend them their support, their falsehood will not be accepted or established as Truth.

Truth can never be tarnished or turned into falsehood. You may be subjected to all kinds of pressure and publicity; but, do not lose courage, do not allow your devotion, faith and steadfastness to decline. Resolve to achieve success in the *sadhana* you have taken upon yourselves. Then, this Sathya will reveal itself, without fail, as your own *Sathya* (Reality).

I do not depend on outer manifestation and actions; I am related to you through the inner principle of Love. If you are to be drawn by outer attractions, advertisement is imperative. For example, if such a Conference or such a Celebration is held in any other place, invitations have to be printed and sent out, personal requests have to be made so that this person or that can attend. Considerations have to be held forth to many so that the invitations may be accepted and the function made a success. But here in the Prashanti Nilayam, no invitation has ever been printed and distributed on any occasion, asking people to come. No one has been specially requested to take part. It is Love, the invitations of the Heart to the heart, that has brought you in tens of thousands to this place. The validity and value of Love are proved by you; Love is the most potent of My powers.

When you light a lamp in your home, you have to go round the homes of others and invite them to come and admire it. But when the Sun rises in all its splendour, there is no need to draw the attention of the world to the event. This is the splendour of the Sun. It will itself command attention. No one need be invited to notice it.

Of course, it is only natural that doubt may arise in you on some occasions based on My form or My words or My action but, when you are eager to know My reality, you must observe in action My teaching and follow Me. Then, certainly, My Divine Reality will be revealed to you. Having looked at this Form through your eyes only, you start guessing and concluding, as your wavering fancy dictates, and lay waste your intellectual and mental efforts; you even allow your devotion and faith to flow into wrong channels. I am advising you against this, with the force of a command.

Swami Karunyananda declared yesterday that he believed for a long time that those who lived in previous Ages were far more fortunate than those of this Age, since they could secure the *darshan* (direct sight) of the Incarnation of the Lord. But he said, it has now become clear to him that there is no generation more fortunate than his; that declaration is true. It is thrice true.

For during no previous Age did man have this unique chance. No organisation of this nature was established, no Conference of this character was held in the Presence and no opportunity was given then to derive *Ananda* through such close association, through conversation and singing together. Undoubtedly, you are all singularly fortunate.

Therefore, do not let the opportunity slip through your hands. Hold fast to it and make the best of it. With steady faith and enthusiastic devotional activity, tread the path indicated and reach the Goal of Realising the Reality.

I bless you that you may attain the Bliss of that Realisation.[1]

◊ ◊ ◊ ◊ ◊

I have come now with the limitation that you need. The Lord's activities are three: Creation, Preservation and Dissolution. They are the characteristic attributes of the Lord. His aims are all *Satwic* (pious) for the protection of the World, the welfare of the World. My exultation is Mine, My prompting is Mine. I will never abide by another's likes or dislikes. I do not pay heed to such. I am that which is the Witness of everyone and everything. All are in my Control; then, who can tell Me what to do? In a few years, years that can be counted on one's fingers, all of you will realise, that I am the embodiment of all *Shaktis* (powers). The wise, the inquiring and the suffering will gather here from all parts of the world. Have the fixity of hold; say, "Whether I succeed in getting from You the external fruit or not, I shall never give up." Do not get dejected when suffering comes and estrange yourself from the Lord, blaming Him for it. The loss will be yours and the repentance will be agonising.

---

[1] *Sathya Sai Speaks*, Vol. 10, pp. 234–38.

You have no hunger. If you have genuine hunger I will not keep you suffering from it. Churn the mind and collect the butter and melt it in the yearning of the heart. When the butter has not melted, the reason is, the warmth of the yearning is insufficient.

I do not appreciate your extolling Me, describing My glory. State the facts. That produces joy. It is sacrilege to state more or less. Demand from Me as of right, the removal of your sufferings. Give me your heart and ask for My Heart; if you give Me only your word, you will get only a word in return. I give you just what you ask for, remember!

When sufferings come, why do you estrange yourselves from the Lord? He gives you suffering, for your good, for the advancement of your devotion. If suffering is granted, you seek *Shanti*; you search for the knowledge of the mystery; you go to ten persons and they each tell you some aspect of the Truth. Without suffering, sweetness cannot arise! When you suffer, if you feel, "The Lord is no longer mine," and stray away, the Lord too will declare, "He is no longer Mine!" Beware.

Wherever you are, when you wholeheartedly seek to do *namaskaram* (obeisance) to Me, My Feet are there, before you! *Sarvata pani padhah* — "Hands and feet everywhere," it has been announced. "Lord, do you not hear My prayer?" if you feel poignantly, My Ears are there! "Don't you see, O Lord?" if you cry out, My eyes are there that instant. Rama, Krishna, Shirdi Sai, This Sathya Sai Baba; that Form is so, this Form is thus — why all such misgivings and doubts? The body is the same, only the dress worn is different. Do not be led away into the morass, by others.

The Lord will never deviate from the word; it may be that you take Me to mean something else. It is My Will that happens always; it is My *Sankalpa* that is being worked out at all times. *Sankalpas* are of three different types: *Yochana sankalpas*, the decision arrived at after long deliberation; *Manana sankalpa*, the decision taken after the desire to do arises; and *Swasankalpa*, where the wish and the fulfilment are like the sound of the shot and the hitting the target, both happening at the same instant.

Do not slander or abuse others or your own selves, as weak, sinful, wicked or low; when you do so, you are slandering or abusing Me, who resides in them and you. All are of the Divine Nature of the *Atma*; all are pure and holy. Some might have erred in using the intelligence and discrimination which the Lord has given and so might have been guilty of "mistakes"; they are not therefore, "sinful." To condemn oneself as "*Papoham papasambhava*" (I am a sinner born of sin), is itself the direct *papa* (sin)! Use your intelligence and march on, putting one milestone after another behind you! Practise *namasmarana* (remembrance of Lord's name) steadily so that it becomes as automatic and as necessary as breathing. Of what benefit is it to be in the same stage of *sadhana* for ever? Take the Form you like, the Name you Love and do *japa* and *dhyana* and no evil thought will arise; wicked thoughts will flee. When they have fled, what remains is the *Atmaswarupa*.

You must lead your lives, according to My words, without the slightest modification. First have faith, then the experience is granted. Even in the case of the previous *Avatars*, that is the order of events, is it not? You worship with faith and you experience Grace. Faith results in Grace, without your being aware of it. You must take in the medicine I give and also follow the diet I prescribe and avoid the things I prohibit.

I always act calmly. I never hurry. I do say, "Let it be so" to every request of yours. You have come into this world to reach the Lord. Ignorant of that purpose, you have hoisted on your head the weight of illusion and you are struggling to unload it, suffering under its weight. What is the use of running after external pleasures and temporary joy? So long as you are caught in this *Avidhya* (ignorance) you can never taste the Bliss of Realisation; you cannot even recognise it much less attain it. But, if you are patient and calm, I shall grant you joy without fail. Do not yield to despair. Even the infant lotus buds will bloom, in their own good time. By the cumulative effect of the good done in many previous births, you have secured this fortune; you do not know how much you have gone through, but, I know! And, whether you know or not, I shall certainly give you your need.

You get the "body" through the *karma* of the past; you get the "type of character" according to the *vasanas* (tendencies) cultivated in the past. The body is the result of *prarabda karma* (to be exhausted in the present life); the *guna* is the product of *Sanchita karma* (which is stored to be experienced in future lives). Do not delude yourself that you are the body, or be fascinated into an attachment for it. But, it is your task to guard it from harm and keep it in good trim. For, is it not with it that you are imbibing the exhilaration of the Bliss of the Lord, the Majesty of the Lord? Therefore, do not deride the body or treat it with contempt. That equipment is intended for your journey towards the Lord; it is the chariot of the Lord; do not neglect or keep it in disrepair.[1]

◊ ◊ ◊ ◊ ◊

5.

The Grace and the Divine Sankalpa (Divine Resolve) of Sathya Sai Baba

My Grace is ever with you; it is not something that is given or taken; it is given always and accepted by the consciousness that is aware of its significance. Win the Grace of your own sub–conscious, so that it may accept the Grace of God which is ever available.

God does not deny any one; it is only you, who deny God. When the gift is proffered, you have to do only one little act, so that you

---

[1] *Sathya Sai Speaks*, Vol. 2, pp. 115–17.

may earn it — you have to extend your hand to receive it. That is the Grace of the subconscious; win it, by teaching it the value of the Grace of God. My Grace is showered wherever you are through My infinite Love, without even calculating or measuring the readiness of your subconscious to receive it and benefit by it. The Grace itself will confer on you the faith and the strength, the wisdom and the joy. I am in your heart all the time, whether you know it or not.[1]

◊ ◊ ◊ ◊ ◊

Every gesture, word and activity of mine, however casual it may appear, is motivated to move you towards the fulfilment of your lives, and endow you with the *Ananda* (Bliss) that your *Atma* (Self Reality) is.[2]

◊ ◊ ◊ ◊ ◊

There is no visible Master for those who are part of Organisations run in the name of Rama or Krishna; but, in this Organisation the Master is here, available for help, advice and direction. You cannot behave in accordance with your whims and wishes here. You have to be vigilant everywhere and at all times. Discard the ego and serve. Don't go about with extended hand, and humiliate yourselves. Ask Me, when you need any help.

Extend your hand only for Grace from God. Ask Grace as of right, not in a grovelling style. Ask, as the child asks the father; feel that God is nearest and dearest. You are the reflections, the images; I am the *Bimba*, the Object so reflected. Can there be any question of difference between the object and its images? You are all I. I am all you. I know I am the *Atma*; you believe you are the body! You are sugar dolls; I am the sugar. Revere any Name; the reverence reaches Me, for, I answer

---

[1] *Sathya Sai Speaks*, Vol. 11, pp. 92–93.

[2] *Sathya Sai Speaks*, Vol. 11, p. 70.

to all Names. Denigrate any individual; it affects Me; for all individuals are expressions of My Will.[1]

◊ ◊ ◊ ◊ ◊

Be simple and sincere. It is sheer waste of money to burden the pictures and idols in the shrines and altars of your homes with the weight of garlands, and to parade costly utensils and vessels and offerings, to show off your devotion. This is deception; it demeans Divinity, imputing to it the desire for pomp and publicity. I ask only for purity of heart, to shower Grace. Do not posit distance between you and Me; do not interpose the formalities of the *Guru–sishya* (Preceptor–disciple) relationship, or even the attitudinal distinctions of the God–devotee relationship, between you and Me. I am neither *Guru* nor God; I am You; You are I; that is the Truth. There is no distinction. That which appears so is the delusion. You are waves; I am the Ocean. Know this and be free, be Divine.[2]

◊ ◊ ◊ ◊ ◊

Is there any end to the list of worldly goods that you crave for? When you secure one, another starts tantalising you. If you do not get that, very often, your hold on the Lord too loosens. If something is lost or stolen from you, you lose faith in Me. I have not come to guard your jewels and your "valuables." I have come to guard your virtue and holiness and guide you to the Goal.

If your goodness is in danger, come to Me. I shall tell you how to cultivate it and reap the fruit. If some one is snatched away by death while on pilgrimage to Khasi or Badrinath, you console yourself that it was an enviable way of quitting. But if you get even a mild attack of headache at Puttaparthi, you start blaming Me. According to you,

---

[1] *Sathya Sai Speaks*, Vol. 11, pp. 147–48.

[2] *Sathya Sai Speaks*, Vol. 10, p. 102.

those who have entered this compound once should not die. If they do, your faith wavers and dwindles. Well, not even an eyelid can open without the Lord's Will. So try to get the Lord's Grace and leave all questions to be answered by Him according to His Fancy.

When the sun rises, all the buds of lotus in the lake will not open out in full bloom. Only those which are full grown can blossom so; the rest have to bide their time and grow. His Grace is the right of all, but it can be won by *sadhana* only. I have no hate or anger in My composition; My Life blood is *Prema*, I am the repository of *Dhaya* (Compassion). Understand Me and My Nature right. The shadow of the Moon in the depth of the lake seems to quiver and shake because of the waves; but look up and you see the Moon, steady as ever. I am always steady, My Grace is ever there. To the outward eye, My action is magic, miracle; to the inner eye, it is all *Leela* (Play). Well, the Hand that creates is the Hand that gives — there is no keeping back. It is always for you and you alone. That is My Truth; know it and be happy.

I have started the work for which I have come down. I have collected the metal, the steel, the stones, the bricks. I have dug the foundation trenches — and the superstructure will rise soon. There can be no interruption. You will see thousands pressing along this road, hundreds on every rock on these hills. The *bhaktas* who are at the Nilayam are sad that they have had no chance of even a *namaskaram* (respectful obeisance) for three months. They feel that those who come from afar and leave in a few days are luckier.

To them I say this: You are deluded by a false sense of values. Why worry so much at not being able to touch these Feet? My Feet are within your reach, at all times, wherever you are. "*Sarvata Pani Pada*" — "Hands and feet everywhere." If you wail in agony, "Don't you hear me?" My Ears are there to listen; if you pray from the depths of your heart, "Don't you see my plight?" My Ears are there shedding

Grace on you. Get out of *Maya* and become *Prema;* then you get *Prema* only from Me.[1]

When the Giver of Grace is here, you run after persons who claim that they got this or the other article from Me or were blessed with this gift from Me! When you have *Kamadenu* (wish–fulfilling cow) here, why seek to know and secure a cow? *Kamadenu* can give you all that you need. When you have *Kalpatharu* (wish–fulfilling tree) here, why bother about fruits on a tree? *Kalpatharu* can give you all that you ask. When you have here the mountain of gold and silver, Meru, why cringe for silver and gold from persons who are themselves beggars? When you have God come among you to support and sustain you, why grovel before crude vulgar entities? Avoid places where they bargain in terms of gifts, donations and payments for Grace and *Upadesh,* for spiritual guidance and transmission.[2]

◊ ◊ ◊ ◊ ◊

You might say that the *karma* of the previous birth has to be consumed in this birth and that no amount of grace can save man from that. Evidently, some one has taught you to believe so. But I assure you, you need not suffer from *karma* like that. When a severe pain torments you, the doctor gives you a morphine injection and you do not feel the pain, though it is there in the body. Grace is like the morphine; the pain is not felt, though you go through it! Grace takes away the malignity of the *karma* which you have to undergo.

You know there are dated drugs, which are declared ineffective after a certain date; well, the effect of *karma* is rendered null, though the account is there and has to be rendered! Or, the Lord can save man completely from the consequences, as was done by Me to the *bhakta* (devotee) whose paralytic stroke and heart attacks I took over some months ago, in the *Gurupoornima* week! It is wrong to say the

---

[1] *Sathya Sai Speaks,* Vol. 2, pp. 90–92.

[2] *Sathya Sai Speaks,* Vol. 10, p. 186.

"*Lalata likhitam*" (what is written on the forehead, i.e., fate) cannot be wiped out; that what one has earned in previous births must be consumed in this birth. Grace can countermand all that; nothing can stand in its way. It is the grace of the "Almighty," remember.[1]

◊ ◊ ◊ ◊ ◊

You may say that progress is possible only through My Grace; but, though My Heart is soft as butter, it melts only when there is some warmth in your prayer. Unless you make some disciplined effort, some *sadhana*, Grace cannot descend on you. The yearning, the agony of unfulfilled aim melts My Heart. That is the *Avedana* (anguish) that wins Grace.[2]

◊ ◊ ◊ ◊ ◊

I am not attracted by learning or scholarship, which does not lead anywhere except towards egoism and pride. I am drawn only by devotion. Bring to Me whatever troubles you have; I shall take them on and give you *Ananda*. When I like My devotees, I like their faults too, though some here turn up their noses and laugh at the peculiar follies and foibles of people who come from all the various States. I am drawn by the Love which brings you here from long distances through great difficulties, which makes you happy in spite of the want of the comforts to which you are accustomed, which makes you put up with the life under the trees or in the open sheds.[3]

◊ ◊ ◊ ◊ ◊

---

[1] *Sathya Sai Speaks*, Vol. 4, p. 225.

[2] *Sathya Sai Speaks*, Vol. 11, p. 296.

[3] *Sathya Sai Speaks*, Vol. 4, p. 32.

Even about Me, there are some who have had a glimpse of the Truth; there are others who have not been able to achieve even that. But, My *Prema* is showered equally on all; I do not reveal or refuse; it is for you to discover and decide, derive Divine Bliss by diving into the depths. How can an ant calculate the depth of the sea? How can a man on the ground describe the features of the pilot of a plane in the sky? Unless you rise to the heights, by following certain disciplines, you cannot experience Godhead. Once you do that, all judgements, all disputations and even sense of victory, disappear.

I know many are puzzled by My practice of listening to your "*korikas*" (wants, wishes, desires), calling you individually and spending long hours with you to satisfy you and to speak to you on these "earthly" demands. They say, no *Avatar* has done this before; it is like catering to worldly things; people come with all kinds of worldly desires and every one is welcomed with sympathy and Love. But, I alone know the basic thirst which expresses itself in these desires and wants, the fundamental discontent.

It is always preferable to approach God for the fulfilment of wants, rather than cringe before men, who themselves are but tools in the hands of God. In his own silent way, God will transform the mind and turn it towards *sadhana* and successful spiritual pilgrimage. He cannot allow His children to lose their way and suffer in the jungle. When you approach God and seek his help and guidance, you have taken the first step to save yourself. You are then led to accept His will as your own. Thus, you achieve *Shanti* (Peace). ...

Do not be under the impression that all these people come to me seeking worldly favours or blessings for worldly advancement or fortunes. At least ninety among a hundred of them ask from Me spiritual guidance only. They do not ask for worldly boons at all. They are eager to be directed along the path of *japa* (repetition of a *mantra* on God's Name), *dhyana* (meditation), namasmarana (repetition of God's Name) or some such *sadhana* (spiritual practice). They are full of *Prema* (Love) for the Divine Principle and the Divine is full of *Prema* towards them. It is a question of *Prema* responding to *Prema*; *Prema* which is saturated with *Sathya*, as *Vivekananda* was saturated with *viveka*.[1]

◊ ◊ ◊ ◊ ◊

Incarnation is for the sake of fostering *Dharma*, for demarcating and directing it and to show mankind the true path of desireless activity. That is the one task I am engaged in, through various channels. Instead of reforming you without your knowledge, it is better to reform you with your own co–operation and knowledge. So, I reveal to you my Glory, off and on, to a little extent, through what you call miracles. I do not engage in them for name and fame; I am miraculous by My very Nature! Every moment of Mine is a *Mahatmya*, a Miracle! They are beyond your understanding, your art and skill and intelligence. I must save every one of you; even if you say, nay, and move away, I shall do it. Those who have strayed away from Me have to return to the fold, sooner or later, for I will not allow them to be distant for long. I shall drag them towards Me. That is My basic Nature, Love and Mercy.[2]

◊ ◊ ◊ ◊ ◊

Some of you may imagine that it is a source of joy for the Lord to take a human form. If you are in this state, you will not feel so. I am always aware of the future, the past as well as the present of every one of you. So, I am not moved so much by pity. Not that I am hard–hearted, or that I have no *daya* (pity). If you bolt the doors fast, how can the rays of My Grace be available to you? "*Swami*," you cry, "I have no eyes; I am yearning to see You. Won't Your Heart melt at my plight?" Of course, this pitiable condition melts *your* hearts; will it not melt *Mine*? But, since I know the past, the background, My

---

[1] *Sathya Sai Speaks*, Vol. 5, pp. 238–40.

[2] *Sathya Sai Speaks*, Vol. 2, p. 132.

reaction is different. If only you knew, you too will react differently. It is the consequence of evil, deliberately done in previous births, and so, I have to allow the suffering to continue, modified, often by some little compensation. I do not cause either joy or grief; you are the designer of both the chains that bind you.

Remove the weight from your head by transferring all burdens to the Lord; leave everything to His Will, His law. Feed your mind with sweet and wholesome food · — *Sathsangha, Sathpravarthana, Sarveswara–chintha* (company of holy, speaking of God, thinking of the Lord of the Universe); then you are full of joy. I am of the nature of Bliss (*Anandaswarupa*); come and take *Ananda* from Me and returning to your avocations, dwell on that *Ananda* and be full of *Shanti*.[1]

◊ ◊ ◊ ◊ ◊

Be devoted to Me and receive power from Me. To the extent to which you enthusiastically quicken up this process of give and take, to that extent you will be successful and happy. Deliver all your anxieties, troubles, travails and desire, to Me and in return receive joy, Peace and strength of mind from Me. During this Advent, only spiritual aspirants and righteous persons are relatives, friends and recipients of My Grace.[2]

I know that those of you who are posted for duty at the outer gates or in the garden, at the *bhajana mantap* (devotional singing hall) or the Shoe Counter, feel jealous of those who are in the inner apartments of the bungalow. Some of you go out on errands into the city and are absent from *bhajana*, etc. I must tell you this. I have no special brand of Grace for those who are at My door, nor do I neglect the man at the gate. In fact, I have no geographical "far" and "near"; My "far" and "near" are not calculated by physical nearness. You may

---

[1] *Sathya Sai Speaks*, Vol. 4, pp. 239-40.

[2] *Sathya Sai Speaks*, Vol. 7, p. 197.

be at My side, yet, far; you may be far, far away, yet, very near and dear. However far you are, if you but stick to *Sathya* (Truth), *Dharma* (Righteousness), *Shanti* (Peace) and *Prema* (Love), you are close to Me and I am close to you. Those are the milestones that mark the road to Me.

When your eyes see a ripe mango fruit on the tree, the tongue recollects the taste, the mind craves for it, the back stoops, the shoulders bend, the hand searches for a stone, the fingers clasp it, the arm throws it; and when the fruit falls, the hand picks it, the teeth bite into it, the throat lets it down into the stomach; there and thereafter it is converted into sustenance as a reward for the effort of all and sent as strength to eye and shoulder, hand and fingers, teeth and tongue. Similarly, when you all cooperate to give Me joy, the reward of Grace will be granted to all.

You are all My Limbs, nourished by Me. You constitute the Sai Body. Sai will send you sustenance, wherever you are, whatever your function, provided you give Sai the things Sai considers sweet and desirable, like virtue, faith, discipline and humility. Be happy that you are a limb of the Sai Body. Do not complain that you are the foot and so have to tread the hard ground. Do not be proud that you are the head and so, up and above. It is the same blood–stream, the stream of *Prema* that circulates in both; the function of each is as valuable as the function of every other limb. The function of each limb is also unique, remember; so do not give room to despondency. Your part is something special, which only you can play. You cannot walk on your head; you cannot think with your feet. Whatever your position, win Grace by your virtue, that is the main gain.[1]

◊ ◊ ◊ ◊ ◊

We are not asking for everlasting Bliss; we ask only for short–lived material pleasures. So, we do not get all that we ask for. What is the

---

[1] *Sathya Sai Speaks*, Vol. 7, pp. 71–72.

reason? Has He no compassion? The child is sick but it asks for many varieties of sweets which the mother refuses to give. Does it mean that she hates the child? Or, is she hard–hearted? Has he lost her affection? The refusal is itself a sign of compassion. For, each person is an invalid, suffering from recurrent birth and death. Granting whatever is asked can only lengthen the suffering. Hence arises the withholding and the denial. And, you too do not ask for the indispensable! You do not pray for the Peace that knows no break. If you do, the boon will be granted.

Of course, you do call. But, do you call on God, or on some one ungodly? God will respond when the call arises from the heart. Your call is fouled by greed, by hatred against others, by the desire for vengeance, by the hiss of envy and intolerance. I know you knock at the door. But, at which door? Keeping the door of your own heart closed, how can your clamour succeed in getting other doors opened? Knock at the door of your own heart. God, the resident, will come into view. *Prahlada* had the faith that God resides in every heart and everywhere. So, when a pillar in the palace was knocked at, the Lord manifested therefrom. Believe that He resides in you and turn your eyes inward.

You complain that God is merciless, hard to please, etc., only because you do not wish to give Him what you ought to or ask from Him what He would gladly give. Tender hearts, holy thoughts, loving speech — these can invoke the Divine *Atma* to manifest into awareness. For, these personify *Sathya*, embody God as *Sathya*. *Sath* means, the Sun, *Surya*. *Thya* means the glory, the splendour. The *Sathya* — the glory of the Sun — nourishes and ripens the grain, which is man's food. Food sustains the vitality, the vital breath. Therefore, *Sathya* has to be adored and propitiated. ...[1]

◊ ◊ ◊ ◊ ◊

---

[1] *Sathya Sai Speaks*, Vol. 15, pp. 285–86.

Do not, like some mental patients, be always worrying about some little ailment or another. Have courage, that is the best tonic; do not give up, before you have to. It is not long life that counts; if you live on and on, a time may come when you have to pray to the Lord to take you away, to release you from travail. You may even start blaming Him for ignoring you and blessing other luckier people with death! By all means, worry about success or failure in achieving the real purpose of life. And then you will get as many years as are needed to fulfill that desire. Yearn, yearn, yearn hard; and success is yours. Remember, you are all certain to win; that is why you have been called and you have responded to the call to come to Me.

What other task have I than the showering of Grace? By *darshan, sparshan* and *sambhashan* (seeing, touching and conversing), you are in that Grace. When that melts and this melts, the two can merge. Treat Me not as one afar, but as very close to you. Insist, demand, claim Grace from Me; do not praise, extol and cringe. Bring your hearts to Me and win My Heart. Not one of you is a stranger to Me. Bring your promises to me and I shall give you My Promise. But first see that your promise is genuine, sincere; see that your heart is pure; that is enough.[1]

◊ ◊ ◊ ◊ ◊

---

[1] *Sathya Sai Speaks*, Vol. 2, p. 70–71.

6.

The Spiritual Practices (Sadhana) that Bhagavan Baba Advises for Devotees

You know there is a rule here that you should come with empty hands, without even the traditional offerings of *pathram, pushpam, phalam, thoyam* (leaf, flower, fruit and water).

Come with clean hands, hands that supplicate, not supply; hands that proclaim that they have renounced attachment to riches; then, I fill them with Grace.

I must say that I accept certain things before giving you that Grace: I demand and take *Sathya, Dharma, Shanti* and *Prema* (I seek the gifts of Truth, Virtue, Peace and Love).

I draw you to Me and then re–form and re–shape you. I am a kind of smith who repairs broken, leaky, damaged hardware. I repair broken hearts and fragile minds, warped intellects, feeble resolutions and fading faith.[1]

◊ ◊ ◊ ◊ ◊

Discard through *sadhana* the attachment to individuality, to sense pleasures; welcome through *sadhana*, the aspiration to expand the heart into the Universal. Do not cloud your minds with cheap desires, transitory hungers and thirsts, that need but morsels or mouthfuls. Yearn for the enthronement of your soul as the unquestioned Monarch of the Universe, when you merge in the Universal; celebrate

---

[1] *Sathya Sai Speaks*, Vol. 14, p. 26.

your triumph over the foes within that hamper your march to victory. Acquire Me as your Charioteer; I shall lead you to that consummation. Earn that unfailing Grace, by your sincerity, simplicity and *sadhana.*[1]

◊ ◊ ◊ ◊ ◊

I appreciate and reward humility, fortitude, sympathy, service, brotherliness, and constant remembrance of God or goodness. When you yearn to have My picture on your heart, you must turn the lens of the camera towards Me, shouldn't you? Turn your intellect, your emotions, your feelings, your activities towards Me, then certainly, My picture will be imprinted on your heart. If your lens is facing the world and worldly things, how can it be imprinted upon your heart?

Of what benefit is this discourse of Mine if you do not receive it into your hearts and act according to it? I find that all the efforts of all these years to awaken you to your duty to yourselves are not fructifying in you. You are like the rocks on the seashore that unflinchingly face the beating of the waves. The rock does not move; the wave will not stop. This predicament should end.[2] Awake and avail yourselves of this unique chance.

◊ ◊ ◊ ◊ ◊

The Sai religion, if the name of religion in its literal sense of binding man to God is accepted, is the essence of all faiths and religions, including those like Islam, Christianity and Judaism. The motive behind the formation and propagation of all these different faiths is the same. The founders and propagators were all persons filled with Love and wisdom. Their goal and purpose were the same. None had the design to divide, disturb, or destroy. They attempted to do good, see good and be good. They sought to train the passions and

---

[1] *Sathya Sai Speaks*, Vol. 8, p. 158.

[2] *Sathya Sai Speaks*, Vol. —, p. 159.

the emotions, to educate the impulses and instincts and direct the faculty of reason to paths beneficial to the individual and society. They knew that the mind, which is the breeding ground of desire and attachment, ambition and aspiration, has to be cleansed and properly oriented.

Sai considers that practice of these disciplines is much more essential than blind faith in a bunch of philosophical theories. No one has the right to advise others unless he is already practising what he preaches. First establish the reign of Love between the various members in your own home. Let the family become a centre of harmonious living, sympathetic understanding and mutual faith.

The holy duty of man is to be ever aware of the *Atma* (Divine Spirit) that is installed in every living being. This will make him conscious of the kinship he has with all. This is the basis of the brotherhood of man and the Fatherhood of God. Cast away the vice of egoism, the evil of greed and the poison of envy. ...[1]

◊ ◊ ◊ ◊ ◊

There are many who declare that they have surrendered to Me. They use the word, *arpana*. They have dedicated their *thanu, mana, dhana* (body, mind, wealth), their all, they proclaim! But, they still continue with their "I did it," "I feel so," "I think so," "I like it," "I do not like it," etc. The I raises its hood so that it may receive homage or praise! Now, it is a big lie to say that you have surrendered! It is sheer falsehood. The word *arpana* is a word that is just thrown about, without any value or purpose, to deceive people who do not dive into its authenticity. How can you surrender something over which you have no control?

◊ ◊ ◊ ◊ ◊

---

[1] *Sathya Sai Speaks*, Vol. 13, pp. 146–47.

You are the slave of your mind, of your passions, of your prejudices; but, yet, you dare claim that you have surrendered your mind, your thoughts, your plans to God! While you are struggling to escape from the coils of the mind and the stranglehold of the passions, how can you dedicate them to Me? No. You need not boast of such bravery, such sacrifice, such devotion. I do not need or ask for such declaration, such devotion. It is enough if you believe that God is everywhere and at all times, and that you are yourself no different from Him. When you are God yourself, to whom are you to surrender what? Think over this deeply and attain to that realisation.[1]

◊ ◊ ◊ ◊ ◊

Be pure in word and deed, and keep impure thoughts away. I am in every one of you and so, I become aware of your slightest wave of thought. When the clothes become dirty, you have to give them for wash. When your mind is soiled, you have to be born again, for the cleansing operations. The *dhobi* (washerman) beats the cloth on the hard stone, and draws over it the hot iron, to straighten the folds. So, too, you will have to pass through a train of travail in order to become fit to approach God. See Me as resident in every one; give them all the help you can, all the service they need; do not withhold the sweet word, the supporting hand, the assuring smile, the comforting company, the consoling conversation.[2]

◊ ◊ ◊ ◊ ◊

Love is the word which indicates the striving to realise the falsehood of the many and the reality of the One. Love identifies; hate separates. Love transposes the Self on to another and the two think, speak and act as one. When Love takes in more and more within its

---

[1] *Sathya Sai Speaks*, Vol. 11, pp. 80–81.

[2] *Sathya Sai Speaks*, Vol. 9, p. 105.

fold, more and more entities are rendered as One. When you Love Me, you Love all; for, you begin to feel and know and experience that I am in all. By means of *dhyana* (meditation), you can realise that I am the resident in all hearts, the urge, the motive, the guide, the goal. Yearn for that vision, that awareness and make it your priceless possession. Then, you have what you often ask Me for — *Sakshatkara* (Direct Vision of Reality). Your Love has to be as pure, as free from the taint of ego as mine so that it can merge in Me.

Of course, it is hard *sadhana*. The mind is too much with you, now. One has to negate and deny, deprive oneself of many expectancies, dive deep into oneself, swim upstream against the current of generations of attachment to worldly things, including the body which one bears. The *gopees* (Cowherd girls) were so filled with the highest type of Love that they saw and experienced the Krishna Principle in every speck of dust and blade of green that they saw. Love of Krishna makes the whole world of Krishna. The denial of everything else is the method of visualising Krishna in all. There is only One, the integer I. When it is repeated once again, we have two. The manifold creation is only He, and He and He, repeated so often. Dust and blade, drop and spot — each is He, He and He alone. And, you are no exception, you are also He. The realisation of this Truth, this identity, this mergence, this is *Sakshatkara*.[1]

◊ ◊ ◊ ◊ ◊

Do you know how much I feel when I find that in spite of My arrival and *Bodha* and *Upadhesam* (Teaching and Spiritual Instruction), you have not yet started this *sadhana*? You simply praise Me and strew compliments; that I am the Treasure–house of Grace, the Ocean of *Ananda*, etc. Take up the Name and dwell upon Its sweetness; imbibe It and roll It on your tongue, taste Its essence, contemplate on Its

---

[1] *Sathya Sai Speaks*, Vol. 11, pp. 96–97.

magnificence and make it a part of yourself and grow strong in spiritual joy. That is what pleases Me. ...

Come to Me, eager to learn, to progress, to see Yourself in Me, and I shall certainly welcome you and show you the way. You will indeed be blessed. All scriptures, all texts, the *Geeta* which is the milk of all the *Upanishadic* Cows, are intended to instill this thirst in you.

The thirst has to be like that of the creeper for the tree–trunk, of the magnet for the iron, of the bee for the flower, of the waters for a fall, of the river for the sea. The pangs of separation must gnaw the heart; the entire being must yearn for union. Do not vacillate or change or try a series of *Nama* and *Rupa* (Name and Form). That will only fritter away time and energy. Ceaseless contemplation of the Lord will give ceaseless taste of *Amritha* to you.

If you do not follow this path, you are doubly to blame; for you have contacted Me. The Form usually creates doubts, for when only the Name is there, you can build around it all your fancies, all that you want, to complete the picture. Do not be misled by such doubts when the Form has come before you; make the moment useful, the life worthwhile.[1]

◊ ◊ ◊ ◊ ◊

Never stray from the path of right, whatever the trouble or temptation. Do not loosen the grip; do not turn back. Do not allow faith to be upset. If you attach importance to riches or children or fame or fortune, you are thereby announcing that you are devoted, not to God, but to riches, children and the rest. If you are devoted to God, how should you manifest that devotion? Let me tell you how. By manifesting Divine qualities, Divine virtues, Divine Love, Divine strength. Become Sai, be Sai.[2]

---

[1] *Sathya Sai Speaks*, Vol. 1, pp. 225–28.

[2] *Sathya Sai Speaks*, Vol. 11, p. 301.

◊ ◊ ◊ ◊ ◊

This is not *bhakti*, this holding a garland in the hand and indulging in paltry conversation in holy places. I do not want nor do I appreciate any one bringing flowers and fruits into My presence. Bring Me the fragrant flower of a pure heart and the fruit of a *sadhana*–mellowed mind; that is what I like most, not these things available outside yourselves for so much of cash, without any effort that elevates the mind. To get a taste for that kind of effort, you must keep the company of great and good men and take delight in good thoughts. By whatever means available, increase the stock of your *Ananda* (Bliss) and improve the quality of *viveka* (discrimination) and try to store as much of these two as possible so that you can draw upon the stock whenever the need arises.[1]

◊ ◊ ◊ ◊ ◊

You are as distant from the Lord as you think you are, as near Him as you feel you are. Well, let Me tell you this. The distance from Me to you is the same as the distance from you to Me, is it not? But, you complain that I am far far from you, though you are approaching nearer and nearer. How can that be? I am as near you as you are near Me.

That nearness is won by devotion, which cannot be steady except after getting rid of "I" and "Mine." When a prisoner is taken from place to place, he is accompanied by two constables, is it not? When man who is a prisoner in this jail moves from one place to another, he too is accompanied by *ahamkaram* and *mamakaram*: egoism and attachment. When he moves about without these two, you can be sure he is a free man, liberated from prison.

Now that I have referred to jail and jail life, let Me tell you something more. You are all under sentence of imprisonment and are

---

[1] *Sathya Sai Speaks*, Vol. 1, p. 75.

in this jail. There is no use hoping for reward when you work in jail; you have to work because you are ordered to; and you must work well too. You cannot argue that rewards are not distributed justly and you are not entitled to desist from your allotted task. If you do so, your sentence will be extended or you will be transferred to another jail. On the other hand, if you quietly accept the sentence and go about your work without clamouring or murmuring, your term is reduced, and you are sent out with a certificate that ensures a happy life, unpestered by constables. This is the attitude that the *jeeva* (individual) must adopt, if he is aware of his sentence and if he is earnest about freeing himself.

Remember, Freedom is your birthright. Concentrate on that and practise the means of attaining it.[1]

◊ ◊ ◊ ◊ ◊

How far have you progressed using the chance of these discourses and the *darshan* and *spharshan* (seeing and touching)? Bring something into your daily practice, as evidence of your having known the secret of the higher life from Me. Show that you have greater brotherliness, speak less with more sweetness and self–control, that you can bear defeat as well as victory with calm resignation.[2]

◊ ◊ ◊ ◊ ◊

The doctor spoke of people who come to Me with various aims; yes; but when some of them do not get exactly what they want, they blame Me and not themselves for wanting things that are not conducive to their progress or for not deserving to get them from Me. Why blame the Sun that he does not illumine your room? Open the doors and the Sun, who has been waiting at the doorstep for just that

---

[1] *Sathya Sai Speaks*, Vol. 4, pp. 57–58.

[2] *Sathya Sai Speaks*, Vol. 4, p. 176.

moment, floods the room with light. You must use your intelligence to deserve the Grace of God. That is the purpose of human effort.[1]

◊ ◊ ◊ ◊ ◊

I ask for *bhakti, shraddha, sadhana* (devotion, faith and spiritual discipline) — purification of hearts — that is all. Only beggars ask for money; I will never associate Myself with the temporary, the tarnished, the tawdry, and the mean. ...

I do not accept from you flowers that fade, fruits that rot, coins that have no value beyond the national boundary. Give Me the lotus that blooms in your *Manasarovara* — the clear pellucid waters of the lake — of your inner consciousness; give Me the fruits of holiness and steady discipline. I am above all this worldly etiquette, which enjoins you to see elders with some fruit or flower in your hand. My world is the world of the Spirit; there, values are different. If you are happy, with faith in God and fear of sin, that is enough "service," enough *kainkaryam* for Me. It pleases Me so.[2]

◊ ◊ ◊ ◊ ◊

Before the festivals of *Dasara*, birthday and *Shivaratri*, every year, I am exhorting you to take up the vow of *seva* (service) as a spiritual *sadhana*. I must say that I am not satisfied with your performance yet. But, I have not given up instructing you and commissioning you for I am hoping that you will catch up with the ideal some day or other. This is an example of the quality of mercy that is natural to Me. That quality makes Me appreciate even the little attempts you make to practise the ideal of *seva*.

Why have you come such long distances, braving all the expenses and troubles of the journey? To be in My Presence and to win My

---

[1] *Sathya Sai Speaks*, Vol. 5, pp. 10–11.

[2] *Sathya Sai Speaks*, Vol. 5, pp. 102–101.

Grace, isn't it? Why then do you seek other contacts, others' favour, once you have reached this place? Why fall into grooves that deny you My Presence and Grace? Forget all else, and stick to the orders that I give; I want only to initiate you into the spiritual path of *seva* and Love. Do not be ashamed that you have been asked to watch a heap of sandals, or carry water to the thirsty, or stand at the gate. The privilege and pleasure consists in the use to which you put your skill and time for helping others. You long for serving Me. Let Me tell you, serving those who serve Me gives Me as much satisfaction as serving Me. Serving anyone is serving Me, for, I am in all.

The relief and joy that you give to the sick and the sad, reach Me, for I am in their hearts, and I am the One they call out for. God has no need of your service; does he suffer from pain in the legs, or ache in the stomach? Try to serve the godly; be *dhasanudhasas* — servant of the servants of the Lord. The service of man is the only means by which you can serve God.

Everyone of you has, I know, the yearning to do *padaseva* (fondly massaging My feet). And, if I give the chance to all who are anxious to get it, what will happen to My feet? And, what a rush there will around Me! In the very nature of things, all those who yearn cannot be satisfied. But, know My feet are everywhere. *Sarvatah pani padham* — "In all places, His Hands, His Feet" says *Geeta*. The *Purusha Suktah* of the *Vedas* says: *Sahasra Seersha, Purusha, Sahasraksha, Sahasrapad* — "The Supreme Sovereign Person has a thousand heads, a thousand eyes and a thousand feet." The heads, eyes and feet of the thousands who gather here, are My Heads, My Eyes and My Feet. Nurse them, respect them, attend to their needs — you have done your *japa*, *dhyana*, and *puja*![1]

◊ ◊ ◊ ◊ ◊

[1] *Sathya Sai Speaks*, Vol. 10, pp. 29–31.

Stick to your faith; do not change your loyalty as soon as something happens or some one whispers. Do not pull down Sai Baba's picture from all the wall and hang some other picture there at the first disappointment. Leave all to Him; let His Will be carried out — that should be your attitude. Unless you go through the rough and the smooth, how can you be hardened? Welcome the light and the shade, the sun and the rain. Do not think that only those who worship a picture or image with pompous paraphernalia are devotees. Whoever walks straight along the moral path, whoever acts as he speaks and speaks as he has seen, whoever melts at another's woe and exults at another's joy — is a devotee, perhaps a greater devotee.

Baba is beyond the keenest intellect, the sharpest brain. Why, even the *Saptha Rishis* (Seven Rishis) failed to grasp the Sublimity of Godhead.[1]

◊ ◊ ◊ ◊ ◊

"Oh, this is my fate, my own past punishing me, I must go through it and suffer it, I cannot escape it"; thus, people get dis–heartened. If it is so inescapable, what is the use of prayer, of *japa*, of meditation, or of the ritual of worship? Win the Grace of the Lord — and all the accumulated burden will be burnt into ashes in a moment! Why blame the Lord for the "writing on your forehead"? It is you who write there and it is you who must wipe out the script. The evil you do, writes; the good you do, wipes! Let your mind dwell on the Lord, and the mist of the past births will melt before the rays of that sunrise; if you do not project those rays, the mist will thicken into darkness.[2]

◊ ◊ ◊ ◊ ◊

---

[1] *Sathya Sai Speaks*, Vol. 2, p. 7.

[2] *Sathya Sai Speaks*, Vol. 2, p. 118.

You need know the answers to two questions only; Who is Baba? Who am I? And the answer is, I am the reflected image of Baba; Baba is the original of which I am the reflection. That is the relationship; that is the bond, whether you know it or not, whether the image is distorted or correct.

You do *dhyana* (meditation), morning and evening; you do *japa* (repetition of *mantra*; you engage yourself in *shravanam, keertanam, smaranam, padasevanam, vandanam, dasyam, archanam, sakhyam* and *atma nivedanam* (hearing, singing, remembering, touching the feet, paying obeisance, serving, worshipping, being a friend and offering the Self) — all for realising that you are but an image, to become a clean, clear image of the Lord, so clean and clear that you merge in Him.

Seva is the adoration of the Lord, as *Vishnu–Virat swarupa* — as having the multifaceted Form and Immanence in the entire Universe. The *Vedas* describe Him as "thousand–headed, thousand–eyed, thousand–footed." The thousands of hands and eyes and feet that have come here for the Festival are all His, the Lord's. Worship Him; that is the purpose of your *Seva*. And He is none else than your own self. Do not count an individual as just an individual; he has God in him, as his Reality. Be aware of that.

I have been offering you advice and directions about *Seva* for some years but I am not satisfied with the extent to which you have been putting them into practice. Your aim should be to please Me, to satisfy Me, to follow My directions. I have come with certain tasks as My Mission. I too have certain vows to fulfil! They have been mentioned in the *Bhagavad Geeta* also. I have to establish the supremacy of *Dharma*; I have to bear the *yoga–kshema* (burden of welfare) of those who are immersed in thoughts of Me alone. So, the best way to please Me is to see Me in all beings and serve them just as you would like to serve Me. That is the best form of worship, which will reach Me.

The Lord may have two or two hundred vows; that is His Will. But, the *bhakta* need have only one vow, to save himself — the vow of total surrender — of *sharanagati*. If you have full faith in the Divinity of every being, the attitude of surrender will automatically be fixed in you.[1]

◊ ◊ ◊ ◊ ◊

Someone asked me during the interview he had, "Swami! May I ask You a question?" I told him I always welcomed questions, for, it was not wrong at all to use Me for solving one's doubts. Then he asked Me, "Swami, can I know from You who You are?" I answered, "But, first, you must know who you are; learn first what you mean when you say I, I, I." That I is this I. The I in that, is the same as This. The difference is due to the degree of manifestation of illumination, to the difference in the power of the bulbs. The Lord is closest to you, He is the mother, father, teacher, friend, guide and guardian. Call on Him, and He responds immediately. From dawn to dusk, spend every minute in His company.[2]

◊ ◊ ◊ ◊ ◊

How do you give Me *Ananda*? By taking to heart what I say and putting it into daily practice. Deciding to move high but attracted by the low, you betray yourself. Improve your character and conduct; when your feelings become cleansed and your impulses pure, then you can see My Form in its Reality. I shall tell you the thing in a nutshell: Make the intelligence that has to understand Me free from crookedness; let is become straight and sharp.

I have now fallen into your grasp, the very Treasure that you have been searching for, because our relationship is *Atmic*, not secular or trained. In all other places, you are fleeced; for the relationship is based on the purse. In some places, it is based on caste or scholarship or some other incidental trait; here, it is the attachment that the

---

[1] *Sathya Sai Speaks*, Vol. 8, pp. 180–81.

[2] *Sathya Sai Speaks*, Vol. 8, p. 169.

Narayana has for *Nara*, the Ocean for the stream, the Universal for the Particular. Here, everyone must become unlimited, escaping from bonds that limit him.[1]

◊ ◊ ◊ ◊ ◊

Come, I am the repairer of broken hearts, of damaged *antahkaranas* (mind, intellect, ego). I am like the smith, who welds, mends and sets right. Ten years ago, a devotee prayed to Me in song, "My heart has gone dry, my lamp has gone out, my path is dark, my brain is confused. Lord, make me fit again for life's arduous journey." The Lord will be waiting outside the door of the *puja* (prayer) room of the *bhakta* (devotee), anxious to fulfil his wish! Verily, he who has the Lord as His Servant, he is the real *Prabhu* (Lord)!

Only, do not allow your faith to falter. Do not become a slave to others; no, not even to God. Test. Test, examine, experience and then, when you find God, demand as of right. But before you get that right, you should appear for the examination and pass, is it not? I set tests not as a punishment or because I enjoy putting you into trouble, but just to give you the joy of passing! ...

You should not also yield to despair or become dejected. It is My *sankalpa* (resolve) that you progress in spiritual development. I have collected all of you and I shall lay the concrete foundation and build the walls and erect the roof and complete the mansion. My *sankalpa* never proves ineffective.[2]

◊ ◊ ◊ ◊ ◊

You clamour for further experience of My Divine Nature and ask that your faith might be strengthened thereby. To know the taste of sea–water, putting a drop on the tongue should be enough; there is no

---

[1] *Sathya Sai Speaks*, Vol. 1, p. 196.

[2] *Sathya Sai Speaks*, Vol. 2, pp. 77–78.

need to drink the whole lot. It is your waywardness, your egoism, your pride that makes you doubt and deny what you have once tasted. Is not one experience enough? Well, let Me ask: how can the limited know the depth of the Unlimited? How can the ant delve into the mountain? It is beyond you to know how or why I create things in My Hand. Or consider this: you have no patience even to put up with the problems of a single family, though the responsibility is obviously yours. Imagine then what My patience must be, to listen to, tackle and solve the problems of tens of thousands of families, with a *Prema* (Love) that is rare even among parents. No. You are incapable of gauging Me. You can never grasp the strength of this super–worldly bond that ties you to Me.

The experience of that bond will come to you unawares. Your duty is to await the moment. Believe and be Blessed. You are now worshipping Shiva or Narayana or Rama or Krishna, is it not? Tell Me how you got started. What experience did you have, before you began, of Rama's *Dhaya* (Mercy) or *Shantam* (Peace) or *Prema* (Love)? Or of Krishna's *Karuna* (Compassion) or *Prema* (Love)?[1]

◊ ◊ ◊ ◊ ◊

7.
The Significance of Bhagavan Baba's Birthday

This year you have named My birthday the "Golden Jubilee" of the *Avatar* (Divine Incarnation), and gathered in vast numbers from all parts of the world. I am sure you have benefitted by the *Sathsang* (holy company). I do not accost one particular date in the calendar as My

---

[1] *Sathya Sai Speaks*, Vol. 2, pp. 101–102.

birthday, for I consider the day when Divinity blossoms in your heart as My birthday in you. Therefore each of you should individually celebrate such a day as My birthday. The day when you resolve to practise My advice, to follow My directives, to translate My message into acts of service, and to engage in *sadhana* — that day is My birthday for you. The 23rd day of November which you now honour as the day on which I was born, is only like any other day if you celebrate it in a routine, ritual fashion. Adore man; the adoration reaches Me. Neglect man; you neglect Me. Of what avail is it to worship the Lord and to suppress man, His counterpart? Love for God must be manifested as Love for man, and Love must express itself as Service.[1]

◊ ◊ ◊ ◊ ◊

Have Love and *Ananda* (Divine Bliss) in your heart. *Ananda* comes from pure sight, pure hearing, pure speech and pure actions.

The day you establish yourselves in this *Ananda*, that day will be My Birthday for you. I must tell you another fact. Swami's Birthday is being celebrated at Puttaparthi because so many thousands come here from far–off places, in spite of the expense and great difficulty during the journey. Do not be under the impression that because it is Swami's Birthday therefore you must come.

I have no desire to have My Birthday celebrated; such trivial thoughts can never enter Me. My only desire is to share My *Ananda* with you, to encourage you to lead lives full of *Ananda*. My Birthday is when you get *Ananda*. My Mission is *Loka samastha sukhino bhavanthu* — "May all the worlds be happy and prosperous." Become aware of the Unity of mankind; promote by love and service the joy and contentment of everyone on earth and fill your hearts with that yearning. Then it becomes, verily, the *Sai Mandir* (temple). From that moment I am where you are.

---

[1] *Sathya Sai Speaks*, Vol. 13, p. 117.

Since this morning many people have greeted Me "Happy Birthday!" No one need wish for happiness for Me, since I am always happy, everywhere. For *Ananda swarupa* (Embodiment of Divine bliss), why talk of happy birthday? You, too, must ever be happy and not wait for the birthday to recur every year to accumulate *Ananda*.[1]

◊ ◊ ◊ ◊ ◊

8.
The Significance of Bhagavan Baba Appearing in Dreams

Here, I must tell you one thing. Which dreams are real? Dreams relating to God are real. You see Me in the dream, I allow you to do *namaskaram* (prostration), I bless you, I grant Grace ... that is true; that is due to My will and your *sadhana* (spiritual practice). If the Lord or your *Guru* appears in dream, it must be the result of *sankalpa* (His will), not due to any of the other reasons which cause dreams. It can never happen as a result of your wish.[2]

◊ ◊ ◊ ◊ ◊

---

[1] *Sathya Sai Speaks*, Vol. 14, pp. 101-102.

[2] *Sathya Sai Speaks*, Vol. 5, p. 197.

Summary

Sathya Sai Baba is the Soul or *Atma* of every being. He is therefore synonymous with Krishna and the embodiment of the *Paramatma* (Supreme Soul). Every being has a portion of the Supreme Bliss and Love of Sai Baba within himself as his soul. When man realizes this, He realizes his oneness with the Divinity of the entire universe.

Chapter 7

Brahma, Vishnu and Maheswara

LORD VISHNU

LORD BRAHMA

LORD VISHNU ON SESHANAG

LORD MAHESHWARA (SHIVA)

Chapter 7

Brahma, Vishnu and Maheswara

Introduction

"Brahma creates the world, Vishnu sustains it, and Shiva destroys it. This process of creation (*stisti*), preservation (*sthiti*) and destruction (*pralaya*) perpetually continues in that cyclic order....

Three types of tendencies or characteristics seem to accrue to every created object. These have been technically designated as *Gunas*: *Satwa guna, Rajo guna,* and *Tamo guna*. These three gunas in their purest form are fundamental entities, the permutation and combination of which produce this world of phenomena. Of these, *Satwa guna* makes for light and lightness, goodness and purity, knowledge and wisdom. It can be likened to the centripetal force. *Tamo guna*, which is the antithesis of *Satwa guna*, is responsible for all that, is dark and heavy, evil and impure, ignorant and deluded. It is the centrifugal force as it were. It is the business of *Rajo guna* to maintain a delicate balance between these two opposing forces. Hence it has got to be in a state of constant internal tension and activity. This restless activity is its chief characteristic and it manifests itself as passion and ambition in the psychological world.

The three deities of the Trinity, correspond to the three *Gunas* in the cosmic play of creation, preservation and destruction. Vishnu represents *Satwa*, the power of existence and preservation. Shiva represents *Tamas*, the power of annihilation. Brahma stands in between these two and represents *Rajas*."[1]

Lord Brahma

"Lord Brahma is traditionally accepted as the Creator of the entire universe. In Vedanta, the cosmic–subtle body called *Hiranyagarbha* is considered to be the Creator, Lord Brahma. An individual's subtle body is constituted of his mind and intellect, i.e., his entire thoughts. The cosmic–subtle–body is the aggregate of all the subtle bodies of all the living beings. The subtle body of an individual is responsible for the creation of his gross physical body and the world of objects that he experiences. In other words, it is the mind, intellect equipment that projects the physical body and the world ....

The manifested world of plurality has emerged from the Unmanifested Reality. To indicate this, Brahma, the Creator is described as being born from the naval of Vishnu (who represents the eternal Reality) when He is shown lying on the great Serpent *Ananta* in the milky ocean.

Brahma is a four–faced God seated on a lotus. The Lord has in His four hands a water–pot (*kamandalu*), a manuscript (*Vedas*), a

---

[1] *Hindu Gods and Goddesses*, Swami Harshananda, pp. 19-20.

sacrificial implement (*sruva*), and a rosary (*mala*). He wears the hide of a deerskin and His vehicle is a swan (*Hamsa*).

The Lord seated on a lotus indicates that He is ever–rooted to the Infinite Reality. Lotus represents the Reality which is the foundation upon which His personality exists.

The four faces of Brahma represent the four Vedas. His four hands stand for the four aspects of man's inner personality (*Antakarana*) viz. the mind (*manas*), intellect (*buddhi*), ego (*ahamkara*), and conditioned consciousness (*chitta*). These four are the ways in which the thoughts function and they are the manifestations of pure Consciousness.

The deerskin worn by the Lord indicates that a seeker, who desires to reach the supreme states of Brahman must first observe austerities. ... Observing such austerities, the seeker must carefully study and reflect upon the scriptural truths which are suggested by holding the manuscript (*Vedas*) in one hand of the Lord representing the *buddhi* (intellect). With such self–control and discipline and having the knowledge of the *Sastras* (scriptures), he must use his physical body in selfless and dedicated service (*Karma Yoga*) for the general prosperity of all. This is indicated by the sacrificial implement held in the second hand (*ahamkar*/ego). When these three spiritual practices are adopted, the mind of the seeker is withdrawn from its preoccupations with the sense pursuits in the external world. Such a mind, which has become introvert and relatively tranquil alone is suitable for concentration (*dharana*) and *japa* (chanting with the rosary (*mala*) provided in the third hand — (mind/*manas*). Meditation is the last process by which the seeker is transported from his finite limited individuality into the infinite transcendental state of God–Realization. This is indicated by the holding of the water–pot (*kamandalu*) — a symbol of *sanyas* — in the fourth hand (*chitta*) conditioned consciousness."[1]

---

[1] *Symbolism in Hinduism* — A Parthasarathy, compiled by R. S. Nathan, pp. 107-108.

Another interpretation is the following: "The rosary represents time, and the water–pot, the causal waters from which all creation has sprung. So Lord Brahma controls time as well as the principle of causation. The sacrificial implements (ladle, spoon, *Kusa grass*, etc.) represent the system of sacrifices which is the means to be adopted by the various creatures to sustain one another. The book represents knowledge, sacred and secular. He is the Giver of all Knowledge — arts, sciences and wisdom. The hand postures of the Lord (*mudras*) are *abhaya* (assuring protection) and *varada* (granting boons)."[1]

"Lord Brahma uses the swan (*Hamsa*) as His vehicle. It signifies that a man of Realization moves about in the world with a unique faculty that a swan possesses. A *Hamsa* (swan), as described in the Hindu mythology, has the faculty to separate pure milk from a sample of milk mixed with water. Similarly, a man of perfection recognizes the one Supreme Truth inherent in the entire pluristic phenomena.

The Lord of Creation must necessarily possess the knowledge to create ... Hence, it is, that Brahma is said to be wedded to the Goddess of Knowledge, Mother Saraswati ...

All creations arise out of *vikshepa* (thought disturbances). This *vikshepa shakti* is Lord Brahma — the total mind — intellect equipment. Man, being essentially constituted of his mind and intellect, has already invoked this *vikshepa shakti* and realized Brahma. Hence worship of and invocation of Brahma is not undertaken by anyone ...

Lord Brahma is not popularly worshipped in India because the idea of creation is repugnant to a seeker of Truth. It is the creation of thoughts that has veiled Infinite Reality. The attempt of all spiritual seekers is to destroy the existing thoughts and maintain this state until the Truth reveals Itself. Hence, Shiva and Vishnu are worshipped more than Brahma ..."[2]

---

[1] Swami Harshananda, *Hindu Gods and Goddesses*, p. 24.

[2] *Symbolism in Hinduism* — A Parthasarathy, compiled by R. S. Nathan, p. 111-112.

Vishnu (Narayana)

"Analysing the human personality, *Vedanta* takes the seeker to discover the state of Pure Consciousness in the innermost depths of his being, which is the one source at once for all his perceptions, feelings and thoughts.

This great Self, functioning as the spark of Existence in each one of us, is the One Eternal Reality. When it expresses through the vehicles of mind and intellect there is the dynamic creature — constantly acquiring and possessing, gaining and achieving good and bad in the world ...

Vyasa describes this great Reality as Sri Narayana who has been shown as resting in yogic sleep in *Vaikuntha*. It is described that in an ocean of milk (*Ksheerabdhi*), Sri Narayana lies in *Yoga-nidra* on a great serpent-bed (*ananta*), protected by the hood of the serpent. He is served by Lakshmi, His consort, who is ever at His feet.

Deep in the recesses of our personality (*Vaikunta*) lies the Infinite Truth (*Vishnu*) upon the Serpent-*Ananta* (the mind) who is depicted as thousand-headed. In all religions, the serpent represents the vicious mind which at one and the same time, can think a thousand thoughts and perhaps, spill its venom through its thousand urges, inclinations, desires and passions. In life it is found that the hooded cobra, to strike its victim, turns its hood away from his body. When the mind is turned towards the world of objects outside, it is capable of spilling its poison onto the world outside. Here in the description, the hoods are turned upon the body of the serpent and it is lying coiled upon itself, forming a soft bed upon which reclines Lord Vishnu (All Pervading). When the multi-headed human mind turns its attention inward upon itself, and the mind lies coiled upon itself, there is the state of a meditator at the moment of his greatest quietude (*samadhi*). At such moments the Infinite Vishnu can be recognized as resting upon such a thoughtless mind held in animated suspension in an atmosphere of breathless devotion. The Lord is in "yogic-sleep." It means that looking from the Pure Consciousness, the world known to us constituted of all the perceptions, emotions and thoughts is not there at all, just as in our sleep we do not recognize the world of plurity. But this is not the ordinary sleep (*nidra*); it is a positive experience of the All–Pervading Reality, and hence it is called the *yoga–nidra*.

Such a vision of the Lord can be experienced by the mind when it turns upon itself; and the mind can gain this steady introvertedness only in an atmosphere of supreme purity. Hence, it is described that He is resting in the "milky–ocean," in the ocean of the milk of human kindness.

Lakshmi (Wealth, Power, Glory) rests at His feet, serving Him. A Man of Realization, who, through meditation has thus experienced the Soul of the Universe in himself, does not thereafter run after the wealth of the world of objects; all glory follows at His heels, wanting to serve Him as His faithful mistress.

Lord Narayana (*Vishnu*) is the One among the Trinity representing the Power–of–Sustenance. He is the One who manifests Himself in the world among mankind at appropriate eras in His various incarnations to rid life of its evil propensities and to make the world ready for greater evolution (see Chapter IV — Rama; Chapter V — Lord Krishna; and Chapter VI — Sathya Sai Baba as incarnations of Lord Vishnu). When this benign Lord wakes up from His yogic–sleep and comes down to bless those who are His devotees, He assumes the form of Lord Narayana ....

Traditionally He is described as blue in colour clothed in yellow, wearing a crown and standing upon a lotus Divine. He has four hands and He holds in them the conch (*sankha*), the discus (*chakra*), the mace (*gada*), and the lotus (*padma*). ... Blue is the colour of the Infinite and whatever is immeasurable can appear to the mortal eye only as blue. ... The yellow represents the earth. Anything that is buried in the earth gathers a yellowish hue, and in fire, earth (mud, silica) glows yellowish. Thus, Sri Narayana represents the Immeasurable, All–Pervading Reality (blue colour), meaning Sri Narayana is the Infinite clothed in matter; He is the Infinite expressed through a form.

When the Self (Atma) thus expresses through a form, an individual (*jiva*) is manifested. Every individual acts and accomplishes in the world, not with the two mortal hands alone, but with a subtle set of four hands. These four aspects that function from within the physical equipments together are called the "subtle body"; in *Vedanta* it is known as the "inner equipment," constituted of the Mind, the Intellect, the Consciousness of them all and the Ego. These four are symbolized in the form–representation of Lord Vishnu having four hands.

The Lord wears a Divine crown on His head to indicate His sovereignty and Lord–ship over all names and forms. He is the sole proprietor of the entire universe.

This mighty Infinite Lord dwells in the core of our personality as the very self in us.

His hands are never empty — each is carrying a symbol together indicating how He carries out His Divine duties as the preserver of the universe. He blows the conch, calling man to live the nobler values–of–life so that he may turn away from all his worldly preoccupations and ultimately reach and receive from Him the Infinite Bliss of unbroken peace and perfection. This "final goal" indicated in our scriptures, is represented as a Lotus.

With a tender anxiety to give the devotee the highest experience of perfect happiness when He calls, man, roaming with his sensuous urges and animal propensities, hears the echoes of the shrill notes of his inner conscience calling him to stop and retire. Generally man has no ears to hear or even when he hears has no heart to obey. He still dashes forth in the quest for sense gratification. It is at such times that, out of sheer love, the Lord wields His mace to knock man down with disappointments, dissatisfaction and a growing sense of restlessness.

Even in spite of these punishments, if the devotee is not turning towards the spiritual path and is not progressively moving towards the final destination, the Lord has the total annihilating power of the discus which can destroy the equipment and lift him from his present life of unhealthy circumstances. This is true of an individual, a community, or a nation. Fascinated by the delusory joys of the sense objects, the human mind may dance forth to live a ruinous life of sense gratifications. And if this material and purely sensuous way of life is continued in spite of the consequent mental tensions and strains, the society dissipates all its higher urges, loses even its common efficiencies and ultimately comes to lose all that it possessed and ends in a pitiful and disastrous fall. This is what history records and common sense ever dictates.

We may even consider the "hand that holds the conch" as the intellect (*buddhi*), the hand that holds the discus as the ego, that which holds the mace as the mind (*manas*), and that which holds the Lotus as the consciousness (*chitta*). The discriminating intellect gives us the call and points out a more rewarding way–of–life, and in case we ignore this silent whisper of the heart and plunge into a life of extrovertedness, the mind gives endless knocks to that personality. If even then, we are not able to realize our folly and withdraw ourselves from the dissipating ways of living, the arrogant ego fettered by these stupidities of the mind, in revolt against the intellect, ultimately drives the individual to its total doom.

On the other hand, in case we are able to listen to the call and surrender our ego and the mind in devotion to the Lord, we can surely come to His sacred feet, and receive the Lotus that He is offering to us as an eternal reward for an insignificant renunciation on our part.

When the inner equipments of the mind, intellect and ego are transcended, the Light and Consciousness that illumines them for us, Itself is discovered as the Pure Infinite Self.

A meditator who meditates thus upon the symbolism represented in the Lord's Divine Form is no more merely gazing at His Divine physical form, but the devotee comes to be transported into a realm of Realization of his own inner True Nature. The Lord is ever rooted in this Divine Brahman and, hence, the Deity is represented as standing on a Lotus."[1]

---

[1] Swami Chinmayananda, *Symbolism in Hinduism*, compiled by R. S. Nathan, pp. 113-120.

The following exerpts are from the Divine Discourses of Sathya Sai Baba:

Maheshwara (Shiva)

"All that is born must die. All that is produced must disintegrate and be destroyed. This is an inviolable law. The principle that brings about this disintegration, the power behind this destruction, is Shiva."[1]

Referring to the illustration, "the matted hair of Shiva proclaims the length and intensity of His *tapas* (austerities and penances), and cobras around His matted hair signify that even the most poisonous becomes harmless because the one that has identified himself with the Supreme has gone beyond all the effects of matter on his senses or organs and has become immune even to the deadliest of poisons."[2] Also the snakes often seen adorning Shiva, refer to the ego which is now seen as a plaything of the Cosmic Consciousness, unable to cause any harm, its poison having been removed.

"The third eye in the midst of the forehead represents the concentration of *jnana* (wisdom), and therefore the absolute power to destroy *tamas* and all its manifestations (darkness, ignorance, etc.) and attributes. ... The blue color of the neck symbolizes the pervasiveness of *maya* or *avidya* (cosmic ignorance). Up to the neck, and beyond the neck is the seat of *jnana* (wisdom, higher intelligence) leading to

---

[1] Swami Harshananda, *Hindu Gods and Goddesses*, p. 57.

[2] V. A. K. Aiyar, *Symbolism in Hinduism*, compiled by R. S. Nathan, p. 67.

Eternity and Immortality. ... The ashes that besmear the body reminds us that this body of which we are proud and obsessed is ultimately bound to end up merely as ashes. ... Ashes can also signify the exhaustion of the *vasanas* (accumulated tendencies) at the mental level.

The trident symbolizes *sama*, *dama*, and *vairagya* (control of the external and internal senses, fortitude in the midst of grief and pain, joy and victory and all dualities, and detachment from the transitory) which dispel and destroy the six qualities which pull us down, namely, *kama* (desire), *krodha* (anger), *lobha* (greed), *moha* (delusion), *mada* (pride) and *matsarya* (envy). By directing the trident mercilessly against these weaknesses, one becomes conscious of the worthlessness of this worldly existence as a slave to these degenerative qualities; and this awakening helps one to forge ahead to the summum bonum of human birth and existence — Liberation ... Shiva, by His *tapas* (penance) and austerities, and consequent wisdom, has conquered the concept of death. ... The tiger–skin apparel stands for *vairagya* (detachment) and absolute unconcern for the body and its supposed needs. The *chinmudra* posture in which He holds His hand teaches us that our ego (index finger) must bend and that our individuality must end as represented by the symbol "zero" which the index finger produces when it bends and touches the middle of the thumb in the *mudra*.[1]

The following excerpts are the words of Bhagavan Sri Sathya Sai Baba on The Trinity: Brahma, Vishnu, and Shiva (as Maheshwara).

◊ ◊ ◊ ◊ ◊

---

[1] Dr. S. R. D. Sastry, *Symbolism in Hinduism*, compiled by R. S. Nathan, pp. 67-68.

1.

The Trinity:
Brahma, Vishnu, Maheswara
(Shiva)

The entire creation is based on three processes: *srishti* (creation), *sthithi* (sustenance) and *layam* (dissolution). The cosmos is kept going by these three processes (*karmas*). Should there not be a director for these processes? You cannot have in this world an action (*karma*) without a doer (*kartha*). The doer and the deed go together.

Who is the doer? What is this action? What is the fruit of the action? It is only when these three are properly understood that the secret of creation can be recognised.

It is easy to criticise the Lord's *leelas* (spiritual actions), but it difficult to understand their inner meaning. Our life should be devoted to understanding the ways of the Lord.

In this understanding, the first aspect to be recognised is *srishti* (creation of the cosmos). What is involved in this process should be understood. For instance, if a giant bridge has to be constructed, a large number of engineers and other personnel are required. Besides a chief manager, there will have to be engineers and men working under him. It is only their combined effort that can build a bridge. In the same manner, for the creation, protection and mergence of the cosmos, three principal agencies are required. The principal authority responsible for creation is known as Brahma. He is in charge of all that is related to creation. Next comes protection. What has been created has to be fostered and protected. The authority responsible for this function is called Vishnu. After growth inevitably there comes the stage of dissolution. There is an authority responsible for laying down the rules for dissolution and enforcing those regulations. This authority is called Easwara (Shiva). Thus there are three authorities who share functionally the responsibility for creation, protection and dissolution. There must be someone who presides over these three functionaries, like the Prime Minister in a Cabinet. Brahma, Vishnu and Easwara are presiding deities for three different functions. There is a supreme authority presiding over these three. This supreme authority was called by *Bharathiyas* (Indians) as *Bhagavan*. Members of different faiths have given different names to this authority. The term that is most widely used in this context today is "God." *Bhagavan* refers to the One who governs all the three functions of creation, protection and dissolution.

In the word "GOD," you have three letters: G, O, D. "G" refers to "Generation" (or creation) (Brahma). "O" refers to "organisation" (that is, keeping creation going) (Vishnu). "D" stands for destruction (Shiva). "GOD" combines the three aspects of generation, organisation and destruction. When people refer to God, they regard Brahma, Vishnu and Shiva as each a God. God is the one who wields the authority over all the three. This Divine entity pervades the entire universe in the form of atoms. "Subtle as the atom, vast as the vastest in creation, the *Atma* pervades everything as atom" (Telugu poem).

Hence, the Divine is called *Atma*. This *Atma* pervades everything and is present everywhere. This all–pervading *Atma* is the Eternal Witness. This role may be illustrated by a simple example: There is light here. There are some who are reading under it, some who are sleeping, some who are talking and some others who are moving about. The light has no connection with all these different activities. The light is only a witness. Likewise, the sun is shining. Using the sunlight different people are carrying on different activities. The sun is totally unaffected by either the good or bad actions that are being done by different persons. Each is accountable for his actions. But the sun shines as a witness to all that is happening. Without the sun none of these actions is possible. The sun is thus the agency that enables the actions to be done but he is not the dispenser of the fruits of those actions. Brahma, Vishnu and Easwara are responsible for enabling the actions to be done, for furthering their fruition and for determining how the fruits should be enjoyed. These three deities have to be propitiated for favours in these respects. That is what has been done on Shivarathi night.

How are they to be propitiated? The methods are indicated in the nine forms of devotion: *sravanam* (singing), *Vishnusmaranam* (remembering the Name), *vandanam* (prostration), *archanam* (worship of images), *padasevanam* (worship of the feet), *dāsyam* (service), *sneham* (friendship), *atmanivedanam* (total surrender).

Today we have to acquire the favour of these deities. With their friendship we can face any troubles just as, if we have friendship of a person in power, we can overcome troubles in life. These deities will help to alleviate the consequences of our actions if they are properly propitiated. For this purpose, the chanting of the Divine name is essential. Equally meditation and penance are necessary. All forms of worship are designed to please the deities.

These deities lay down regulations for observance by the world in respect of their specific functions. These regulations are like the traffic rules and guideposts and the road signs that indicate to people using the roads how they should behave.

For instance, there is Brahma. As Creator he lays down the laws relating to actions and how the consequences of these actions affect people in their lives from birth to death. In addition, he also effects changes in the administration of these rules. On the basis of this function, the Brahma principle is operative everywhere. The very term "Brahma" means "pervading." The pervasiveness of the Brahma Principle is cosmic.

"Vishnu" also means that which is all–pervading. The Vishnu Principle permeates everything. Wherever the creation principle of Brahma is present, there the sustaining principle of Vishnu is also present.

Where there is protection there is also punishment. This means where Vishnu is present, Easwara is also present. ...

The cosmos is governed by the three principle deities. I am letting you into a secret. So far as Creation is concerned, propitiate Brahma and establish links with the deity. As regards protection, establish links with Vishnu (by propitiating Him). With regard to destruction, establish association with Easwara (Shiva). However if your heart is totally pure, you can establish direct connection with God. You need not approach the lesser deities. For this, there is a way. That is the way of total surrender. Through surrender you can establish a direct link with God, heart to heart. ...

The three presiding deities over creation, protection and dissolution are the Trinity — Brahma, Vishnu and Shiva. But there is a fourth entity — the Overlord (*Srionayakam*), who is above these three. He is God. He can overrule the trinity. How? By mitigating the magnitude of the consequences of *karma*. He can counteract any kind of situation. That is the Divine prerogative of God. He can create anything, protect anything. He creates and brings about its dissolution.

Therefore, God should be regarded as having control over Generation, Organisation and Destruction. To realise God, you have to surrender yourself completely. When the surrender is total, a direct link with God is established. Without such surrender propitiating the lesser deities is a waste of time.[1]

◊ ◊ ◊ ◊ ◊

The four stages of *Pranava* (Om) are associated with the deities Vishnu, Brahma, Rudhra and the *Paramatma*. Vishnu means that which is omnipresent. The visible universe is suffused with beauty and beauty is God. Since the universe is the body of God, the Supreme Person, Vishnu is also described in the scriptures as "He who delights in decoration" (*Alankara Priyo Vishnu*). The material Universe is saturated in harmony, law and symmetry and is therefore charming and fascinating. Through this attraction, the external world, the universe, draws man into various paths and exertions. The five elements, the five senses, the five vital airs and other phenomena

---

[1] *Sanathana Sarathi*, April 1995, pp. 85-98.

teach man various lessons to mould his nature. So the objective world can be taken as his *Guru*.

Vishnu is the deity who fosters and feeds, who moulds and masters. Moreover, He is the guardian of the Cosmos, the *Jagadrakshaka*. The scriptures teach man to sanctify the waking hours — *jagrat* stage — for they belong to Vishnu, and are charged with the Vishnu–principle. They exhort man to avoid wicked deeds, polluting thoughts, and all types of errors and failings.

During the dream stage, we can experience Holiness and Bliss, only when we engage ourselves, while awake, in steady, pure, unselfish activities. In dreams, we see diverse objects and persons, strange worlds, of skyscrapers and castles. From where did these emerge? Through whom were they presented? *Prajnanam Brahman*, the Supreme Consciousness, is the basis for the creation of this variety of dream appearances. *Brahma* is the deity that creates. So, the dream state is the *Brahma*–phase of consciousness.

Then, the deep sleep stage. Here, the experiences gained during the waking hours or gone through in dreams do not impinge on man. They have all been extinguished. *Rudhra*, the deity into whom the Cosmos ultimately merges, is therefore associated with the *sushupthi* (deep sleep) phase.

Next, we have the *thuriya* or the fourth stage, the stage of *Atma*–Consciousness. When the salt doll is dropped in the sea, it reaches the bottom and is dissolved. The same happens to the seeker of the *Atma*. He is dissolved. He becomes one with that which he sought to know. He cannot return and describe the experience.

"The *A* of *Om* is the *Vishwa*; the *U* is *Thaijas*; the *M* is *Prajna*" — this is another interpretation in the scriptures. *Vishwa* is the Waking, *Thaijas* the Dream, *Prajna*, the Deep sleep stage. The *Pranava Sadana* (the spiritual exercise of meditation on *Aum*) is therefore very important for seekers. The *Vedas* prescribe the repetition of the *Pranava*

(Aum) while studying holy texts, reciting the Name of the Divine, carrying out daily duties and offering gifts.[1]

◊ ◊ ◊ ◊ ◊

The *Karma Kanda* reveals that the Law of *Karma* affects everything that has a body and not merely human beings alone. For instance, even the Trinity — Brahma, Vishnu and Rudhra — cannot avoid the consequences of *karma*. By their actions they are demonstrating this Truth to the world. For instance, like a potter, Brahma is continuously creating things in this Cosmos. This is the unceasing work. Why is he involved in this? Because he has a distinct body. Assuming the body for performing *karma* and discharging his *Dharma* (Righteousness) through his *karma*, he is setting an example to the world.

Vishnu comes down in human form whenever *Dharma* declines on the earth and is in danger of extinction. Facing the censure of the wicked, punishing evil–doers and protecting the good and the innocent, and receiving the praise of the devotees, Vishnu is carrying out His duty of protecting *Dharma* and reforming mankind. It may be asked, "Why should Vishnu go through this ordeal as the protector of *Dharma*?" It is not an ordeal. It is only a demonstration of the duties that are related to the assuming of a certain form. *Easwara* (Shiva) covers Himself with *vibhuthi* (sacred ash), dwells in the burial ground and subjects Himself to various rigorous disciplines. Thus even Brahma, Vishnu and Maheswara, by their actions, have been setting an example to mankind as to how to make human life purposeful.[2]

◊ ◊ ◊ ◊ ◊

In the waking state, the senses have free play. The gross body is most active then. In the dream stage, the senses subsist in their subtle

---

[1] *Sathya Sai Speaks*, Vol. 15, pp. 18-19.

[2] *Sathya Sai Speaks*, Vol. 16, pp. 43-44.

form. The mind revels in its fancies then. In the dream, the subtle body is active. It creates many attractive and astounding scenes and incidents for its own edification. In the deep sleep state, the mind along with the subtle aspects of the senses are submerged in the ego or the causal body. This is the *shoonya* (vacant) stage, according to *Vedantic* terminology. It is vacant because there is no positive gain associated with it. It does not confer awareness of the *Atma* (Divine Self) and the Bliss of that Awareness. That can happen only in the fourth state after the *sthuula* (gross), *sushuma* (subtle), *karana* (causal). That state is named the *Maha Karana* (supercausal). The waking state is the gross region of *Brahma*, the Creator, when activity abounds. It merges in the dream, the Vishnu region, when mere *sthithi* (existence) abounds. That too merges in deep sleep, when both dissolve and lose their identity in *laya* (Rudhra).

The fact to remember is that every individual, every day, experiences *Shrishti* (Brahma, Creator), *Sthithi* (Vishnu, Maintenance) and *Laya* (Rudhra, Dissolution). But, he fails to recognise it and benefit by the experience. He mistakes birth as creation and death as dissolution. This is sheer ignorance. One has to transcend these three changes and establish himself in the stable unchanging *Maha Karana*, the *Atma*.[1]

◊ ◊ ◊ ◊ ◊

Creation, preservation and merging are the three forms of the Divine Will. By *karma* (action) yoga, you grasp the meaning of creation and the created; by *bhakti* (devotion) yoga, you understand the preserver and the preserved; by *jnana* (knowledge) yoga, you merge into the principle from which you have emerged.[2]

◊ ◊ ◊ ◊ ◊

---

[1] *Sathya Sai Speaks*, Vol. 16, pp. 65-66.

[2] *Sathya Sai Speaks*, Vol. 7, p. 22.

God is not involved in either rewards or punishments. He only re–flects, re–sounds and re–acts! He is the Eternal Unaffected Witness! You decide your own fate. Do good, be good, you get good in return; be bad, do bad deeds, you reap bad results. Do not thank or blame God. Thank yourself, blame yourself! He does not even will that creation, protection and destruction shall take place. They follow the same law, the innate law of the *maya*–ridden universe.

This electric current, for example, can be used by us, to turn the fans and give us coolness in this sultry weather; it can be used to give light, to magnify human speech and take the sound nearer to you; it can be made to produce many copies of a printed sheet. In all these cases, it creates. But, if you are so overcome by all the good that it does and your admiration goes a little too far and you grasp the wire that carries it to you, you are killed! The current creates; it protects; it destroys; it depends on how we utilise it.[1]

◊ ◊ ◊ ◊ ◊

In a way man is the very Trinity — Brahma, Vishnu and Maheswara. Vishnu is symbolic of *satwic* attribute, Brahma that of *rajasic* attribute and Maheswara of *tamasic* attribute. As long as man contains in himself all these three attributes *satwa*, *rajas* and *tamas*, he is the embodiment of Trinity.[2]

◊ ◊ ◊ ◊ ◊

In this human body, constituted by the five elements, God dwells in the form of the three *gunas*. *Bharatiyas* adore the Trinity — Brahma, Vishnu, Maheswara. The Trinity are not embodied beings. No one has ever seen them. Nor is it possible to experience them in any way. The Trinity dwell in the human body as the three *gunas*: sattwa, rajas and

---

[1] *Sathya Sai Speaks*, Vol. --, p. 43.

[2] *Summer Showers in Brindavan* (1993), p. 44.

tamas. The three qualities are forms of the Divine. Brahma is responsible for creation. The process of creation is subtle and cannot be perceived by any of the senses. This transcendental process is taught by the mother. All are creations of the mother. Hence, the Upanishad declares: "Revere mother as God." The mother is to be adored as Brahma, the Creator. Revere the mother, serve the mother and trust the mother. This symbolises worship of God.

Next comes the father. He protects the child, takes care of upbringing and leads him to God. This protective function is attributed to Vishnu. The father symbolises Vishnu as the protector. Hence the injunction: "Revere the father as God." Thus the mother and the father are images of Brahma and Vishnu.

Then there is Easwara. He is called *Bolasankara.* He gives whatever one prays for. He never says "no" to any supplicant. Such an embodiment of Truth cannot be hidden — to experience this embodiment of auspiciousness (Shiva), *tamas* is the means. The *tamas* quality is usually associated with slothfulness and indolence. But this is not the proper meaning of *tamas* (as an attribute of Shiva). Shiva's role is to lead man on the right path to realise his divinity.

The Trinity, in the form of the three *gunas,* are present in every human being. This is borne out by the scriptural aphorisms *Easwara–sarvabhoothanam* (the Divine dwells in all beings), *Isavasyam idam jagat* (the Lord is the indweller in the cosmos). When the significance of the three *gunas* is understood, the nature of the Trinity can be understood.[1]

◊ ◊ ◊ ◊ ◊

---

[1] *Sarathana Sarathi,* Nov.-Dec. 1995, p. 282.

2.

Vishnu: Narayana

The *Geeta* speaks of *bhakti, jnana, karma,* as *yogas* and by *yoga* is meant what *Pathanjali* intended to mean (*chitta vritti niroda,* that is, the stilling of the agitations of the mind–stuff). Vishnu is the supreme exemplar of this calm, for He is "*shanthakaram bhugjaga shayanam,*" the very picture of peaceful calm, though reclining on a thousand–hooded serpent; the snake being the symbol of the objective world with its poisonous fangs. Being in the world but not of it, not bound by it — that is the secret.[1]

◊ ◊ ◊ ◊ ◊

Brahma's lotus is not a stalk that grows in mud and rises above the waters to catch the rays of the sun and blossom, but the many petalled Lotus of the Heart, each petal being the direction in which a particular tendency attracts the individual.[23]

◊ ◊ ◊ ◊ ◊

God is called in His Cosmic form as Vishnu, who permeates everything in the cosmos. God is the cause and the cosmos is the effect. You must try to understand the various attributes of the Lord. Vishnu is depicted as having a conch in one hand and a wheel in another. In a third hand he carries a mace and in the fourth a lotus.

---

[1] *Sathya Sai Speaks,* Vol. 6, p. 95.

[2] *Sathya Sai Speaks,* Vol. 2, p. 260.

[3] *Sathya Sai Speaks,* Vol. 2, p. 260.

What is the esoteric significance of all this? The conch is a symbol of sound. Hence, God is described as the embodiment of sound. The wheel (*chakra*) symbolises the wheel of time (*kalachakra*). The Lord is the master of Time and Sound. The mace signifies strength or power. This means that the Lord holds in his hand the strength of all beings. The lotus in the Lord's hand is a symbol of the heart. This means that the Lord holds in His hand the hearts of all beings.[1]

◊ ◊ ◊ ◊ ◊

What is *Vaikunta*? The Lord's abode is described in various ways as *Vaikunta, Kailasa, Swarga,* etc. ... All these are crazy fancies. What is the abode of God? The Lord told Narada: "I reside wherever my devotees sing My glories." The Lord dwells in the hearts of devotees. This is His main address. All other places are "branch offices." Any message addressed to the Divine Indweller in the heart is bound to reach God.

Vaikunta, as the abode of God, means a place which is changeless. Many things may change in a man, but his heart is changeless.[2]

◊ ◊ ◊ ◊ ◊

Vishnu means, *sarva vyapi* (He who is everywhere). So, His residence *Vaikuntha* (heaven) must be everywhere. You can gain entry, by knocking with the correct password on your lips. Your heart can become *Vaikuntha,* if you but cleanse it and purify it and allow God to manifest in it. *Vaikuntha* means "the place where there is no shadow of grief." When God manifests in your heart, all is full and free.[3]

---

[1] *Sanathana Sarathi,* September 1993, p. 226.

[2] *Sarathana Sarathi,* February 1996, pp. 39-40.

[3] *Sathya Sai Speaks,* Vol. 8, p. 4.

◊ ◊ ◊ ◊ ◊

Vishnu (whose incarnation is Krishna) is said to ride on a bird called Garuda. In fact, it is the heart of man that is spoken of as a bird; the heart yearns, it carries the thought of God; it moves swiftly to where He is. If your son is in USA, it goes to where he stays. Man turns to God, at all times and in all places. For the essence of man is Divine.[1]

◊ ◊ ◊ ◊ ◊

Vishnu is the God that symbolises the universal aspect of the Divine Principle in the Universe as well as beyond it.

Rtham, rhythm or Righteousness is the very breath of Vishnu, for, it sustains the stars, it stabilises society, it ensures advance. Vishnu is that aspect of the Trinity that is concerned with sustaining, fostering, stabilising, strengthening. So, Vishnu has to incarnate often in order to save and salvage the world. He has to re-establish *rtham* (right or Righteousness, morality), so that the world may sail on an even keel and reach the harbour of Liberation, so that the world may be transformed into a Prashanti Nilayam (Abode of the Deepest Peace).[2]

◊ ◊ ◊ ◊ ◊

That permanent basis, Brahman, when it gets mixed up and combines with these impermanent or transient people who come and go, then you get the picture of the world like the picture you see in a cinema. That is why we say, *Sarvam Vishnu mayam Jagat*. This process, by which the untrue or transient pictures and the true and the somewhat permanent screen are together combining and giving you an impression of permanence, may be called the *Vishnu maya* of the

---

[1] *Sathya Sai Speaks*, Vol. 8, p. 169.

[2] *Sathya Sai Speaks*, Vol. 10, pp. 8-9.

Jagat. The word *Vishnu* here should not be understood to refer to an individual wearing his insignia like the *Sankha, Chakra* and so on. The word *Vishnu* here stands for omnipresence.[1]

◊ ◊ ◊ ◊ ◊

Likewise, Vishnu pervades the cosmos as His body. All things in the cosmos are limbs of the body of Vishnu. Hence no one should have any aversion to anything in the universe. He should not hate anyone, because the same Divine is present in you and in everything in the universe.[2]

◊ ◊ ◊ ◊ ◊

Vaishnavites consider that Vishnu carries four insignia in His four hands — *sankha* (conch), *chakra* (discus), *gadha* (mace) and *padma* (lotus). The conch is a symbol of sound. This means that the entire universe is in God's Hand. The *chakra* (discus) symbolises the Wheel of Time. The inner significance of this is that God holds Time in His grip. The lotus is a symbol of the heart. God holds in His hand the hearts of all beings. The mace is a symbol of prowess. God is the possessor of all power and strength. This is the esoteric meaning of the weapons attributed to Vishnu.[3]

◊ ◊ ◊ ◊ ◊

Narayana is the Lord of Waters; (*naram* means water). But, what is the water of which He is the Lord? He resides in the heart, and His presence when recognised melts even the stoniest heart and the water

---

[1] *Summer Showers in Brindhavan* (1972), p. 75.

[2] *Sanathana Sarathi*, November 1992, p. 270.

[3] *Sarathana Sarathi*, April 1992, p. --.

emanates from the eye as tears of joy, gratitude and fullness! His Presence is said to have been recognised by man, when he is suffused by sympathy, making him sad while another is sad and joyful when another is fulled with joy. Narayana is He who brings tears of joy to the eyes! That is the function of your tear glands: to express internal joy; not to weep like a fool or a coward.[1]

◊ ◊ ◊ ◊ ◊

Usually, when you are asked where God is, you point to the sky or some such distant place and say He is there, as if He is just a Person and has a definite place of Residence. But *nara* (man) himself is *Narayana* (God), each one of them; *Madava* is *manava*, each one of the species. So the number of Gods is thirty–three crores, as given in the *Sasthas* or, as can be calculated today, much more. It is delusion that has induced *Narayanaswarupa* (embodiment of God) to imagine and behave as if he is just a *nara* (man). To remove that delusion, there are various means suited to the needs of each sufferer. But all the treatment and all the struggle is to achieve the experience of being *Narayana* and discard the limited, bound, relative entity, *nara*. That is the one harvest yielded by all the various processes. Until one understands oneself, the delusion and the resultant grief cannot be ended.[2]

◊ ◊ ◊ ◊ ◊

The *guru* is the person who discovers that you have fallen into a wrong road that leads to further and further darkness. For, he knows the right road and he is full of love for all who strive to escape the travails of the night, without lamps to light their steps. This is a day when the First of *Gurus* is remembered with gratitude. He is called

---

[1] *Sathya Sai Speaks*, Vol. 2, p. 135.

[2] *Sathya Sai Speaks*, Vol. 1, pp. 153-54.

Narayana, because *Narayana* is the reality and if you do not get a *Guru* from outside yourself, if you pray, the *Narayana* inside you will Himself reveal the road.[1]

◊ ◊ ◊ ◊ ◊

Nara (man) and *Narayana* (God) are the two wires, the positive and the negative, which combine to bring electricity through. *Nara* will co–operate with *Narayana* and become the vehicle of Divine Power, if he has acquired the two qualities, *Sathya* (Truth) and *Prema* (Divine Love).[2]

◊ ◊ ◊ ◊ ◊

The five elements abide in Narayana, God. There can be no seed without a shell or husk. The husk is the Cosmos; the seed is God. They are both interrelated, and abide together. One must try to understand this fact through steadfast inquiry, *jnana.* The ignorant ascribe validity to the husk; the wise probe into the basic *Atma.* The ignorant person believes that the Universe is all that is, and reduces himself to a status worse than an animal. Animals harm only other animals; but the ignorant person causes injury to his own self![3]

◊ ◊ ◊ ◊ ◊

Naram means "water" and *nayanam* means "eye," and the implication is that only tears can win God for you. That is the inner purpose and meaning of the *Narayana mantra.* Other *mantras* (sacred formulae) too have their own latent meaning, like this one. Just as a

---

[1] *Sathya Sai Speaks,* Vol. 5, p. 189.

[2] *Sathya Sai Speaks,* Vol. 1, p. 68.

[3] *Sathya Sai Speaks,* Vol. 15, p. 138.

G and an O and a D add up, not to the sound Geeodee, but to God,
so also A, U and M, meaning *Bhur Bhuvah* and *Suvah*, the three planes
of existence and consciousness, add up to the *Pranava, Om*. So too,
Narayana is the Lord of the *Naram* in the *Nayana*, who is won by tears
of repentance and who rewards you with tears of joy. Win Him and
then He becomes as visible as all this; in fact, He is all this, only you
do not see it so.[1]

◊ ◊ ◊ ◊ ◊

Constant practice with full faith
will transmute
nara into Narayana,
manava into Madava
(human into Divine);
for Narayana is your real nature,
Madava is your real essence.
You are but a wave of the sea;
know it, and you are free.[2]

◊ ◊ ◊ ◊ ◊

Now, there are some who say that *jeeva* will be *jeeva* (individual
soul) and *Deva* will be *Deva* (God) and the two can never be the same
or merge. If that was true, then, what is the use of *japa, dhyana,
sat–karma* (good deeds) and all the other varieties of *sadana* (spiritual
discipline) recommended by the *Sastras* and the sages? There is no
doubt that *Nara* (man) can become *Narayana* (God); "*Thwam*" (Thou)

---

[1] *Sathya Sai Speaks*, exact volume and page number unknown.

[2] *Sathya Sai Speaks*, Vol. 10, p. 165.

can become "*Thath*" (That). That is the doctrine of the *Upanishads* and the experience of the saints.[1]

◊ ◊ ◊ ◊ ◊

Summary

Everyday every individual and the universe experiences the creative process through action and thought in the waking and dream states making use of the gross and subtle senses, mind and body. This all–pervasive transcendental process involving the *rajasic guna* or attribute (passionate, active) is called Brahma.

Also everyday the individual and the universe experience the process of sustenance and protection, also called organization. Whatever has been created, one's own body or anything in the universe, needs to be sustained and protected for at least some time. Vishnu, the embodiment of *Dharma* (Righteousness) and the five great elements (earth, fire, water, air, ether) is symbolic of the *satwic guna* or quality (equanimity, calmness) and is commonly experienced in the sleep state or subtle mental state as boundless, peaceful existence.

Maheswara (Maha Easwara, Great God), also known as Shiva, Easwara and Rudra, is experienced daily by all in the deep sleep state or during a meditative state when the individual merges into the *Atma* having no

---

[1] *Sathya Sai Speaks*, Vol. 4, p. 103.

experience of individuality (ego, mind) or dream; one is merged in the causal body. Maheswara is the Divine process responsible throughout the universe for dissolution or destruction of every created form and is symbolic of the *tamasic guna* (latent, quiet and inactive) in the sense of leading the individual to the awareness of his innate *Atma* through destruction of ignorance.

The goal of human life is to transcend in awareness these three states to the super–causal (*Maha Karana*) state — that is, awareness of oneself as the *Atma*, the Blissful Divine Self. From this awareness one would see that Brahma, Vishnu and Maheswara are the processes involved in the *maya*–ridden universe, propelled by *karma*, and one is witness to them.

Chapter 8

Durga, Lakshmi and Saraswati

GODDESS KALI DURGA

GODDESS LAKSHMI

GODDESS SARASWATI

Chapter 8

Durga, Lakshmi and Saraswati

Introduction

Some of the aspects of the Divine as the Mother Energy or Primordial Power (*Adi Shakti*) or *Devi* or *Aum* have been named in Hinduism as Durga, Lakshmi and Saraswati. The worship of these three aspects during special days of the year called Navarathri has the purpose to destroy the evil tendencies inside the mind so that the inner and outer worlds may have peace and joy. Through continuous spiritual practice (*sadana*) one would be able to tap the inner resources (represented by these three aspects) and thus elevate oneself to purer realms of Divine Truth. These three Divine aspects being all pervasive are within one's own body.

"The source and sustenance of all creation, whether at the level of matter or life or mind, is one and one only. It is *Shakti* (energy). Brahman the Absolute of Vedanta and Shakti or Devi of the Tantras are identical. When that energy is in a static condition, with neither evolution or involution, when the universe to be created is not even in a seed–form, as it were, it is called Brahman. When it starts evolving into this creation, sustains it, and withdraws it back into Itself, it is called *Shakti*. ... If Brahman is likened to the word, Shakti is its meaning. If Brahman is like fire, Shakti is its burning power. The two are inseparable: one in two and two in one.

In the Hindu mythological literature, ... this energy is always pictured as a female deity, the Devi, as the consort of its counterpart male deity. Each member of the Trinity has his Shakti or Devi as his consort: Saraswati of Brahma, Lakshmi of Vishnu, and Parvati of Shiva ...."[1]

Durga

"Literally Durga means one who is difficult to approach or difficult to know. Being the personification of the totality of the powers of the gods, She is naturally difficult to approach or know. However, being the Mother of the Universe, she is the personification of tender love, when supplicated.

Of the several aspects of Durga ... Yoganetra (meditation–sleep) is her power of sleep, taking recourse to which Lord Vishnu rests between two cycles of creation. She is praised as responsible for the creation, sustenance and withdrawal of the universe. She is the mysterious power, the very personification of knowledge, wisdom, and memory. She is pleasant and beautiful. At the same time, she is terrible also ....

---

[1] *Hindu Gods and Goddesses*, Swami Harshananda, pp. 77-78.

She is the physical universe. She is the mysterious power of Vishnu, the original cause, as also the power that deludes beings (*maya*). It is only by pleasing her that one can hope to get spiritual emancipation. She is residing as the intellect in the hearts of human beings. She is the all devouring time. She is the very personification of all that is auspicious and good. She is ever engaged in protecting her children. Kali, the terrible, with a garland of human skulls around her neck, is another of her aspects ... Durga has three major manifestations: Mahakali, Mahalakshmi, and Mahasaraswati — the three major manifestations of the One Supreme Power — Maha Ishwari according to the three gunas (*Tamas, Rajas, and Satwa*).

Mahakali is the personification of the *Tamasic* aspect of Durga, the personification of *Maya*. Unless she is pleased and voluntarily withdraws, the Lord in us will not awaken and destroy the powers of evil which are trying to destroy us."[1]

"Man, the imperfect, the bound, the sorrowful, has a thousand enemies within. He is riddled with negative thoughts, fears, yearnings. These are selfishness, jealousy, meanness, prejudice and hatred — just to mention a few. The *sadak* (spiritual aspirant) must get rid of these lawless villains within. In Mother Kali's (Durga's) *Kripa* (Mercy), these destructive masters are to be annihilated. No amount of soft persuasions can avail. ... There must be a deep determination, adamantine resolve, and a fight — royal — within, as sanguine as Kali's ferocious sword dripping with blood and unless the *sadak* is willing to wear about his neck the skull–*mala* (necklace) of these murdered false values, there can be no peace or order in the within.

Invoke the Mother Terrible to help us annihilate within all negative forces; all weaknesses, all little–ness. It is these that have removed us from our own selves — the Supreme *Parameshwara Swarupa* (God), which we all are.

Now a mere elimination of our weakness in itself is no permanent achievement, for if the bosom is empty, again they will enter by the

---

[1] Hindu Gods and Goddesses, Swami Harshananda, pp. 104-110.

back doors. ... We must equally emphasize the positive side in our right effort."[1]

Durga may have 4, 8, 10 or 20 arms. In the illustration in this book, she has 10 arms. The conch or *sankha* held in her second left hand symbolizes *Om*, the *pranava*, signifying that she and each of us is the embodiment of Divine energy and intelligence. Durga blows the conch, calling man to live the nobler values of life so that he may turn away from all his worldly preoccupations and ultimately reach the Divine and receive from the Divine unbroken peace and perfection.

In her top left hand, she holds the trident (*trisula*), symbolic of the three *gunas* (qualities), *tamas, rajas* and *satwa*, that control nature (including man) until they are destroyed through effort and grace, allowing man to manifest his pure Divine nature. The trident also may symbolize the Divine Presence and power in the three aspects of time — past, present and future.

The skull in her left hand indicates her power over all false and evil values and her ability to destroy them, as well as her power over time which ultimately dissolves everything, including the human body.

The bell in her left hand signifies the Divine *pranava, Om*, that is always ringing, calling in so many ways, urging the human intellect to awaken to realize the existence of the Self.

---

[1] Swami Chinmayananda, *Symbolism in Hinduism*, p. 153.

"She wields a mace in her right hand to knock man down with disappointments, dissatisfactions and a growing sense of restlessness. Man dashes forth in his quest for sense gratification with no ears to hear the Lord calling or heart to obey even if he hears, so out of tender anxiety to give the devotee the highest experience of perfect happiness, she wields the mace.

Even in spite of these punishments, if the devotee is not turning towards the spiritual path and is not progressively moving towards the final destination, the Lord has the total annihilating power of the discus (or dagger) which can destroy the equipment, and lift him from his present life of unhealthy circumstances. The lotus in the right hand indicates the final goal of life, the Infinite bliss of unbroken peace and perfection.[1] "The cobra in her left hand signifies that even the most poisonous becomes harmless because the one that has identified with the Supreme has gone beyond all the effects of matter on his senses or organs and has become immune even to the deadliest poisons."[2]

"Durga is seen annihilating Mahisasura, the he–buffalo, which represents the jungle law that might is right. He is the ruthless brute force that does not brook any opposition when selfish ends are concerned .... At the subjective level, Mahisasura stands for ignorance and stubborn egoism. Its subjugation and conquest are possible only when the *sadhaka* (spiritual aspirant) pools all his energies together and fights it with a tenacious will. Since God helps him who helps himself, the intervention of the Divine power in his favour is always there. This is known as *Vijaya Dasami* during the Navaratri Festival, the victory over the five senses of perception and the five senses of action.

The lion, Durga's mount or vehicle, represents the best in animal creation, particularly courage. The spiritual aspirant requires great courage to subjugate the animal tendencies and ego. To become Divine, one must keep one's animal instincts, ego, etc., under complete

---

[1] *Symbolism in Hinduism*, Swami Chinmayananda, compiled by R. S. Nathan, pp. 116-117.

[2] Ibid., p. 67.

control; thus Durga riding the lion symbolizes this complete control
over the lower nature.[1] When this is achieved, Goddess Lakshmi is
sure to bless us with all prosperity. Once the undivine qualities have
been conquered and eliminated, the concept of "want" undergoes a
change and even drops off. That is the highest prosperity."[2]

Lakshmi

"Lakshmi, the power and consort of Vishnu, the preserver, is
represented as the power of multiplicity and goddess of fortune, both
of which are equally necessary in the process of preservation ... .
Lakshmi is the goddess of wealth and fortune, power and beauty ....

Lakshmi is usually described as enchantingly beautiful, standing
on a lotus and holding lotuses in each of her two hands and adorned
with a lotus garland ....

Her four hands signify her power to grant the four *Purusarthas*
(goals of human life): *Dharma* (righteousness), *Artha* (wealth), *Kama*
(pleasure), and *Moksha* (liberation, beatitude).

The lotuses, in varying stages of blooming, represent the worlds
and beings in various stages of evolution."[3]

"Wealth does not mean only money. It also incudes the nobler
values of life, the powers of the mind and intellect, moral and ethical
qualities, etc., which constitute the spiritual wealth. These are the types
of wealth to be acquired before one's initiation into actual spiritual

[1] *Hindu Gods and Goddesses*, Swama Harshananda, pp. 110 and 112.

[2] *Symbolism in Hinduism*, compiled by R. S. Nathan, p. 276.

[3] *Hindu Gods and Goddesses*, Swami Harshananda, pp. 82-85

learning and knowledge. That is why Lakshmi is worshipped in the second set of three days during the Navaratri Festival after Durga and before Saraswati.... Lakshmi pours out wealth to the community ... wealth does not come by its own accord. The capacity to earn wealth remains as an inherent power in man and it has to be drawn out through self effort (*purushartha*).

The story given in the *Bhagavata Purana* is that of the churning of the ocean of milk by the Gods and the Demons for obtaining nectar. One of the many precious things that came out of the ocean while churning was Goddess Lakshmi symbolizing the creation and development of ethical and cultural values of life in one's bosom, when one's pure, *satwic* mind is churned by the process of self–reflection and contemplation upon the Higher Self.

"Lakshmi holds lotuses in her hands symbolizing that the realization of the Self is the Supreme Goal to be gained by man."[1]

Saraswati

"Saraswati is the Shakti, the power and the consort of Brahma, the Creator. Hence she is the procreatrix, the mother, of the entire creation.

She is considered as the personification of all knowledge, arts, sciences, crafts and skills. Knowledge is the antithesis of the darkness of ignorance, hence she is depicted as pure white in colour. Since she is the representation of all sciences, arts, crafts and skills, she has to be extraordinarily beautiful and graceful ... *Hamsa*, or Swan, the vehicle of Brahma, is usually associated with her ... The Swan is supposed to possess a peculiar power to drink milk alone from a mixture of milk and water and leave the water alone behind, representing the power

---

[1] A. Parthasarathy, *Symbolism in Hinduism*, pp. 195-196.

of *viveka* (wisdom, discrimination) and hence of knowledge; the ability to absorb the good and reject the evil.

Being the consort of Brahma, the Creator, she represents His power and intelligence, without which organized creation is impossible

....

The four arms show Her unimpeded power in all directions, or Her all-pervasiveness.

Being the Goddess of learning, it is but proper that Saraswati is shown holding a book (*pastaka*) in her left hand representing all areas of secular sciences. Mere intellectual learning without a heart tempered by higher feelings, sentiments and emotions, is as dry as sawdust. So she holds a *veena* (lute), on which She actually plays to show the need for the cultivation of fine arts. Then there is the *aksmala* (rosary) held in the right hand. This symbolizes all spiritual sciences, or *yoga*, including *tapas* (austerities), meditation, and *japa* (repetition of the Divine name)."[1]

"Saraswati literally means 'the one who gives the essence (*sara*) of our own' Self (*Swa*). Sitting on the lotus symbolizes that the teacher is well-established in the subjective experience of the Truth. Holding the scriptures in Her hand indicate that She upholds that the knowledge of the scriptures alone can take us to the Truth. The four hands represent the four aspects of the inner personality of man, viz. *manas* (mind), *buddhi* (intellect), *chitta* (conditioned consciousness) and *ahamkar* (ego)."[2]

Saraswati represents an enlightened one in *samadhi* as well as a true teacher who can distribute knowledge of the Infinite to disciples for their enlightenment. This

---

[1] *Hindu Gods and Goddesses*, Swami Harshananda, pp. 78-81.

[2] *Symbolism in Hinduism*, p. 191.

Divine state is a state of perfect freedom from the little ego and rediscovery of the Supreme Self.

The Dassera festival (*Navaratris*) is celebrated throughout India and other countries by Hindus for 10 days. During the first three days Kali–Durga is invoked to kill the demons that reflect negative tendencies within man. During the next three days, Goddess Lakshmi is worshipped to cultivate the Divine qualities and wealth such as love, kindness, devotion, patience, endurance, nonviolence, etc., which are within man. Goddess Saraswati is worshipped during the next three days as the final stage in man's spiritual evolution, so that Divinity may manifest through study of the scriptures and constant reflection and meditation. After these three stages are gone through in life, on the last day, Vijaya Dasami Day, the devil is burnt down, indicating the transcendence of the ego.

The symbolism and mythology around the Truth of the Divine Mother (Devi or Shakti) in Hinduism is vast. The three aspects briefly discussed in this introduction, namely, Durga (Kali), Lakshmi and Saraswati, represent only a minor but important part of the revealed knowledge of the Divine Mother Energy.

The following words of Bhagavan Sri Sathya Sai Baba reveal more knowledge about the Divine Mother in creation.

◊ ◊ ◊ ◊ ◊

1.

Durga, Lakshmi and Saraswati
(An Overview)

In daily life and in nature we come across a number of examples to illustrate the Divine Nature of this Mother Principle. The cow converts her own blood into milk which gives sustenance to us all. She is considered a *Mathru Moorthi* (Embodiment of the Divine Mother) because of this. The earth keeps us in her bosom and gives us protection at all times. The earth is also known as a *Mathru Moorthi*. Then there are the *Angiras*, the many fluids emanating from our own body that digest our food. This *Rasa Swarupini* resides in our limbs and activates our body. She sustains our life and therefore she too is considered as a *Mathru Moorthi*. The *Maharishis* have taught us what is desirable and what is undesirable in our life, the *Sreyo Marga* and the *Preyo Marga*, through various *Sastras*. That is why these *Rishis* are also *Mathru Moorthis*. The teacher, the preceptor, who imbibes in us *Sujnanam, Vignanam* and *Prajnanam* (three types of knowledge) is also a *Mathru Moorthi*. Therefore, the cow, the earth, the *Angiras*, the *Rishis*, the Preceptor — all these five are the very embodiments of the Divine Mother.

The Mother is the *Sarva Sakthi Swarupini* and it is in order to declare to the world this Divine aspect of the Mother, the *Navarathi* festival is celebrated. In these nine days we adore and worship Durga, Lakshmi and Saraswati. What is the basis for this three fold aspect of the Divine Mother?

Durga is *Shakti Swarupini* — the physical, mental and spiritual powers are conferred by her. Lakshmi endows us with all types of *Aiswarya* (Wealth). These are *Gnana Aiswarya* (Spiritual Knowledge), *Prana Aiswarya* (Life Energy), *Vidya Aiswarya* (Worldly Knowledge).

Saraswati gives us the power of intellect, the power of discrimination, the power of word.

Our Mother is truly an embodiment of Durga, Lakshmi and Saraswati. She confers on us all types of energy and power. She provides us with all manner of wealth and helps us grow and prosper. She also aspires for her children to earn fame and name through their education. All these three Divine principles come and merge in our own mother.[1]

◊ ◊ ◊ ◊ ◊

In the very first instance, you should try to understand what this nature is. Nature itself is *Jagadisa* (Lord of the World). There is only one entity who is the master of all. That is the *Satchidananda Swarupa* (Embodiment of Being, Awareness, Bliss, *Atma*). In every object in the universe, the principles of *asthi* (existence), *bhathi* (shines) and *priyam* (pleases, is useful, lovable) are common. Only the name and form bring about this complexity. We are believing, unnecessarily, in the names and forms which are temporary and lose faith in the permanent aspect of things, which is Divinity. This is a great mistake. The day we give up this wrong path and take to the right one, we will begin to realise who God is.

Prema Swarupas (Embodiment of Love)! We should believe firmly that nature itself is God. It is wrong to assume that God dwells somewhere we cannot see. Have the conviction that all human beings are verily different forms of God. These nine days of Navarathri are celebrated in order to help you to realise the different aspects of nature.[2]

◊ ◊ ◊ ◊ ◊

---

[1] Sankirtanam, pp. 2-3.

[2] Sankirtanam, p. 13.

Prema Swarupas! God is in us. All the energies and all the powers are in us. We have to recognise this Truth and conduct ourselves properly. There is no separate heaven or any other world elsewhere.[1]

◊ ◊ ◊ ◊ ◊

Likewise, Durga and Lakshmi are resident in our own being. Only they are invisible. Without them no function of the body can take place, you cannot see, you cannot talk, you cannot walk or perform any act. Just as a mother, who has given us this birth, teaches us various types of *vidya* (knowledge), our physical body in which is resident these three Divine Principles is also like a mother. Human beings are the children of these three mothers. They are invisible, inseparable, unmanifest. Only when we manifest all these powers which are within us can we call ourselves true human beings. Until we can express these faculties, fully, we cannot call ourselves true human beings.[2]

◊ ◊ ◊ ◊ ◊

The significance of Durga, Lakshmi and Saraswati has to be rightly understood. The three represent three kinds of potencies in man: *ichcha shakti*, will power, *kriya shakti*, the power of action, and *jnana shakti*, the power of discrimination. Saraswati is manifest in man as the power of speech (*vak*). Durga is present in the form of dynamism (the power of action). Lakshmi is manifest in the form of will power. The body indicates *kriya shakti*. The mind is the repository of *ichcha shakti*. The *Atma* is *jnana shakti*. *Kriya shakti* comes from the body, which is material. The power that activates the body that is inert and makes it vibrant is *ichcha shakti*. The power that induces the vibrations of *ichcha shakti* is *jnana shakti*, which causes radiation (of

---

[1] Sankirtanam, p. 7.

[2] Sankirtanam, p. 14.

energy). These three potencies are represented by the *mantra*: "Om Bhur–Buvah–Suvah." *Bhu* represents *Bhu–loka* (the earth). *Buvah* represents the Life force (also means Conscience in man), *Suvaha* represents the power of radiation. All the three are present in man. Thus, Durga, Lakshmi and Saraswati dwell in the human heart.

Men are prone to exhibit *rajasic* qualities like anger and hatred. They are the menacing manifestations of Durga. The extolling of the Divine in song and poetry and the pleasing vibrations produced by them indicate the power of Saraswati. The pure qualities that arise in man such as compassion, love, forbearance and sympathy are derived from Lakshmi.

When people worship Durga, Lakshmi and Saraswati externally in pictures or icons, they are giving physical forms to the subtle potencies that are within them. The unfortunate predicament of man today is that he is not recognising the powers within him and developing respect for them. He goes after the external, attracted by the physical forms. The relationship between the material and the subtle has to be understood.

The remedy for man's ills is contained within himself. But man seeks remedies from outside. ...

Likewise, people today tend to ignore the Divinity within them, but hanker after many external objects. There is no need to go in search of the Divine. Men must develop firm faith in the Divinity within them. All that is needed is to turn the vision inwards to experience the Divine within.

Men engage themselves in many outward spiritual practices (*sadana*). These must be internalised. All scholarship is of no avail if there is no realisation in the heart. The scholar may expound the texts, but lacks the internal experience. One who has mastered the *Vedas* may be able to explain the words, but cannot recognise the *Veda Purusha*, the Supreme Person hailed by the *Vedas*.

When a person goes to a temple, he closes his eyes in front of the idol, because what he seeks is an internal vision of God and not a sight of the external form of the idol. God is Omnipresent as proclaimed in the Geeta. God is One, though names and forms may differ.

Though people live in the phenomenal world and carry on their activities, they should perform all their actions as an offering to please the Lord.

What is it you should do during these ten days of the Navaratri festival? Convert your *ichcha shakti* (will power) into a yearning for God. Convert *kriya shakti* into a force for doing Divine actions. Convert your *jnana–shakti* into the Divine itself.[1]

◊ ◊ ◊ ◊ ◊

Man has been equipped with *iccha shakti* (will power) for this very purpose — to will the good, the ennobling and the elevating. The two other *shaktis* gifted to him are *jnana shakti* (the power to know) and *kriya shakti* (the power to act). To make the interdependence of these three *shaktis*, here is an example: "Your wish to drink a cup of coffee is so insistent that you will to have it fulfilled. But, mere *iccha* (will) cannot produce coffee. Next, you use your *jnana* (wisdom) and provide yourselves with a stove, a quantity of water, sugar, milk and coffee powder. But still, your original *iccha* is unrealised. Next, you use *kriya* (action) and prepare the coffee you wanted and knew how to make."

Well. The *iccha shakti* wills to attain God, let us say. Mere wish is too weak to gain the goal. *Jnana shakti* advises you not to despair. There are ways by which you can win. It lays before you various *sadanas*. *Kriya shakti* takes these up and inspires you to act, to persevere in practice, until you attain the objective. Unfortunately, 99 men out of 100 use only the *iccha shakti*; they stop with the wish; they do not pursue and attain the bliss that waits. Their faith falters; they do not march on boldly. The *iccha* prompts you to earn a first class in the examination, but the *jnana* is ignored and the *kriya* is left undone. If a

---

[1] *Sanathana Sarathi*, November 1994, p. 283-85.

thousandth of that eagerness is shown in *kriya*, in the test, the first class can be secured easily.[1]

◊ ◊ ◊ ◊ ◊

A life built upon desires (*sankalpa*) cannot last. The mansion of desires must be converted into a Mansion of Divine Will (*Iccha–Bhavanam*). When the Will Power (*iccha–shakti*) (Lakshmi) is converted into the power of action (*kriya–shakti*) (Durga), it results in *jnana–shakti* (the power of Wisdom) (Saraswati). It is through this Divine Wisdom that spiritual liberation *Kaivalyam* is secured.

The Navaratri festival should not be observed as a festival for worshipping the consorts of Vishnu, Shiva and Brahma. These Goddesses symbolise Divine potencies. All these potencies are derived from Vishnu. The entire cosmos is a manifestation of the myriad forms of Vishnu. People must recognise this oneness underlying the different forms. All beings breathe the same air as their life–breath. Likewise all the five basic elements are common to all. These elements are the stuff of Nature. But in the *Paratatwa* (the Supreme Principle, the Divine), these do not exist. The elements are mortal. The Divine is immortal. To proceed from the mortal to the immortal the easiest means is the cultivation of Divine Love (*Prema*).

The heart is like a sky wherein the clouds in the form of thoughts hide the *buddhi* (the intellect) and the Mind representing the sun and the moon. *Vairargya* (Detachment) is the means to get rid of thoughts and the desires arising from them. The *Devi Puja* (Goddess Worship) performed during Navaratri is intended to get rid of worldly attachments and divert the mind towards God.[2]

◊ ◊ ◊ ◊ ◊

---

[1] *Sathya Sai Speaks*, Vol. 14, p. 184.

[2] *Sanathana Sarathi*, December 1992, p. 305.

In the worship of the deities during Navaratri, every day, one of them should be worshipped, not externally but with one's heart and soul. Bodily actions are ephemeral. The body derives its value from the spirit within. Hence it should be regarded as a sacred temple.[1]

◊ ◊ ◊ ◊ ◊

Navaratri is celebrated in honour of the victory that the *Para–Shakti* (the Goddess of Energy, immanent in the Microcosm and the Macrocosm) achieved over the *Asura* or Evil Forces, as described in the *Devi Mahathmyam* and *Devi Bhagavatham*. The *Para–Shakti* is in every one as the *Kundalini Shakti* (dormant spiritual energy), which is able to destroy when awakened, the evil tendencies inside the mind; so, the *Navaratri* is to be dedicated by all for the propitiation of the outer as well as inner Divinity, in order that the outer and the inner worlds may have peace and joy. By means of systematic *sadana* it is possible to tap the inner resources that God has endowed man with and elevate yourselves to the purer and happier realm of the Reality.[2]

◊ ◊ ◊ ◊ ◊

Bharatiyas have been celebrating the Navarathi festival from ancient times as a mode of worship of *Devi* (the Divine as Mother). They worship Durga, Lakshmi and Saraswati during these nine days. Who are these three? They are three forms which have fascinated man. Their esoteric significance is represented by three potencies (*shaktis*). They are: *karma, upasana* and *jnana*.[3]

---

[1] *Sanathana Sarathi*, November 1994, p. 290.

[2] *Sathya Sai Speaks*, Vol. 7, p. 159.

[3] *Sanathana Sarathi*, November 1994, p. 282.

The Vedas declare that wherever the mind wanders, there the three worlds will be perceived. What are these three worlds? All are familiar with the pronouncements in the *Geeta* and in the *Gayatri Mantra*. The three worlds are: (*Bhu, Bhuvah, Suvah*: the *Bhuloka, Bhuvarloka* and *Swarga*). These three are present in man: *Adibhoutika, Adidaivika* and *Adyatma*. These were worshipped as three Goddesses by our ancients: Durga, Lakshmi and Saraswathi.

Every form is that of Durga — the deity that is associated with energy (*shakti*). There is infinite power within man, power that is beyond comprehension and which is Divine. But he makes no effort to recognise it. If man did not have this power, how could he have gone to the moon? What is the power that makes the earth revolve round itself? It is not any machine or *mantra*. The power is within the earth itself. This energy, present in man and in other objects, has been characterised as Cosmic energy. What is this Cosmic power? The sun derives its energy and effulgence from this Cosmic source. It is the same Cosmic source that accounts for the power of the human mind and the marvellous power of the eye to see the most distant stars.

With this power of sight, man is able to see the entire creation. There is no greater power than this. Thus, man is endowed with all powers. But this boundless power is being recognised and exercised by each one according to the level of his development. The same electrical energy is used for a variety of purposes: for heating, lighting, operating a fan, etc. Likewise, the Divine Cosmic energy in human beings is used by different persons for varied purposes. This energy is latent in all beings. Because of his ability to manifest the Divine, boundless Cosmic energy, man is described as a manifestation of the Divine (*Vyakti*). Humanness consists in the manifestation of what is hidden and invisible in man.

This energy in man is a primordial power (*adi shakti*). It is termed *Om*. This power permeates the physical world (*prakriti*) of matter. This is known as *bhu*. There is another power which animates this material substance. This is the power of vibration. It is termed *prana shakti*, the life force. It is this life force which activates every part of the human body. This is termed *buvah*. Lakshmi symbolises this power. Lakshmi is the embodiment of that power which enables a human being to see, to hear and to do many things. Lakshmi represents the power to see what is good, to hear what is good, to speak sweet words, to entertain good thoughts and to do good deeds. The Lakshmi Principle accounts for all the good, happy, auspicious happenings in the world.

The third form of energy is symbolised by Saraswati. She is regarded as the Goddess of Speech (*Vak–devata*). Lakshmi is *Pranaswarupini* — the embodiment of the Life Force. Durga is *Shakti–Swarupini*, the embodiment of physical energy. These three in their unified expression represent the *Atmic* principle.[1]

◊ ◊ ◊ ◊ ◊

All this talk of the Consorts of the Lord, of Lakshmi, Saraswati and Parvati being the wives of the Trinity, are absolutely silly. They reveal only the *samsaric* (worldly living) glasses that you wear, the projection of your worldly fancies on the "heavenly families," the weaving of stories on the human model for the satisfaction of human cravings. These names are only convenient expressions for the *Shakti* (Divine Power) that is immanent in Godhead. For example, Lakshmi is the personification of *Dhaya* (Mercy) or the Grace of Vishnu; that is why she is said to dwell on His breast! So too, Parvati is half the body of Shiva, inseparably incorporated in Him! The powers of Creation, Conservation and Dissolution are co–existent and continuous in Godhead. You may ask how the three can co–exist. Well, look at electricity! The current can create, conserve as well as dissolve, all at the same time, and to the same extent. These *Shaktis* (Divine Energies) are similarly pictured as inseparably associated with the three aspects of the Absolute. Man's duty is to achieve unity with the *Shiva–Shakti* for he is but a spark that has emanated from it; he is but a flame of the Eternal Fire.[2]

---

[1] *Sanathana Sarathi*, November 1994, pp. 287-88.

[2] *Sathya Sai Speaks*, Vol. 1 p. 223.

◊ ◊ ◊ ◊ ◊

During the Navaratri festival, for the purpose of eradicating one's demonic tendencies, the deities were worshipped with kumkum (sacred red powder). The red powder is a symbol of blood. The meaning of this worship is offering one's blood to the Lord and receiving in return the gift of peace from the Lord.[1]

◊ ◊ ◊ ◊ ◊

This is the message of *Navaratri*, the Nine Days' Festival celebrating the victory of the Primal Energy. That energy, when it is manifested in its *satwic* (quiet) aspect is delineated as the Great Teacher and Inspirer, *Maha–Saraswati*; when it is *rajasic* (active and potent), the great Provider and Sustainer, *Mahalakshmi*; when it is *tamasic* (dull and inactive), but, latent and apparently quiet as the Great Dark Destroyer and Deluder, *Maha–kali*. Since *Shakti* is all–pervasive, omnipotent, infinitesimal as well as all–comprehensive, it can be contacted everywhere, in outer nature or inner consciousness. Prahlada told his doubting father: "Why doubt, discuss and delay? Seek it anywhere; you can see It." It is near and far, before, behind, beside and inside everything, in the known and the unknown world.[2]

◊ ◊ ◊ ◊ ◊

Navaratri means nine nights. Darkness is associated with night. What is this darkness? It is the darkness of ignorance. The purpose of the *Navaratri* celebration is to enable man to get rid of nine types of darkness which have taken hold of him. When a reference is made to *Devi*, it signifies the unified form of Durga, Lakshmi and Saraswati. The three together represent Shakti. Shakti is the energy that accounts

---

[1] *Sanathana Sarathi*, November 1994, p. 290.

[2] *Sathya Sai Speaks*, Vol. 7, p. 160.

for all the phenomena of nature (*prakriti*). Nature is energy and the controller of that energy is the Lord.

Nature (*prakriti*) is made up of the three qualities, *satwa, rajas* and *tamas*. Saraswati represents the *satwa guna*, Lakshmi represents the *rajo guna* and Parvati (Durga) represents the *tamo guna*. As *prakriti* (nature) is made up of these three qualities (*satwa, rajas* and *tamas*), to get control over nature, man has been offering worship to Durga, Lakshmi and Saraswati. These are not goddesses but deified symbols of the three qualities.

To acquire the grace of the Lord, man has to offer worship at the outset to *prakriti*. On the one hand you need human effort and on the other you have to acquire the grace of the Divine. *Prakriti* (nature) and *Paramatma* (the Omni–Self) are like the negative and positive poles in electricity. However powerful the Lord may be (as positive pole), there can be no creation without *prakriti* (representing the negative pole). The basis for creation is *prakriti*. For instance, however good the seeds you may have with you, without planting them in the ground you cannot reap the fruit. The role of nature in the creative process is similar.

When man forgets God and desires to enjoy the benefits of Nature, he becomes ultimately a demon like Ravana who brought about his own destruction. To secure the grace of the Lord, one has to have purity of the heart, purity in speech and purity in action. This triple purity is described in *Vedantic* parlance as *tripurasundari*. Lakshmi, who is the embodiment of all prosperity, is represented by the heart. The mouth represents Saraswati. Purity in action (*kriya suddi*) is represented by Durga. The observance of the *Navaratri* celebration is to get rid of the darkness in which man is enveloped, by cultivating the triple purity of thought, word and deed.

The human body emerged from Nature. Nature has two forms: *apara prakriti* and *para prakriti*. Apara *prakriti* includes eight forms of wealth (*ashta aiswaryas*), and *kama, krodha, moha, lobha, mada, matsarya* and the three mental faculties in man: *manas, chitta* and *ahamkara*. *Para prakriti* (the higher nature) represents the consciousness in man. Without the life force (*prana*) and consciousness (*chaitanyam*) man is only a corpse. True humanness consists in controlling the five elements which make up the lower nature (*apara prakriti*) and merging in the higher nature represented by the life force and consciousness (*chaitanyam*).

The *Navaratri* has been divided into three parts: the first three days being dedicated to the worship of Durga, the next three days to the worship of Lakshmi and the last three to the worship of Saraswati. All Hindu festivals have a sacred purpose. Unfortunately, nowadays the festivals are observed only with external rituals without understanding their inner meaning. In the performance of all forms of worship there should be steadiness of mind and body. Only then concentration can be achieved. Today men are unable to maintain steadiness of body and mind.

... The basic significance of *Devi Navaratri* is the adoration of nature (*prakriti*). *Devi* refers to *Bhudevi* (Mother Earth). All the vital requirements of man can be found in the Earth. Those who travel to the moon have to carry with them the oxygen, water and food they need from the Earth. None of these can be found on the moon.

Students! The progress of modern technology, by polluting the atmosphere with carbon dioxide smoke, is causing threat to life on earth. This smoke has already created a hole in the ozone ring above the Earth which has been serving as a protective cover against harmful radiation from the sun. If the ozone layer is destroyed, the effect of the sun's rays may be disastrous. All nations are now worried about this threat. All that needs to be done to avert this danger is to reduce the pollution of the atmosphere caused by automobiles and industrial effluents. The uncontrolled development of industries has to be checked. Development should be in the common interest, to promote the welfare of all.

The Navaratri celebration is an occasion for revering nature and considering how natural resources can be used properly in the best interests of mankind. Resources like water, air, power and minerals should be used properly and not misused or wasted. Economy in the use of every natural resource is vital. Pollution of the air has many evil consequences. The inner significance of observances like *Nagara*

Sankirtan and *bhajans* is to fill the atmosphere with sacred vibrations and holy thoughts.[1]

◊ ◊ ◊ ◊ ◊

The world is a manifestation of the three *gunas* (*satwa, rajas, tamas*). The Divine is worshipped as *Devi*. The term *Devi* refers to the feminine aspect. The term *sthree* is used to denote a woman. There are three syllables in this term: *sa, tha* and *ra. Sa* symbolises the *satwic* aspect of a person. The *satwic* quality is the very first quality that manifests in man. The feeling of love develops from the mother. It is impossible to describe the nature of maternal love. The mother converts her own blood into love and gives it as milk to feed the child. Therefore, the first quality represented by *sa*, is the *satwic* quality.

The second syllable is *tha*. This does not represent *tatwa* or *tamas*. Anil Kumar described eating and sleeping as characteristic of the *tamasic* quality. This is not so. In the term *sthree*, the syllable *tha* represents bashfulness, modesty, self–esteem and such traits which are characteristic of women. Shyness is a predominant trait in women. They attach great value to their honour and reputation. It is because of these sacred qualities that their *tamasic* aspect is significant. The common view regarding the *tamasic* quality does not apply to them.

The third quality, symbolised by the syllable *ra*, is *rajas*. Such qualities as sacrifice and high–mindedness in women reflect the *rajasic* aspect of their nature. When necessary, women will be prepared even to sacrifice their lives to safeguard their honour. Without regard to the difficulties and troubles they may encounter, women are ready to make any sacrifice to protect their honour and self–respect. When the *tamasic* elements attempt to subvert the *satwic* qualities, they are ready to combat and vanquish them.

The term *Devi* thus represents the Divine power which has taken the *rajasic* form to suppress the forces of evil and protect the *satwic*

---

[1] *Sanathana Sarathi*, November 1992, pp. 267-69.

qualities. When the forces of injustice, immorality and untruth have grown to monstrous proportions and are indulging in a death–dance, when selfishness and self–interest are rampant, when men have lost all sense of kindness and compassion, the *Atmic* principle, assuming the form of *shakti*, taking on the *rajasic* quality, seeks to destroy the evil elements. This is the inner meaning of the Dasara festival.

When the Divine Goddess is in dreadful rage to destroy the wicked elements, she assumes a fearful form. To pacify the dreaded Goddess, Her feminine children offer a worship to Her with red *kumkum* (sacred red powder). The Goddess, seeing the blood–red *kumkum* at her feet, feels assured that the wicked have been vanquished and assumes Her benign form. The inner meaning of the worship of *Devi* with red *kumkum* is that thereby the Goddess is appeased. During the ten days of the Dasara, the demons (*rakshasas*) in the form of wicked qualities have been routed. *Rakshasas* do not mean demonic beings. The bad qualities in men are the demons. Arrogance is a demon. Bad thoughts are demons. Ravana is depicted as the king of *Rakshasas*. He is said to have ten heads. He was not born with ten heads. Who is this Ravana and what are his ten heads? *Kama* (lust), *krodha* (anger), *moha* (delusion), *lobha* (greed), *mada* (pride) and *matsasya* (envy), *manas* (the mind), *buddhi* (intellect), *chitta* (will) and *ahamkara* (the ego) — these ten constitute the ten heads. Ravana is one who has these ten qualities. Each one can decide for himself whether he is a Ravana or a Rama according to his qualities. Rama is the destroyer of the bad qualities. When engaged in this act of destruction of bad qualities, He manifests His *Rajo–guna*. But His *rajasic* quality is associated with His *satwic* quality. Even in cutting off Ravana's ten heads, Rama showed His Love. This was the only way Ravana could be redeemed.

When the Lord metes out a punishment, it may appear harsh. But what appears externally as *rajasic* is in reality *satwic*. In a hailstorm, along with rain there will be hailstones. But both the rain and hailstones contain water. Likewise, there is *satwic* quality even in the Lord's *rajasic* actions. Similarly there may be *satwic* quality even in *tamasic* actions. These depend on the time, place and the circumstances in which the Lord acts. Butter can be split with a finger. But a powerful hammer is needed to break a piece of iron. The Lord deals with *satwic* persons in a *satwic* way. He applies the *rajasic* weapon against *rajasic* persons.

People worship the Lord, attributing dreaded forms and qualities to the Divine (*Roudrakara*). This is not proper. The Divine has only one attribute: the embodiment of Love. It has been said: "Love is God. Love pervades the Cosmos." Hence, one should not view the world from a worldly point of view. It should be viewed through the eyes of love.[1]

◊ ◊ ◊ ◊ ◊

Lakshmi represents the protecting aspect of Nature. When Durga (*Kali*) has destroyed the demonic qualities, Lakshmi purifies the mind. Then there is purity in speech represented by Saraswati. The worship of Durga, Lakshmi and Saraswati is thus undertaken to get rid of the impurities in the mind and purify one's thoughts, words and deeds.

Nature (*prakriti*) is the embodiment of the Divine. Man perceives Nature and experiences Nature, but is unable to recognise the Divinity in Nature. To see the external manifestations of the Divine and yet fail to recognise the Divine is a sign of stupidity. Man sees Nature in the form of the Universe, which is the Cosmic form (*Virata–Swarupa*) of Vishnu. Has the Lord any particular form or abode? No. He is everywhere. He is you and you are He. The day you recognise this, you will comprehend God. If you want to see the Divine in you, you have to use your *buddhi*, just as you need a mirror to see your own eyes, which are able to see everything else in the world. It is folly to seek the Divine elsewhere. God is nearer to you than your own mother. With purity of heart, you can experience the Divine within through your intellect. Love is the means to have this experience for Love is God.[2]

---

[1] *Sanathana Sarathi*, November 1991, p. 351.

[2] *Sanathana Sarathi*, December 1992, p. --.

◊ ◊ ◊ ◊ ◊

The cosmos has three forms: the gross, the subtle and the causal. The physical universe represents the gross form. The subtle form is the mind and subtler than the mind is the *Atma*.

A human being has five sheaths. These five sheaths have been grouped into three. The gross sheath is the *annamaya kosa* (food sheath). The three *kosas, pranamaya* (vital sheath), *manomaya* (the mental sheath) and the *vijnanamaya* (the intellectual sheath) together constitute the subtle sheath. The causal sheath is the *anandamaya kosa* (the bliss sheath). Even the last sheath does not represent total bliss, because there is a higher entity above the *anandamaya kosa*. This is known as *mahakarana* or supracausal entity. This is the *Atmic* principle.

Because every individual has these three bodies, he is called *tripurasundari*. Every human being has these *tripuras* (three cities). The three *puras* are the body, the mind and the heart. Since the *prakriti* element, which is feminine in nature, is present in greater measure in the body, it is termed as *sundari* (a beautiful damsel).

During the Navaratri festival *Tripurasundari* is worshipped. Unfortunately, from ancient times people have been observing only the external forms of worship without understanding the inner significance of these festivals. The entire cosmos is a temple. The Lord pervades the cosmos. Nature (*prakriti*) teaches the spiritual truth about Navaratri. Realise the love of Sai through spiritual practice. The Lord has to be realised through *sadana*. *Sadana* does not mean adoring God in a particular place or in a particular form. It means thinking of God in all that you do wherever you may be. It may be asked whether this is possible. The answer is that it is possible by dedicating every action to God.

During Navaratri there is a form of worship called *Angarapana pooja*. In this form of worship, all the limbs of the body are offered to the Divine in a spirit of surrender (*saranagati*). Surrender means offering everything to the Divine and giving up the idea of separation between oneself and the Divine. There can be no true surrender if there is a sense of separation. There must be the conviction that it is the same Divine who dwells in all beings (*Ekam Vasi Sarvabhuta–anta–atma*).

In the performance of *Angarapana pooja*, there is a form of self–deception. When a devotee says, "*Netram Samarpayami*" ("I offer my eyes to the Lord") and offers only a flower to the Lord, he is indulging in a kind of deception. The proper thing would be to say that he is offering a flower. Actually *mantras* like "*Netram Samarpayami*" are intended to indicate that one is using his eyes only to see God. The real significance of the *mantra* is that you think of the Divine in whatever you see or do. Therefore, the true meaning of the *Angarapana pooja* is to declare that you offer all your limbs in the service of the Lord. This means that whatever work you do should be done as an offering to God. Nowadays selfishness is rampant among devotees and they love God not for God's sake but only to get their selfish desires fulfilled. As long as selfishness prevails, the Divine cannot be understood.

The Navaratri festival should be used as an occasion to examine one's own nature whether it is human, animal or demonic, and strive to transform the animal nature to the human and divinise the human nature. Wisdom cannot be acquired from outside. It has to be got through inward *Sadana*.[1]

◊ ◊ ◊ ◊ ◊

A debt is an obligation arising out of what one has received from others. We can easily identify these debts in the human body; different Divine Forces are present nourishing and protecting it. This Divine Energy permeates the entire body; it is called the *Rasa* (Divine Essence). We owe a debt of gratitude to the Divine which has not only endowed us with this precious human body but which also sustains it. We shall be able to enjoy these gifts of the Divine only if we discharge this debt to the Divine. How is this to be done? It is by

---

[1] *Sanathana Sarathi*, November 1992, pp. 270-71.

rendering service to other bodies saturated with the same Divine, by doing righteous deeds and consecrating all actions in the service of society. The debt to the Divine has to be discharged in full in this life itself or during many future lives. The earlier we repay this debt, the sooner we shall realise Divinity.

Next, the debt to the *Rishis*: By selfless investigations and experiments the sages discovered for mankind the paths to be followed for bettering our lives here and attaining mergence. They have laid down the types of right action that will help man to lead a good and worthy life and successfully strive for Self–realisation. These guidelines and codes of conduct have come down to us in the form of *Sastras* (spiritual sciences). The *Sastras* also deal with rituals and forms of worship for propitiating the Divine. The sages have taught how man can proceed from the human to the Divine. Such codes have other names elsewhere. But, whatever the name, these are essential for human survival.

When man strays from these codes, he is subject to many calamities. Man will have to pay the price now or later for violating these codes. Because the sages of yore have given man these precious guidelines for a righteous and sacred life, we repay the debt by respecting these codes and observing the injunctions laid down by them.

Today, instead of honouring and following the *sastras*, people are dishonouring and violating them and committing many wanton sins in the process. When we follow the path laid down by the sages, we can lead exemplary lives and reach the full height of human potentialities.[1]

◊ ◊ ◊ ◊ ◊

---

[1] *Sathya Sai Speaks*, Vol. 16, p. 133.

2.

Durga: Kriyashakti (Power of Action) / Prakritishakti (Power of Nature)

Durga represents the prodigious power of Nature (*Prakritishakti*). As against this power of nature is the *Para–Shakti* (the Power of the Spirit). When spiritual power is predominant, the power of Nature is kept under control. When spiritual power is weak, the power of nature becomes predominant. This is illustrated by the example of smoke and fire. When smoke is predominant, the fire is suppressed. When the fire is blazing, the smoke vanishes. Hence, to enhance the power of the Spirit and limit the power of nature, man has to cultivate *vairagya* (detachment). To the extent the power of nature is under control, to that extent spiritual power grows.[1]

◊ ◊ ◊ ◊ ◊

Durga represents Mother Nature (*Prakriti–Mata*). To overcome the demonic qualities arising out of the influence of nature, the power of nature has to be invoked. This is the meaning of the worship of Durga. Nature is the protector as well as the chastiser.[2]

◊ ◊ ◊ ◊ ◊

---

[1] *Sanathana Sarathi*, December 1992, p. 304.

[2] *Sanathana Sarathi*, December 1992, p. 310.

We should believe firmly that the energy that we have in our body is a form of Durga. We should not waste this energy. We are also wasting our energy through our bad looks, bad words. This is reprehensible. We should transform them into sweet and serene words and acts. We have taken up this kind of celebration in order to understand and resolve that we do not waste our energy in a frivolous manner. This is the most important aspect of these celebrations. We have to pray: "Oh! Mother, you are residing in me in the form of energy. May you flow through me so that I can use it only for proper things."[1]

◊ ◊ ◊ ◊ ◊

The supreme energies of *Ichcha, Kriya* and *Gnana* are embodied in the Divine principles of Durga, Lakshmi and Saraswati. *Kriya shakti* is the source of all wealth and prosperity, but this is an all—embracing expression. Our act of inhaling and exhaling is wealth, our looks are wealth, our words are wealth — all these are various types of wealth. Perceived in this manner, one can understand the all—pervasive nature of the Divine.[2]

◊ ◊ ◊ ◊ ◊

---

[1] Sankirtanam, p. 15.

[2] Sankirtanam, p. 13.

3.

Lakshmi: Ichcha-Shakti

Ichcha-shakti (the potency of Will) arises from thoughts. This *ichcha-shakti* is the source of several other potencies like intellectual power, the discriminating capacity and others. To develop this *ichcha-shakti* (Will power), one has to worship *Devi*. This calls for the cultivation of *thyaga* (renunciation or detachment). For instance, if one has a desire for various drinks, he can bring the desires under control by giving up, to begin with, the desire for some of them. Thereby the Will power (*iccha-shakti*) is developed and in due course it becomes easier to give up other desires. In *Vedantic* parlance this is described as *Vairagya* (renouncing all attachments). *Vairagya* is not abandonment of hearth and home and retiring to a forest. It means developing Godly thoughts and reducing worldly feelings. It is when this balanced development takes place that one acquires control over the powers of Nature (*prakriti-shakti*).[1]

◊ ◊ ◊ ◊ ◊

The food that you take is the very form of Lakshmi. We should not waste even a small particle. We should eat only as much as we need. Even water should not be wasted. All the five elements are of the form of Lakshmi.[2]

◊ ◊ ◊ ◊ ◊

---

[1] *Sanathana Sarathi*, p. --.

[2] *Sankirtanam*, p. 16.

4.

Saraswati: Jnana Shakti (Power of Pure Knowledge and Pure Speech)

Saraswati is a Goddess, the Consort of *Brahma*, the Creator; you are the votaries of a Goddess, whom every one worships; She confers wisdom and liberation. Be true to the highest boons She confers. Do not be contented if you give some food for the worldly hunger of the senses. Do not lower your ideals for the sake of cheap fame or vulgarise public taste. Instead of *loukika sringaram* (worldly enjoyment), give *aloukika Atmanandam* (Bliss of the Self). Contribute to the expansion of love, the purification of motives, the enlargement of sympathy, the tolerance of difference, the respect for individual striving.[1]

◊ ◊ ◊ ◊ ◊

The power of wisdom is Saraswati. She is *Sabda Brahmamayi, Characharamayi, Jyothirmayi, Vakmayi, Mayamayi, Nityanandamayi, Paratparamayi, Srimayi* — all these eight types of wealth emanate from Saraswati. She teaches all the types of *Vidya*. Her vehicle is *hamsa*, and this truly is a representation of the inhaling and exhaling activity, which is symbolised in the sacred *mantra*, "*Soham*". Saraswati is *Vak*

---

[1] *Sathya Sai Speaks*, Vol. 4, p. 37.

Swarupini. This power of speech itself is Saraswati. She is also *Veda Swarupini.* Saraswati resides in your own self.[1]

◊ ◊ ◊ ◊ ◊

The *Atma* or Conscience is the source of all your strength. The reality is manifested in you by the *So–ham* that is produced by every breath. This *So–ham* is also known as *Hamsa Gayatri. Hamsa* (the Swan) is credited with the capacity to separate the milk from the water with which it is mixed. *Hamsa Gayatri* is recited to separate the body–consciousness from the Spirit (the *Atma*). Gayatri signifies the mastery over the senses. Gayatri has two other names — Savitri and Saraswati. Savitri is the master of Life. Saraswati is the presiding deity for speech, *Vak.* The *Gayatri mantra,* "Bhur, Bhuva, Suvah," refers to the body (*Bhur*), Life, (*Bhuva*) and *Prajna* (*Suvah*) or Awareness. "*Bhur, Bhuva, Suvah*" does not refer to three worlds outside man. All the three are in him. Hence, man is not an ordinary being. He is the embodiment of the Cosmic Divine Consciousness (*Chaitanya–Swarupa*).[2]

◊ ◊ ◊ ◊ ◊

Similar mistakes are made about other deities. For instance, Saraswati is represented as a Goddess riding on a swan. Saraswati is the Goddess of Speech. Speech is based on the inhaling and exhaling of breath. In this process of respiration, the sound *So–ham* is produced and when it is repeated regularly, you have the sound *Ham–so,* which is identified with a swan. The inhaling and exhaling process is the chariot on which the Goddess of Speech moves.[3]

---

[1] Sankirtanam, pp. 13-14.

[2] *Sanathana Sarathi,* June 1993, p. 154.

[3] *Sanathana Sarathi,* October 1995, p. 259.

◊ ◊ ◊ ◊ ◊

Saraswati does not represent only literature but also the Goddess who gives us perfect Bliss or *Ananda*. She will root out the impurity in man and make him sacred and pious. This Saraswati will establish the *Atma thatva*, and is the stream connecting man with God. We must consider her as the stream flowing internally and never as the stream flowing externally.[1]

◊ ◊ ◊ ◊ ◊

Saraswati is the *Shakti* of Brahma, the First Member of the Trinity, who is the source and sustenance of all creative activity. Gayatri — the vital *Vedic mantra*, which prays to the Source of Light, to illumine the Intellect of the aspirants — is also a facet of that *Shakti*.

The *Gayatri mantra* (*Vedic* prayer to illuminate the intelligence) is a universal eternal call from the heart of man to the embodiment of Love and Light. It is the very basis of the educational effort in all lands and at all times. But, people have now ignored Saraswati and Gayatri; they have installed, Lakshmi, the Goddess of Wealth, in the altar of Education. The emphasis is on soft furniture, soft curricula, soft tests, and soft treatment for the idle and even the mischievous.[2]

◊ ◊ ◊ ◊ ◊

Gayatri is described as having five faces. The first is "*Om.*" The second is "*Bhurbhuvassuvah.*" The third is "*Tatsavithur Varenyam.*" The fourth is "*Bhargo Dhevasya Dheemahi.*" The fifth is "*Dhiyo–yo nah Prachodhayath.*" *Gayatri* represents in these five faces the five *Pranas* (life forces). *Gayatri* is the protector of the five *pranas* in man. *Gayatri thrayathe ithi Gayatri* — "Because it protects the one who recites it, it is

---

[1] *Summer Showers in Brindavan* (1972), p. 181.

[2] *Sathya Sai Speaks*, Vol. 13, p. 79.

called `Gayatri`." When *Gayatri* acts as protector of the life–forces, she is known as *Savitri*. *Savitri* is known in the *puranic* story as the devoted wife who brought back to life her husband, Sathyavan. *Savitri* is the presiding deity of the five *pranas*. She protects those who lead a life of Truth. This is the inner meaning.

When one's intelligence and intuition are developed by the recitation of the *mantra*, the activating deity is *Gayatri*. When the life–forces are protected, the guardian deity is called *Saraswati*. Because of the protective roles of *Savitri*, *Saraswati* and *Gayatri*, in relation to life, speech and the intellect, *Gayatri* is described as "*Sarvadevata–swarupini*" — the embodiment of all goddesses.[1]

◊ ◊ ◊ ◊ ◊

Vidya (knowledge) must teach man to turn to God and discover that Nature too is God. *Vidya* must awaken the consciousness latent in man and become aware of the *Atma* (Self) that underlies all its levels. *Vidya* claims to increase man's knowledge. What is that knowledge worth? Without character, that knowledge is best cast into fire. The educated person is now more vicious, more greedy, more crafty than the uneducated! This knowledge encourages him to exploit and exterminate others. This knowledge pollutes and poisons the world. It destroys peace and prosperity all over the world. Words! Words! Words! The plethora of words! Nothing is practised; no one acts.

Today the student world is tossed in confusion. Not only in confusion but in downright insanity. They wear white clothing; the hearts are still dark.

> *Heads are full of evil thoughts;*
> *Ears are open for scandal tales;*
> *Eyes delight in peeping unseen;*
> *Minds crave for wicked plots;*
> *Reason pursues plans to cheat.*

---

[1] *Sathya Sai Speaks*, Vol. 16, pp. 36-37.

When Vidya *perceives these in man,*
It will not stay a moment there.

...

Frogs hop on the lotus but they do not inhale its fragrance or taste its nectar. But bees come from afar and imbibe both. So the question of our reaching out to God depends on the fashioning our mind has already received. But man can modify his mental condition by means of constant practice of righteous actions. When we are good, our surroundings too tend to be good. When we hold a rose in the hand, the group around us also gets the fragrance.[1]

◊ ◊ ◊ ◊ ◊

The *hamsa* (a legendary swan) has the property of separating the milk from the water and drinking the milk only. So too, Paramahamsa (realised person, who has achieved Truth) can separate the Illusory from the Real and experience the Bliss, communicated only by the Truth.[2]

◊ ◊ ◊ ◊ ◊

A *jnani* (a Self–Realised One) will feel that the *Atma* immanent in every one is his own *Atma;* he will be happy that he is himself all this; he will see no distinction between man and man for he can experience only unity, not diversity. The physical differences of colour, caste, and creed adhere only to the body. These are but the marks of the external body. The *Atma* is *nishkala,* that is to say, it has no parts; it is *nirmala,* blemishless, unaffected by desire, anger, greed, affection, pride and envy; it is *nishkriya,* activity–less. It is only *prakriti* (Nature) that undergoes all these modifications or at least gives the impression that

---

[1] *Sathya Sai Speaks,* Vol. 15, pp. 198-99.

[2] *Sathya Sai Speaks,* Vol. 7, p. 180.

it is so modified. The *Purusha* is but the eternal witness, the ever–inactive, the modification–less.

Of what can you say, "This is Truth"? Only of this — which persists in the past, the present and the future, which has neither beginning nor end, which does not move or change, which has uniform Form, unified experience–giving property. Well, let us consider the body, the senses, the mind, the life–force and all such. They move and change; they begin and end, they are inert, jada. They have three *gunas, tamas, rajas* and *satwa*. They are without basic Reality. They cause the delusion of reality. They have only relative value; they have no absolute value. They shine out of borrowed light only.

Absolute Truth is beyond the reach of Time and Space, it is *A–parichchina*, that is, indivisible. It does not begin; it is always and ever existent; it is the basis, the fundamental, the self–revealing. Knowing it, experiencing it, is *jnanam*. It is *A–nirdesyam*, that is, cannot be marked out as such and such, and explained by some characteristics. How can something that is above and beyond the intellect and the mind be described through mere words?

It is also termed *Adrisya*, invisible to the eye, the optical apparatus that undergoes change and that is very limited in its capacity. *Brahman* can never be grasped by anything elemental and physical; through *Brahman*, the eye is able to see, so, how can the eye perceive *Brahman* itself? The mind is bound by the limitations of time, space and causation. How can the *Param–atman* who is superior to these and unaffected by them, be limited by them?

... The basic Truth must be kept constantly before the mind's eye. Wants should not be multiplied. Time should not be frittered away, no, not even a minute. The craving for one pleasant thing will give rise to another still more pleasant thing. Cut at the very root of desire itself and become master of yourself. The renouncing of desire will take you fast to the pinnacle of *jnana*.

The *jnani* or the Liberated person will be unaffected by joy or sorrow, for how can any event produce reactions in him who has wiped out his mind? It is the mind that makes you "feel"; when one has taken a drug that deadens the consciousness, he feels no pain or even joy, for, the body is then separated from the mind. So too, wisdom when it dawns separates the mind and keeps it aloof from all contact.

By special discipline, the turbulence of the mind can be calmed; as a result of this, it becomes possible to taste the bliss of the Atman, free from its pulls. The mind attracts him outwards and offers only external objective joy. But, the wise man knows them to be fleeting. For him the *Atma* is enough to fulfil all desire for happiness — complete and permanent. So he will have no need for the external world.

The *jnani* will acquire some special powers too, through his beneficent resolutions, his beneficent promptings and purposes. Through these, he can attain whatever he wishes. The greatness of the status of a *jnani* is indeed indescribable, beyond imagination. It is of the same nature as the splendour and magnificence of the Lord Himself. Why, he becomes the *Brahman* that he has always been. That is why it is declared, *Brahmavid Brahmaiva Bhavathi, Brahmavid Apnothi Param.* That is to say, "He who has known *Brahman* becomes himself *Brahman;* he attains *Brahman*–hood." The fact that this world is unreal and *Brahman* alone is real must become patent; then, all impulses are destroyed; ignorance is demolished. The gem of *jnana* has been stolen by the mind; so, if it is caught, the gem can be regained. The gem entitles you to the status and dignity of *Brahman*, which you assume immediately.

The great souls who have won this *Atmajnana* deserve worship. They are holy; for they have attained *Brahman*, the right of every one in the world, however great or whatever the *tapas*. That is the Kingdom they seek, the honour they aspire for. This is the great mystery, the mystery elucidated in the *Vedas, Upanishads* and *Sastras*. The solving of this mystery makes life worth while; it is the key to liberation.[1]

◊ ◊ ◊ ◊ ◊

---

[1] Jnana Vahini, pp. 24-25.

Summary

Durga, Lakshimi and Saraswati are symbols of Divine potencies existing within the gross material, subtle and causal bodies of human beings and pervading the universe, derived from the primordial energy (*adi shakti*). Man, as he is composed of Divine Energy in his every aspect, is Divine. It would benefit him to use his intellect to realize and act in accordance with this Truth. It is Saraswati, the energy aspect that confers knowledge of the *Atma*, that makes one a *jnani*, a liberated one.

On *Vijaya Dasami*, October 21, 1996, Sai Baba said during His Discourse: "Durga is within your heart as Power and Energy, Saraswati is the energy of your speech and Lakshmi is the energy evident when you use your two hands to perform beneficial, sacred actions."

Conclusion

"The great exhortation of the Vedanta is that each and every soul, in whatever sphere of the Universe, shall rise above all mortality to the realization of *Brahman*, that is to say, that the personal soul shall come to realize that it alone is Reality, the process being a gradual expansion of consciousness. All relative ideas and relationships about which consciousness builds itself in the weaving of desire must be transcended. The state of progress and becoming, which is the soul's constant experience, must attain its climax culminating in Pure Being and Absolute Perfection. Then, all ideas of birth and death will have ceased to be, and time will have sunk into eternity. Sensation will have forever passed into beatitude, all progress will have died out, for That which progress tends will have been realised. Then all the fraud of personality will have vanished with its relative freedom and bondage of will. For Infinite Freedom has then been attained beyond all struggle, beyond all desire, and beyond all bondage. When the personal soul realises the Supreme, then verily it is Brahman. "Tat Twam Asi" — "Thou Art That" — is the spirit of all Vedanta teaching that being the "OM TAT SAT" or the state of immeasurable knowledge, eternal experience and unfathomable bliss.

The Hindu conceived of the Truth in the categories of the real and the unreal. Thus something may exist being however at the same time unreal in the highest understanding of reality. Whatever is relatively real or possesses aspects of reality, is of the essence of Brahman. Man exists as personality. Higher than man are the Gods and the Devas and other superior beings. The reality of all is Brahman with this as the background, the mind immediately recognises the synthesis of Hinduism. Polytheism, Theism, Monism, all are one in the vision of the Highest. The Gods are personal forms or aspects of Brahman and because Brahman is real, even so are they real. They are "idea forms" of Brahman. More real are they than men, relatively speaking, because they are more immediate forms and emanations of the Infinite Reality and more conscious of reality than men. The humblest Hindu peasant knows this.

According to the needs of time and place and the surrounding circumstances and according to the varying necessities of human mind, these spiritual imaginings of Brahman vary. Sometimes Brahman is conceived of as the Divine Father or the Divine Mother or as the Eternal one rapt in meditation, or as the Terrible One, the personification of Infinite Force, or as the Preserver or the Destroyer or as a Divine Incarnation full of sublimity. The incarnation is the God–man who realises and preaches the state or consciousness of Brahman. He is God born as Man. There are in Hinduism innumerable gods or visualizations of Brahman which the human mind has made unto itself, but underlying the apparent Polytheism is a great Monotheism and ultimately a spiritual Monism. In the end, as every Hindu knows, all these seemingly different deities are one, first because they are manifestations of the one and the same reality and secondly because they represent the consciousness of Brahman in different aspects. So there is ultimately only one Personal God. All the Gods are One Person in that they have the same divine consciousness and because all are Brahman. But there is still a higher purpose. The majority of men recognize the personal God in their own particular objectification of Brahman. It may be Krishna, Buddha, Rama or even Chaitanya, even as with the Christians it is Jesus the Christ. There is no clash in religion in India, however varied the religious belief or worship, that is the reason the state is a secular state, no distinction being there on the ground of religion. Instinctively, every Hindu worships all the Gods bowing to the Great Ideal of which each one is a separate embodiment. We therefore see in India, a Hindu passing before the Church — recognizing there the existence of the Supreme Being and inwardly accepting that it is the "dwelling of God." He sees the underlying oneness and unity of the different concepts recognizing

Brahman in them all. It is a racial characteristic, a racial inheritance. This vision is peculiarly Hindu in the understanding of religion. Thus every God in Hinduism represents aspects and symbols of the One Eternal Reality.

Therefore, the Indian Polytheism is the highest Monism in the essence. The many forms of henotheism or the deification of any one representation of Brahman as Super–Personal God is also, as a consequence, Monism in the essence.

Monotheism itself becomes a spiritual Monism for eventually the individual soul finds that its own reality is the same as that of the god worshipped. "Whom then to worship?" asks the Hindu. He says that the worshipper and the worshipped and the ideal of worship and all the Gods and all the souls are One. It is because of this unifying supreme outlook of the Vedanta that devotees can sincerely worship all the Gods or take any one God as his chosen ideal of worship. The Impersonal Brahman within their own soul offers equal assurance that all religions and all religious philosophies lead only to the same goal. Thus India, seemingly so divergent in her religious beliefs, traditions and customs, is one in this great thought. In the vision of the Hindu, even a stone has the divine substance in it.

The final conclusion of Vedanta is that all these Gods are visions and personifications of Brahman, created by the soul itself. All stand for various "torch–light ideas" of the human mind. As man develops, his conception of the Gods grows, but the Gods do not change. Brahman is ever the same. It is man who changes, it is man who grows. Finally the soul in its most luminous insight discovers that even as all great ideas are only aspects of one all–including Truth, even so are the personal Gods manifestations of the same divine Nature and Consciousness. All external forms of divinity are superimpositions by the inner Divinity of the Soul upon the special vision it entertains at any given time. Ultimately all superimpositions die out and all the Gods merge in their true nature, the One and Indivisible only Brahman, only Reality remains. And the Gods are Brahman, and the soul is Brahman, and the Truth is Brahman. Verily the Universe is Brahman, and all paths, however diversified in the religious ideas and worship, lead to the same goal, Brahman, whether the worshippers are Hindus, Christians, Mohammedans, Buddhists or Zoroastrians, or the followers of any other prophet.

No wonder therefore that the Hindu philosophy teaches the importance of the Soul and Its reality, and therefore on death the body becomes a useless mass of flesh prone to destruction and disintegration, and therefore the Hindu believes that after the soul has departed and mixed itself into the Divine, the body is like a discarded piece of old cloth fit to be rejected and burnt. How foolish therefore is the concept that the soul will remain waiting till the day if liberation dawns when all the dead will rise and till that time the body also will remain to join the soul. After the death the soul mixes with the Super Being of which it forms a part; the body which covered the soul is thrown down as waste as soon as the soul has departed."[1]

Sathya Sai Baba is Himself the embodiment of the deities He has discussed as well as the embodiment of the Supreme Brahman. We are grateful to Him for sharing His wisdom and knowledge so that each may benefit through increased awareness and realization of one's own innate Divinity.

---

[1] Pramila Jaykar, *Symbolism in Hinduism*, compiled by R. S. Nathan, pp. 83-86.

Appendix

Hindu Gods and Goddesses – Swami Harshananda; Sri Ramakrishna Math, Mylapore, Madras.

Symbolism in Hinduism – Compiled by R.S. Nathan; Central Chinmaya Misssion Trust, Bombay.